Johnny Angel Is My Brother

A Psychic Medium's Journey

Cheryl Booth

ISBN :1-4196-1804-0
Library of Congress Control Number : 2005909523

To order additional copies, please contact us.
BookSurge, LLC
www.booksurge.com
1-866-308-6235
orders@booksurge.com

Johnny Angel Is My Brother

Table of Contents

Johnny's Ongoing Legacy & Amazing Communication From Heaven

Hello! Allow me to introduce you to one of my very favorite people, my brother, John Howard Booth. Even while the manuscript was in the editing process, Johnny's energy was so incredibly evident around me, letting me know he, too, was excited that this book is finally going to be shared with the world, and was supporting all my efforts. I'll share just three outstanding examples of this, because they even blew *me* away, and I've been involved in this work for over twenty years!

Johnny passed into Spirit in 1985 and his communication with me through other mediums, signs and direct "Wake up and smell the coffee!" messages continue to grow stronger and more amazing to me with each year that passes. From the time we first met in this physical incarnation, we had a strong, special telepathic communication. I believe John is a highly evolved soul (like many who enter this Earth sphere with extreme challenges), who chose to limit his spoken words while here, but he has certainly been extremely vocal and visually in evidence ever since his transition. Let me explain.

Once my editor had this manuscript, I released being obsessed with it and began focusing on doing readings again. I was brought into an investigation by a family, involving the murder of one of their own. Upon their request, I traveled with them to the scene of the crime, to try and tune in more specifically to details that might assist the detective working on this case. The young woman whose life had been taken was a firefighter, and as we turned onto the road that would lead us to the station where she worked, my focus was directed to the corner of an intersection where I saw a diner named *Johnny Angel's*! I smiled and pointed to it, telling the family that I knew that meant my brother would do everything in his power from the other side to help make the reading as strong and accurate as possible. So that was #1. The reading was quite powerful and I know John's energy definitely helped me, as he so often does.

Less than a week later, I was visiting a friend I had not seen for several months, catching her up on the book and sharing stories about Johnny. She usually has her TV on, often tuned to the *Game Show Network*. A rerun of *Who Wants To Be A Millionaire* continued to play, but she muted the sound. Just as I was sharing some information about John, "something" drew my attention to the TV screen, exactly at the moment they showed the names of the next ten contestants. JOHN BOOTH was the second name! Now, the timing of that was obviously no accident. I seldom watch that channel, and for his name to pop up on a rerun, no less, just in time for me to see it, well, all I could say was, "Hi, Johnny! Thanks for being so clear! Lots of people ask for signs from loved ones in your dimension, but this is just too cool!"

The third instance of his presence all around me happened about two weeks later. I took the book cover artwork into a local healing center I frequent, *Ceragem* (check out their website www.ceragem.com and be sure to scout around—they have centers in many cities and offer FREE treatments on this amazing massage therapy bed, about which I'll share more in Chapter Thirteen on Healing). Because the *Ceragem* bed has helped me so much, I was moved to tell the owner I would be including a mention of it in my book. I had never met him before; he is often out of town. He looked at the cover and smiled. "I used to be a musician," he said, "and I once worked with the original 'Johnny Angel', the fellow the song was written about." Now I ask you, friends, could all three of these incidents be mere coincidence? I don't think so! In fact, I *know* much more is going on here!

So, I share this early on to let you know what a terrific soul my brother is, to get a glimpse into how blessed I am to share these ongoing connections with him. I am so thrilled to share our story with you in the pages that follow. Many people get goosebumps when I talk about Johnny. Don't be surprised if *you* get them as you read about him. It's all good so just relax and receive, because it's healing energy super-charged with love!

Enjoy!

Acknowledgements

I am so grateful to all the wonderful people who contributed their stories, energy and support to this book. God bless you each and every one. Since it's my first "solo" book, the Acknowledgements are rather lengthy (this was a long time manifesting, and I had lots of help along the way!) If I've inadvertently omitted you from the following list, please know you always have a place in my heart.

I have already dedicated this book to my parents and Johnny, but cannot omit them, ever. You are in my thoughts and heart daily. I so treasure and love you all. Thanks for all you do to help me keep going!

Special thanks to my older brother Don for believing in my talents, musical, psychic and otherwise, when other family members thought I was simply "unusual" or downright weird. You have always been there for me, Don. I love you very much.

Aunt Kathy, Millie and all other family members and friends in Spirit who understand, appreciate and assist me with this work...you inspire me and sometimes when I need a pick-me-up, you tell the best jokes! I love you all!

I am grateful to everyone at BookSurge who helped this book come into print, most especially Andrew Roskill. Also, a very well deserved "Thank you!" to Thom Kephart, Sharon Crocker and Julie Burnett.

Major thanks to *everyone* who purchased advance copies of this book to fund its publication and promotion. It wouldn't be here now without you!

Major kudos and appreciation to John Edward, George Anderson, Rosemary Altea, James Van Praagh, Kelsey Grammer (for providing years of wonderful entertainment through his acting and direction, and now his producing of the show *Medium*) and all others who have positively contributed to raising people's awareness of mediumship and helping to show that life on Earth is far from the end. Blessings to you all!

I must acknowledge the generosity and support of Amy & Harold Nicely for allowing me to be their psychic telephone between dimensions, and for contributing to the realization of this book in such a significant way!

Thanks to Sherri Mills-Anderson, Dave Mills and to one of the most amazing communicators from Spirit I've ever had the opportunity to work with, their brother Jim Mills.

I am extremely grateful to Jennifer Selberg, Barbe Ratcliffe, David and Sheila Podolak, and Sam and Sue Stratton for all their help and support. Thanks for your long-time support, believing in me and in this book!

My long-term buddy, Keith Jennings in L.A., thanks for sticking with me, and never giving up on our connection, even though many months have gone by between our phone calls at different times over the years. You're the *best*, my fellow Scorpio. I cherish our friendship!

I'm grateful to my Tucson friends. Carol Maywood, bless you for so graciously allowing me to use your casita when I head south to rest and recharge! A round of applause to my writer friend Sinclair Browning for including my story about my mother in *Feathers Brush My Heart (Warner Books, 2002)*. She also writes great mysteries and thrillers! Check out her website www.sinclairbrowning.com. Write on, Zeke!

Thanks to my astrologer Philip Comi for being a good listener, good friend, and all around good egg! By the way, if you're searching for a *wonderful* astrologer, although he's in Phoenix, Philip can do a variety of charts for you wherever *you* are. Like myself, he has many long-distance clients. He also teaches great classes, in person in Phoenix, as well as via the internet. For details, call 602-808-8884. (At the time of this book's first printing, his website was still under construction, but keep checking in on it: www.philipcomi.com)

Thanks, Frank Baranowski, (currently a resident of Heaven) because I know you still help me find ways to spread my message in this dimension whenever you can. Blessings to you for that, and for having had me as a guest on your KTAR radio show *Mysteries Around Us* several times. I know you're having a great time "over there" lifting spirits through enlightenment and laughter, just like you did here!

I so appreciate the guidance and unfailing support of Ann Albers, my wonderful psychic colleague and friend (www.visionsofheaven.com). You're the best, Ann, and I'm happy to call you my "adopted little sister!" Heaven knows how many other times we've been connected in past lives, and I'm sure it's always been fun and growthful!

Harry Lynn, Merlin E. and Brian Hurst are three gentlemen whose patience, expertise, wisdom and support I shall always cherish. Thank you!

A big "Thank You!" goes to Ellen and Skipper on beautiful Whidbey Island, WA...two of my favorite people in this lifetime as well as the one in that convent, many moons ago. You ladies are a great source of inspiration to me!

Words are simply inadequate to express my gratitude to my wonderful family & friends in Spirit as well as my guides, among them, Edgar Cayce, Dr. James Martin Peebles, Mark Twain, Norma Jean, Archangel Raphael, Jaeron, Merlin and The Brotherhood of Light.

Heartfelt thanks to so many of you for being there for me when times were tough, for not allowing me to give up hope on this book, my dreams and my gifts. Special nods to Nina Sartini, Linda Moran and TT Nelson, because ladies, you were there with support and encouragement on so many levels, several times. I simply cannot thank you enough.

To three of my dear friends who recently crossed into Spirit: Tess M., Linda C. and Pete H., you are missed by many, and I am grateful to feel your visits more strongly and frequently as time goes by.

I especially want to thank my wonderful clients and friends who have been kind enough to send me validations of details that came through in their readings...that's a large part of what keeps me going! Of course, I'm always grateful for the wonderful word of mouth referrals so many have been gracious enough to send over the years.

Thanks to all who have welcomed me into their homes when my work allows me to travel to great places! In Chicago, this includes Matt and Lauren Trapani, their wonderful kids & whole family. Also big thanks to my dear friend Valerie Decker, gratitude to Joy Schaad for opening her beautiful bed & breakfast to me (located in Chicago just north of Wrigleyville—*Joy's Joy, A Victorian Bed and Breakfast*. For rates & more details, call 773-528-3443 or you can email joyschaad@aol.com). Also thanks to Merle Gross for her hospitality, and hello and thank you to *all* my friends and clients in Chicagoland! That includes Diane Willis and Chicago IANDS (International Association of Near Death Studies)—you're the best! It has been my pleasure to be a speaker and to perform *Medium, Rare* for this group's national convention. Visit their website for more details on Near Death studies and all their fascinating speakers & meetings—http://chicagoiands.org Also, many thanks to my friend and fellow intuitive Dawn Silver and *Healing Earth Resources* in Chicago.

And finally, thanks to each and every reader of this book. My hope is that it touches and inspires you to share your own stories and to enjoy the journey, each and every day!

Prologue

With the recent success of the TV show *Medium*, the unique film *What The Bleep Do We Know*, and a virtual plethora of other series and movies currently cropping up about metaphysics, the supernatural and paranormal, it's evident the public is open to learning more about this field than ever before. Not to mention bestselling books about and by psychic mediums including John Edward, George Anderson, Rosemary Altea and others. This wave of interest has opened the path for many books, which express many theories, opinions and experiences. I encourage you to always seek and embrace what rings true to you. There may be certain things you read in other books, or in this one, which feel like truth to you and there may be a few things which you find hard to swallow. Go with your gut, always! I never want to come across as having all the answers. I believe when we stop learning and growing, it's time to "head 'em up, move 'em out" and go back to the Light. So what you'll read in this book is a sharing of my own experiences and beliefs, never a campaign to convince you that I'm an "authority" on paranormal events or metaphysics. I just like to give people something to consider and perhaps find comfort from a similar experience in their lives.

Many recent TV series and movies tend to stress how those in Spirit can help those still on the Earth plane solve mysteries and murders, get closure with loss, and many other wonderful gifts they can pass along to us. While I believe this is all true, I also believe they have many fascinating activities in their own dimension. So I'll be sharing some of those insights they've imparted to me, again for your consideration. We'll know for sure when we get there, won't we? While here in Earth School, we need to stay most focused on creating our own reality and doing so in ways that serve our soul contract...the motivating factor which compelled us to show up here in the first place! For me, as for many of my clients, knowing that loved ones are never totally removed from us, that the soul is eternal, has certainly brought me lots of hope and comfort over the years. It is my intention that this book will do the same for you, as you read some of the stories they've related to me about that side of things, as well as their willingness to help us with this one.

In case you're wondering, this book doesn't contain pat answers about what temperature it is in Heaven, nor what exact age those in that dimension "always are." Hey, if it's truly Heaven and we all have free will, seems to me that's probably open to interpretation of the individual soul. I've included messages that those in Spirit have sent to their loved ones here about their experiences on that side of things; please just know I'm not promoting it as "the Gospel according to Cheryl."

I hope you enjoy and are inspired by this book, which chronicles my journey from being a stubborn kid in a Pentecostal household whose precognitive dreams spooked my poor mother to no end, all the way through to my adult life as a psychic medium and hypnotherapist. Because he was and is, such a beautiful guide to me, I could not do that story justice without including my brother John's personal story.

John was born with severe cerebral palsy. He was and is a major blessing in my life and I'm grateful for having had the opportunity to learn so much from him. Our life together convinced me that beings who enter this Earth plane with overwhelming challenges are often extremely evolved souls. Johnny has always provided me with inspiration and guidance. He's been in Spirit since 1985, yet continues to be one of my strongest guides. This book would not be in your hands today if not for his loving energy and influence.

There is much to learn from the beautiful souls who are here dealing with such challenges as Downs Syndrome, cerebral palsy, epilepsy, muscular dystrophy, and other such birth conditions. I encourage you to make time in your life to get to know some of them, for it will bring you a great blessing. These beautiful beings almost always exude a pure, happy, unconditionally loving vibration, and are a pleasure to be around. Johnny very seldom complained about anything, and helped me learn not to take my own gifts and advantages for granted. I feel so honored to have been a member of his Earth family.

In order to accurately depict our joint journey, it is necessary to "go back to the beginning." If you've been touched by an Earth angel like John yourself, you will relate strongly to a lot of this. If you haven't, perhaps you'll make an effort to meet some of these beautiful beings, then see what you can learn from those teachers "in disguise."

First, however, I'm going to present some case studies of readings I've done in recent years. For those who wish to develop your own psychic abilities, it is my intention that this book will encourage you to pursue that. There are many books, CDs, and videos already out there which can help you. Again, find your truth and run with it! And F.Y.I., I've already started a separate book about that for adults, as well as a Playbook for Psychic Kids.

Those in Spirit have told me many times that until there is at least "one medium per square mile" on the Earth plane, they will continue to do their best to reach their loved ones here through many means, including "butting in" on readings of their loved ones' acquaintances and friends. They have much to share and convey and need Earth-based folks willing to be the "psychic telephone" between dimensions to assist in this work. Although not everyone in Spirit communicates through mediums, there are many who do, so our network here needs to increase to handle the demand.

There are only a few personal testimonials in this book. There are several on my website, and I thank all the wonderful folks who have provided those for me. Also, you will find *many* references to great books, websites and movies throughout this missive. If the topics intrigue you, write 'em down! In future editions, I may include a reference/bibliography section, but for now, grab 'em as you go!

Thank you for reading this book. If you feel it helps you and can help others you know or meet, please spread the word and thank you in advance for doing so.

Some of Cheryl's Case Studies

Please note: In case studies, as well as all accounts of client's readings and testimonials throughout this book, unless express permission has been granted to use actual names, identities have been disguised to protect their privacy. In some instances, the portraits presented are composites and in others, identifying biographical details have been either omitted or changed.

The Mountain, The Song, & The Phone Call

Note: Sherri Mills-Anderson has granted me permission to include her moving testimonial, as well as the conclusion to this particular case, here. Actual names are given and their experience is quite touching. Sherri's testimonial is at the end.

In 1997, a brother and sister came to me for a reading. Their older brother had been missing for two years. The last time anyone saw him alive was on a camping trip in the Colorado mountains. This fellow was considered a great outdoorsman, an extremely experienced mountain climber, so when he started up the mountain one afternoon, his son and his brother thought nothing of staying at base camp, telling Jim they would see him upon his return.

He signed in at the highest-level ranger station, and that's the last anyone heard from him. As I began to tune into Jim's energy, I got the familiar chills I experience when those in Spirit are talking with me. The very first thing he transmitted was, "You have to tell my family that my physical body is dead."

So I took a deep breath and shared this with them. The sister began to cry. Even though they knew this was probably the case, there was a hopefulness that perhaps somehow, someway, for some unbeknownst reason, Jim might have simply decided to disappear and start life over somewhere else. Maybe he had amnesia. All kinds of things must run through families' minds in this sort of case, any possible way to hang onto the belief their loved one might still be alive keeps them going, yet always wondering.

He went on to give many accurate details about his life and his family. In fact, his brother and sister came back a couple of weeks after that with a topographical map and Jim pinpointed an area where he said his body had struck a ledge in the fall he took, and it would be found in a crevace. His brother, also a mountain climber, identified that as being the most sheer, treacherous side of that mountain and told me rescuers refused to search there, out of fear of losing the search team's lives. Jim was aware of all this, but insisted in that reading and every subsequent one I did for his family, that his body would one day be found. He really wanted this to happen, especially for his kids' sake, so they could get closure and move on.

At the end of the first reading, Jim's sister said, "Cheryl, I'm not asking you this to test you or anything like that. Jim has given so much great evidence, I believe you really are in touch with him. But would you mind just asking him if he has anything to say about a phone call and a song, please?"

I nodded, and telepathically sent up the request. Jim came back quickly with, "*Rocky Mountain High.*"

My left brain to this day still tries to interject while I'm doing readings, and that day was no exception. It guffawed, basically, and tauntingly said, "Oh, Cheryl, come ON! That's just what you want it to be because it was in Colorado. How obvious will that sound, if you say that?"

I was about to cave in and ignore it when it felt like Jim was jumping up and down inside my head, overriding that dubious, nagging voice.

"NO! Cheryl, you've *got* to say, 'John Denver's *Rocky Mountain High.*' *Please* just say it!"

So I did. His sister started crying again and through her tears said, "Oh, my God! Wow. The day after Jim disappeared, his girlfriend got a phone call and that song was playing. But nobody was there!"

My chills intensified.

"We always wondered if it was his way of letting her know he had gone on into Spirit. And now I believe that's right."

"Yeah, so do I!" I replied. "Your brother is certainly one of the most powerful, accurate communicators I've ever connected with. Wow!"

I believe Jim is such a great communicator from that dimension, because communication was his field in *this* one. He was a television reporter and producer, and did a lot of stage acting. So it was something he's very comfortable with, which is a great blessing to any medium.

This particular case study has an interesting conclusion. Eight years after that first reading, I got a call from Sherri, his sister. We had been in touch over the years and I'd done a number of readings for the family. But the call I got the week of September 19, 2005 was very unusual, and extremely gratifying.

She left me a message that said, "Cheryl, I had to call you. Yesterday, some guys who do extreme repelling were working their way down Jim's mountain, right where he showed you on the map. One of them thought he saw some clothing, and thank God they decided to investigate. They found his body under some snow, along with his backpack, containing his I.D., so it's a positive match. Thank you so much, Cheryl. That's the good news, even though it's stirred up more grief, in some ways." She paused, her voice understandably a bit shaky. "We're planning a memorial there next week. I'll talk with you more when we get home."

I am so thankful to Jim for being the terrific communicator he is and for never giving up on believing his remains would be discovered. The more I told his story over the years, the more *I* believed he would be found, too. Now his family can finally have true peace in knowing he is in the Light and has been, this entire time.

This is the testimonial of Sherri Mills-Anderson, reproduced as she wrote it. She has entitled it *Following the Trail of Memories*:

"In the majestic southwest mountains of Colorado, in the Sangre de Cristo range (which means the "blood of Christ"), Jim Mills came to the end of his life. This is a sacred place for many vision quests.

Jim Mills' last climb was August 17, 1995. My younger brother Dave was with him, but they separated on the way up, because Dave felt an accident was imminent. He just got the inner feeling that "it was the wrong day." Jim proceeded, but never returned to base camp that day.

Enter Cheryl Booth. I sought her out in 1997 due to her excellent reputation as a psychic medium, and her ability to help find missing persons. Dave and I met with her for a reading and she said Jim was there in Spirit. She explained that a bird had spooked him and he'd fallen off the mountain, landing on a ledge and then in a crevace, far below. Jim said it was "a dumb mistake."

I've had readings off and on with Cheryl in the eight years since that first contact, where she has always brought in Jim's spirit and the feeling that we were getting closer to the discovery of Jim's remains. He always insisted his body would be found, so that the family could get closure and peace about this. Cheryl even circled the area on a topographical map, with Jim's guidance, as to where his body was located.

In February, 2005 at a group gathering where she was giving messages, Cheryl told us Jim's remains would be found soon. The ten-year anniversary of his disappearance was August, 2005, and on September 11, 2005, his remains were spotted on the mountain by local climbers. Our family received the call we had waited for so long, from the Sheriff's Department.

They said after the fall in 1995, Jim had settled on a ledge after falling between three hundred and a thousand feet. This was very close to the area Cheryl had marked on the map.

Our family is forever grateful to Cheryl Booth for bringing us peace in this process, through her accuracy and comforting nature. She let us know Jim was safe in the Spirit World, and that his personality was still intact. Cheryl has amazing talents as a psychic medium, and has taught me so much about the afterlife.

On October 1, 2005 our family scattered Jim's ashes on the same mountain where for all those years, Native American spirits protected him.

Thank you, Cheryl Booth, for we now have closure and peace, just as Jim wanted." Sherri Mills-Anderson

"Tell my son, Steven, I love him"

One night a woman called to book an appointment. "I'd like to talk to my best friend who passed away recently," she said.

"Well, I'll do my best," I replied. "I can never guarantee anything, you understand. Those in Spirit must be willing to come through, and not everyone in that dimension chooses to do the communication."

She said she understood, and we scheduled the appointment for about two weeks down the road. About a half hour before she was to arrive, there were incredible goosebumps running up and down my spine and arms. A man's voice began talking inside my head.

"I'm so glad they're coming," he excitedly said. "Please tell them to tell my son, Steven, I love him. And encourage him to start swimming again...it's such a good catharsis for him. I know he's mad that I left; he needs to join a teenagers' group so he can talk to others his own age about all this..."

I interrupted him. "Please, friend...please wait until your friends are here so I'm sure to include everything you wish to say to them. I don't want to forget any of this. I know you're excited, you just need to wait a bit. They'll be here in just a few minutes."

He agreed, but his presence lingered. As soon as the woman and her college-age daughter arrived, I ushered them to the reading area. We sat down and I did my usual centering invocation for protection and guidance to serve everyone's Highest Good. Then I looked at her and said, "There's a gentleman in Spirit who's been here for nearly forty minutes. He is very excited to tell you lots of things, mostly about his son, Steven." I went on to repeat all of the information he had given already. Her mouth fell open and her daughter stared at me with wide eyes.

"Does that message make sense?" I asked.

"Yes...oh, yes! We're just shocked...."

"Okay, wait...here comes some more, now...." The man went on to give more evidence, which obviously resonated about his family. Then he said something I wanted to verify. "He's talking about Michael's wife. He keeps saying, 'Michael's wife'. Do you understand this?"

She shook her head, "I, ah....Michael is another son. He's just a young boy...."

My invisible friend piped in stronger. I smiled, and looked at her. "He says *you* are Michael's wife. This is your husband, isn't it?"

She burst into tears of relief and release. "Oh, my God! Yes, yes! Cheryl, I wasn't trying to deceive you. Michael was my best friend *and* my husband. I wasn't sure exactly how this works...this is so incredible!"

"That's all right," I assured her. "Healthy skepticism is a good thing. I'm glad he's such a strong communicator. That always makes my job easier."

We went on to have a powerful, healing communication, which was exceedingly detailed and accurate. If only *everyone* in Spirit were as good at the communication as Michael! They all transmit messages in complete thought forms, it's simply that some have more focused intention and energy. When that occurs, the entire message comes through, clear as a bell. It's such a pleasure to help facilitate people's healing and growth. At times like these, I realize how blessed I am to do this work.

An Eye-opening Healing

In 1996, I was doing readings at a metaphysical bookstore in Phoenix, one day per week. This was something I enjoyed, and proved to be a good way to meet new clients. Some "regulars" came to see me once a month or so. I always encouraged them to wait at least that long, and began to give them "homework" whenever it felt appropriate, so they could take positive action and monitor their growth. To become empowered, rather than reliant on me or anyone else, other than self. Sometimes it's helpful to check in with someone you trust to get an objective sort of "progress report" but it should never become addictive.

Cecile was one of my regulars, who visited with me every two or three months. This lady is incredibly psychic herself, but like many of us, she doesn't always trust the information she gets for herself. Many of us need a detached, objective listener occasionally, a sounding board. If that were not the case, there would be no therapists, no counselors, no psychics, and in many cases, no best friends! We tend to become too emotionally attached to our circumstances, so that we can't clearly see or accept the logical solution to situations which we have created. During those times, we may wish to seek more objective guidance.

One day, Cecile came into the bookstore for a reading. One of her sons in the Spirit World had been a very clear communicator on several occasions, usually giving great evidence that it was indeed him, along with comforting, helpful messages. Today, however, my guide Jaeron was the vocal one in my head. At this time, Jaeron was one of my main guides. He and I shared a Revolutionary War lifetime where he was a doctor and I was his apprentice and adopted son. I'll write more about him in a future book about past lives and guides. For now, suffice it to say that he often spoke through me directly, so I basically channeled him; other times, we'd have a telepathic conversation I'd relay to my clients, much the same as during my mediumship work.

Jaeron spoke about Cecile's husband in no uncertain terms. He adamantly addressed this man's health condition. I was surprised, since I had never met Cecile's husband, and was shocked Jaeron was talking so freely about him. Having been a medical doctor in his last earthly incarnation made Jaeron excellent at pinpointing various diseases, sometimes offering herbal remedies, dietary changes or exercise routines. When passing along any type of health guidance, I always encourage my clients to undertake "due diligence" by reading up on the information shared and/or to consult with an expert in that field prior to trying anything. That way they make an informed decision. I in no way, shape or form do any prescribing; rather, it's a sharing of potentially helpful information.

Jaeron's voice rang out in my head, "Tell her Bob must have eye surgery immediately or he will lose his eyesight. You must tell her this right now, Cheryl!"

I paused. This point blank, no-nonsense health message was very unusual at this point in my reading career. "Bob is your husband's name, is that correct?"

"Yes, it is," she confirmed.

"Well...is he having any trouble with his eyesight, or..."

My guide became exasperated with me. "Oh, for Heaven's sake! Don't beat around the bush, there simply isn't time! Ask her about his recent headaches, tell her there is pressure on the optic nerve...stress that he must have surgery done immediately or he will most assuredly go blind! Tell her!" he insisted.

I cleared my throat. I've never played upon people's fear in order to get them to take action. Neither was Jaeron. He was just explaining what he knew to be a circumstance which could be remedied by surgery. His uncharacteristic urgency made it plain this must be done rapidly.

"Ahm...okay, Cecile, here goes. My guide, Jaeron, is aware of something serious in connection with Bob's vision, and he basically demands that I tell you about it, okay? Has Bob been having a lot of headaches, recently?"

"Well, yes, he has. His eyes are real tired, and he's been talking about getting some new glasses."

"He needs more than just new glasses. The information I'm getting is that he needs laser surgery right away, or he may well go blind. He needs to get this checked out with a specialist in the next couple of weeks. No longer!" Jaeron's prodding caused me to blurt the information out more bluntly than I intended.

Cecile's eyes grew wide as she nodded her head. "I understand. You've been so accurate before, Cheryl, I'll tell Bob he needs to go get this looked into right away."

"Oh, that's great. Thank you...I'm sorry it came out so strongly, but Jaeron is powerful when he's got important news, and he is very insistent about this. Let me know how it turns out, won't you?"

"Of course. Thank you. We'll see you soon." She waved, and walked out hurriedly.

I took some deep breaths to get centered for the next client. I thought about this reading several times over the next few days. About three weeks later, Cecile walked back into the store. Her smile lit the place up.

"Oh, Cheryl, guess what? Bob went to a specialist, and you were right! There was a mass pressing on the optic nerve. Fortunately, it was operable. When the surgeon saw that, he said, 'Sir, you're going to need laser surgery right away, otherwise you'll lose your eyesight.'" She squeezed my hand. "Thank you so much!"

"Oh, my God, well...thank *you* for the update! That was such an unusually strong message..."

"Well, that's a *good* thing! Bob doesn't put much stock in readings and such, but when I told him how powerful this message was, he made an appointment right away. In fact, he's already had the surgery...he's doing really well. Thank you again!"

"My pleasure. I'm so glad it turned out this way." I was quite moved, and sent a mental "Thank You telegram" to Jaeron on the spot. The chills on my arms confirmed his receipt of it. About a month later, Cecile was back, along with a man I realized must be Bob. She gave him a playful little shove in my general direction, and stayed at the front of the store, looking at candles and books as he made his way back to my reading table. He was carrying some eyeglasses.

"Hello, Cheryl. I'm Bob." He stuck out his hand, and I gladly shook it.

"Oh, hello, Bob! So nice to finally meet you. Your wife is such a lovely person. I really enjoy talking with her."

"Well, yes. I, ah..." He was obviously a bit nervous, and suddenly held out the eyeglasses to me. "Here. Look at these. This is what I used to wear. See how thick those lenses are? Just like looking through pop bottles, aren't they?" he joked.

"Yes, indeed. That's a pretty strong prescription, for sure." Since no one was waiting for a reading, there was no rush. I let him take his time to say whatever else was on his mind.

"Well, I just...I'm not a big believer in psychic stuff. Or I wasn't, until this happened to me. Cecile thinks the world of you, and when she told me what you knew about my eyes, well, something in me just knew it was the truth. Thank you! You saved these!" He pointed to his eyes, then grabbed my hand to vigorously shake it again.

I laughed. "Well, you're certainly welcome. But Bob, please understand, *I* didn't save your eyes...and I didn't know about your condition...a guide I work with gave me the information to share with Cecile. If I knew about everyone's conditions, I don't think I could walk down the street and lead anything resembling a normal life, do you?"

He nodded. "No, I guess not. That makes sense. Do you just have to turn it off, sometimes?"

"That's exactly right, I have learned to turn it off when I'm focused on doing something else in the physical world. I got the information for *you* because Cecile was here, just waiting to receive whatever information would come through for her highest good that day, and the highest good of her family. That's all she ever asks about, getting helpful information for those she loves. Even though she didn't mention you specifically that day, you had the most pressing need. I'm so glad it worked out for you! Do you have to wear glasses at all now?"

"Just real weak ones, when I read. Nothing like these." He laughed as he pocketed the old specs. "It was a pleasure meeting you, Cheryl. I'll get a reading myself sometime, now."

"Well, that would be great, Bob. It was a pleasure to meet you, too. See you soon."

Bob's experience certainly opened *my* eyes once again to the fact that God moves in wonderful, mysterious and magical ways. Sometimes it's through a minister, a teacher, or someone time-traveling in the guise of an angel; other times it's through nonphysical beings, or through the skilled hand of an eye surgeon. As you believe, it is done unto you. Your faith, indeed, will make you whole.

Those days of bookstore readings were certainly interesting, and one major personal reward I received during that time was making the connection with a colleague who has become an incredible friend, one whom I admire very much. Ann Albers, another psychic, healer and author, was also doing readings in that store then. We both were there at separate tables one day, which was unusual since they normally had only one reader at a time. During the busy holiday season, they doubled up.

During a slow stretch, we started talking to each other and after about ten minutes of fun comparisons of our work, I walked over and sat down as if I was her client, assuring her I'd leave the minute a *real* client appeared. Interestingly, none did for quite awhile, and we really established a bond. I told her about some past life stuff I was picking up for her, and she gave me some "hits" she was getting for me. We laughed a lot. It was like visiting a family member you've missed, but haven't seen for a long time. In fact, to this day, many years later, I often refer to Ann as my "kid sister." She is younger chronologically, and that's the only criteria for this nickname. Her abilities as a reader, healer, teacher and author are amazing. You can learn more about Ann Albers, her work and *her* books by visiting her website www.visionsofheaven.com

Ann is the first (and longest term) friend I met in Phoenix who also works in this field, and therefore totally understands things anyone else might consider too "out there" to believe. I'm so grateful we have such a wonderful connection and am proud to call her my friend.

The Little Girl, Forest Street and Denny's

Unfortunately, not every story has a happy ending in my line of work. However, I have a commitment with Spirit that if I can assist in bringing closure to those left here on the Earth plane, I will do so.

A few years ago, I received a call from someone in Ohio. "Cheryl, the police here are baffled by a little girl's disappearance. She's only five years old. Could you try to tune in and see what you get, please?"

That's all that was said. I promised to get back in touch if I got any information. Then since I had time, I meditated on it, then received a message to go lie down. Many times in my dream state, clarity comes forth, especially where missing people are concerned. In this dream, I clearly saw the name "Denny." I also saw a street sign which said, *Forest Street*, and a park. In my dream "movie" I saw police searching a dumpster in this park, and finding the little girl's body. I saw a headline of the local paper, and noticed the date was day after tomorrow.

I woke up a few minutes after that and called my contact back to relay the information. I told her I was sorry I didn't have better news, that in cases like these, part of me prayed I would be wrong. After giving her the details from the dream, I heard a gasp on the other end.

"Cheryl, she was last seen at a *Denny's* restaurant. And there is a park nearby...Forest Street runs along one perimeter of the park!"

"Please share this with the police as soon as possible, and see what happens. And let me know what happens, okay? Thanks."

I got a call two days later. All the details had borne out. I was sad, but remembered the words of my dear mentor, Brian. He had told me years before I would be doing work finding missing people, primarily missing children. Even though this case had not involved the use of a map, Brian had a vision of me working with maps quite a bit, as I did with the Jim Mills case. I'm starting to do that more and more. My mentor used to say, "Cheryl, don't be distressed. Even if they are not alive when they're found, just think about this...at least the parents won't watch the door every minute, wondering if their child is still a hostage, being tortured, or if they're ever going to come home or not. People need closure. It's all right."

Brian was right, but I was not ready to do this work when he first foresaw it. It took me several years, actually, to feel ready to invite these types of investigations. Thank God the police have become more open to working with psychics in cases such as this. May God bless all parents and families who have ever been through a similar situation. This is absolutely one of the most difficult experiences a human being can endure.

Free License

A married couple booked a reading a few years ago and when they arrived, it was immediately evident to me the husband wasn't that open to being there. He sat with his arms crossed tightly over his chest, which can be a real energy blocker. Such body language shows someone guarding his heart chakra, most likely a strong skeptic who is not going to be very open to messages from the other side.

His father came through first of all, and when he gave his son some specific details like his name and his military background, the gentleman on my sofa began to relax a bit. Yet I could feel that this was not the main person these folks had come to connect with.

I felt a new energy sending me information, so I asked them, "Who is Morgan? I have a young lady here talking about her sister Morgan."

The woman took a deep breath and her eyes began to tear up. "Our daughter's name is Morgan. Who's talking to you now?"

As I looked at her, I realized this was the person they both wanted to hear from the most.

"It's your other daughter, the one who's been in Spirit now for a few months, she says. She's telling me she passed away in a car accident."

The mother nodded, the father looked stunned. Their daughter went on to give accurate details of her life here on the Earth plane, including her own name and specific personal messages, some of which she requested they pass along to her sister, Morgan. It was a very moving, healing session for all concerned. As we were winding up, even after we had already headed toward the door, their daughter asked me to please tell them one more thing.

"Can you hold on just a moment, folks? She has one more thing she wants to tell you." I listened closely, then repeated verbatim what she was saying to me. "She says, 'Tell them I think it's hysterical what happened to my license.' Is that meaningful to you?"

They both looked shocked, yet again. So much so, they couldn't respond immediately. In my mind's eye, their daughter in Spirit held up her driver's license so I could see her picture on it. Then she stamped "Suspended" across the front of it and laughed again. I relayed all this.

"My gosh," her mother said softly. "That would be her sense of humor, all right." She explained that this wonderful young woman, who was such a clear communicator she made my job a breeze, had gotten a speeding ticket about a week before she died. Obviously, she never made it to traffic school nor responded to the charge, so nearly a month after her passing, the DMV had sent a notice to her home, stating that her license was suspended until she made things right!

I heard her laughter ringing through my head. "Just let 'em try to come get me and make me sit through traffic school or court *now*!" she hooted. This brought a smile to her parents' faces. Those in Spirit will often interject a bit of levity, usually with their unique sense of humor shining through, to try and help those left here grieving lighten up, just a little bit. This was a step toward allowing the healing for her family to grow. I'm grateful to this young woman for coming through so strongly. We've had a few follow-up readings with other family members over the years, and she never fails to give wonderful evidence of the soul's continued existence, and of her interest in the Earth lives of her family.

Of all the various types of losses I've seen over the years, my heart especially goes out to parents who lose their children. That's simply something no parent is ever prepared for, to outlive their child. Joel Martin and Patricia Romanowski wrote a wonderful book about medium George Anderson, concerning his work with such situations called *Our Children Forever*. It contains messages from children in Heaven that they have sent back to their parents through George's gift. Many people have found tremendous comfort from reading that book. To me, that's the highest calling of a medium is to willingly serve as a beacon of light on the path toward comfort and understanding for those who are in grief. I've recommended it to many parents. Perhaps you know someone who would benefit from it.

Young people who die suddenly in accidents such as this are quite often very clear communicators from the other side. They don't need any "recharge" time for their soul to recover from their earthly experience, as do some older folks who dealt with debilitating illnesses or many hard circumstances in their most recent lifetime. Many of these young accident victims have also come through strongly for their families, to let them know they exited the physical plane immediately, and really didn't experience any pain or suffering. I believe when the soul knows it's time to "check out" we do that quite readily. It's not unlike one of my favorite movies, *Ghost*. The soul often seems to stand there looking at the body it just left, much the way we observe clothes that simply don't fit anymore. I believe the screenplays of *Ghost* and other films along these lines may have been channeled, in a sense. There's a lot of information in that particular movie that really resonates with what I've learned and experienced over the many years I've done this work.

Others in Spirit who have left suddenly have told me that once they've had a chance to adjust to their return to the Light, they often decide to 'sign up" for various jobs or duties. Several young people who crossed in accidents such as the young lady from this study, have commented that they now work on teams in the Spirit World who welcome new "crossovers" and help them acclimate to their new surroundings. Some have even spoken of taking on the appearance of paramedics in order to help the news sink in fully to the new arrivals.

Another great movie about the afterlife you might watch is *Defending Your Life*, starring Albert Brooks and Meryl Streep. Yet another is *What Dreams May Come*, starring Robin Williams. Both have interesting takes on what it might be like in that dimension. There are others, far too many to list them all. I mention just a few that have had pure moments of truth for me. I always urge folks to seek those moments out for themselves.

"What Time was that Reading?"

Debbie is a regular client with whom I became friends. One night she called me, very wound up, in a positive way.

"Hey, Cheryl! I really need to see you to check in on something!"

I laughed. She was so animated she was nearly out of breath. "Okay, we can do that." I took a moment to check in. "Well, you've met someone, haven't you?"

"Yes!" she practically shouted. I moved the receiver away from my ear, smiling. Debbie had been praying for a special someone for a long while. She's such a warm, intelligent woman, I had been praying right along with her. She really deserved happiness. She came over the next Saturday and we went right into the session.

"Oh, I see you at the computer. You met this guy in a chat room, huh?"

"Jeez, Cheryl! You're something else. Yes, that's right. His name's Joe."

"This feels really good already, Deb. Is he coming out here to meet you? He's from back East, right?"

"Right again! And some of my friends are freaking out because they want me to insist he stay in a motel instead of with me. But we've talked for hours on end. He's emailed me his picture....he's called me from his work, I've called him there...he's an engineer for a well-known company. Do you get anything else? Should I go through with this? He wants to come out for a visit in a couple of weeks."

After tapping in a bit more to Spirit's commentary, it seemed like a big "green light go-ahead" was called for. I was very pleased for Debbie, and just when I thought our session was over, Spirit gave me those familiar chills. I paused, closed my eyes and listened. Then I looked at her and asked, "Do you know if Joe has a brother named Tom?"

"No, I don't. We haven't really discussed siblings....just his kids, work, things like that, mostly."

"Well, someone in Spirit is insistent there is a Tom. It's either a brother, or someone very close to Joe, who he reveres as a brother. And Tom is apparently going to give you and Joe his blessing in your relationship. So that's positive! Check it out and see what happens." I smiled.

She was beaming as she left. "I'll let you know. We're going to firm up plans on the phone tomorrow."

That was Saturday. The following Monday morning at about 7:45, my phone rang.

"Cheryl, it's Debbie. I couldn't wait to call you!"

"Okay, okay....breathe, slow down! What happened?"

"We made plans for his visit. Then I remembered to ask about Tom. I said, 'Do you have a brother named Tom?' There was this long pause. 'Well, I did,' he finally said."

I got chills. "Oh, Debbie...Tom's passed over, isn't he?"

"Yes. And that's not all. He was Joe's favorite brother, whose opinion was incredibly important to him. Joe asked me, 'What time was that reading Saturday?' Cheryl...it turned out that at the exact half-hour you and I were doing the reading, Joe was at Tom's graveside, talking with him! He asked him to give him a sign, to be his guardian angel of sorts, if this relationship between us is a good thing. Can you believe it?" She was ecstatic.

"Well, yes, after years of doing this, I can. Spirit is marvelous! I'm so happy for you, Debbie. Was Joe convinced that was a sign?" I smiled.

"Oh, yeah. Now more than ever, he can't wait to come out here!"

We talked a bit longer, and as I hung up I thanked Tom and asked him to continue to bless this couple's meeting any way he could. Spirit moves in mysterious, and sometimes quite romantic ways!

"You Light Up My...Living Room?"

One morning I awoke very refreshed after a good night's sleep, prepared to give my best effort to a reading scheduled to start at ten a.m. I had plenty of time to do my meditation, eat breakfast and tidy up the house. I should have been completely able to focus on what was coming up, but suddenly I felt the irresistible urge to go lie down again. I knew some sort of dream communication was trying to come through, so I set my alarm to insure I would wake up at least twenty minutes before my client arrived. All she had told me was that she was hoping to hear from a friend of hers who had recently passed away.

Almost immediately after closing my eyes, I went into a deep dream state. I was startled to find myself in what appeared to be a young man's bedroom. Whoever's room this was, he was most likely in his early twenties. I deduced this from the posters on the walls, the various things adorning his dresser and so forth. I sat down to wait for what would happen next, when there was a knock at the door. I opened it, not at all sure what to expect.

An older African-American lady was there who smiled kindly at me, then said, "I've brought my grandson Eric to see you for a reading."

"All right. Thank you," I motioned her to come in, but she shook her head and reached back around herself to catch the young man's hand.

"He's a little skeptical about all this, but I told him he just needs to talk with you and relax. I believe he will loosen up if you just spend a few minutes talking with him. I'll catch up with him later."

"I'll do my best," I ventured a smile at the young fellow. His grandmother gently pushed him through the doorway, then she walked down the hall. He acted as though he owned the joint, and I realized it was *his* bedroom. This was certainly not my typical setting for a reading! But knowing I was somewhere in a "neutral zone" between Earth and Spirit planes, I just did my best to go with the program. He stretched out upon the bed, and without really knowing why or exactly what I was doing, I found myself reaching into my pocket, then lightly drizzling salt all around him, like a police chalk outline of a murder victim. I was aware it was sea salt, which I often use to neutralize energy in homes when I do house clearings for clients, or when I move into a new dwelling myself.

He quietly watched me, then started asking me a few questions about my background, how long I had been a medium, and so forth. I felt like *I* was being interviewed, rather than giving him a reading! He had a great sense of humor, but I could sense he was hesitant about this whole process. I did tap into a few things that I told him I'd like to share with him, so I pulled up a chair next to the bed and for a few minutes, we had a conversation. I don't remember all the details, but what does stand out in my memory is that at one point he sat straight up and looked at me. He had piercing, clear dark eyes, and when he smiled, the dimple on one side of his face showed very deeply.

"All right, lady. That last thing you said was right on target. You're the real deal. I can work with you."

And with that, I awoke. How strange! "First time for everything, I suppose," ran through my mind as I made my way to the living room to do my last minute preparations before the "earthly" reading was scheduled. When I answered the doorbell, an attractive young Hispanic woman was standing there. She extended her hand shyly, and confirmed that she was Gina. I invited her in.

Shortly after we sat down, I *had* to ask her, "Gina, I just had a very unusual experience right before you got here. I had a vivid dream of a young African-American fellow named Eric. His grandmother brought him to see me for a reading, and it was obvious to me we were in the Spirit World for this meeting. I believe he was murdered, because of certain things that happened in the dream. He was pulling my leg about being a medium for awhile, then I said something that really hit home, and he told me he would be happy to work with me, that he felt he could trust me. He was a handsome guy, with a deep dimple on the right side of his face when he smiled. Does any of this make sense to you?"

She became extremely pale. I asked if I could get her a glass of water, and she numbly nodded. Once she had taken a couple of sips, she reached into her purse and silently handed me a brochure from a memorial. There was Eric, from my dream, smiling at me from this piece of paper! And it had the details of his funeral, three weeks before, along with his name, "In Memory of Eric Lawson."

This was pretty astounding instantaneous confirmation for me, even after having done readings for over ten years at this point in time! Gina proceeded to tell me that Eric was her fiancée, and that he had indeed been murdered in a drug deal gone sour. I asked her not to give me much more detail, as I would prefer to have him do that for us. After I said the prayer I always open every reading with, to get my energy focused in, Eric came through with flying colors, validating many things, mentioning many of his family members by names and reciting recent events which had been going on in their lives, as well as Gina's. At the end of the session, she promised to stay in touch and told me she would definitely share the tape recording of the session with his family. She also confirmed that Eric's grandmother, whom he loved dearly and who had been heavily involved in his upbringing, was in Spirit World, too.

Eric was so delighted to finally have found someone able to hear him and understand the messages he was sending, he actually "hung out" with me for a few days! I kept telling him he needed to go on and start living fully in the Light, that I was happy to help deliver messages to his loved ones as they might choose to come see me, but that he had lots to do in that dimension now. Still, he let me know he was around once in awhile, playing with the volume on my stereo, making the lights blink, different little signals that were similar to a practical joke of sorts. I knew he was simply excited to know someone on the Earth plane could get his signals, and that he had probably been trying to send them to his loved ones, to no avail. People in grief often write off such things to imagination, or just wishful thinking that a loved one who's gone on is actually trying to get their attention.

About a week after Gina's session, I was doing another reading and at the end of it, my client asked me if those in Spirit ever talk to me when I'm "off duty." I laughed, and told her it had taken me a few years of doing this work to realize I had to draw extremely clear boundaries at times, in order to have a normal waking life and stay focused in this reality. So I had learned to tell folks who were persistent that sometimes "the meter wasn't running!"

"However, there has been a very persistent young man around recently, who just won't let up. He doesn't mean any harm, he's just excited that I can hear and feel his energy..."

At that moment, my halogen floor lamp, which had a dimmer switch, dimmed all the way to blackness, then slowly illuminated all the way back up. I saw the knob on the side of the lamp turning ever so slowly. This was not a random "flickering" but a very deliberate show that Eric was putting on! I laughed and told her he was obviously flattered by my mention of his antics, and had decided to show off a bit.

Her eyes were quite wide as she hurriedly gathered her purse, mumbled, "I have to go, now" and scooted for the door as fast as she could without actually running. I couldn't blame her!

I had a serious talk with Eric after that, telling him he simply could not run off any clients or guests and he really needed to start working with his guides and angels on that side of things to move in a direction that was going to serve his Highest Good. I enlisted the help of his grandmother, and the pranks soon stopped. Once in awhile, though, when I tell this story, I feel his fun, upbeat energy in the chills that I feel up and down my arms. This is a guy who really appreciates being remembered! Other members of his family came to me in the next few years after Gina's initial reading. He is another example of an excellent communicator whose life was cut short at a young age, and his messages are exceptionally clear and powerful. As much as I appreciate a good joke now and then, I'm grateful he's calmed down now and is moving forward in his work on the other side.

So, now that you've gotten a taste of the types of readings I've done, I feel it's time to let you know how this all started, many years ago. There are many more encounters with those in Spirit that are included in the pages which follow, but much of it is about my dear family and how I came to rise above my mother's fear and mistrust of my psychic abilities. My brother Johnny was there "back in the day." He's still a major guide and influence for me, truly a remarkable soul I feel you'll enjoy meeting through this book. His story deserves to be told, and our mutual saga is one which is impossible to separate.

This book is lovingly dedicated with unending gratitude to my brother John, the most beautiful soul I've ever had the pleasure of knowing personally. For me, Johnny is the purest definition of a "soulmate," in this lifetime, and many others. It is also to honor the memory of our parents. If not for the love and guidance of all three of these remarkable beings, during their time on the Earth plane as well as from the Great Beyond, this book wouldn't exist. Thank you, my dear family, for without your support and encouragement, I would not be following my path in the way it has unfolded. I love you all beyond measure!

Cheryl

Part I

Beginnings

Chapter One

The Skeptic

Manhattan Beach, California, July 29, 1985:

Do have a seat. I'll just fix us some dandelion tea, shall I?"

I nodded, "Yes, that would be nice."

Although the British gentleman was pleasantly cordial, I was uneasy. A nervous shiver ran down my spine. It was rather chilly for someone not used to the ocean's moist evening air.

For nearly three years, I'd been a North Hollywood "Valley Girl," bouncing around from one living situation to the next, kind of willy-nilly. The ocean's power really had a pull on me, and I hoped to live closer to it someday. As negative ions roll in off the waves, their vibration was supposed to calm you down. I hoped this would be the case tonight, temporarily transporting me out of the frenetic pace of "La-La-Land." Since moving to L.A., I'd worked in several aspects of the entertainment industry. I started out as a singer and actor and was now moving more toward the production end of things. I'd heard everything imaginable from agents, writers, producers, directors, actors, musicians; most of them full of big lines with egos to match. So what could a so-called "psychic medium" throw at me that could top that?

I relaxed slightly, took a few deep breaths and gingerly sank back into the flowered easy chair. Something rattled around in the back of my mind about the ocean enhancing meditation, focus, clarity; I'd also heard it could intensify psychic awareness. Even though I always felt calmer at the beach, you couldn't prove the rest of that by me; most likely a lot of "hogwash" as my dear old Dad used to say. Maybe that's why this fellow lived so close to the water, to further convince clients he was more "in tune." Whatever! The chair was comfy, and some peace and calm felt great after driving for miles on the always hectic 405 Freeway.

At first, I figured Mr. Hurst must be rolling in dough to have such a nice beach home, but upon closer examination I realized this part of the house was actually an "add-on" or a guesthouse. I wondered if he was getting rich by pulling the wool over the eyes of gullible, grieving people. Or was he merely renting this part of the larger home? I was on a self-appointed mission to check him out. If he proved to be a fraud, I vowed to begin working to debunk psychics in general.

The friend who recommended him may have been fooled, but not me, brother! During my long drive there that night, I'd strengthened my resolve to remain a hard-core skeptic. I'd only given him my first name on the phone when we set the appointment, more than three months ahead of time. He must keep busy, being booked that far ahead. I had deliberately parked way down the street from his home so as not to give him any clues. I was skeptical, but not totally closed off. I had read about Edgar Cayce, and even had lots of precognitive dreams as a kid. That is, until my mother made me quit telling her about them, because it scared her too much when they'd come true. But this was different, someone claiming to actually be able to communicate with the dead? Preposterous! But try as I might to stay on my guard, something inside me really wanted to like this man.

Brian Hurst smiled warmly at me from his kitchen. He certainly looked harmless; average weight, height; regular clothes. His face was open and friendly, with wide green eyes that seemed to see right through you. My mother had possessed that same shade of clear, green "all-knowing" eyes. His home seemed normal; no weird voodoo masks, statues or oddball paintings. Nopc, nothing out of the ordinary, no way out-there, spiritual "woo-woo" stuff.

He carried a full tea service back to the living room, laid out to perfection. The tea steeped in the multi-colored pot; there was honey, lemon and milk, along with some little cookies. He whipped this up so quickly, I wondered, "Could he have known I was a tea drinker before I even arrived?" Nah, that was silly, probably just part of his usual routine. After all, the Brits do love their tea!

He sat down, took a delicate sip, and briefly explained what I might expect. I stirred my tea, listening politely. Next, he said a short prayer, which quite surprised me. The church I was reared in totally negated anything like this. Call it a reading if you want, it was a "séance" as far as they were concerned, and immediately classified as being "of the devil." Images of old movies where phony psychics moaned and swayed and things flew around the room flashed through my mind. Yet something in Brian's manner assured me I was in no danger whatsoever.

For a moment he gazed at me so pointedly I wondered if he was trying to read my mind. Then he broke the silence. "You're from somewhere in the Midwest, aren't you? The snowplows were out in the winter and quite often you didn't have to go to school because it snowed so hard."

"Ah, yes, that's right." Inwardly I remained unimpressed; he could have guessed that from my face. I'd often heard I had a "Midwestern girl look," whatever *that* meant. Odds were, he could hit more than fifty percent accuracy with clients using that statement, given the transient nature of Southern California's population. The Doubting Thomas within my mind smirked, "Okay, yes, you're very charming and all, but you're gonna have to do a lot better than that, buddy!" He suddenly startled me by jumping up.

"Oh, excuse me, Cheryl...it *is* Cheryl, isn't it?"

"Yes, that's right. What's wrong....?"

"Oh, dear," he intoned apologetically as he crossed back to the kitchen. "I forgot to unplug my refrigerator. Just a moment." He pulled the plug then returned to his seat. "You see, it oftentimes hums on the same frequency that the spirits send messages through. That can make the communication much more difficult to pick up."

He smiled as if all he had just said and done were perfectly logical. Inside my head *The Twilight Zone* theme music hummed loudly, "du du du du, du du, du du..." Now, *this* was finally getting weird, more like what I expected. Granted, I had been a music education major, not heavy into scientific stuff like sound waves and frequencies, but come on! This was pretty bizarre. Oh, well, at least I could laugh off all this freaky stuff all the way home! Amused, I decided to give him ten more minutes before taking off. I'd simply pay him for the time spent and have a nice, relaxing night.

"Did you have an aunt who lived on the outside edge of Kansas?" His voice abruptly interrupted my thoughts. When I looked over, his head was tipped to one side a bit, eyes closed, as though straining to hear some unseen person.

"Well, actually, yes." I cleared my throat, which was suddenly dry. "My favorite aunt lived right on the western border of Kansas, in a town called Goodland. That's correct." I was rambling now, as I hadn't expected my aunt to give me a message. I loved her dearly, but she hadn't been on my mind for some time. If any valid information could indeed come through this fellow, I had dared to hold out a tiny hope that I might hear from one, or both, of my parents. He smiled, sensing he was on the right track. My heart skipped a beat. This was getting a bit eerie, but I was absolutely riveted to my seat.

"Well, this dear lady is in Spirit, you see, and she's got a white dog with a black spot on its side there with her, and she's saying, 'We're not in Kansas anymore, Toto!'"

"Oh, my God!" I gasped. My aunt had a penchant for white poodles and her favorite, a standard named Pierre, had a large black birthmark on his side! To top it all off, she knew that my favorite movie from the time I was tiny was *The Wizard of Oz*. She'd even given me a set of L. Frank Baum books. Where was this guy getting this information? Though disconcerted, I was now thoroughly fascinated.

"Kathy, who is Kathy?" he asked, peering at me. My vocal cords felt frozen. I couldn't reply before he grinned and continued, "Oh, that's *your* name, is it then, Auntie? Aunt Kathy?"

I managed to eke out, "Yes, that's her name!" I cleared my throat again, and tried to clear my head as well. I took a deep breath and tried to slow down my racing heart. What was going on here? Was I going to faint, shout, or just sit there like a zombie? Brian went right on having a good time conversing with my deceased aunt, while I tried to get a grip.

"She says she's been moving little things about in your home lately, Cheryl, like your keys, nothing major. Just trying to get your attention, let you know she's around. Not to scare you or anything. She became rather frustrated when you couldn't figure out what was going on. She's tried talking to you several times, she says, but you can't seem to hear her." He chuckled as though sharing a private joke with her, then filled me in. "She says, 'Don't take this personally, Cheryl, not many of you on the Earth take the time to learn to hear us.' But she adds that she thinks *you* will, one day," he beamed at me.

I was so stunned, the next few minutes went right over my head. Good thing he was tape recording this session, because I remained in shock for the better part of the next half-hour. In fact, I mentally "time-tripped" backward several years...

Aunt Kathy had always been a rebel, the middle child of three daughters born to my maternal grandmother. Grandma had labeled Kathleen "feisty, bull-headed and ornery." Strangely enough, my mother had assigned those same attributes to me at a young age! I strongly recalled a "table-tipping" session when visiting Kathy one summer. I was eleven years old and my ten year old cousin and I were on a week-long visit with our aunt. The scene replayed like some mini-movie in my mind.

That quiet, hot Kansas night, we had just finished washing the dinner dishes. TV was especially mundane that night, and Aunt Kathy sensed we were restless. Her boys had left home long ago, and I think she got a kick out of having a couple of kids around at that point in her life. My cousin and I were playing checkers, arguing out of boredom, when a noise distracted us. What was our eccentric aunt up to now? She winked at us as she moved a small telephone table to the center of the living room. Next, she lowered the lights and whispered conspiratorially, "Bring three chairs over here from the kitchen, girls. How would you like to see this table dance?"

Wide-eyed with wonder and doubt, we decided to humor her. Aunt Kathy was always fun; you never knew what she'd do or say next. She cussed like a sailor, smoked like a chimney, and her heart was bigger than all outdoors. We loved her madly because she was so unique, very different from our mothers, her sisters. She made us laugh, and often gave us new things to think about. She was so unlike our Moms, sometimes it was hard to imagine they really were sisters at all. Like right now! Intrigued, we moved the chairs into a triad fashion around the little ordinary, two-tiered table.

Aunt Kathy enjoyed having a captive audience. In retrospect, I know she would have been one hell of an actress! I don't know if she ever tried these tricks on her husband, probably not. Uncle John was a retired, soft-spoken farmer with simple tastes, who would have undoubtedly written off such antics as nonsense. He pretty much kept to himself during our visits. "Aunt Khaki," (my baby nickname for her, which she refused to give up when I got older) was in her element now. Her eyes danced with mischief as she led us through this ritual.

"Now, put your fingertips just lightly on the edge of the table right in front of you," she demonstrated, "like so, that's right. Now, focus on the table...we're going to ask it a couple of questions. Are you ready?" She looked at us, one at a time. We gulped bravely, trying to look cool as we nodded in the affirmative. "Okay, Table...tap once for yes, twice for no. Do you understand?"

The table (thankfully) did nothing. I let out an involuntary sigh of relief. Aunt Kathy was far from finished, however. "I said, once for yes, twice for no, Table. Now, if you understand, *dance*!" she commanded. Slowly, the table seemed to shudder, then it distinctly tapped once.

"AAAAHHHH!!!" My cousin and I yelled in unison. Aunt Kathy just grinned. I decided it must be a big trick, and quickly looked under the table leg to see if her foot was propped there, but saw both feet neatly tucked under her chair.

"What'sa matter, Cheryl? Afraid?" She challenged. She had reverted to an eleven year old herself, it seemed! She knew I was a tomboy who couldn't stand being called "chicken" in any way, shape, or form.

"No, not me! Not at all! I just thought you were messing with us."

"Nope. So, what do you want to ask it?"

My cousin and I exchanged looks. She seemed more frightened than I, because she couldn't even squeak out a word. I took a deep breath, and decided to be a player.

"Okay, t-t-t-table..." I stammered. "If you're so smart, tell me, is this right?" I paused in order to work up a worthy test for our wooden fortune teller and to brace myself so I wouldn't yell again if and when it answered. "Okay, here goes: my middle name is Elizabeth."

"THUMP, THUMP!" answered the Table. Two for "no!" I had inherited Grandma's middle name of Ellen. This time, I had been watching closely. Aunt Kathy's feet were definitely under her chair the whole time.

My cousin finally found her voice and asked a couple of questions. I came up with a few more and the table faithfully dance-thumped correct yes/no answers. No longer afraid, we were mesmerized. Aunt Kathy suddenly grew tired of the game and wanted to be sure to insert a "disclaimer" for her sisters' benefit. She knew we would talk about this at home! She stood up with a flourish.

"Girls, that's enough, now. Can't be wearing this ol' table out, y'know. But I want to show you something *really* amazing." She crossed to the bookshelf and came back with a large Bible, holding it reverently. "See this Good Book?" We nodded. She carefully placed it on the center of the lower shelf of our magic table. "Put your fingertips back on the edges, girls, just like before." After we did, in her best theatrical gypsy voice, our aunt commanded, "All right, Table, dance!"

The formerly active table was now sound asleep for all points and purposes; back to its boring "day job" of being plain old, stationary wood. Aunt Kathy raised her voice and once again ordered, "Table! I said *dance*!" It remained perfectly still. Dead to the world.

She shoved her chair back, jumped up, triumphantly pointed to the Bible, clapped her hands and whooped like a tent revival preacher, "The Word of the Lord, girls! The Word of the Lord!"

She was a character, all right. I knew in my heart my aunt wasn't messing with "dark forces." She was a wonderfully kind, generous woman. She also knew how to play it smart where her sisters were concerned. She knew we wouldn't be able to keep this story from our mothers, both "God-fearing Christians," who would undoubtedly criticize her for corrupting our young minds with such heathen carryings-on. So she basically covered her tail with the Bible finale'. Way to go, Kathy!

Gradually, I focused back on the present time. Here she was tonight, nearly two decades later, talking away as though she'd never left the face of the Earth; conversing with me through this stranger from England. Fascinating! Brian told me he would repeat verbatim whatever she said to the best of his ability, that those in Spirit often transmitted thoughts much more quickly than he was able to convey them, so he sometimes had to ask them to slow down a bit and focus on one clear idea, one thought at a time. In my aunt's case, however, she apparently had this communication "wired" because it just *flowed*.

She gave several recent personal details from my life that only I would know. She even mentioned that I needed to put air in my left rear tire before I headed home or I just might have a blow-out on the freeway. Three people at various stops that same day had pointed out that exact tire and I'd ignored their advice. As I had parked nearly a block from Brian's door, there was no way *he* could have known that. I was a believer by this point; this was the real deal. Now I excitedly asked my aunt questions, chiming in with verification as he relayed her messages.

"Aunt Kathy," I cut in at one point, "I love you so much and I'm very grateful you're here tonight. Thank you! Is my Mom there? Can she give me a message, too?" A tear ran down my cheek; my mother had passed away in 1971 when I was fifteen, nearly fourteen years prior to this sitting. My Dad followed in 1983. There was a distinct pause, then Brian seemed to pick up a slight Midwestern accent as he repeated her answer.

"Well, honey, just because someone dies, it doesn't make them a genius."

I was stunned by that reply. Aunt Kathy continued, "Your mom, well, you know how strong she believes, how the church was everything to her and all. See, there are different levels of spiritual awareness over here, too, hon. People bring their belief system back to the light and some choose to grow and stretch, and some don't. Pretty much like the Earth. Someone has to be willing to open up their mind to new ideas. Now, that genius comment was not a dig at your mom. You know I love her to pieces! I'm not saying I'm any Albert Einstein, either. It's just that I was always more open to this sort of thing, remember?"

I certainly did. There was that dancing table, for one thing! This all made sense to me somehow, it *felt* true.

"But you listen here, Cheryl Ellen...er, is she saying Ellen?" Brian was checking to make sure he heard her correctly.

"Yes, my middle name is Ellen, that's right. When I was a kid, if they really wanted my attention they used both names."

He laughed, really appreciating the fact I was giving him encouraging confirmation now. Why not? He had more than proven he was genuine!

Aunt Kathy continued, "Well, dear, now that you're ready to hear from us over here on this side, I'm going to tell Dolores how important it would be for you to hear from her directly. I'll do my best to convince her nobody's gonna be mad at her. God doesn't get mad at us. He doesn't waste His time on that vengeful, jealous God stuff they teach in most churches. Here's the truth—GOD IS LOVE. That's one thing they got right. They should spend much more time on that idea right there, in my opinion."

I nodded my head in complete agreement. I'd always had a hard time picturing God arbitrarily punishing innocent people and countries by creating impoverished conditions or handicaps. My own little brother had created that question in my mind at a young age, and...

"Cheryl?" Brian gently interrupted my thoughts. "I'll repeat the question; you went off somewhere for a moment, didn't you, dear? Your aunt mentions someone named John...who is John, please?"

Caught off-guard, I blurted out, "Oh, dear God! John is my younger brother." Not a word had been said up to that point about my sweet baby brother John. I was nervous as to what might come forth next. I needn't have been. Without question, it proved to be the most comforting evidence I have ever received from a reading.

Brian sat up, tilted his head even more, leaned his torso over to one side, and his wrists pulled back in a contracted fashion. My mouth fell open, because this man, sitting there with his eyes closed, was perfectly mimicking my little brother's usual physical position when he sat up in his wheelchair!

Before I could offer any explanation as to my brother's condition, Brian described it perfectly. I sobbed uncontrollably as he relayed, "He was born with severe cerebral palsy, quite severe...oh, my, yes...so sad...he was very sadly hit, that's what your aunt says, yes...His wrists are contracted just so, and his spine is crooked. He's in a nursing home, your aunt says, and she knows you're very worried about him because he's so sick right now."

I was weeping openly at this point, because I had so much guilt over not being in a financial position to care for my brother, whom I loved so much. He required around-the-clock care and Dad and I had finally placed him in a nursing home four years ago. We had to make him a ward of the state to get him admitted, thereby giving up all say-so in how his care was managed. One of the first things they did upon his admission was to insert a feeding tube. His health had gone downhill ever since. Leaving him in that home was one of the hardest things I ever did. Dad himself needed to go into a retirement home at that time. He was nearly eighty years old and could no longer care for the house. Upon his encouragement, I had moved to California to seriously pursue my dreams of making it in "show biz," but the guilt gnawed at me constantly, harping "There should have been *some* way you could have done more for John, Cheryl!"

"Cheryl? Your aunt wants you to listen closely to this next bit, will you try? I know it's hard, I know you're sad." Brian couldn't have been more sensitive. I felt I'd known him for years; after all this amazing evidence, how could I feel otherwise? "You know your brother is quite ill right now, yes?"

Wiping my eyes with my shirt-sleeve, I whispered, "Yes. I worry about him all the time, pray for him a lot...he's been in the hospital so much, lately."

"Well, Aunt Kathy says you're not to spend so much time worrying about him, hon. She calls you 'hon.' John is getting ready to make his transition to Heaven and she says when he sleeps, he's practicing manifesting there on the other side. She says, 'Hon, over here, John is absolutely *perfect*!'"

"Oh, thank God!" I cried, this time with tears of joy. I knew in my heart this was the truth. I knew it beyond the shadow of a doubt. For the first time, I felt truly happy for my baby brother. He was finally going to escape that little twisted body of a prison, which had never seemed noble enough to contain his incredibly sweet, loving soul.

That night in Brian's living room, I felt I'd received a direct dispensation from God; finally, some solid comfort for all the loss I had endured; both parents, my favorite aunt, and now my beloved brother was apparently going to join them very soon. But it was okay, because he would be *perfect* in the Spirit World!

I hugged Brian and thanked him profusely at the end of the sitting. He was obviously touched and emotional himself. "Oh, it's so rewarding when it flows, Cheryl. Your aunt is an exceptional communicator. I wish all those in Spirit were able to speak so clearly."

I knew I'd found a wonderful friend whose gift had truly blessed me. Brian mentioned he held group sittings in his home once a month, and encouraged me to stay in touch. I promised to do so, then immediately drove to the nearest gas station and put air in that low rear tire!

John died August 10, 1985, just twelve days after that extraordinary reading. Because of that extremely powerful session and its impeccable timing, (I was beginning to learn there are *no* accidents in this life), I was able to bless John and release him willingly, with very little remorse. After all, how selfish to dwell on my own loss, when his soul had finally obtained ultimate emancipation after twenty-five years of being trapped in that little, crooked body. Instead, I rejoiced with the Angels because I knew he could now fly among them, sing with them and dance upon the stars.

What I didn't know at that time was that our true journey, our mission together, was just beginning.

Chapter Two

The "Show Me State"

What better place for a skeptic to hail from than Missouri? "Show me," "Make me believe," "I'll believe it when I see it!" These are the supposed credos of Missourians. In my private practice and at lectures, I'm often asked about my childhood, especially about when my psychic awareness began. So let's "start at the very beginning."

My birth was more than a month overdue. Being late for many things became typical through early adulthood, until I learned to stop creating that situation. As to my debut in this lifetime, perhaps I simply wanted to be a Scorpio rather than a Libra! Some of my astrologer friends today present a strong case that each soul chooses a sun sign in order to be endowed with certain characteristics which will assist the soul in its Life Objective. No matter how the "Powers that Be" factored into my belated birth, I know my dear mother was more than ready for me to make my entrance in November, 1955!

I was a "blue baby," born with the umbilical cord wrapped around my neck. Did this traumatic entrance set me up to stifle my voice? Well, I spent most of my young years in the company of my elders and with the exception of what my mother deemed inappropriate outbursts of psychic and/or intellectual insights, I was most usually seen and not heard. So did that early manifestation of holding back my voice, breath and opinions affect me? Certainly such things are worth consideration, simply because it can assist one in moving on and becoming more productive in one's present life. Today, in addition to working as a medium, I'm also a certified hypnotherapist. In sessions involving Time Line therapy and past life regression, I've learned that many times something centered around one's birth circumstances sets the tone for future development.

Since my late teens, I've used my voice to earn the major portion of my living. I joined my first band as lead singer at age eighteen; I acted in theatre for many years and worked for several years as a radio announcer and voiceover artist. Today I love speaking to large crowds, putting on seminars and workshops about self-empowerment and spiritual growth. And of course, in my private practice whether giving a reading or guiding a hypnosis session, I'm always talking! I'm grateful I "found" my voice. I know that was one of my soul's lessons in this life, and brother, did I get it!

We lived in North Kansas City until I was nearly three years old. That first house resembled a home you'd see in *Leave It To Beaver*. For us, as for most of the nation, the mid-'50's were a peaceful, happy time. Like many adults, my parents both smoked. Mama stopped soon after I was born, however, because her baby girl had this habit of grabbing everything. I nearly pulled the poor woman's earlobe off once by grabbing a dangling earring! So those types of jewelry went away. Secondhand smoke was a totally foreign concept back then. She simply didn't want her baby to be burned, so she gave up cigarettes, cold-turkey. Daddy continued to smoke, but only while working in the yard or the garage, never when carrying or playing with me. I quickly became the apple of his eye and thus began our life-long mutual admiration society.

Definite evidence of my intuitive talents showed up even by the tender age of two. Most of this I know due to the frequency with which these stories were told to family members and friends. Much of what my mother considered cute at first grew into curiosity, then in the absence of a logical explanation, curiosity transformed to worry, then fear. At that point, the stories stopped being circulated. I never forgot them, though. What follows are just a few examples.

My oldest brother got married when I was not quite three. He and my brother Don were Mom's kids from her first marriage. The newlyweds visited us frequently on weekends, and usually Don was there, too. He lived with us part-time, and with his Dad sometimes. One of the activities we shared as a family was playing canasta. Now, I was about two and a half when I learned this card game. I'm told I played quite well, often winning, even though bidding is an integral component of canasta. My folks were always apparently surprised by my understanding of the principles involved. Honestly, I don't remember much about this. Could it be linked to a past life as a card shark? I'm jesting now, attempting to keep this light as I point out several rather unusual activities and behaviors I exhibited from a very young age. Many young children have similar gifts, even more pronounced than mine were "back in the day." After all, souls are evolving, mass consciousness is elevating, and it's about time! The kids coming into the Earth plane experience these days are amazingly advanced in their inner knowing. Young children simply don't have the "walls" up yet which stop them from acting on intuition or gut instinct. That's why I love teaching psychic development to young people. I learn so much from them! [If you have a psychic child you'd like to encourage to embrace and positively develop their gift, I'd suggest reading *The Wise Child* by Sonia Choquette.]

It was pretty peaceful during my first three years in the Booth family. My mother doted on me, reading storybooks to me quite frequently. In fact, one day she became convinced she had a prodigy on her hands. I loved her attention and like all children, especially loved making her proud of me. One day she was reading me a familiar story when I exclaimed, "This time, Mama, let me read it to *you*!"

She laughed, "Sure, you're a big girl, go right ahead."

I began "reading" perfectly, word for word, turning the pages at the right place, glancing up to see disbelief growing on her face. This was fun! I was impressing my Mama, one of my favorite people!

As soon as my father set foot in the door that night, she grabbed him by the arm and led him to his favorite chair.

"Sit down, Walt. You're not gonna believe this. Our little girl is a genius! She can read, I tell you. The child is only two, and she can *read*!"

I grinned up at Daddy as he gave me a quizzical look.

"Oh, you can read, can you, baby? Hmm, that's great." He patted his lap, told me to get my storybook, climb up and read to him. I promptly obeyed. Another chance to show off, to perform for my other favorite person in the world!

My father had a limited education, but was extremely savvy and street-smart. Largely self-educated and a great judge of human nature, he was also a pretty good detective. He encouraged me as I read, watching carefully as I moved my eyes along the page, just like Mama did. Then suddenly, he turned the page before it was time!

"Hey, Daddy! No! Stop! Go back to the other page! I wasn't done," I pouted.

"Oh, sorry. Well, let's just go on from here. Start with this word, honey," he pointed helpfully at a word midway down the new page.

"I can't! I don't know it. I only know the story if it stays in order."

"Oh, really? So, you just know when to turn the pages because the pictures go with the part of the story you're saying?" He raised an eyebrow as he grinned at my mortified mother.

He'd realized I had a somewhat uncanny ability to memorize and recite from a young age. When it came to music and stories, my memory was pretty photographic. He chuckled lightly, tickled to have busted my mother's chops. She was not amused at first, but soon realized it was pretty funny how she had jumped on the "wunderkind" wagon so soon. I could tell neither one was mad at me, so I happily finished "reading" the story and enjoyed the rest of the evening.

The television became my favorite babysitter, as it did with many Baby Boomers. My mother saw nothing wrong with letting me sit for hours, glued to kids' programming. I remember watching *The Wizard Of Oz* in one of its first TV airings, and how fascinated I was. The flying monkeys and the Wicked Witch of the West didn't terrorize me as much as they did my mother! I loved the songs, and immediately identified with Dorothy, searching for her home and acceptance. The Scarecrow was my favorite character, and I clapped and hooted whenever Ray Bolger fell down only to magically get back up again. He seemed to have rubber legs!

Music has always moved me. I constantly sang nursery rhymes and such until I began to absorb the catchy jingles of commercials. My mother swore the first song she ever heard me sing was the Hamm's beer commercial theme, "*From the land of sky blue waters...!*" Daddy sure got a kick out of that one, because that was one of his favorite brands.

Another story repeated and handed down about my early childhood development was with regard to my vanity. I suppose my mother gets some of the credit for this, as she loved to doll me up. She was a talented seamstress (a gift I never inherited and always admired) and she received many compliments on the beautiful dresses she made for me. Much to my dismay, people fawned over me, oohing and ahing at the outfits, and they always raved over my naturally curly golden locks. It irritated me when strangers wanted to touch my hair. (They were invading my aura, but I didn't understand that then, of course. Think about that the next time you start to pat a child you don't know on their head!)

I contracted chicken pox around age two. I had already survived German measles, but these pox things were nasty! They put mittens on me and taped them closed to keep me from scratching at them; several spots were on my face. My conceit about my looks became most obvious one day when Mama came rushing into my bedroom as I stood wailing before the mirror.

"Cheryl, honey! What on earth is wrong! Why are you crying

so?" She took me on her lap and patted my back soothingly, genuinely concerned.

I sobbed and pointed to the aberration in the mirror. "Because.... because that don't look like Cheryl! She's ugly!"

She choked back her laughter, fearful of setting me off again, and assured me the ugly old pox would disappear soon, as long as I promised not to scratch them. She wisely hung a cloth over my bureau mirror, promising to take it down when I was all pretty again.

About that same time my parents decided we needed a bigger home, so my father began looking. He'd find a house in our budget, then take Mom and me to check it out. I somehow knew when we'd walk into a house it would not be where we'd wind up. I began saying, "We're going to live in a pink house with a fireplace."

My parents found this very droll. Mama began telling her friends about this, but usually added, "That Cheryl! I swear, she's already so spoiled! Her father absolutely dotes on her, and here she is telling him she wants to live in a pink house with a fireplace. Can you imagine? I don't know where she gets her notions."

Now, I firmly believe I said, "We're *going* to live in a pink house" not "I *want* to live in a pink house." I believe I had a precognitive dream and was just telling them what it showed me. One day Daddy called from work and said he was taking us to see a house he thought would be just perfect. He drove us to Gladstone, a suburb further north than we had looked so far. We pulled into a driveway with a "For Sale" sign. I looked up at the house and began laughing and clapping my hands.

"This is it! This is our house!"

My parents looked at each other. Mama raised an eyebrow and said, "Well, Walt, it's *pink*, that's for sure. I hope you didn't spend a lot of time trying to find a pink house just to make her happy. It's huge! Probably way out of our price range..."

Dad laughed. "No, it's really not, they're anxious to sell. And it just so happens to be pink, too." He playfully pinched my cheek. "And what's inside the pink house, Punkin'?" He pointed to the roof.

"Oh, Daddy! A chimney...it has a fireplace! Come on, let's go see!" I scrambled over my mother's lap, trying to bolt out of the car and hurry into what I was certain was our new home.

"That's right," my father chuckled. Mama shot him a look. "Well, it's just pure coincidence, Dee. They say it's a great school district, too. Come on, let's take a look. There's a huge back yard, a finished basement and three bedrooms. Lots more space, right?"

Mama nodded and opened the car door. She was apparently

weakening. My Daddy could talk her into almost anything and when the two of us joined forces, she usually found it easiest to give in.

"It won't hurt anything to go inside, honey," my father continued convincing Mama. "You'll like the realtor, he's a real nice guy."

By this time, I was standing on the small porch, impatiently waiting for my parents. Long story short, we bought the pink house with the fireplace and that's where I lived for the next eighteen years.

Around the same time, Mama and I went on a shoe shopping expedition. She was determined to find me a pair of Oxford style saddle shoes, worn by almost all the little girls back then. She was so excited to finally have a daughter to dress up. My brother Don was fourteen when I was born. So not only was I the first baby in a long while, I was her only girl. My father's first marriage included three daughters who were already grown long before I was born. So he longed for a son in many ways, while my mother wanted her long-awaited daughter to be a perfect little lady, complete with popular clothes, immaculate manners and grooming. When I turned out to be a rollicking tomboy, she was extremely disappointed. But I'm getting the cart ahead of the horse, here. Back to the shoe story.

That patient young sales clerk brought out every pair of saddle shoes he had in stock in every size close to fitting me, but none worked. They either pinched my feet or slipped right off.

My mother sighed, "Well, I guess we'll just have to go somewhere else tomorrow, Cheryl. I didn't know you'd be so hard to fit. Thank you, young man." She gathered her purse and came over to grab my hand. I was standing in a corner, looking at a life-size doll "model" who was wearing saddle shoes.

"Her shoes will fit me, Mama. The dolly's shoes. See?" I pointed, beaming. "They're like the others, but hers are my size."

"Don't be silly! Those must be one of the same sizes you just finished trying on. They're not going to take those shoes off that doll just to satisfy one of your whims. Come on, it's time to go home."

I began to cry. "But, Mama! I know these shoes will fit. I *know* it! Can't we try them, please?"

She glared at me. "Now, you stop that right this instant, young lady! We've wasted far too much of this young fellow's time. Let's go!" She yanked at my arm as she looked at the salesman apologetically. "I'm so sorry, sir. She's very strong-willed. Her father and I spoil her too much. Thanks again." She pulled me along behind her as I gazed longingly at the doll.

He called after us, "Well, ma'am, it's really no trouble. I don't have any other customers right now, and hey, maybe the little girl is right, wouldn't that be a hoot?" I smiled at him, he was nice! He winked at me. "Stranger things have happened. Gosh, she's got me curious now. No harm in trying, is there?"

He smiled as my mother shrugged her shoulders and with a sigh, sank into a chair. By now she was accustomed to people wanting to see me smile. He sat the doll down in a chair and slipped her shoes off. I hopped into the chair next to her and extended my feet so he could make the transfer. The doll was about my height. I somehow felt like she "told" me her shoes would fit me.

"There you go, young lady! Walk around and see how those feel," he winked again.

I hopped down. Lo and behold, the shoes fit perfectly!

"Look, Mama, they fit! They feel good. Can we get them, please? Can we?"

Unable to hold a frown for long, my mother laughed. She bent down to check the placement of my toes in the shoes. ""May we?' not 'can we?'" she clucked her tongue. "Oh, land o' mercy, child...you drive me to distraction! Honestly, I don't know where you come up with this stuff. How did you know...? Never mind. Hmm...they sure do fit, don't they?" she looked to the salesman for confirmation.

He grinned. "Yes, ma'am, they sure do. That's one smart little girl you've got there!"

"Yes, too smart for her own good, sometimes," she said with a wry smile. "Okay, honey. They're yours. Wanna wear 'em home?"

"Oh, yes, please!" My toes wiggled happily inside my shiny new shoes. I silently conversed some more with the funny doll while my mother made the purchase. Of course at that age, I was totally unaware that the voice I heard in my head was most likely a guide, not the doll herself.

That story was one of those told many times, much like the pink house saga. I don't want to paint my mother as the "heavy" all the time. She was a wonderfully caring woman. There were actually times she was quite pleased to show me off. On some level, she must have felt I had the potential to be the next Shirley Temple, because she loved rolling my naturally curly hair up into thick sausage curls. Sometimes she'd get me all spruced up and we'd go to her favorite grocery store, which was owned by a man with a funny name, Izzy Glass. Always reminded me of Fuzzy Wuzzy. I'm sure his full name was Isador, but to all his friends, he was "Izzy." He loved it when I'd come into the store with Mama. They'd stand me up on the end of the checkout counter and have me sing all manner of nursery rhymes and songs from TV and radio. *The Mickey Mouse Show* was in its heyday then, and I thought I was as good as any of those ol' Mouseketeers! I was always a great mimic and learned lyrics quickly.

While performing on the grocery store "stage," people would applaud and often lay a few coins by my feet. Although that embarrassed my mother, I remember a glint of pride in her eyes during those early performances and she'd encourage me to scoop up the change and put it in my piggy bank when we got home.

Grocery stores were the source of many funny stories between Mama and me during those early years. One time I was looking at toys while she moved on to shop, and I became frightened when I looked up and couldn't find her. I ran up and down the aisles, finally seeing the backside of a woman Mama's size, wearing a coat that looked like hers. I flung myself at her legs, sobbing, "Mama, I lost you!"

She turned around good-naturedly and I was surprised to look up into the smiling face of a lovely African-American lady. Mama had rounded the corner with her cart just in time to be embarrassed by her daughter yet again. The woman was very gracious and quite amused; it was really not a big deal to anyone except Mama.

Another time we were coming out of the store. We had a 1956 two-tone Chevy Bel Air. I loved that car! It was copper and cream. The day in question, there was an identical car parked right next to ours. Back in those days, it was not common practice to worry about locking the doors of your car or your house. A simpler time, indeed! I headed for our car. Mama had her arms full of groceries, and said, "Cheryl! Get in *our* car. That's not ours!" She headed around to the driver's door and got in.

I protested, "But, *this* one's ours..."

"Don't argue! Get in so we can go. I'm tired."

I obediently climbed in, looked around and realized the upholstery was slightly different than our car, parked right next to us. I wistfully looked at it, wondering if this meant we were trading vehicles with some stranger. Grownups sure did some odd things!

Of course, when her key didn't work in the "copycat" car she realized I was right, and urged me to hurry up and change. Fortunately, no one else saw that, so she was not too embarrassed. In fact, we all laughed about it later when she shared the story with my father!

One thing that was not so funny was that we were on a pretty fixed budget. Daddy worked as senior mechanic and shop foreman for a Sinclair Oil refinery downtown. We always seemed to have to make the money stretch. Mama's strength was not numbers, something I *did* inherit from her! Math has never been my strong suit. Several times, at the check-out line, when the clerk announced the total bill, a puzzled look would come over my mother's face. When she didn't have enough money, she'd look down in shame, gather her composure and decide which items to have voided off. If only they'd had pocket calculators back then, Mom! I share this simply to show you how readily my mother absorbed shame and guilt. It was something she had been brought up to do. So when she was harsh with me about my antics, I know that most of the time, she was trying to protect me from experiencing those emotions by embarrassing myself.

We all loved that pink ranch house. I had my own room, and there was a full finished basement. The back yard was huge, stretching out over an acre. It was lush and rolling, with two gently sloping hills accented with bushes. Mama planted irises, jonquils and roses. When they were in bloom, it was a symphony of color! There was a tall cottonwood tree toward the back fence, two weeping willows, and a large oak tree that became my favorite for climbing in later years.

I have many fond memories of the first years in that home. My parents loved Lawrence Welk. As we watched his show, I climbed up on the fireplace hearth and made it my stage, trying to dance around like Bobby and Cissy. I was my parents' personal floor show entertainer, and quite a cut-up. This was a mystery to them, as was my singing. Neither one of them seemed to have a musical or theatrical bone in their body. In fact, my mother admittedly "couldn't carry a tune in a bucket." I found out in later years that my father was actually a good lyricist when he was younger, and he always did have a strong love of music. For the most part, however, I was a bewilderment to them.

I remember swinging for hours in the backyard, singing at the top of my voice. Periodically my mother would yell out of the screen window, "You're too loud, Cheryl Ellen. Calm down." I'd try, then I'd get caught up in the song and the volume would be back before I knew it. Daddy teasingly called me "Little Leather Lungs." He loved it when I sang.

One day a neighbor waved as we were getting into the car. "Hey, Dolores! Hi, Cheryl. Say, we really love your singing, young lady!"

"Thank you, Mrs. Spencer," I smiled.

Mama shook her head, "Oh, mercy, I'm sorry if she's so loud she bothers you..."

"Bother? Oh, no! She's got a good voice, right on key. She seems so happy when she's singing, makes me happy to hear her. You keep it up, honey!" She winked at me and went inside.

Mama just looked at me and shook her head, her most typical response to me these days. Singing and acting out songs, shows and plays would be a major theme in my life. Because of my love of performing and lack of common interests with her, I'm certain she sometimes wondered if I were from Mars or at the very least, suspected that I may have been switched at the hospital. Except there was no denying I was the "spitting image" of my father. Even in looks, she couldn't relate to her daughter. Once she was talking to her youngest sister and asked, "Mary Catherine, don't you think Cheryl looks like me, even a little bit?"

Her sister gave me the once-over, pausing just long enough so that Mama would take her seriously. "Well, sure she does, Dee! She looks like you from here up!" She held her palm flat out against my eyebrows and howled with laughter. Mama was not amused.

It's true that my mother was a strict disciplinarian. However, many years after she died, I found her diary, kept during the first three years of my life. The entries about my health, growth and learning convinced me beyond the shadow of a doubt that she fully loved me. As I grew older, she had a hard time accepting that I was so different from anything she'd expected. That was the main source of our communication problems. Her own upbringing was less than pleasant at times, and I'll address that a bit more later. Dolores Voncille Booth was a great human being, loving and generous to a fault. What happened next in our family was an extremely difficult blow for us all; but mostly, I remember how hard it hit my mother.

Chapter Three

"Heeere's Johnny!"

When I was four, Mama began talking about "expecting" to her friends. I wasn't sure what this meant at first, but felt it was some happy surprise or secret, because she always smiled and talked about it in hushed tones when I was around. One day she called me to her and as she placed her hands on her growing belly, she told me she was going to have a baby soon. I squealed with delight.

"Oh, a baby brother, I'm going to have a baby brother! I had a dream about this!" I was so excited. "Can we name him Johnny, please, Mama?"

She laughed, "You and your crazy dreams! Why are you so sure it's a boy, Cheryl? And what makes you want to name him Johnny? Oh, I know! Because your little boyfriend's name is Johnny, huh?" she teased.

Johnny was the name of a little boy for whom she babysat. He lived just down the street and we had lots of fun together. He was certainly my best friend then; but there was more to this than wanting to create a namesake for him.

I was sitting by her on the couch and carefully laid my ear against her tummy, where she told me the baby was growing. "No, Mama, not because of *that* Johnny." I listened closely to her stomach. "I just know that's my brother's name, his name is John. That's what he told me in the dream, and that's what he still says now. We have to name him John. Maybe we'll call him Johnny, but his name is John. Please, can we name him that?"

"Oh, my Lord, Cheryl. The baby is not talking to you. How could he? Or she? Listen to me! You've almost got me convinced it's a boy. You're mighty persuasive with that imagination of yours! God will decide if it's a boy or a girl."

My face fell, recognizing yet another instance where she didn't believe me. She saw my disappointment and lifted my chin with a finger. She smiled, "But listen here, I promise you, if it *is* a boy, we'll call him John, that's a good name. Your Daddy and I haven't even talked about names, but I'm sure that's fine with him. Whatever *you* want, usually is! And if it's John, we'll give him Howard for a middle name, same as your Daddy's. There. Are you happy now?" Thrilled about her new baby, she couldn't stay coarse with me for long.

"Oh, yes, Mama! Thank you! I already love my baby brother! I can't wait for him to be born so we can play together!"

I skipped off happily to share the good news with the neighborhood kids. I'm sure she sat shaking her head, wondering where I got such wild ideas. She must have hoped having a younger sibling would calm me down, minimize what she considered my many harebrained ideas, complete with imaginary voices and friends. She probably thought I spent too much time alone, so I made up all my "stories" to entertain myself. It was true, having older parents and siblings, I preferred the company and attention of adults, or was usually most content playing alone. But I was never truly alone!

She was due in a couple of months, growing anxious and more than just a little nervous. One day she was downstairs doing the laundry and I was upstairs watching TV. Suddenly she let out a bloodcurdling shriek. I ran downstairs as fast as my feet could fly to find her standing transfixed, pointing in horror at my dollhouse, which sat under the stairs. Puzzled, I looked inside to see a tiny little garter snake slithering around. I reached to pick him up.

"STOP! What do you think you are doing?" She was literally shaking, and white as a ghost. This was my first experience seeing my mother's deathly fear of snakes.

"Well, he's just a little garter snake, Mama. Daddy showed me some in the back yard. He's not poison. I'll just put him outside...."

"You'll do no such thing." She still had not moved an inch. "You go get Mac. Go get him *now*! Run!"

Since my little brother was on the way, I thought maybe that had made her go a little crazy. Daddy teased her about some of her cravings. I didn't know how pregnant ladies were supposed to act. The MacFaddens lived across the street. Mac worked nights, so Mama knew he would be home. I looked up at her, dumbfounded. All this commotion over a harmless little old garter?

"Go now, Cheryl Ellen. GO!"

"Yes, ma'am!" I scooted up the stairs, and heard her yell up after me to be careful as I crossed the street.

Now it was *my* turn to be embarrassed. After ringing the doorbell, I sighed and explained to my neighbor what was going on. He chuckled, closed the door and held my hand as we went back to my house. He bravely removed the "deadly" garter snake and Mama's face slowly changed from white as a sheet back to its natural color. I was beginning to see how adults were afraid of a few things in life, so in a strange way, this incident created a bond between my mother and me. It let me see that she wasn't always in total control of every situation, and that somehow made me love her that much more.

She was forty-three at the time and I wouldn't find out until years later that during her pregnancy, she slipped and fell on the way to a doctor's visit. She always blamed herself for that, and felt her age was another major contributing factor in John's physical condition.

I heard the story of my baby brother's birth many times. When her water broke at the hospital, she recalled the doctor was present in her room. The intense labor pains suddenly got much worse. Having giving birth three times before, she sensed something was wrong this time around. The doctor's behavior confirmed this was the case, because rather than allowing the birth to proceed normally, he held back the baby's head and began yelling at the top of his lungs, "STAT! Get me a nurse, STAT!"

She must have passed out from the pain, because she didn't remember much else until she woke up after delivery and worriedly looked around.

"Where's my baby? I want my baby!" she screamed. The birth had been so excruciating, she felt certain the baby was stillborn.

The nurses assured her the baby was fine, it was a boy. They would bring him in to her soon, but they were running a few tests right now.

"What's wrong with him? What kind of tests? What's the matter with my baby? Please!" she sobbed. "Why did the doctor hold him back so long? I don't understand. Please bring him to me...."

The nurses comforted her, "There now, Mrs. Booth. Your baby's all right. You just rest. We'll bring him in, in a little while. Try to get some rest. You've just had a real rough time."

Basically, the doctor soon told her and my Dad that John had suffered a "birth injury." There were many complications including some brain damage, and he would most likely be retarded. She cried all during this explanation, her only desire to hold her newborn.

"But where is he? I have to see him, doctor, to hold him. I have to know he'll be all right. Why don't they bring him to me?"

"Well, Dolores, he seems to be having a series of seizures..."

"What?!? Oh, my God, no! My tiny baby, having seizures!" She sobbed hysterically, "Please, I've got to see him!"

They gave her something to calm her down and hours later, mother and son were reunited. Complemented by a shock of thick, black hair, and blue eyes a few shades darker than mine, John's chubby little face looked pretty similar to my baby pictures. The resemblance to our father was striking in both of us! I noticed that his tiny fists were tightly closed most of the time, but the adults didn't comment on that much. It must not have seemed strange to them. As my mother held him, she felt he was absolutely beautiful. A blessed gift from God, a special child.

Once news reached our relatives that a handicapped child had been born, there were many adult discussion held in corners of the hospital waiting room. I heard bits and pieces of conversations, some of which involved my father being advised to "give the child to a special home." I was horrified, but my fears were quickly put to rest. I was so proud to hear my father reply that he would never, ever do such a thing. This was his son, not some monster to be hidden away!

My Aunt Kathy showed up to support her sister's family during this difficult time, and relieved my brothers and sister-in-law who pitched in and did their best to keep me entertained and busy. My father looked very worried the whole time. It seemed to me like everybody wanted to talk to him, the doctors, nurses, our family. Aunt Kathy was so funny, such a warm, big-hearted person. I was glad she had come to stay with us for a few weeks. She told me stories that day in the waiting room, then at one point, stood up and looked me in the eye

"Okay, young lady. Let's go talk to your Daddy for a minute. The doctors seem to be done yacking at him." She took my hand and we headed toward the chair where my father sat slumped forward with his head in his hands. She cleared her throat.

"Ah...Walt?" He started, and she squeezed his shoulder reassuringly. "I'm sorry, Walter. Are they giving you much hope right now?"

He shook his head dejectedly. "No, they don't really know what the hell's going on, Kathy. That much is clear. Damn doctor ought to be sued. I blame him!" His eyes were full of angry tears. "Holding a child back like that, what the hell was he thinking?"

"I don't know, dear." She sat me on his lap, and he automatically hugged me tightly. I hugged back with all my might. My Daddy was my hero, and I'd never seen him cry before. Aunt Kathy pulled up a chair beside us and handed him a tissue. "What I do know is a special child like this requires a lot of care. I wish I could help you more, but right now this is the best I can do." She took an envelope from her purse, and pressed it into his hand.

"What's this? Oh, no, I can't take this from you..."

"Yes, you can, and you will! This is my big sister we're talking about here, the one who took care of me when I was a snot-nosed kid. I owe her a lot! You and Cheryl mean everything to her and Johnny will, too, now. We've had a good year with the farm. I had this little bit tucked away for an emergency and I can't think of a better one than this, can you, Cheryl?" She looked at me, trying to keep my father from being so embarrassed.

I shook my head solemnly. "It's a 'mergency, all right. John will be fine, though, Daddy, you'll see." I patted his cheek, and he kissed the top of my head as he gave my dear aunt a grateful look.

"Kathy, you're the only one who's offered anything more than lip service. God bless you! Somehow, I'll pay you back, don't worry."

"The hell you will!" My aunt grinned and quickly stood up. "That's a gift, Walter, not a loan. It's my choice to offer it. 'Sides, I wish it was a lot more. You two go see Dolores now. Tell her I'll be back tomorrow, I have to get some rest. See ya back at the house, okay? I'll fix us something real good for supper." She turned on her heel, threw her hand up in a cheerful backward wave at us and was gone.

Dad opened the envelope and caught his breath as he counted out five new one hundred dollar bills. "Your aunt Kathy is good people, Cheryl. Don't you ever let anybody tell you any different. God love her!"

Even though some of my mother's other relatives helped out by donating their time and energy to getting her situated to life at home with her special son, Aunt Kathy was the only one who ever offered any financial support in a time of great need. She made several visits during those early years of John's childhood to help out any way she could. Once she even performed CPR on him and brought him back to life after a particularly violent seizure. My brother Don told me about this, many years later. He remembered how Aunt Kathy wondered aloud afterward if she had truly done John and us a favor by keeping him alive in his condition. Without a doubt, she absolutely *did*!

Doctor and hospital bills mounted; the medications with which they kept trying to control John's condition were all expensive. Their diagnosis read, "cerebral palsy, caused by 'severe birth injury.'" Even though my father wanted to sue the doctor, my mother would not hear of it. She always maintained God sent Johnny to us that way for a reason. She internalized her own guilt, which manifested in her own ill health years later. The medical "wizards" never addressed the seizures or gave them a name, although I've learned through spiritual guidance many years later that he also suffered from epilepsy.

They prescribed Phenobarbital at first, but John was allergic to it; he had even more severe seizures while on it, sometimes one every ten minutes. Eventually they put him on Dilantin and Mysoline, which worked pretty well for many years. It's truly a miracle he survived such a rough beginning, but John had a specific focus for being here. Our immediate family and so many others were blessed and enriched by his presence in our lives.

Shall We Dance?

All of us had a lot of adjusting to do with the new baby and his special needs. I was so happy to have him home, I'm sure I was the only one not in the least worried about how things would turn out. At four years old, everyone's an optimist! I was thrilled to have a companion to help me deal with the adults who often misunderstood me.

He was home for about six months when the following incident took place. I spent a lot of time talking with him from the first day he came into the house, and I felt very protective toward him. One afternoon he was lying on the couch, surrounded by a huge "nest" of soft pillows. Mama was in the kitchen, fixing dinner before Dad came home from work.

"Come on, Johnny, let's dance like they do on Lawrence Welk," I whispered as I gently picked him up and firmly supported his head and bottom, just like Mama did.

I began the best waltz attempt sans accordion that my feet could muster. I actually felt graceful, not clumsy like in ballet class. This was fun! Johnny's eyes were dancing brightly as he trustingly smiled up at me.

As we rounded the edge of the living room for about the third time, I giggled with delight. My baby brother and I were dancing! I had prayed for a playmate for so long. My Sunday School teacher said, "God answers prayer." I finally felt like I had proof positive cradled in my arms. I didn't have the foresight to know I should have prayed for our mother to stay busy in the kitchen for another couple of minutes, at least until the dance was over. Suddenly, I felt her staring at my back. I turned to see her ashen face.

"What on earth do you think you're doing?" she whispered in horror.

"We're dancin', Mama, Johnny likes it. Look, he's smiling!"

"Put him down." The command was quietly controlled, but over five years' experience with that tone of voice warned me to obey, pronto.

"Yes, ma'am," I whispered as we did one last 1—2—3 to the couch. As I was about to lay him down, she swept in and grabbed him, propping the pillows up around him, ever so carefully.

"Mama, I just..."

The sting of her backhand slap across my cheek left me breathless. She pushed me out of the way so she could inspect her baby more closely as my eyes filled with tears. She didn't understand. I would never hurt Johnny. It seemed so familiar to dance with him, and he'd been laughing, too...

"Don't you ever, *ever*, do that again, do you understand me, young lady? Do you?! Don't ever pick him up when I'm not in the room! Do you hear me? Answer me!" The words echoed in my brain with added emphasis because she was shaking me so hard.

"Yes, Mama. YES!" I wailed. She stopped rattling me back and forth and I was able to breathe again. "But he's okay. Really he, he liked it."

Her eyes narrowed. "I don't know where you get your ideas sometimes, child. Honestly! Whatever made you pick John up like that?"

She held me still at arm's length and looked me square in the eye. "Cheryl Ellen? I asked you a question. What made you pick him up? I know you know better."

I looked down at my toes and mumbled.

"What? You look at me, young lady, and repeat what you said." She cupped my chin, forcing me to look into that piercing eye contact which burned emerald hot right into my soul. "I told you I don't know how many times, John is a 'special' baby. The Lord put him in our hands to take care of. He isn't like other children, you know that by now. He's what they call 'handicapped.' You've seen his seizures. How would you have felt if he'd had one 'cause of what you were doing, huh? Answer me!"

I sniffled, "But, Mama, he wouldn't have. Anyway, we've danced like that so many times before..."

Her eyes flew open wide. "You've picked up my baby other times, before today?" There was doubt, however, because she rarely left his side for more than a few minutes at a time.

"No, I mean..."

She took a deep breath. "What do you mean, honey?" Softening a bit, she wanted to let me continue, hoping against hope for some logical explanation from her energetic, imaginative daughter.

"I mean when we were big, we used to dance together."

She stared right through me, knowing I was too innocent to quickly make up a lie about this, but not understanding where the words were coming from. I didn't quite get it either, then. The answer came out twenty-five years later in a past-life regression session which would trigger my intense interest in hypnotherapy. All I knew at that young age, in that moment, was John and I had indeed been dancing partners before. Somehow, somewhere else. She cleared her throat as she straightened his blankets and arranged the pillows.

"All right. Stories are fine for bedtime, Cheryl Ellen, but don't fib to Mama. God doesn't like children who fib. Remember that. You could have hurt your brother, don't you know that?"

I *didn't* know nor really believe that, but in order to keep this circular conversation to a minimum and hoping to avoid another round of literally being "all shook up," I gave the required response.

"Yes, Mama. I'm sorry."

"Well, all right. Long's you understand. Go on outside and play, honey. I know you love your baby brother, but you...well, you need some fresh air, and he needs sleep. He may never be able to play with you like the neighbor kids. Probably won't." She seemed to be talking to herself more than to me. "The Good Lord sent him to us so we could learn a lesson from Him." She smiled for the first time since walking in our waltz. "I won't tell Daddy what you did if you promise me you won't do that again."

My father never laid a finger on me; she was always the disciplinarian. Only once when we first moved into the pink house had my father and I had a "fight." It amounted to me telling him to "shut up" while I was running around the back yard and he was warned me not to get too close to a leaf fire he was tending. He promptly grabbed a switch from the weeping willow tree and without even stripping the leaves from it, he lightly swatted me across the back of my legs. But my little heart and pride were injured. My Daddy, my hero, had hit me! I ran weeping and wailing to Mama, "Daddy hit me with a fuzzy stick!"

It's funny in retrospect, and became another oft-repeated story in the Booth household. But since that time, his implied displeasure at my naughtiness was usually enough to keep me in line.

"Okay, Mama. I'm sorry. I'll go play next door. Will you call me for supper?"

She playfully swatted my backside as I skipped toward the door. "Don't I always, honey? You be a good girl, now, you promise? Be careful. Try not to be such a tomboy and rough-house so much."

I nodded and ran outside. I turned to wave at her from halfway across the yard, but she was sitting on the couch by Johnny, looking down at him. From the distance through the picture window I thought I saw tears running down her face, but I wasn't sure. She didn't sound mad anymore, so why would she be crying? I decided I probably was seeing wrong because I'd carefully hidden my new glasses again, hoping she wouldn't make me wear them to play outside.

Mama's words ran through my mind a few times that afternoon, but I didn't really believe her. John was my long-awaited baby brother. I loved him. He just *had* to be able to play with me, that was part of the deal. When the neighbor kids had to go inside, I moved to my own backyard and climbed on my swing-set. I began another silent, inner talk with The Man Upstairs.

"Hey, God, it's me, Cheryl. Sorry if I'm bothering You. Thank You for everything, 'specially Johnny. I hope You're having a good day. I gotta ask You, though...don't you remember? I've asked You about this a million times already, but I'm gonna ask again...please make Johnny well. I know You can, or I wouldn't ask. Thank You!"

I said many prayers like this over the first few years of Johnny's life. I'd spend hours daydreaming about all the things I wanted to teach him. Simple, fun things about being a regular kid, like how to spin in circles on the grass 'til you're so dizzy and out of breath you fall down giggling. Or stretching out on the grass then rolling down the steep hill in our backyard. But I'd make sure he wore some old clothes for that, otherwise Mama would get hopping mad at both of us. Grass stains were one of her pet peeves.

"Little girls don't play rough like that, Cheryl," she'd admonish while scrubbing those stains for all she was worth. "Why don't you stick to playing house and dolls instead of playing ball and pretending to be pirates with all the boys?"

"Aw...that's no fun, Mama. I'm as good a runner as the boys, and I learned how to play whiffle ball today..." but I could tell she wasn't listening.

By now, I knew she hated my tomboy antics almost more than the stained, ripped clothing they often caused, so I kept most of these experiences to myself. But when John was big enough to do all this, too, she'd *have* to approve. She'd want me to teach him to be good at this stuff. He was my ticket away from *Barbie, Tiny Tears* and all those boring creatures whiling away their lives, collecting dust on my closet shelf. And tea parties? Yuck! Dressing up in those itchy, lacy dresses she loved to make me wear, sitting there with a bunch of other little prim and proper girls who seemed like stiff little dolls come to life themselves with their cutesy manners their mothers loved, their pinkies delicately poised as they poured the imaginary tea and politely intoned, "One lump, or two?"

God, how I hated that game! Give me stick ball, or the TV reenactments I so loved; hanging by my knees from the swing-set bar, *anything* but those boring, goofy tea parties and talking to a bunch of expressionless dolls and phony baloney prissy girls.

"C'mon, Johnny," I'd whisper when nobody else was around. "You just gotta get well and be okay so we can play together outside. It's a lot more fun that this sissy stuff Mom makes me do. You just gotta get better, okay?"

And he'd look right at me and smile. I knew he understood me, I *knew* it. Our best secret was that we always could communicate perfectly, no matter what anybody else thought. I knew he heard everything I said and got it—BINGO!—just like that.

As the years went by and his vocabulary didn't extend beyond a few words, I felt quite safe confiding my deepest, darkest secrets to him. He'd never snitch to "Sergeant Mom." But I always swore him to secrecy, just in case his power of speech miraculously increased. Who knew? One of those times at the altar when Mama and all the preachers were laying hands on him and begging God to make him rise up and walk, God might just decide to turn on his voice box first. He might, just to shake 'em up. Why not? He *was* God, after all. People didn't always get exactly what they prayed for, I learned that more and more as I grew up. Sometimes the things they *did* get were better for them than what they thought they wanted ever could have been.

Just like Johnny. He turned out to be the best friend I ever had, even though we never did spin around in circles together or laugh as we rolled down the lush grass in our hilly back yard. I began to do those things on my own, now giving more attention to the sensations involved, then I'd describe the experience to him later. Or I'd play ball as his proxy, thinking, "This one's for Johnny!" as I smacked a base hit or the exciting home run. Him not being able to do that alongside me didn't matter so much as we grew closer. I was always happy just to share his company. He was my best audience whenever I felt like singing or being dramatic. He never rolled his eyes at me like our parents tended to, usually muttering something under their breath like, "Where does she get this?"

"Well, she's *your* daughter!" Followed by laughter. My parents loved me, that was always evident. But when it came to understanding me and unconditionally accepting me for who I was, *that* was an aching void Johnny very neatly filled in my life.

If I wanted to be positively goofy, John didn't care. He let me be who and whatever I felt like being at any given moment. And he was the kindest, gentlest, most patient friend and teacher I would ever have.

As for Mama, she never lost the weight from her last pregnancy. In fact, she began to gain, growing increasingly heavier. She was about 5'7" and had always been able to carry a bit of extra weight without anyone really noticing. Now, however, I saw her struggle at first to fit into various clothes, then she simply gave up, donated those and bought a few new things in a bigger size. Eating became her solace, her one physical comfort after Johnny's birth. She'd go through phases of dieting, but nothing ever worked for long.

Having a November birthday meant I couldn't begin kindergarten until the following fall, closer to the age of six. Shortly after I turned five, I began to complain of headaches, earaches and blurry vision. Mama may have written some of this off to sibling rivalry at first, but when the symptoms persisted she took me to the pediatrician. After a thorough exam, he declared I should be taken to a specialist. He said there was a severe infection in my ear, which might require surgery.

My mother's face fell. *This* on top of her newborn's drastic birth condition? Knowing the way she believed then, I'm sure she wondered if God was testing her faith. The specialist pronounced I required immediate mastoid surgery. In those days, this was a delicate operation. Johnny needed Mama around the clock, so she was unable to be with me overnight in the hospital. I know she was extremely conflicted over this. She gave me a jar full of nickels and instructed me to call her every morning and evening from the pay phone just down the hall from my room. Daddy promised to come see me as often as he could, but he felt he needed to be home with her and his son overnight. The afternoon I was checked in, he stayed for quite awhile, sitting on the edge of my bed, telling me stories and jokes. Through the blinds, I could see it beginning to get dark. Daddy cleared his throat and stood up.

"You have to be strong now, Punkin. The doctors and nurses will take real good care of you. You'll have to be a big, brave girl and say your prayers. You'll be home before you know it." It looked like he had a tear in his eye. This seemed so hard for him. I reached up and patted his cheek.

"I'll be fine, Daddy. The angels and the nurses will look over me. You go home and take care of Johnny and Mama. Don't worry 'bout me."

He laughed. "You're something else. It's just, well, we both need to stay with the baby in case he needs to come back to the hospital for something. You know his seizures can be so hard. So honey, you promise you'll be okay and get all better right away for your old Dad?"

" 'Course I will, Daddy. You and Mama take good care of Johnny. I'll be home soon. It's okay."

He bent down to kiss the top of my head. "That's my brave Cheryl. I'll come see you every day. And don't you forget to call your mother, five times a day if you want to," he pointed to my jar of nickels. "She'll have a fit if you don't!"

We both laughed. "I promise."

"Good girl. Now, you better get to sleep. They're going to come get you bright and early for your operation. Mama and Johnny and I will be here when you wake up for sure, okay? Good night, sweetheart." He kissed me again and squeezed my hand.

"Love you, Daddy. Tell Mama and Johnny I love them, too. See you after they fix my ear!" I bravely gave him a big smile as he waved and walked out the door, but I was scared inside. It was the first time I'd ever spent the night away from home, away from my parents. I could tell my Daddy felt helpless, so I didn't want to worry him anymore.

The surgery was a success. The thing I remember most was how nice the staff was to the poor little kid who had to stay overnight all by herself. I worked this to the max! I would get them to stay in my room and tell me stories every chance I could. I had to get so many shots to prevent infection, they began to apologize to me. They got the biggest kick out of my daily treks to the pay phone. I would stand up on the seat to reach the dialer, drop in my nickel and talk away.

My folks had told me to be sure and call any time, and I took them literally! In fact, they finally had to tell me not to call *quite* so much... two or three times a day was just fine! Mama's favorite phone exchange was when I called her the day after the operation. The nurses told me I'd get to go home the next day, so I was really excited. Mama sounded real happy I was coming home, too.

"We'll be there right at noon to get you, honey! It'll be so good to have you home."

"Yes, I can't wait. How's Johnny?"

"Oh, he's fine, sweetheart. He's fine. I keep telling him what a brave big sister he has." I could hear the smile in her voice. She was proud of me!

"Oh, it's not so bad, Mama. The nurses are real nice. Only thing is, my rear-end feels like a pincushion from all the shots!'

She burst into laughter. This child of hers was certainly precocious! "Oh, it'll heal, honey, don't you worry. Sleep on your tummy for now and get a good night's rest. We'll see you tomorrow. Love you!"

"I love you guys, too. Sweet dreams, Mama. Kiss Johnny for me. Bye bye."

I hung up and gingerly climbed down, not wanting to fall on my sore derriere! I was happy I had made Mama laugh. She didn't laugh too much these days.

Even though the nurses had been real sweet, I hated the hospital. I vowed never to spend any more time in one than was absolutely necessary.

Chapter Four

Growing Pains

"Fly Me To The Moon..."

As a child I had many vivid dreams, several of which proved to be precognitive. Mostly about a relative who was going to visit, or something that would happen soon. My parents thought this was cute at first. I also experienced a lot of deja vu in the classroom, often knowing exactly what the teacher or a classmate would say or do the split second before it occurred. I believe this came from dream "projection" in some cases.

A recurring theme from the age of about three was my flying dreams. Many young children experience these, so that was nothing unusual. However, there was a peculiar pattern to the ones I had. So unusual, I vividly recall it to this day.

I'd be deep asleep when I'd look around and realize I was out in our back yard. The stars were out, the night air felt cool and welcoming. I was flying up in the air about twenty feet high. I could touch the ground if I chose, but flying was much more fun! In the absence of a backyard swimming pool, I would have great fun in these flying dreams, doing the backstroke across the sky, far above the ground. My favorite game was to pretend I was in the circus because I could effortlessly do backflips high over our clothesline, always landing perfectly. I imagined an audience roaring its approval. Or I might choose to walk along one of the thin wires as the ringmaster announced, "Ladies and Gentleman! Direct your attention to the center ring high wire and observe Cheryl, the Terrific Tightrope Walker!"

Our back yard had two major downhill slopes. In my dreams, I'd float to the top hill, touch down, and then sprint with all my might toward a bush that was about four feet high, located at the crest of the second slope. Always at the last possible second, just by thinking it to be so, I'd magically spring upward and float gracefully over the prickly bush, never even grazing a leg.

These early astral projection experiences were wonderful. In the beginning, I'd "get out" of my body at least once a week. The only thing that scared me was coming back into my body, and that was because of the noise. For some reason, when I'd be pulled back into my physical form, this pattern would occur: I'd hit the bed very hard, forcefully slamming back inside my body, in effect. Next, I'd bounce up as though I'd hit a trampoline, smack flat up against the ceiling, then back inside my body. So there was a loud "WHAM!—BOOM!—WHAM!" effect. That noise would frighten me, and I'd wake up crying.

On several such occasions, I yelled for my mother, telling her the thunder had scared me. At first, she'd look outside, then seeing clear skies, would assure me it was just a bad dream, there was no storm. After awhile, these became episodes she thought of as "the girl who cried wolf."

This pattern went on for a few years, but the frequency decreased. One night my mother made sure I was fully awake, then turned on all the lights in my room and told me in no uncertain terms I was to stop this nonsense and quit disturbing everyone's sleep.

"You're a big girl now, Cheryl. You're eight years old, for goodness sake! You need to stop imagining such things. I know all children have nightmares sometimes, but this is ridiculous. Besides, even if it *is* storming, you're safe inside the house. Nothing can hurt you. You're going to wake Johnny up with all this hollering and you wouldn't want to do that, would you?"

"No, ma'am. I'm sorry."

"Well, then, next time this happens, you just tell yourself it's nothing to be scared of. Mama's tired of this game. I won't come running for this anymore, you understand? So get it through your head. No more." She snapped off the light with a sigh and went back to bed.

"Yes, Mama," I called after her. But what I didn't understand was why she wouldn't listen to my stories about my flying abilities. When I'd try to explain I was just confused by coming back inside my body, she'd cut me off cold. Was I so strange, such a freak-show, that my own mother didn't believe me? Did she think I was some kind of weirdo? I began to keep more of my dream activity to myself, and consequently to suppress and stifle it. What's the point of telling an adult who won't listen anymore? Or when she did, she looked at you as if you were an idiot? An "idjit" was Mom's slang for it.

I had lots of heroes as a kid, my Dad being the most obvious, most reality-based. He was fifty-three when I was born, but to me he was ageless. We had tremendous fun and always seemed to understand one another pretty well. I found out years later we had more in common than I realized. He was the psychic one of my parents, but during my childhood this was never acknowledged or discussed. He had learned early on that such talk made Mom extremely uneasy.

Other heroes in my formative years came from television, movies and books. Like most children, I loved cartoons and comic books. Superman was always my favorite of that genre. I also had an intense love of mythology, Greek, Roman, Norse, it didn't matter. All mythology, especially the parts about the heroic quests, intrigued me. This puzzled my mother, but she was glad I was an avid reader and not always glued to the television. Some folk songs with legendary heroic conquest themes impressed me enough to try my best to reenact them.

The story of John Henry, the "steel driving man" who helped build the railroads, really captured my attention. That he would challenge a machine seemed incredibly brazen and heroic. Always one to root for the underdog, I sang this song over many times, at home, in the car, not just in music class at school. One of his lines to the railroad magnates who favored machine versus manpower was, "I'll die with a hammer in my hand, Lord, Lord..."

One day when I was about seven, I decided to "become" John Henry. I was not supposed to play with my father's tools, and I knew it. But how in the world could I realistically *be* this strong hero without a hammer? Impossible! So I snuck into the garage, grabbed my father's ten pound sledge hammer and drug it into the front yard. I may have been sneaky in obtaining my prop, but that love of an audience made me throw caution to the wind. I took it right down to front and center stage (or yard, in this case) where all the neighbors and drivers (and eventually even my mother) had a birds-eye view of this wild child singing and doing her best to swing this heavy hammer.

At first, I was content to simply drive the head of the tool into the ground and be satisfied with the resounding "Thud!" But as the dramatic flow of the song built, I began lifting it above my head and swinging it with all my might, even succeeding in putting it clear behind my back and bringing it up over my head. Wow! What a big "Thwack!" that made when it smacked the ground! I began to believe I was superhuman...sort of like when Clark Kent morphed into *Superman*. I lost sight of John Henry, and became enamored of my own strength and power. I should go to the carnival and hit one of those things that rang the bell so you could win big prizes! This was so cool!

Just about that time, I lost control of the hammer and clunked myself soundly on the back of my head, which knocked me out cold! I'm surprised I didn't hear birdies twittering in circles around me when I came to, like in the cartoons. Instead, I heard my mother sobbing, and realized I was on the ground, cradled in her arms with a crowd of neighbors gathering around us.

"Oh, dear God, let her live! Please bring my baby back to life...."

My eyelids fluttered and I gazed at her through a cloudy mist. "Hi. Don't cry. I'm okay, Mama."

"Oh, thank you, Jesus! Cheryl, you're all right! Thank God!" She hugged me tightly until her "anger adrenaline" kicked in and she held me at arm's length so we were making serious eye contact. The neighbors who had been concerned began to back away, sensing a storm brewing. The crazy little Booth kid hadn't succeeded in committing a bizarre suicide, and was apparently so hard-headed she didn't even have a concussion, so the show was over! Also, most of them had heard my mother's yelling at me more than a few times, and knew they'd better clear out.

After a stern lecture about staying away from Dad's tools, emphasized by several solid swats on the rear, I was sent to my room. John Henry no longer seemed like such a good hero. I had a sore head *and* a sore rear end! My pride was more than a little injured, too. What a rotten way to end my swell performance art. Maybe from now on, I'd just keep tying one of John's baby blankets around my neck like a cape, and run at top speed, arms outstretched, pretending to fly like Superman. I sure wouldn't touch any stupid ol' hammers for a long time.

Meanwhile, John's first few years on the planet were certainly no picnic. His seizures were lessening, but his spine was extremely curved. Our parents took him to a series of chiropractors and osteopaths. We learned about physical therapy for the handicapped and I actually liked helping Mama move his arms and legs, especially because there were little songs attached to some of the exercises. I recall one that went, "Let's all fly like the birdies fly, up and down, and up and down...." as we moved his arms in tempo. Mama encouraged me to sing because from an early age, John responded to music, especially to my singing. He would smile, sometimes throwing his arms up in the air as he would giggle and coo. So he fast became not only my very best friend, but also my most appreciative fan. After all, he was a captive audience, so I guess he figured he may as well enjoy it!

John always responded positively to massage. Because of his reaction and enjoyment of it, many years later I would study massage, which in turn opened the door to working with various healing modalities. My mother's former brother-in-law was a gifted osteopath who helped John tremendously. We drove for hours to Hiawatha, Kansas, sometimes on a weekly basis, so Johnny could receive a treatment. Johnny's poor little spine was so crooked compared to mine. He didn't have much control it all, he couldn't sit upright without support. When held on someone's lap with his head hanging down, he could only lift his head with much encouragement and a lot of straining of his underdeveloped neck muscles. This took several minutes of concentrated effort on his part. Actions I took for granted every day were a major event for him.

Dr. Glenn was a wonderful osteopath with a tremendous healing presence. Even though he lived far away, Mom believed so strongly in his abilities. So from the time John was quite small until he turned nine or ten, we'd journey there as often as possible. The doctor would begin by doing some slow stretches with John's arms and legs, rubbing the limbs to increase circulation. Then he'd gently adjust the spine. I watched closely many times, and my interest was not wasted on Dr. Glenn.

"Here, Cheryl. This is what I call a spinal walk. Watch me, then you try, okay?"

Johnny was lying prone on the doctor's adjustment table, his face to the side. Dr. Glenn placed his thumbs on either side of John's sacrum, then began "walking" up toward the neck, almost rolling slowly along the spine, one vertebra at a time. Alternating first one thumb, then the other. John made some of his "happy sounds." He always loved positive touch. The doctor smiled encouragingly at me. "Your turn. Just nice and slow, nice and easy."

I placed my hands where his had begun, and began mimicking the light rolling "walk." John looked at me when I got up to his cervical area, and smiled. I grinned back, "Does that feel good, huh, Johnny?" He smiled again, laughing this time. When John laughed, it was such a natural, joyous sound it always made me laugh, too. Dr. Glenn joined in, and patted me on the head.

"So, are you going to become a doctor, Cheryl? You have the gift, from what I can see."

I looked down at the floor, ashamed I didn't want to be part of his wonderful profession. "No, sir. I might be an actress or singer. Maybe a teacher. I just don't think I could sew people up, or see all the blood and stuff. I'd probably get sick."

When I was about eight or nine, I briefly considered becoming a nurse or doctor, but I really had a strong distaste for "blood and guts." I even hid my eyes during the shoot-outs on *Gunsmoke* and back in the early 1960s you rarely caught a glimpse of anything resembling even a *simulated* bloodstain on that show! I didn't care for hospital shows, either. Violence and operations were just never my cup of tea.

The doctor laughed. "Well, that's perfectly all right. The world needs musicians and teachers, too! But I know one thing, you sure can make your little brother feel better by working on his back. You learn quickly. You can help John a lot by just doing this once in awhile for him. It'll help him relax."

"Oh, sure! I love helping Johnny. I'd do anything for him." I was massaging my brother's hand, trying to get him to relax his fingers, which were tightly contracted most of the time.

"That's easy to see. You two love each other very much. You're a great big sister." He was making some notes on John's chart. "Now, I need to talk to your Mom for a minute, so why don't you go outside and play with Melissa for awhile? I bet she's out there wondering when you'll come see her new swing-set." Melissa was his daughter, and we were in the same grade. We always had fun together, so I happily ran outside.

Looking back, I realize this experience was really my introduction to the healing power of touch. I'd seen "hands-on healing" services at our church, but this man was the first person I knew who made people feel better for a living, just by using his knowledge and his comforting, sure touch. As I write this book today, I remember him fondly. He's been in Spirit World for some time now and I wouldn't be a bit surprised if he's involved in some type of healing there, as well. I'm grateful to have known him, and bless him for being so helpful to Johnny and our family.

Just a few days after this particular visit to Dr. Glenn's, I was singing to Johnny, who was lying in his usual place on the living room couch. He'd been making noises and singing along in his own fashion, so we were both in great moods. Mama was running errands, and Daddy was outside tinkering on his truck. I finished our little "concert" and went over to talk to Johnny. As I sat down beside him, I noticed his eyes glazing over a bit, beginning to roll back slightly. This was the physical cue that he was about to seizure. No one ever told me to try what happened next, but Someone worked through me that day. I calmly reached behind John's neck, and began slowly and deeply massaging just above and all around the lowest cervical vertebra (C-7). I talked to him in a soothing voice as I worked, and held his hand with my free hand.

"It's okay, Johnny boy. Stay with Sissy. Don't go away, don't be scared. I'm right here. Come on, it's okay..." All the while, I kept rubbing his neck, looking at him. His eyes slowly came back into focus and amazingly, he relaxed his arms. Usually, they would lock in a bent position while his hands flailed and jerked around helplessly during a convulsion. His whole body usually became a small, knotted hurricane of sorts that shivered and quaked.

When I was very small and unused to his seizures, I'd cry and scream for Mom or Dad if they weren't present, because I thought he surely was going to die. The whole family eventually learned to talk soothingly to him until it was over, and tried to hold one of his hands if possible. Just ride it out with him. But this time it was different. Johnny smiled directly at me. There hadn't been one shiver or tremble. Maybe Dr. Glenn's influence had guided me, or perhaps a Hand even bigger than his utilized me as an instrument to help prevent that seizure. Whatever the case, gratitude washed over me in waves. I hugged Johnny and we talked and prayed. When I say "we" talked, it was more like I babbled and Johnny listened, laughing and jabbering as I sang out, "Praise the Lord!" several times. To me, this was as good as being in a revival meeting!

When I shared this story with our parents, Mama gave me one of *those* looks. But the next time it happened, she was there, and she made way for me to sit with him. I suppose she figured it couldn't hurt to let me try. And it worked again!

She turned to me. "Well, I'll be, Cheryl Ellen. That's a miracle of sorts, it really is." Her eyes smiled and released the intense, inquisitive look reserved for when I'd say or do something that seemed to make her wonder yet again if they'd switched babies on her in the hospital. "Show me what you did there, honey, will you?"

My mind offered a silent prayer, "Oh, thank You, God! She believes me this time!" I was elated. "Sure, Mama, you just hold his neck real gentle, but firm, then you rub it like this." I demonstrated the massage technique, and she copied it. We taught it to my father, too. So we all learned how to watch closely for signals, "catch" the seizures and were successful in deflecting them many times. This was always so gratifying for all of us, to see John so relieved and happy. The look in his eyes and his beautiful smile were especially priceless during these episodes. Our parents would often discuss how hard those awful convulsions must be on John's heart. I figured they were right, but more than anything, it tore me up to watch him suffer through that violent agony. The neck-rubbing discovery considerably lessened the helplessness we'd always felt, and we all praised God for His Goodness and Wisdom.

On a personal level, my interest in the healing power of touch was steadily increasing. And Mama? Well, she was obsessed with getting her son to speak. She talked to him continuously. One of the physical therapy "tricks" that was recommended to us was to put a small dab of peanut butter on the roof of his mouth. This was to encourage the tongue muscle to work. Johnny would get a funny, puzzled look on his face, and of course we would be standing by with water in case he had problems, but he would eventually lick the sticky stuff off, smacking his lips and making sounds to show us he thought it tasted good. Mostly, "mmm, yummm." Pudding was one of his favorites. We also got him to lick *Tootsie Roll Pops* to exercise his tongue. Being a sugarholic, I certainly didn't mind always having a few of those suckers around the house!

One of the earliest treats I remember Mom giving me was a piece of white bread slathered with butter, then sprinkled with lots of sugar. She'd hand it to me with instructions to go outside and eat it. Because she was raised during the height of the Depression, and I'd heard stories about rationing, I knew that when she was a kid, these things were considered priceless. So she thought this was an extra-special treat. I have twelve fillings which prove how much I loved sugar!

When Aunt Kathy visited, they used to laugh and carry on as she told stories from their childhood. She told how they once snuck into the cellar as little girls and ate great spoonfuls of raw flour. Since it was rationed, they figured it must be delicious! Naturally, they both became really sick. Another story helped me understand why my mother couldn't abide drinking milk. During the Depression, even as a little kid she knew cream was also a precious commodity, just like flour. I guess she thought it would be like drinking liquid gold or something. So at a family dinner, with guests present, when peaches were served as dessert, a small container of cream was passed around. When the pitcher got to my mother, she poured *all* the contents onto her peaches. Her mother punished her by making her consume all the rich liquid. She got very ill once again, and never drank milk of any kind after that.

My maternal grandmother, Bertha, was quite the strict disciplinarian. Hey, Mama had to learn it somewhere, right? I share middle names with Bertha Ellen. I was always *so* grateful they gave that to me rather than Bertha! Going through school as Bertie, Big Bertha or Bertha Butts would not have been fun. Even the name she saddled my mother with was heavy. Dolores is a beautiful name, but its main translation is "pain." This was somewhat prophetic with respect to my mother's adult life.

This next story of my mother's childhood seems funny in retrospect but would be considered child abuse by today's standards. At the time of this incident, Bertha loved reading Gothic novels. My mother was about eight years old, her sister Kathleen close to five. After playing for awhile at a neighbor's house one day, Kathleen came home to discover her older sister tied to the front porch post!

"Oh, Dee, what happened?"

"Sshh!" my mother whispered. "Listen, Kathy. Do me a big favor. Mama's real mad at me. I said something that set her off. This clothesline hurts my wrist. Just sneak into the kitchen and get a big butcher knife."

Kathy was always a rebel. Her eyes must have sparkled. "We gonna cut you loose?"

"Yeah, that's right. But you have to be real quiet, and hide the knife somehow. Be careful not to hurt yourself. And Mama can't know what you're doing, okay?"

Kathy grinned. "Be right back."

She went in to find their mother seated in her favorite easy chair, reading one of her big romance books.

"Kathleen, where are you going?" My grandmother asked, her eyes never leaving the page.

"To get a glass of water in the kitchen, Mama. Then can I go play some more?" Kathy innocently asked.

"Sure. Just be home before sundown and suppertime."

Kathy knew better than to even bring up the subject of her sister on the front porch. She didn't want to remind their mother of her prisoner, knowing once she was immersed in a story she tended to forget things for a while.

Kathleen turned on the water to cover the sound of the drawer opening. She got a butcher knife, and carefully carried it behind her back as she sidled past her mother, just a few feet away from her. Grandma didn't even notice her younger daughter going back outside.

Needless to say, my mother was cut loose and the two sisters ran off to play. When they came home, however, Grandma tied *both* of them to the clothesline pole! Yes, it was another day and age. Seldom would my mother speak harshly of hers. She was the eldest daughter, and must have felt a strong obligation to her mother. Whenever Aunt Kathy visited us, though, she always told it like it was. They would both be reduced to tears they laughed so hard at those memories. Thanks to Aunt Kathy's honesty, I learned that my mother had been a fairly precocious child herself!

I received my fair share of spankings growing up, usually for "smarting off." In retaliation, I would hold my breath as long as possible so as not to cry, and Mama would just spank me harder. I guess she felt if I didn't cry she hadn't gotten her point across. We played those games for several years. I don't want to give you the wrong impression. My mother was not a cruel woman at all. She was extremely compassionate and kind. When I think back on the punishments I received, I now know she was simply dealing with me the way she had discipline modeled to her. Thank God she never tied me up! Banishment to my room was normally what followed a spanking, but there I could read and escape into a fantasy world, so I really didn't mind.

Johnny's entrance into our lives softened her in many ways. She was less likely to argue with me for too long if he was in the room. His very presence made all of us feel blessed and peaceful. Later on I would come to believe he was more evolved than any of us who may have thought ourselves more fortunate simply because we could walk and talk like "normal" people. He taught us all so much patience and love. That's what he was all about.

Johnny truly had a great love of food and favored certain tastes. He was diagnosed with an allergy to milk; it seemed to prompt even more seizures, and it nauseated him. So we found soy substitutes, no easy trick in those pre-health food store days. There were just a couple of nearby drug stores which carried cans of this. When I think of soy milk's popularity today, it makes me smile. I actually enjoy it now, but back then Johnny didn't like it and I didn't blame him. I thought it smelled nasty as Mama filled his bottle with it. I was a huge fan of milk and felt sorry for him that he couldn't enjoy it like I did. Mama began to worry about him becoming malnourished, so started supplementing the liquid with baby food, and soon replaced what I called "the fake milk" altogether. Most of his food was bottled baby food, or as he grew, we created blender-ground versions for him of things we were having for lunch or dinner. It took a good hour to feed him until he was full, but our mother was tireless and full of patience when it came to tending to John. She would cradle his head in the crook of her arm and talk to him while spooning the food into his small mouth. He would make his yummy sounds for the things he liked the most, and spit out the ones he did not. Not that different from any other baby! It's just that we were slowly beginning to understand a difficult fact—feeding him and attending to him like a baby was a necessity that would apparently continue throughout his life. Sometimes she'd let me help feed him. When he was about three or four, we discovered he loved those little Vienna sausages. This was an easy source of protein, so we fed them to him often. I learned the only thing you had to be careful of was not letting him mistake your finger for a sausage!

A few well-intentioned relatives continued to encourage us to place him in a home, saying that this intensive amount of care-giving would detract from our own enjoyment of life. Thank God my parents didn't listen to them and recognized John for the wonderful blessing he was!

On the few occasions he was fussy, Mama would say, "now, now, now, John" over and over as she rocked him. He would almost always settle down pretty quickly; those words seemed like a soothing mantra for him. When he was about three or so, I believe his first words were, "now, now, now" but Mama was thrilled! Her baby was talking, despite the doctor's grim outlook regarding any power of speech or the brain activity to support it ever developing.

John's other early words were also quite simple. Once in a great while he'd bestow a great gift upon our mother for all her faith, love and hard work by saying, "Mama." She used to tell her friends this meant more to her than a treasure chest of gold. Most frequently, though, he chose to say, "I good," because we were continually reinforcing to him what a good boy he was. And he *was*! According to Mama, compared to "normal" babies who cried a lot, he was very quiet, never really complaining unless he was legitimately hungry, wet or feeling sick. He smiled a lot, which made us love him all the more. We figured if he was so happy, given all he had to deal with in the physical world, we should certainly strive to be happy, too.

His other big catch phrase early on became, "I go!" Then he would throw his arms with those little contracted wrists high into the air, squealing with delight. He totally understood the concept of "going" somewhere in the car. We had a Rambler station wagon for many years. My Dad was a big *AMC* fan and chose this particular vehicle because it was one of the first in the 1960s to offer a front seat that fully reclined. That meant we could put pillows around John, fasten him in tightly and travel around together. Car seats were not enforced in those days, and there was no way John could have sat up in one, anyway. His lack of muscle control would not allow that.

I paid close attention to things that my little brother was drawn to. He would stare right into bright white light. I decided it must remind him of when he was in Heaven. He seemed hypnotized by it when one of our parents would be holding him, and he'd be anywhere near an overhead light fixture.

As far as we could tell, his favorite color was red. Maybe it was the brightness of it, but he responded the most to toys of that color. One of his favorites was a cute little stuffed red fox. He'd laugh and coo when we held it up for him, and hugged it as best he could under his one of his small stiff arms when we placed it there.

He also loved the sound of running water and really enjoyed being given a bath. He would strain to move his head in the direction of the sound of water. That took a great deal of effort on his part, so I knew it meant something special to him. Again, he was an excellent teacher from a tender young age. I discovered much later that water conducts Spirit energy.

When Johnny was born, we were attending a local Baptist church, not far from my elementary school. Basically, it was Mom and I who attended, and when he was big enough she would bring Johnny along. Our father was not impressed by the minister there. He had grown up in the Southern Baptist faith in Virginia, and was used to evangelists who were powerful, pulpit-thumping showmen. I liked Sunday school, however, and displayed an early talent for memorization of Bible verses, even winning little awards for being able to recite the books of the Old and New Testament in order. Another chance to perform! What a little ham, even in church!

My best friends in kindergarten were identical twin brothers, Danny and David. We spent many recess periods playing and laughing. I began to beg Mom to let me invite them over to play at the house. She was happy I was making new friends in school. Kindergarten had been pretty traumatic for me. The very first week, one mean little girl burst my bubble and informed me Santa Claus was not real, that your parents did all the gift-giving and lied about the man in red. It was all a big fake, and I should get a clue. I remember going home and wailing as my mother held me upon her lap, trying to comfort me. She was surprised to learn why I was so upset.

"Well, honey, Santa is just a legend, like one of your comic book fellas. But he's a good legend, and..."

I interrupted. "I don't care that Santa's not real so much. I'm mad because you think I'm stupid!" I burst into tears all over again.

"What? I most certainly do not! You're such a clever little girl, Cheryl. Why on earth would you say that?"

I sniffed, "Because you lied to me and I believed you. I didn't think you and Daddy would ever lie to me, so I believed you about Santa.

So you must think I'm really stupid." I was afraid to ask if there was anything else I'd been deceived about. My trust in my parents was shaken for the very first time.

I wasn't the only one whose faith was shaken up during this timeframe. The Baptist congregation didn't give my mother much hope that Johnny would ever be healed, be normal. She was desperately seeking a miracle for his sake, as well as to assuage her own guilt over his condition. When I asked about inviting my twin friends into our home, I had no idea this would be the catalyst to a whole new level of faith and hope for her.

Mom agreed to let the boys come over for a couple of hours one night after school. She called their mother, an energetic, tiny woman named Vesta, to make sure that was all right. She seemed pleased the boys had made a new friend and quickly agreed.

We began spending more time together, and our mothers developed their own friendship. Soon, Vesta told my mother about the church they attended. She said the preachers there laid hands on people who were sick or afflicted and that many were healed as a result of God's power flowing through them. Mama admitted this sounded really encouraging, given the dismal attitude of the Baptists. Vesta invited us to come to The Evangelistic Center Church in downtown Kansas City as her guests. This was known as a full-Gospel, non-denominational church. We were to discover it was much different than anything else we had ever encountered. I immediately loved the building because it had formerly been a theatre. There were comfortable padded fold-up seats and a large, carpeted stage area where the preachers paced and jumped, clapping their hands and shouting at times as they gave the sermon. The high ceilings made for wonderful acoustics. There was even a balcony, but I was not allowed to sit there. The teenagers ruled the roost up there.

The people in the congregation engaged in worship services where they "praised the Lord" by holding their hands up and gently swaying back and forth, often talking in other tongues. Sometimes this portion of the service lasted for nearly an hour at a stretch. Of course, the natural performer in me looked at it as a unique form of entertainment at first, but I soon learned how seriously my mother took it all. I also realized it could take a physical toll on one to stand for that long. No wonder some of the adults seemed to go into a trance.

Mama would always roll Johnny down the aisle in his little "hoed" wheelchair for the healing portion of the service. This lightweight, simplistic chair was so named because it resembled the slant of a farm hoe; you leaned it back while wheeling it so it could easily accommodate John's inability to sit up straight. It was somewhat like a lawn chair with wheels; its back had webbing, there was a slightly padded seat and a very basic footrest. You moved it along at a forty-five degree angle, so it was basically a streamlined stroller.

Our mother was on a mission, insatiable in her belief that God could "make Johnny whole." The ministers and congregation at Evangelistic Center always welcomed our family, including Johnny, with open arms. I saw some incredible healing done there. Mom began to search the scriptures for a sign as to when Johnny's healing would be complete. She found somewhere in the Bible that seven was considered God's "perfect number" so she began a quest; she set her vision of her son's healing taking place during his seventh year of life on Earth.

We began to go to church both morning and evening, most Sundays. Mom really wanted Dad to come with us, and his love of her, along with curiosity as to what made this church so different finally got the better of him. Some of the traveling missionaries who came to speak there reminded him of his old Southern Baptist tent revivals, so he began to go with us more often than not. It was about that time that my father gave up his long-time habit of drinking beer. I don't recall him ever drinking anything stronger when I was a child, but he certainly enjoyed his beer! So for him to give it up, I knew God and/or Mom were really getting to him. He didn't smoke much anymore, either.

It was a long drive to church, about forty minutes, to the "other side of the river" from our house. It was south of the Missouri river in the old downtown district. Having grown up in the "burbs" I was unused to the poverty and grittiness of the inner city. So I looked out the car windows, fascinated by this different lifestyle.

Now, my father was born in 1902 in Virginia. Growing up in the early 20th century in a Southern stronghold, he had some prejudices thrust upon him from a young age. In later years, I called him "Archie Bunker" quite a bit; in fact, he looked a little like Carroll O'Connor! He didn't appreciate this reference, but to a degree, it was true. For example, we'd be a few blocks from the rougher parts of downtown and he'd say something like, "Lock your doors, now, we're going through jigaboo country."

I would ask why he was afraid of the black people and called them names, and he'd just tell me to be quiet and do as he said. As time went by I became extremely confused by all this, because once in awhile, he got a kick out of taking us to a black church. It was as if he suddenly became colorblind. He loved the music there, and seemed to feel right at home. He admired the strong preaching style exhibited in those churches. There were some lovely African-American families who attended Evangelistic Center. Because my father knew them and had the same faith in common, he accepted and respected them. It was a strange conundrum. I'm not making excuses for him; I simply found this contradiction very odd.

When I was a teenager, Dad told me how when he was in his teens, his older brothers invited him to a special private meeting. He was about sixteen years old and was a member of the Free Masons, so he thought it would be a similar type of gathering. He was shocked to learn it was a Ku Klux Klan meeting! He said he ran out of the door as quickly as he could, ashamed his brothers were part of such goings-on. So you see what I mean? A man of contradictions Selective prejudice, you might call it.

The Archie Bunker identification came about because by the early 1970s I'd heard him make various slurs about many minorities and ethnic groups, including "homos," and the "snooty Limeys" he'd served with in World War II. That last one really struck me as comical given the fact that the Booth family descent is most likely around seventy-five percent British! I pointed this obvious hereditary link out to him, but he'd just snort.

The point is, I loved my father, prejudice and all, because he loved us without reservation, and did the best he could by us. John was his only son, and he especially accepted him unconditionally. Dad would no more have heard of shipping John off and away from the family than he would have permitted that to happen to me.

The thing that impressed me deeply about this new church was their seeming obsession with *The Book of Revelation*. They seemed to take great delight in sending out scary messages about the Second Coming of Christ and what would happen to all the wicked sinners who were not born again. They harped on it so much I began to have horrific nightmares, which made Jesus' return seem to be a frightening event, rather than a welcome one.

In fact, one day when we were about nine years old, Danny and David were over playing in our back yard along with me and some other neighbor kids. Mom and Vesta were sitting outside, watching us, and Johnny was there in his wheelchair. He always loved to hear kids playing and laughing.

Suddenly, there was the loudest "BOOM!" I had ever heard up to that point in my life. It seemed to hang in the sky, and I looked up, feeling certain the Heavens were about to open. Danny, David and I were all on the same page about this Revelations stuff, because we all immediately fell to the ground and began shouting and crying things like, "No, no, Jesus! Don't come and make us go to Heaven yet! We don't want to go! We're just kids...."

Needless to say, our mothers were both embarrassed and speechless. Maybe they even had some of the same thoughts cross their minds! We learned from the news later that night, what we had heard was one of the first sonic booms ever to take place in Kansas City. Funny what fear can do, isn't it? Especially fear where God is concerned, since God is truly only LOVE. But back then, I was forced to be a disciple of the concept of a vengeful, punitive God. That's what the preachers preached, that's what my family seemed to believe, so I went along with the program. I must say, I was quite relieved to realize that boom was man-made. The next time I vowed not to let it scare me at all.

"Is the Little Boy Asleep?"

Because John was so special to us, we never had anyone outside the family baby-sit him, not until I went to college. In fact, we were all pretty happy to pack up into the Rambler any time we needed to go anywhere. John loved going on trips, whether long ones or just to the market. Our parents would often leave me in the car to watch him while they went shopping. I'd read to him, or sometimes we'd listen to the radio. Something out of the ordinary began to catch my attention on these outings. The first few times it happened, I probably didn't notice. But it began occurring so frequently, I realized something special was going on.

People would walk up alongside John's side of the car, and look in. They'd smile at me, and say, "Isn't he precious? Is the little boy sleeping?"

John might choose to make the great effort to turn his head and smile up at them. Whether he did this or not, I politely answered that he was handicapped. Many times they would say things like, "oh, what a shame" or "well, God bless you kids." I'd thank them, and watch them walk off. What was so unusual besides the frequency of this event, was the fact that their car was usually parked quite far from ours. I began to wonder if my little brother had some sort of magnetic force field he was sending out that people couldn't resist. Doing the energy work I do today, I've come to believe John was healing people with transmissions of love, even then.

At church, many people would take one of his little hands in theirs and kiss it. He was always sweet, never offended by their attention, unlike me who hated to have her hair messed with. I realize now that my brother's mission here was not so that *he* be healed, but that he dispense healing energy to those around him. I wish our mother could have understood that while we were growing up.

Someone gave us a copy of Dale Evans Rogers' book *Angel Unaware* when Johnny was about five years old. Mom read it to me, then I reread it myself, over and over again. Sometimes I'd read it out loud to Johnny. It tells the story of Dale and Roy Rogers' daughter Robin, a beautiful child with Downs Syndrome, who lived a very short time, but blessed their family profoundly. That book seemed to help Mom a lot. I still recommend it to people today who have a special needs child in their life. It helped open up the eyes of our understanding.

Dad was getting better about going to church with us more often. When I was six years old, he came home one day with a sad look on his face.

"Dee, sit down."

Mom was cooking, it seemed like she was always cooking or tending to Johnny. One look at Dad told her to turn off the stove and join him at the kitchen table. He proceeded to tell her how he'd been forced to take an "early retirement." He had just turned sixty, and had been under the impression he would be working at Sinclair until he was sixty-five. He was a supervisor, after all. Suddenly that day, though, a younger man had shown up and taken his place, with no notice at all. My father was devastated.

Mom hugged him and reminded him that God would provide. She'd get a job somehow or he would find part-time work. God would show us the way. She calmed him down and said we'd pray about it in church that week. I remember feeling a little scared that night. I knew something pretty major had occurred, but wasn't sure what it meant yet.

Her friend Vesta introduced Mom to *Tupperware*. She was a saleslady for this company and convinced my mother she should give it a try. So for awhile, Johnny and I were part of the *Tupperware* party circuit. I'd help Mom load her products and samples into the Rambler, then we'd buckle John in and away we'd go. My job was to make sure Johnny was safe and happy, and then I got to help her set up her display, and often was called out to do the drawing for the door prizes.

Johnny and I enjoyed this quite a bit. We looked at it as an adventure of sorts! I especially liked going to homes that had pets, because our mother was not fond of house pets. She was raised on a farm and believed animals belonged outdoors, never in the house. In fact, I was allergic to dogs and cats at that time, so she had a built-in excuse to avoid letting me have one. One afternoon at a very nice lady's home, John and I were in the back bedroom waiting for the party to be over. A cute puppy wandered in, and I began to play with it. My eyes teared up and I sneezed a bit, but I didn't care. I sat up on the edge of the bed next to my brother and took his hand, stroking it over the dog's back. I always liked to let John experience things that I enjoyed.

"Look, Johnny, it's a dog! You're petting the dog. Isn't it cute?"

He smiled. The puppy was fluffy and soft, and licked his hand. My brother laughed out loud and suddenly, I got fired up about trying to increase Johnny's vocabulary.

"Johnny, it's a DOG. Say DOG. Dog? D-O-G. Dog, dog, doggie, dog...." and on and on.

My poor little brother turned his head away, but I turned it back so he could watch my mouth while forcing him to listen to my inane repetition of the word. I had recently seen *The Miracle Worker* on TV, so I was on a mission with a little acting thrown in, yet again! I held his fingers over my lips so he could feel the movement and got down on my knees so he could see me forming the word. This went on for about twenty minutes or more. I was obsessed. I was going to teach my brother a new word so we could surprise our mother, no matter what.

Suddenly, Johnny did something which amazed me. He took a big sigh, looked right at me and distinctly said, "Dog." He looked at me as if to say, "Are you happy now?"

I whooped and hollered. "Wow! Wait 'til we tell Mom! Say it again, Johnny. Please? Please, say it again, Johnny!"

He sighed and said the word two or three more times before he rolled his head away. This seemed to bore him, but *I* was ecstatic. I babbled to Mom about it the whole time we were packing up the *Tupperware*. She smiled patiently, just wanting to get back home so she could start supper.

In the car the familiar feeling of her disbelief overtook me. I begged Johnny to say "dog" for our mother. He just looked at me and smiled really big, then looked away. The thought I read from him was, "That was just for you, Sis. I wanted you to stop bugging me!"

I felt betrayed. Mom was sick and tired of hearing me repeat the word over and over and told me to be quiet. Johnny was starting to let me see glimpses of abilities he held in reserve. More of these would surface over the years, and I'd develop the theory that he was perfectly happy just the way he was, but certainly could have spoken more and done more if it had served his soul contract's purpose. That night, however, I was simply ticked at him! How could he bail on me like that? Making me sound like an "idjit!" He was supposed to be on *my* side. It may have been our first and only sibling disagreement!

Something inside of me made a shift about that time. I decided if my brother could talk when he wanted to, then I could avoid sneezing around pets when I wanted to. A stray calico cat came up to me on the porch one day after school. I talked to it and petted it. Taking a deep breath, I thought how nice it would be not to have my eyes tear up and itch; to not have to sneeze because of playing with this cute animal. Suddenly I realized I was not sneezing or itching! I even held the cat up to my face and took a deep breath, just to be sure. I rubbed my cheek against its fur. No tears, no sneeze!

I grabbed the kitten and ran inside. "Mom! Look at this cute kitty I just found! May I give it some milk, please?"

This was a familiar song and dance. For years I would beg to feed, then keep stray cats and dogs, and "no, because of your allergies, Cheryl," would always be her standard response. She looked at the cat and wrinkled her nose slightly. Animals belonged *outside*. In her book, cats should be in the barn, catching mice. Still, she was not coldhearted. This little kitty looked a bit ragged and mewed hungrily.

"All right, Cheryl. Go ahead and give it a little saucer of milk out on the porch."

"Really? Thanks! Um, Mom, could I please keep this one? Please?"

"You know what those critters do to you, young lady." She saw the pleading look in my eyes and sighed. "This should be clear to you by now, but here it is again. Okay, then. I'll make you a bargain. If you can go two whole hours with no sneezing and puffy eyes, we might try to keep it. That make you happy?" She smiled, confident my allergies wouldn't let her down.

"Yes, ma'am. I have a feeling this time I'll be just fine." I grinned confidently.

Long story short, that day mind triumphed over matter and/or pet dander. I walked up and down the length of our driveway for the full two hours, holding and petting the cat and saying over and over to myself, "don't sneeze, don't cry. Don't sneeze, don't cry." It's really my first recollection of doing self-hypnosis, of sorts! I have never been allergic to animals since. After much begging and especially after getting my feisty father to side with me, she gave in.

He teased, "Well, Dee, you *did* say she could keep it if she went two hours without a reaction. The girl seems healed! It's a miracle, praise the Lord!"

"Callie" made herself right at home. She was no trouble and seemed very smart, as far as I was concerned. What I loved most about her was the way she fiercely protected Johnny. Anytime someone she didn't know would get near him, the hackles on the back of her neck would go up. Sometimes she'd hiss and spit if a sudden movement was made toward him by a stranger. She even perched on the corner-post of his crib and watched over him as he slept. I concluded that many animals are much more intelligent than some people. This sweet cat knew how special my brother was! She never got in his face, and Johnny loved it when I'd help him pet her, she was so soft. A couple of years later, while my grandparents were visiting, I believe my mother put them up to pretending to need a "good mouser" for their barn. So reluctantly, I watched them pack her into their car and drive off. They promised me visiting privileges and my grandfather renamed her "Kansas City Kitty." She lived for several years on their farm and always seemed happy there when I saw her, so that made it a bit easier. Still, I longed for a pet. I noticed how friends' dogs were always nice to Johnny, too, always being gentle and protective toward him. There's a picture of him with a sweet little dog named Sam in this book. Animals possess an innate intelligence and respect that I came to believe certainly supersedes human understanding. They love us unconditionally, and since Johnny also loved everyone and everything with no strings attached, no wonder they adored him! (I've done some animal communication in recent years, which is addressed in Chapter Fifteen).

Meanwhile, Dad was not happy about his wife working. He tinkered with fixing things up around the house and yard to keep himself from going nuts. He and my mother began taking Johnny to garage sales with them once a week while I was in school. It became a hobby, a cheaper form of window shopping, which could involve some creative haggling. They actually had a lot of fun doing this!

About that time, a new car wash was built down the street from us. Dad complained how it would bring more traffic into the neighborhood. One day after he ran an errand, he came home quite excited. All at once, the car wash had become his salvation.

"Dee, Cheryl! Guess what?"

We hadn't seen him this excited in a long time. He'd been retired for several months and seemed to be losing interest in life in general. It was a joy to see him so animated.

"I stopped in at the new car wash because I wanted to see what it was all about, y'know? The owner was there. We got to talking, and it turns out he wants me to run it for him!" He fairly beamed.

My mother was unclear on what this meant. "What do you mean, 'run it' for him?"

"Manage it. Keep the stalls cleaned out, collect the money every day. Work on the machines if they need it. Maintenance, all that. It's only part-time, but it'll help. Isn't it great?"

She was onboard now. If Walt was happy, the whole household would be happier. "Sure, sure, honey! Wonderful! When do you start?"

He dangled a rattling keychain. "I already did! We just hit it off and he hired me on the spot. So I'll be home in a couple of hours. Just wanted to tell you where I was. Gotta go get a feel for the place." He kissed her on the cheek and tousled my hair. "Daddy's got a job, hot damn!' He did a little jaunty step out the door toward the car. The old Walt was back and how!

Mom and I smiled at each other. God was indeed moving in mysterious ways! Over the next several years, I became an expert at rolling quarters emptied from the coin boxes, then helping Dad take them to the bank. The car wash never brought in tons of money for us, but it gave my Dad something to do and more importantly, made him feel like an active contributor to the welfare of our family again. He worked there part-time for nearly fourteen years.

Throughout all of these family changes, Johnny was constantly cheerful, a loving, wonderful presence. He seldom cried nor was sick. Mom taught me to change his diapers, which didn't thrill me, but since it was him, it was okay.

I was quite sensitive to odors as a young child. If someone sitting near me at school threw up, I would usually get the dry heaves simply from the smell blended with that weird red chemical sawdust the janitor sprinkled on top to dry it up. Knowing this about myself, I devised the best diaper-changing plan I could. Stinky diapers were the main ones with which I had a problem, so upon confirming Johnny had "gone Number 2" I would back up where there was lots of fresh air, fill my lungs and hold my breath the whole time I removed the offensive diaper, tucked a clean one around him and ran full tilt to the bathroom to flush the nasty contents away. It's a wonder I never passed out! And those were the days of cloth diapers, so Mom insisted I rinse the diaper out in the clean toilet water afterward. Not a favorite chore, but hey, this was my baby brother. And he was always so sweet and accepting. Plus, the more I practiced holding my breath, my "personal best" got up to nearly two minutes without getting light headed!

Mom would laugh to see me running down the hall, full diaper extended at arm's length while I grew progressively redder in the face. I was a strange kid in many ways, but Johnny didn't mind. I always felt comfortable being myself around him. Our parents noticed our bond; they frequently commented on how he lit up as soon as he heard my voice in a nearby room. And although Mom encouraged me to play outside as often as possible, sitting and reading aloud to Johnny was one of my favorite past-times.

One day I was reading the Bible out loud to him and our mother stood in the kitchen doorway, listening. Johnny kept his eyes on me as I read and held his feet, sometimes massaging them with one hand. I was somewhere in the Old Testament in the middle of some dramatic tale, probably David taking on Goliath, when she interrupted me.

"Cheryl, why are you talking that way?"

I looked up, startled. "I'm just reading normal."

She shook her head no. "You're using some strange accent...it sounds Irish. Why are you doing that?"

Mimic that I was, I seemed to pick up Celtic accents easily. However, I had been unaware of reading with one just then. After years of trying to explain my "strangeness" to my mother, I'd learned it was sometimes easier to just shrug my shoulders and say, "Oh, I dunno. Sorry." So that's what I did.

She raised an eyebrow, wiped her hands on her apron and returned to her cooking. Johnny smiled. Apparently he had enjoyed the accent, so I continued reading the same way only at a lower volume. Looking back, I know that in many past lives I had British, Scottish and Irish links. Seems that part of my Higher Self must have really enjoyed those lives and using the lilting accent or brogue so much, snuck it in even when *I* was unconscious of speaking that way. As that young child however, I simply chalked it up to my "weirdness" which always puzzled my parents.

Kids at school had begun to label me that way, too, because I enjoyed engaging teachers in conversation, often asking what they considered "bizarre" questions about literature. I loved reading, mostly biographies. I was tested in the second grade and my teacher's eyes were quite wide when she reported my reading comprehension was at the 10th grade level.

Mom was always proud of my grades, and when this additional report was sent home she immediately did one of the most supportive things I remember her ever doing for me. She drove me down to the big library in North Kansas City, about twenty minutes from our house. Clyde and Edith Lay lived across the street from us, and proved to be invaluable friends. Edith was a librarian at the North Kansas City branch, and she suggested Mom bring me in and help me get my own card because the selection was so much bigger than the smaller local library. My mother got her own card, too, and we would go at least every other week. I devoured books, many times reading into the night way past my bedtime. I loved it so much I would sneak a flashlight under the covers and pore over mythology, biographies, mysteries and such. I read the entire Laura Ingalls Wilder series, and adored Mark Twain. In fact, I consider that wonderful Missouri author one of my guides, these days!

John got to hear many of the stories I read, simply because I was such a ham. Some of the first acting I ever did was for him, using accents and dialects, creating characters and making sound effects. It was great fun. He would listen peacefully for hours, or as long as my voice held out, sometimes commenting, "I good!" or "now, now, now" or making his own sound effects. His seizures were under much better control at this time, which was a major relief for all of us.

We were now going to church as often as five times a week. I'm not kidding! There were Wednesday morning services, which I was exempt from when school was on. Then there were Wednesday and Thursday evenings, Sunday morning and evening and occasionally a Tuesday night when a missionary or out-of-town evangelist dropped by. Johnny endured being rolled down the aisle to have hands laid upon him each and every time. Mom never missed an opportunity for this, and I began to hope that God would heal him more for her sake than John's. I missed seeing her smile real big like she had when I was tiny. She always seemed a little sad these days.

As for me, I relished basking in my little brother's presence. He was always cheerful, sweet and loving. I just felt good all over when I hung out with him. Many years later, I came to believe that those who are born with such severe challenges are very evolved beings, who not only come to work through any of their own soul issues, but to set examples to others, to teach us patience and understanding as we observe their courage and consistent cheerfulness. In Michael Newton's books, *Journey of Souls* and *Destiny of Souls*, he talks about people being in the same "soul group" or family. I believe Johnny and I most definitely fit into that category, and have gone through many lifetimes together. In fact, I believe "soulmates" can take on various forms, not always having to fit into the romantic category. Johnny is certainly the closest thing to a soulmate I have ever had, and I couldn't ask for a better one!

Chapter Five

Parents & Other Heroes

My brother Don lived with us off and on during my childhood. He fixed up the basement and made it into an apartment, placing really cool travel posters of exotic, faraway places on the wall, like Greece and Italy. Don was one of my early heroes because if not for him, I would not have been able to go to many movies, concerts, circuses and other fun events. He was the only family member to strongly encourage and appreciate my natural bent toward music and acting. He bought me my first piano when I was ten years old. I'm so grateful to my brother for nurturing my creative side, which some other family members considered capricious or a waste of time. "Thanks" is simply inadequate to express my gratitude to my dear older brother for the valuable role he has played in my life.

As Johnny and I were growing up, my parents were naturally consumed with John's care. They had to be very budget conscious. I believe more than anything else, they simply didn't realize how starved I was for culture. But Don did, thank God! He took me to many events and I loved going places with him. When I was five, he encouraged my parents to allow me to take dance lessons. I endured these for awhile, never understanding nor shining in ballet; in fact, I was pretty much a klutz in the twinkle-toes department! But I did find tap dancing fun. I was in a few recitals, but it wasn't really my cup of tea.

About the same time, someone in the family got the bright idea I should learn the accordion. I don't remember who or why. It was likely an outpicturing of our love of Lawrence Welk! So a three-quarter size instrument was rented and I was on my way to reading notes and playing the vertical keyboard. I liked this much more than dancing, and went so far as to win a tiny trophy at my first music recital.

Johnny would laugh and "sing" along in his own way when I made music. It's definitely a universal language which dissolves all speech barriers. Many special needs kids, including autistic ones I have known through the years, all respond very happily to music. My parents didn't fathom where my musical abilities came from, although I found out many years later my great-grandfather on Mom's side had played the banjo. About age eight, I became obsessed with the idea of owning a guitar. The accordion hadn't held my attention more than a couple of years, so I was told I had to buy any new instruments with my own money. I'm sure my parents thought that would be the end of that. Didn't they know me better than that by now?

I was on a mission! I sold *Grit* newspapers to the neighbors, did chores around the house, raked leaves and mowed our yard and those of the neighbors who "hired" me, sold lemonade and did other kid-typical money-raising activities. When I had saved the $11.99 plus tax the drugstore wanted for a shiny new acoustic guitar, Dad drove me there and I proudly made my purchase. Looking back, that first guitar was actually not a bad instrument. In the '60s, you could get a decent sounding real guitar, not just a toy, for that amount of money. Dad was especially proud of my initiative in going after what I wanted. He bought me a book of Hank Williams' songs (one of his favorite country singers) and suggested I teach myself a few. We went to the music store and I got a chord chart book to teach myself where to place my fingers. I learned about frets and tuning. This was quite different from the accordion and fun, to boot!

My father was always a Grand Ol' Opry fan, and to further the advancement of our mutual admiration society, by the age of nine I could play and sing *Your Cold, Cold Heart, Jambalaya, You Win Again* and a host of other Hank tunes. Dad enjoyed this so much he didn't even mind when I insisted on packing the guitar along in the car. I would often sit there in the Rambler's back seat, strumming and singing to Johnny while our parents ran errands, like shopping. One of the few movies I remember Dad taking me to see was the young George Hamilton in the movie of Hank's life, *Your Cheatin' Heart.*

Dad was always going to thrift stores, or "salvage stores" as many were called back them. Some were actually very early versions of antique marts with an open, outdoor feel. He bought me some of my first records, among them a set of 78 rpms of Beethoven's Fifth Symphony, conducted by Arturo Toscanini. I still have these relics, as well as *South Pacific* on 78s with Mary Martin and Ezio Penza. My father was proud of finding these "jewels." I believe he paid all of a quarter for each set! At least he did what he could to encourage my musical leanings, and I was grateful for that. As for Mom, she never responded to my singing very much, unless it was hymns.

I had many heroes. My mother only had a handful of them that I was aware of. Along with the rest of the world, she was profoundly affected by the death of one she held in exceptionally high esteem.

Friday, November 22, 1963: Along with millions of Americans, I remember certain details of that day quite vividly. Never mind that three days prior I had just turned eight years old. Something like that sticks with one for a lifetime. That Friday afternoon, I was seated in my second grade class. The P.A. intercom crackled, and we heard our principal take a somber breath.

"Teachers and students...I am incredibly sorry to announce that President Kennedy has been shot and.... the President of our country has just died."

There was an audible gasp from Miss Sewell, our teacher. We kids looked at each other in confusion and shock. Died? President Kennedy? I looked over at a picture of him we had on the classroom wall. He was so handsome, so young. There must be a mistake! How could he be dead? This was totally foreign to me. Who would shoot the President? And why?

All of these questions whirled around in everyone's mind that day, regardless of age. I caught something about a man with a gun and was given my first exposure to the word "assassination." The rest basically became a blur. The principal added that school would be dismissed early so that we could be with our families. The buses would collect us shortly, and more announcements would be made. Miss Sewell was now weeping openly. She instructed us to gather up our things, and to bow our heads in silence in honor of our fallen leader.

It was all so surreal. My thoughts immediately went to my mother, home alone with 3 year old Johnny. President Kennedy was someone I knew she greatly admired. They were the same age, and she really thought he was going to do big things for the U.S. I prayed God would help her, as this news was apparently traveling like wildfire. I remember walking through our front door and calling out for her. Johnny was asleep on the couch, always able to find peace, no matter what was going on in the outside world. There was no response from Mom. I looked in the kitchen, in the garage, then I heard very quiet sobbing coming from her bedroom.

"Mom?" I tentatively peaked in the doorway to find her standing on the second rung of a step-ladder, paint brush still in hand. She had begun texture painting her ceiling by hand, an arduous job, to say the least. When my mother wanted something a certain way, though, there was no stopping her. Except for this news. I wondered how long she had been frozen there on the ladder, tears streaming down her cheeks.

I walked over to her. Although I usually called her "Mom" at this age, to be more cool, like my peers, I reverted to saying, "Mama?" as I gently reached up for the paint brush, which she numbly released. Placing it in the roller pan on the floor, next I reached up for her hand. "C'mon, Mama. Let's go sit in the living room, okay? C'mon. I'm here now."

She burst into great heaving sobs. "Oh, dear God, Cheryl. They killed John Kennedy. What kind of world is this?"

I felt my mother lean on me for the first time in my life. I was so glad I was home for her. Dad must have been working at the car wash and hadn't heard the news yet. I decided I'd go get him as soon as she was calmer.

She turned on the TV and we watched in utter disbelief as they showed the convertible driving through Dallas. It was impossible, yet here was documented proof this awful thing had really happened. After twenty minutes or so, she seemed calmer so I got up to go fetch Dad, but just then he pulled into the driveway. By the look on his face, I could see he had heard by now, too.

We mourned with the rest of the country as everything seemed to grind to a halt. The unthinkable had taken place. Lincoln was the only President I was familiar with who had been shot. My awareness of his death came more from being teased by the older kids about our last name for several years.

"John Wilkes Booth is your great grandpa, I bet. He shot Abraham Lincoln! Aren't you ashamed?"

At first I would deny that we could have been related. I would try to explain that even if we were, his actions had nothing to do with me. This seemed to egg on my tormentors, however, because the teasing continued. So out of frustration, I eventually reached the point where I would say, "I claim his brother Edwin, the greatest Shakespearean actor of the 19th century, but I disinherit John Wilkes." Kids would then look at me like I was crazy, or with just a blank stare. They'd usually shake their heads, and walk off, but at least the teasing usually stopped. *Usually*. Bullies are often hard to defeat with intelligent repartee, so the black humor inside me decided the blunt approach might work best. My stock reply soon became, "You better shut up or I'll shoot *you*." That pretty much ended the ribbing from all concerned. I got some strange looks from those within earshot for awhile, but kids forget quickly, and my violent threats were never taken (nor given) seriously.

I began to read about Lincoln, and realized there were many parallels between his life and assassination and that of JFK. This was long before I had any awareness of reincarnation. Yet something about all this history repeating itself in so many similar ways was eerie to me. I was heavily into doing all kinds of craft work at this time, so I paid homage to these two fallen presidents by first carefully burning the edges of a picture of each of them from a fancy Presidential coloring book I bought, then decopauging (laminating images to wood) them, side by side, to a board. I added one of each of their more famous quotes below their image, and that plaque hung on my wall for several years.

We put our lives back into gear, slowly but surely. Mom took to calling Johnny "John-John" after the President's brave little son. Dad found a new hero in LBJ. Mom and I were not impressed with this Texan. Something about him didn't strike me as quite honest, and he sure wasn't handsome like JFK. But my father believed he would help wipe out the Commies once and for all. Dad was a Navy veteran, twice, in fact. He first joined when he was just seventeen years of age, in 1919. You'll read more about that later on.

Dad always said he didn't see much action as a young sailor, but he loved being on ships. So much so, that when World War II broke out, he re-enlisted, at the age of forty! Well, as he admitted to me much later, it was a combination of patriotism coupled with an unhappy first marriage and the fact that two of his three daughters had already left home. So serving in the Navy seemed like a logical thing to him, a way to escape an unhappy home life. My father always looked a good deal younger than he was, so lots of his fellow sailors didn't know his true age at first. When the secret leaked out, many of them affectionately called him "Pops" even though he didn't look old enough to deserve that title. He was injured in active service on Shore Patrol and as a consequence, suffered with arthritis the rest of his life.

My Dad was not a big complainer, however. At least not while Mom was around. She continued to sell *Tupperware* part-time, explored selling *Stanley* home products and *Avon*, but primarily busied herself keeping the house and taking care of us.

My father was only 5'7" tall. He swore up and down he was an inch taller but I know better, because I could look over the top of his head by the time I was twelve, and I was measured at school as being 5'8"! Walter Howard Booth could be a bit cocky sometimes, probably very much so when he was a young man. Seeing us together, lots of people thought he was my grandfather, but that didn't bother me. Our age difference was no big deal to me. It was who he was inside that I always related to the most.

One of the funniest incidents I remember about my Dad happened one sultry 4th of July. Fireworks were legal and all the rage back then. Dad always got me some snakes, sparklers, fountains, Roman candles and bottle rockets, along with several types of firecrackers. He would put on quite the private pyro-techniques display for me in the backyard. Mom hated this, but she knew he realized he'd never be able to do this with Johnny, so I was the next best thing. As I got older, he gave me more responsibility, like lighting certain things on his cue. I thought it was really cool. He taught me to blow up ant hills (Sorry, little guys! My respect for all life was not developed then, obviously. Hope you crossed over to ant Heaven just fine). We'd toss a lit 'cracker into the end of an open crossbar tube on my swing-set and it would echo like a cannon. I got into these little war games so much that I saved some money and bought my own G.I. Joe and tank. Mom was truly ready to give up on me ever being a lady when I did this in favor of playing with Barbie!

Anyway, the 4th of July before I entered the 3rd grade, my Dad went on a fireworks shopping mission. Mom, Johnny and I were out on the front patio, watching traffic and neighbors go by, fanning ourselves and drinking iced tea. Dad pulled in and parked along the end of the yard. By the way he swaggered up the drive with a big grocery bag brimming over, I knew he had scored some pretty cool stuff. He had a cigar clamped between his teeth and he grinned at me around it.

Suddenly, Dad took off like a bat out of hell, throwing the bag as far away from us as possible. It all happened so fast I was mystified. I soon understood his actions as the bag began to spew out sounds and sparks. I realized the ash from his cigar had fallen in and ignited it. My mother alternated between laughing and gasping for breath.

I sat there in silence and my father was sitting nearby on the grass, grateful for the agility he still possessed. "God! That was stupid!" He shook his head at his own error. "I just forgot the damn thing was lit." He was trying to kick the habit and would often chomp on an unlit cigar for awhile..

My mother snorted, "Well, it's a good thing you got a clue when you did or it would've blown your fool head off." She broke into new peals of laughter and Dad soon joined in. Johnny was grinning at them both as if he didn't quite get the joke, but he was glad they were happy.

Dad looked over at me, sullenly sitting there. "What'sa matter, Squirt? Your old Dad's okay. Not still scared for me, are ya? Not my girl. They've all gone out, honey, look." He pointed at the smoldering remains of the bag.

I pouted, "I'm not scared. And I'm glad you're okay. It's just...."

"Just what, Honey?" he asked with concern.

"It's just that they weren't pretty at all in broad daylight. What a gyp!" With that, I stormed into the house as my parents dissolved into more howls of laughter. So my father went out once again, and brought home a few more fireworks to ease my disappointment. I didn't see a cigar around him for several months after that.

Speaking of cigars, I was somewhat allergic to the smoke, but I didn't mind Dad smoking them nearly as much when he started saving the bands to redeem them for various sporting goods items for me. Certain tobacco companies ran similar promotions to keep their customers hooked via other types of rewards. Mom was not at all happy about my first football and softball gear. To appease her when she realized her tomboy daughter showed no signs of becoming a real "little lady," he also traded several cigar bands in and got a huge family Bible, complete with reproductions of Michelangelo paintings.

Mom had her own version of this redemption thing going on, but hers was S & H Green Stamps. They even had a store where you'd go trade in books full of stamps. We got some pretty neat stuff and I always liked going there. My parents found creative ways around not having a full salary coming in every week. I never really felt deprived. Our income bracket would have been considered lower middle class. We lived in a safe, clean neighborhood, had nice neighbors and Dad always kept our vehicles in great running order. Johnny was largely responsible for reminding us not to take what we had for granted. He was so happy with so little, who were we to want more?

Many kids my own age bored me with their endless pettiness. Don't get me wrong, I longed for their acceptance, and usually had a small circle of friends. I usually didn't mind good old solitude, though, because I actually enjoyed my own company. Oh, sure, I went through bouts of loneliness, but I didn't feel most kids my age understood my jokes or viewpoint, so usually kept those thoughts to myself. It was easier. The only time I'd let much of it out was when I'd have conversations with John. *He* always understood and accepted me unconditionally.

Whenever I began feeling that my life was that of a loner and sometimes boring, all I had to do was try to put myself in John's place. His only interactions were with the family, church members and the occasional visitors to our home. He never seemed to be bored, though.

I decided he had infinitesimal patience and resolved not to feel so sorry for myself.

My main outlets of expression were music and my writing. I loved to create stories, essays and poems. My writing began in earnest in second grade. I ambitiously wrote my first "book" entitled *The Adventures of Tim McMullin.* Hand-printed, of course, it was all of twenty pages long. The main story line dealt with the hero, Tim, forever being taunted by the local bully, Bruce. However, at that age, for unbeknownst reasons, I spelled his name "Bruise!" Maybe a past life memory of being beaten black and blue by such a tormentor? Anyway, in the end, clever Tim always managed to outwit good ol' Bruise. This little book amused my mother to a degree, but she puzzled over why I was so fascinated with writing about a little Irish boy. I couldn't explain it either, it just seemed natural to me, like writing about the kid next door. My father didn't really pay that much attention to my schoolwork. He knew I got good grades, liked school and was happy most of the time; that was what he considered a good educational experience.

At a third grade Open House held around Thanksgiving, my teacher was so impressed with one of my little story/essays that she posted it on the wall. It was a five or six page story complete with drawings...a story about a young Indian boy whose father carefully taught him to tan hides for clothing and teepees, how to build a lean-to, how to hunt, fish, and be a brave warrior. It was rather detailed, and written in the first person, speaking from the boy's point of view. I think this intrigued my teacher more than the descriptive accuracy. What follows is my recollection of a brief conversation between my mother and teacher at that particular Open House.

"Oh, Mrs. Booth, Cheryl has such a vivid imagination! She reads so much! She says you take her to the library at least once every other week, is that true?"

"Well, yes." My mother was in conflict about my literary addiction. She loved the fact I was bright, yet recently had tried to discourage me from reading so much, and so high above my grade level. She felt it would surely confuse me. I would often take a book up into my favorite climbing tree and read for hours. I was still doing the late night "under cover" reading whenever I got the chance! Reading was my great escape. It fed my imagination.

By third grade, I was already out of the Teen/Juvenile category and perusing the Adult books at the library. It was about this time that my infatuation with medieval times and the Arthurian legend began. I proudly carried around a copy of *The Once and Future King* by T. H.

White, which I read and reread so many times I couldn't count them. Due to its size in hardcover form, most of my playmates thought it was the Bible at first glance. No one else toted around such a big book; consequently I was pegged as "odd" by my peers at a pretty young age. I didn't care. If odd people read such great stuff, then odd I would remain! Merlin turning Arthur into animals to teach him things, Arthur and the Knights of the Round Table fighting for right not might...ah! Now *that* was a mystical, noble life!

Let's rewind back to that Open House experience. I began to tune out the adult voices. In a daydream or sorts, I wandered over to look at some of my classmate's work during the course of the women's conversation. Some of the artwork on display was pretty good. I had recently begun drawing knights and horses and wanted to see if my work was "up to speed."

My teacher called, "Cheryl, please come here, dear. Your mother and I have been talking about your story here, and we're curious. Did you read a story about the Indians, other than what we studied in class? Some sort of historical novel, or maybe you saw a pioneer or Indian show on TV recently, anything like that?

I shook my head. "No. I've been reading about King Arthur, mostly. I keep looking for more books about that. I love learning about medieval times!"

My mother said, "But honey, why on earth would you write this little story as though you were an Indian boy? That just strikes us as a little...well, unusual. We thought you got that idea from another book, maybe?" She almost sounded hopeful.

Innocently, I shot her theory down. "No, Mom. You remember my Tim McMullin book last year?" She nodded wearily. Poor woman! Her daughter wrote accurately about things for which she had no logical base of knowledge or experience, and I realize now this probably frightened her to some degree. That lack of understanding usually expressed itself via silence, which I mistook many times for anger. I wasn't sure what I'd done to upset her, but on many occasions she would be very quiet after a question and answer session such as the one going on at that moment.

"Well, this story sort of wrote itself, just like the stories about Tim. I don't know how, exactly, but that felt like I really lived in Ireland in the 1800s, it was easy to write. And this one here, it...well, it felt like I really *was* that Indian boy. I knew just how to write about what he learned and saw. I felt like I was him, and he was me. Isn't that funny?" I looked at her and pushed my glasses back against my nose.

All through elementary school, I wore exceptionally unattractive eyeglasses with pointed edges. Probably because that style of frames was in our price range. And this was in the day way before designer glasses. These spectacles contributed even more to my oddball, bookworm image. Today's kids would call me a "nerd!"

"Yes, that's very funny, Cheryl. Hysterical." But she wasn't smiling. "I don't know, Miss Sewell. Cheryl does this type of thing a lot." She sighed. "I don't understand it, really. But if she says she didn't read it somewhere else, or see it on TV, then she didn't. One thing I know about my girl for sure, she's no liar."

Startled, my teacher said, "Oh, please, Mrs. Booth, don't misunderstand me. I was not implying Cheryl plagiarized the story. I just thought she may have read something or seen something on television that inspired it. It's so intricately written for a student her age. She's actually very gifted." She smiled at me, then patted me on the head. "Have you thought about testing her this year for the accelerated program? I even believe she could easily skip a grade or even two, if you're interested."

"No, no, I don't think so. Her father and I don't want to give her airs. She needs to fit in with her own age group. We're happy with her progress. She just does some strange things once in awhile, like these little stories. We don't understand it, but maybe we don't need to." She extended her hand to my teacher. "Thank you for talking with me, and thanks for putting Cheryl's story up on the wall. I hope people enjoy it." Mom didn't look like she really meant that. I was confused. My teacher was proud of my writing, why wasn't my mother?

We left and drove home in the familiar, stony silence. That night is clearly etched in my memory. From my adult perspective and the hypnotherapy training I've pursued, I realize those two stories were clearly past life memories which came back through my writing. Reincarnation was considered a foreign, evil concept by my parents, and was never discussed. In fact, I never heard the word spoken in our home. So at that tender age I had no basis for what I wrote. I just knew it felt true to me, and that people seemed to enjoy reading it.

All children are very intuitive. Humans are intuitive beings. It's part of our nature. However, many times parents stifle a child's psychic abilities simply because they don't understand them. There is a fear and mistrust associated with certain types of information coming from a child, and "in the best interest" of that child, many parents put a tight lid on psychic activity. Mine certainly did. It was not to be cruel, it was just that their parenting "tool box," if you will, didn't include instructions on how to deal with a kid like me. If you'd like to read a great book by another author who was an intuitive child who turned out just great, check out *Second Sight* by Dr. Judith Orloff.

In high school, I would become an avid reader of the books of an author named Taylor Caldwell. I especially liked her book *The Captains and the Kings,* which was a thinly veiled fictionalization of the Kennedy dynasty. About ten years later, I read several books by Jess Stearn, among them *The Search for Taylor Caldwell's Psychic Lives.* Mr. Stearn knew her personally and took her to a hypnotherapist at one point in time, because as she got older, she was losing her hearing. The hope was that it could be improved by hypnotic suggestion. Mr. Stearn also suspected Ms. Caldwell had some incredibly interesting past life experiences, mainly due to the fact that her writing was so factually accurate, yet she always insisted she never researched any of her historic novels of various eras. She said it was as if someone was talking through her when she wrote, and she simply went along with it. Under hypnosis, his suspicions were confirmed, and it came out that she had lived in many of the times in which she so vividly wrote. This was all the more credible because Ms. Caldwell did not (on a conscious level) believe in the concept of reincarnation! She apparently became more open to the possibility as time went on. It's an excellent book, as are all of hers. She was certainly a prolific writer! So, who knows? In retrospect, even way back then in grade school, I, too, may have been "channeling" a bit through my writing!

On my tenth birthday, my brother Don gifted me with my first real piano. I was thrilled! A neighbor gave Mom a recommendation to a piano teacher and we started in on lessons right away. A lot of the accordion stuff came right back as I found I remembered the notes of the treble clef. Technique and finger building skills challenged my left hand to work pretty hard, but I kept at it. Johnny loved listening to me practice.

I really enjoyed playing by ear and being a "TV child," the first tunes I picked out were television theme songs. *The Addams Family* song was great fun and Johnny always grinned when I did the finger snaps. Mom was not impressed, not even when I figured out the slightly complex theme to *Mission Impossible*, one of the shows we watched on a weekly basis.

"I don't think your teacher intends for you to waste your time playing junk from TV, Cheryl Ellen. You'd better practice those little songs in your books so you're ready for your lesson."

"Okay, Mom," I sighed. "It's just that those tunes aren't much fun.

Most of 'em are just made up exercises, around and around the same five notes in each hand. Boring!"

"Well, young lady, if you want lessons, you'll darn well practice the songs in the books your teacher tells you to work out of. Those books and those lessons cost good money. So you just let that other nonsense go, y'hear?"

"Yes, ma'am."

So I secretly picked out fun stuff "by ear" when I knew she wasn't listening to me. Once I knew enough notes to begin playing simplified classical pieces and eventually buying some popular sheet music, I was much happier about the lessons! As for Johnny, he loved it anytime I would sit down and play the piano, whether it was by ear, doing my finger exercises, classical, rock, Broadway, it didn't matter. His Sissy was putting on a concert for him, as far as he was concerned, and he often sang along in his own special way.

My tenth birthday was also the year I got my first real bike. Dad insisted I ride around in the back yard for quite a few weeks until he felt that I was ready to take on the street with defensive riding. His youngest daughter from his first marriage had been struck by a driver while riding her bike. She was not seriously injured, thank goodness, but it was an experience that Dad never forgot.

Riding around the backyard was painfully boring until I discovered the momentum I could build up by starting at the top of the highest hill and pedaling for all I was worth as I flew over the second hill and cut some wild corners. All of this when Dad wasn't watching, of course!

That fun came to a screeching halt one afternoon when I misjudged a high speed turn at the base of the lower hill. The front wheel spilled right into a window well, throwing me over the handlebars and luckily, into some soft grass. Dad happened to witness that, however. He figured if I got into that much of a spill in the back yard and survived, the street couldn't be much worse. So soon I was rocketing all around the neighborhood, up and down the huge, winding hill of 74th Terrace. In retrospect, it's clear I led an idyllic childhood during those first eight years in the pink house (which by that time Dad had painted yellow, Mom's favorite color).

I recall how much I enjoyed summers spent playing team sports with the neighborhood kids, or exploring the undeveloped little stretch of woods just about a mile from our house. Many peaceful mornings I'd quickly eat breakfast, do my chores then hop on my bicycle, a sack lunch tightly clutched in one hand.

"Just be back in time for supper, honey, before it gets dark, you hear?"

"Yes, ma'am," I'd dutifully reply, then pedal madly for the ultimate freedom. Roving through this little wooded glade with a small brook running through the middle of it seemed like a slice of Heaven. It was probably my first natural form of meditation. I'd lean my bicycle against a tree on the outside edge of my "forest." In the 1960s in that part of Missouri there was little danger of kidnapping, let alone someone stealing a child's bike.

The majority of today's children don't have that freedom my generation took for granted...to come and go without worry. What a world, where safety is now considered a luxury. Where fear of terrorism and awful crimes like kidnapping always keep us on high alert. A shame, isn't it? What of our inalienable rights, life, liberty and the pursuit of happiness? Shouldn't that include a child's ability to travel safely throughout her/his neighborhood, playing with abandon? I pray the world can return to that, someday, somehow. Please join me in knowing this world has the adaptability for peace to be restored on every level. Universal Consciousness can achieve so much. So much fear is promoted and projected through the media. If we choose to focus on our own divine rights and protection rather than the bombardment of negativity we are hit with in the news each day, I believe that one day, we can reclaim our freedom.

I certainly took my own safety for granted at the time; looking back on this experience now, I wouldn't trade it for anything. I'd lose myself in playacting for hours on end, pretending to be a famous explorer or sometimes thinking I might become a botanist, checking out the various types of leaves and underbrush. I got poison ivy a couple of times until I learned to recognize and avoid it. I also ruined more than one pair of sneakers attempting to jump across the widest "gorge" in the stream. My poor mother! I think her tomboy daughter got into more dirt than either of her sons from her first marriage!

There were some wonderful wild blackberry bushes in those woods, too, and my neighbors and I would eat them to our heart's content. Sometimes I had company on these outings, but more often I went alone. I actually preferred it that way. Those woods were magical to me, and I'm very grateful I had that opportunity to play outdoors so freely in such a healthy environment!

One summer, I experienced winning my first contest. Because of the sweltering humidity, many days I stayed inside and hung out with my little brother. Times like these, Johnny and I often watched a sequence of cartoons. Well, *I* would watch, he would mainly just listen and I'd tell him what was going on if it was particularly funny. I loved Bullwinkle, Quickdraw McGraw, Bugs Bunny and the Warner Brothers gang of goofy characters. John's favorite summer perch was on the couch wearing only a diaper and plastic pants, and we had the fan going full blast. So he was keeping cool, but didn't exactly have a bird's eye view. I was the one most interested in cartoons, anyhow. John just liked to be in the same room as me.

One of our favorite shows was a local one which featured a large dog puppet as the "host." They were having a weekly contest, and the dog would pull an envelope out of a basket, they'd read the name, then make a phone call to award the winner some really cool toys and prizes. I decided I would win this, no matter what.

I thought about what would make the dog grab my envelope instead of the others. I knew Dad had some long business envelopes in his room, so I went and got one. Most of the ones in the basket looked like the smaller kind. So I carefully addressed my #10 envelope, put in the required contact information, asked Mom for a stamp and marched to the mailbox. She found this amusing, since she'd never won "a darn thing."

The next week on the day of the drawing, I could swear I saw my long envelope in the basket, but the camera was too far away to read the writing. The puppet dog told some jokes as he fumbled around in the pile, then, he *did* it! He pulled out a long envelope. I was sure it was mine! I began jumping up and down excitedly. Mom came running from the kitchen to see what all the commotion was, and just then the phone rang.

"Quick! Answer the phone, Mom! Get it! Get it! Please! I just won! The dog pulled my envelope! It's them calling, I just know it!"

"Calm down, child. Mercy!" She snorted. "That dumb dog didn't pick your envelope, you just simmer down." She went over and lifted the receiver. "Hello? Yes, this is Mrs. Booth." She looked over at me as I held my breath expectantly.

"Yes, Cheryl is my daughter and she sure did send in an entry to your show. You mean she *did* win? Well, I'll be." She slowly held out the phone to me. "They want to talk to you."

"Whoopee! I *knew* it!" I ran and took the receiver. "This is Cheryl. Uh-huh. Yes. Oh, thank you! Yes, if you tell her how to get there, we'll come get my prize right away! Thank you, sir!"

Mom took the phone again, and patiently wrote down the directions to the toy store where we would go to redeem my prize, shaking her head from side to side in disbelief. I think on some level, she may have thought I put some kind of "spell" on that dog, but this particular time, I really believed it was simply the size of the envelope! Later that night, my parents drove us over to the store. I won a *Golferino* set (this was a little man on a golf course who hit little ball bearings into a series of holes as you aimed him and pushed a lever to make him swing), a yo-yo and some other cheap little toy that didn't have much staying power. It broke so early on, I honestly have no recollection of what in the world it was. What I do remember is how excited and proud I was to have won, and how great it felt to take my prizes home. Contests would always have a fascination for me, and this paid off on three different game shows for me when I became an adult and was living in L.A. But that came much later!

Around most of my peers and in the classroom, I was typically very introverted. I grew up around the company of adults, and preferred it. I was used to carrying on conversations at their level. We had taken Johnny for so many kinds of evaluations by this point in time; the doctors and other "experts" were never hopeful about his potential for improved development. Mom took the dour news the hardest. I always got the feeling she blamed herself for his condition. By now, I knew deep inside that John's worth and wisdom exceeded anything a silly physical test or even an IQ test could ever measure, even if he'd been able to take one of those. He always laughed at my jokes and impressions. He was aces in my book!

I decided to become Johnny's "secret" recreation director. I felt like he must get pretty bored, living out his life in his wheelchair, on the couch, or in bed. So every chance I got when our parents were otherwise occupied, I'd race up and down the hall pushing him at top speed in his wheelchair. He laughed and sang, "ah-ah-ah-ah" as he bounced along. I realized thrills in his life were few and far between. This motivated me to hunt around in the garage for other forms of wheeled transportation that could be modified to accommodate my baby brother.

One day I found my old red wagon collecting dust over in a corner. I pulled it out to front yard and hosed it off, realizing it was just the right size to hold Johnny and a few comfy pillows. As I shined it up, I concocted a plan. Mom stepped outside to see what had become of me.

I had already thought about how to present my idea. I smiled up at her as I wiped the beads of water off the wagon. "Hi, Mom! Look what I found! I figured Johnny might like to be pulled around in this. Watch!" I jumped inside to show her how spacious it was. "Plenty of room for some pillows, huh? It's only fair he should have a toy like this. After all, I've got my bike. And this wagon is just going to waste." I looked hopefully up at her.

She actually took the time to inspect it, looking the wagon up and down, then surprised me by agreeing! "You know what, young lady? That is great idea! Let's go get some pillows and you can give your brother a little ride around the driveway, real careful, now, y'hear? He'll probably love playing with you like that. He loves his Sissy Cheryl so much." She scurried inside, a happy smile lighting up her face. I was stunned at how easily my scheme was unfolding!

Soon I was pulling Johnny around the yard under our mother's watchful eye. I knew I would have to build her trust slowly to work my up to my *big* plan, which was to pull Johnny to the top of our twisty, hilly street. I loved rocketing down those hills on my bike. Someday, I would take Johnny up to the top hill, hop on the back of the wagon, and we'd fly down the hill. What a thrill *that* would be for him! But it would have to be at a time when Mom had no clue what I was up to. It required careful planning, and timing it when she was busily distracted, and wouldn't see us, like maybe when she was downstairs doing laundry, or away from the house, running an errand. This would be Johnny's and my secret!

So for days I told him about my plan, waiting and watching for the perfect opportunity. He looked right at me as if he understood. We were conspirators, as far as I was concerned. It was all just a matter of time now. A few weeks later, "we" saw our chance. We were in the yard, and Johnny was already comfortably nestled inside the wagon. Mom was beginning to leave me alone with him for longer stretches of time now. She came out and announced she was going to the store, but she'd be back in about a half hour.

"You take good care of your little brother now, Cheryl. Your Daddy's mowing the back yard, but you go get him if you need anything, all right?"

"Yes, ma'am. Johnny and I will be just fine. We'll have fun!" I almost snickered with anticipation, but managed to hold my enthusiasm level down so as not to raise any suspicion from Mom. I felt like my heart would burst out of my chest, but I innocently smiled and waved at her as she backed out into the street. Making sure she was out of sight, I slowly began to pull the wagon along the street in the opposite direction from which she had gone, up the fun hill. This would probably be the closest thing Johnny would ever get to a roller coaster ride, and I just knew he would love it.

He looked up at me trustingly as I assured him this was our big moment. We climbed the hill leisurely. I whistled to cover my nerves. I knew some of our neighbors were snoopy and didn't want to give away our plan by rushing willy-nilly down the street. Not too many people were around, though, as it was mid-afternoon and most folks were still at work.

Finally we got to the top of the hill. I knelt down beside my brother so we could make eye contact. "Okay, Johnny buddy, this is it. We're going to *fly*! Are you ready? Ready to go? Go, go, go!"

That did it! John's little hands flew up in the air as he crowed, "I go! I go!"

"You got it, kiddo. Hang on!" I climbed on back and made sure I had a firm hold on the wagon's tongue to steer it. I draped myself over my brother's body, figuring I'd make a pretty good safety shield. Kids are so crazy! Lucky for me that insane *Jackass* show wasn't on TV when I was a kid, or Heaven knows what other dangerous stuff I might have put my little brother and myself through! Pushing off, we began careening down the hill. The wind took my breath away as it whistled past my ears.

"Uh-ah-uh-ah," Johnny rattled as we moved. He was grinning, so I knew he was having fun, too. We made it all the way down the really big hill and part-way up the next smaller hill. That one was within easy visibility of our house. As we slowed down I hopped off and steadied the wagon. I took a few moments to straighten the pillows a bit and brushed Johnny's hair smooth with my fingers. Then I began pulling my precious cargo nice and easy again, as if the whole adventure had been very slow-paced and gentle. Of course, I realize now I could have gotten us both pretty banged up. Thank God there was at least one angel riding with us that day!

Our parents never knew about the wagon ride, nor was I foolish enough to ever brag about it. The asphalt surface of the road was a lot bumpier and much more unpredictable than our driveway. Why no cars came along behind us is a mystery and a blessing. So I figured now it was back to the occasional fast wheelchair ride inside the house. We had successfully achieved our own version of *Mission Impossible*, and it was back to life as usual. Johnny and I had one really strong secret between us now. Even if God did give him full speech one day, I didn't care if he tattled. It was worth it to share the glory of a forbidden thrill ride, even just the one time!

As he grew, more routine grooming came into play for Johnny, just like with any little kid. Daddy usually cut his hair with the clippers while Mom held him. I begged them to let his hair stay long because I thought he looked cuter. But in the summer, it was always a "butch" haircut, cooler for Johnny and easier to take care of. Even basic stuff like brushing teeth was a special event for my brother. Johnny didn't understand the concept of rinse and spit. If we gave him water after brushing his teeth, he'd just swallow it! So we began brushing them with just a tiny bit of toothpaste followed by just a little bit of water.

When we took him to the dentist, they put a special rubber block between his upper and lower teeth to keep him from biting while the doctor was working on him. I always did my best to explain to him why all this was necessary. He cried sometimes and I didn't blame him. Heck, lots of kids cry at the dentist! And when they're sticking all kinds of weird stuff in your mouth it's scary. Our dentist was really nice, though. He always let me sit in a chair next to Johnny and hold his hand as I talked to him about all kinds of things, trying to distract him from the unpleasantness that was going on. He always seemed to appreciate it. I just took it as part of my natural role of being his big sister protector.

Our father was an excellent carpenter and extremely inventive. As Johnny grew, Dad saw his extra length and weight were making it more tiresome for Mom to feed him. She always held him in the crook of her arm, his body draped across her lap while she fed him with the other hand. Dad was always bringing home used TVs and old radios from garage sales and those salvage stores he loved so much. He usually got them running, too. I remember he had a board, which tested the tubes to see if they were good. This was *way* before the digital age! Once he got things up and running, he'd usually sell them at a garage sale for a profit. Pretty nifty!

I was very surprised one day to walk out to the garage and find him gutting a big stand-up TV he had recently brought home. The insides were on the floor and he was sanding down the cabinet. He saw my wide eyes and winked at me.

"Making a surprise for your baby brother, Cheryl. You'll both just have to wait and see what it is." He loved to put me in a state of suspense.

"Huh! Well, he sure can't watch *that* set!" I pointed to the abandoned parts. I couldn't for the life of me see what was so valuable about that cabinet. "Have fun, Dad!" I shook my head and ran off to play. Sometimes my father seemed as kooky to me as I must have seemed to my mother. Maybe *that's* where I got it from!

I came back home a couple of hours later and was surprised to see wheels mounted to the base of the TV cabinet. Dad had fashioned a big, roomy wheelchair. It was bulky, though. I knew we would never be able to fit it in the car. He continued working away, humming a little ditty to himself.

"Um, what's the plan here, Dad? This is really cool, but don't you think it's kinda, well, kinda big?"

"This right here," he stood up and patted his invention, "This is your brother's new feeding chair."

"His what?"

"Observe and be amazed." Dad sat down on an old stool, rolled the chair back and sat the back of it, its "neck," so to speak, between his legs on the stool. I saw that he had tacked on an extension there specifically so the chair would balance this way. "See? Now your Mom can reach around the side like this, while Johnny's leaning back, and feed him. He's starting to get too big for her to hold him and feed him. You know he has to be at an angle to swallow easily, so, voila! What do you think of your old Dad now, Cheryl?"

I ran over and hugged him, giving him a big kiss on the cheek. "I don't think you're old at all. You're the best Dad in the world. It's perfect!"

"Well," he chuckled, "perfect is a little strong at the moment. I have to make some cushions for it, but it will make life easier for your mother. And I think Johnny just might like it, too."

"He'll love it and so will she! You're so smart, Dad."

He beamed at my praise and shook his head. "Aw, shucks, ma'am, t'weren't nothin'!" He sounded like a character from *Gunsmoke*. I knew he was pleased with his creation and happy I saw the usefulness of it. The feeding chair was a big success and served us well for many years. In fact, there's a picture in this book of John in his chair.

This retirement stuff seemed to suit Dad pretty well by now. Working at the car wash a few days a week and tinkering in the garage in his off-time suited my father just fine. He later gutted a beautiful vertical radio and created a "pulpit" for our Michelangelo Bible, prettier than many I had seen in churches. This held a place of honor in the living room for years, standing just under a picture of Jesus, which hung on the wall. I loved that picture of Christ because He was smiling, not sad and dejected as so many paintings depicted Him.

My father and I discovered that besides looking a lot alike, we had another strong common bond. When I was in first or second grade we had the first strong occurrence of what he would call "sympathy pains." I learned later on I was empathic, and Dad and I were linked this way.

It seemed like we almost always knew when the other one was hurt or sick, even if we were far apart. Like one day at school, I remember shouting out, "Ouch!" whereupon my teacher and the whole classroom turned to look at me.

"What's wrong, Cheryl?" she asked.

I turned beet red. There was no way to explain what I had just seen in my head. The moment just before I had yelled, I had seen a little movie of my Daddy working in the garage. He was hammering something then he turned suddenly and the hammer fell out of his hand, striking him upon the foot. At the exact moment it hit him, I literally felt his pain and shouted. Everyone at school thought I was strange enough without going into *this*. So I did what seemed appropriate. I fibbed.

"Oh, I'm sorry. My foot went to sleep and it woke up all of a sudden. Guess I got a cramp. Sorry, ma'am."

Several of my classmates snickered, but my teacher didn't join them. "That's all right, Cheryl. Sometimes we can't help it when those things happen. Maybe you should take a walk and get a drink of water. I'm sure it will feel all right in a minute."

"Yes, ma'am. Thank you." I scurried out the door, relieved to be away from the mocking eyes of my peers. As much as I liked performing, when I was just being little old psychic me, I didn't like all that attention.

Upon arriving home, I went straight to my father and stamped my foot in anger.

"Why did you drop that old hammer on your foot earlier, Daddy? That hurt and it got me in trouble today!"

"Well, it hurt me, too," he said matter-of-factly. Then it hit him what I had just said. "Hey! How did you know I dropped it? What are you talking about?"

"Oh, I got a picture of it happening, like a little cartoon or movie or something and as soon as it hit your foot, *my* foot hurt and I yelled. Teacher was nice, but the kids were jerks!" I pouted.

He stared at me for a moment, then sat down and took me on his lap. "I'll be more careful next time, honey. I'm sorry you feel it when I get hurt. When you're sick, I feel it, too. So we both better stay well, huh? You and your Pop's got what I guess they call sympathy pains for sure. Ain't that odd?"

This connection would last throughout our lives. We almost always knew when the other was calling on the phone, in any kind of danger or feeling ill. My father was quite psychic; he simply didn't know what to call it. In fact, I don't even remember the word "psychic" ever being used in our home when I was a kid.

I took great delight in creating games to test my intuition. On a conscious level, I didn't know what I was up to, but something inside urged me to develop this "sense." I had always enjoyed various versions of solitaire, and one day decided to try a new card game. I took all the aces out of the deck, turned them face down and mixed them up. Somehow, I knew to place my palm over them and when one felt "hot" or "itchy" I knew that it would most likely be the one I was looking for. Usually I sought out the ace of spades. One day I found it twenty-two times in a row. That scared even me, so I discontinued playing for some time.

Speak Up!

Church was such a big part of our lives in those days. People there loved Johnny and wanted to touch him or hold his hand for a moment each time we walked in the door. I'm convinced he was sending them healing, rather than the other way around! The sermons were long and I'd often read my Bible if I found them dull. The worship service, standing up, holding up your arms and praising the Lord out loud, sometimes lasted for nearly an hour and became physically tiresome. Speaking in tongues went on a lot. There would be a lull in the praise service, and someone would often be moved to talk in this unusual manner. Following that, someone else would often get the "interpretation" and share with all of us what had been said.

Johnny would often sing along in his own way. Sometimes I winked at him when our parents were busy worshiping, trying to get him to smile. One particular Sunday, he threw me a curve. Looking right back at me he grinned, threw up his hands for a moment and very clearly shouted, "HalleLOOyah!" I was in shock. Had I just imagined this?

I looked at Mom and Dad, but their eyes were closed as they swayed back and forth, hands in the air, praising away. So many people uttered this word I'm sure it never occurred to them it could have been their poor little speech-impaired son.

I felt like shaking my head or cleaning out my ears. He'd better not be pulling something funny here, like he did with "dog!" Like saying something so just *I* could hear it, then making me look like a fool by not repeating it when I bragged on him. I moved closer to my little brother and knelt beside him.

"Okay, now that's a lot more syllables than 'I go' and 'I good.' Would you mind repeating that, Johnny? C'mon, give me another 'hallelujah!'"

He smiled and amazed me again by shouting it even louder, twice in a row! "Hallelujah! HalleLOOyah!"

Excitedly, I tugged on Mom's dress sleeve. She was irritated at first, but I just pointed to her son and asked him to say it again. This time he didn't shortchange me.

"Hallelujah!" John shouted triumphantly.

I thought our mother would faint from joy. "Walt! Walter! Johnny just said 'hallelujah!' Oh, dear Lord, he said 'hallelujah!'"

Dad was ecstatic when he heard his only son let go with several more repetitions of this long word. The church folks were thrilled, too. One of them said something like, "Well, maybe God will unlock the child's vocal cords instead of raising him up to walk!" If that happened, I wouldn't have cared if Johnny spilled the beans about all the secrets I'd shared with him.

I believe something shifted inside all of us that day. From that day forth, Johnny had a new vocabulary word and it was a doozy! I firmly made up my mind he only said what he *wanted* to say, when he wanted to say it. That was just fine with me; I was thrilled he could say it so perfectly. No doctor could explain the big gap in articulation between his previous chosen words and this near tongue-twister. Something more was going on inside Johnny's head and heart than any scientist or doctor could measure. God had His Hand upon him.

Sometimes when there would be a long silence in the house, Johnny would let forth with a resounding, "Hallelujah!" and get us all laughing and thankful for our blessings. He was a little minister of love, sure enough.

Mom considered a major part of *her* ministry cooking dinner for visiting missionaries. She was a wonderful cook! That was one skill her mother taught her. I always loved going to Grandma's when food was involved, and her eldest daughter was no slouch in the kitchen, either. I pronounced them both to be "good cookers" when I was little. My mother's ongoing battle with her weight really began in earnest after Johnny's birth. She would snack the entire time she was cooking a meal and sometimes when I got up in the middle of the night for a glass of water, she'd be sitting at the table, eating right out of the ice cream carton. I knew she was sad a lot, so I figured the food must make her feel better somehow.

My personal favorite ministers who came to "sup" with us were from England. Reverend Robert Hartley and his wife were lovely folks. They were most appreciative of my mother's cooking talents and always encouraged me to play the piano and sing a hymn or two for them. I've always had a fondness for British people and loved speaking in a replica of their accent for weeks after they had gone on their way.

I missed the hymns from our Baptist church because they had a clear melody and chord structure. I could always find the harmony. The Evangelistic Center music program was run by the head minister's daughter who wrote many original songs and attempted to teach them to the congregation. These were mostly Bible verses set to music. Some were catchy, but many sounded alike to me.

I thought Mom had been acting strange lately. When her sisters came to visit she made them go in the bedroom with her, saying she had to show them something. When they came out, all the ladies looked so solemn. I had no clue what my mother was going through at that point, but figured it was private and she'd tell me and Daddy if and when we needed to know.

She amazed us all one day shortly after Johnny's initial "Hallelujah!" experience. Perhaps she felt that since her son had found his voice, so would she. She approached the ministerial staff, declaring she wanted to sing a solo. You may remember the statement that she "couldn't carry a tune in a bucket"? I was flabbergasted and prepared to be not just a little embarrassed. I couldn't stand it when people sang off-key. In the midst of the worship service with everybody doing their own thing it didn't matter; standing up in front of the entire church with the help of a microphone was a totally different ball game.

She picked a modern Christian rock song called *I've Got Confidence*. I had no idea why she chose it, but it was a cool song and if I wasn't impressed by her voice, I was by her taste. She got me to play along with her at home, then she practiced a couple of times with the church pianist.

The Sunday she was scheduled to sing, my father's younger brother and sister-in-law happened to be visiting from Virginia. We all piled into the car and headed to church. Dad had warned me to be supportive so I put on a happy face, telling Mom she'd be just great, while my insides churned. More than anything else, I didn't want her to be embarrassed. This was far more important than my anxiety over her lack of stellar vocal ability. However, this was clearly important to her so maybe God would somehow loan her a beautiful angel's voice for a few minutes. I crossed my fingers and wished the best for her all the way across town.

Church was jam-packed that day. The building held at least 500 people and it looked like every seat would fill up. My prayers intensified as we made our way down to a middle aisle where there were enough seats open for all of us as well as an aisle seat open for Johnny's chair.

When it came time for her solo, Mom's hands were shaking a bit as she walked down the aisle, clutching the sheet music for dear life until she nervously handed it to the accompanist. She climbed the four stairs to the platform and took her stance behind the pulpit. Nodding that she was ready, she put on a brave smile and began singing for all she was worth, off-key as usual.

I decided to focus on her courage and stop being so critical. I knew I could sing well, but I didn't have any desire to sing a solo in this church. It was such a family affair in the ministerial department, it always struck me as a clique. I didn't feel like opening myself up to that kind of criticism. Yet my mother, who couldn't sing a lick was here, front and center on an actual stage, giving God her best effort. So who was braver? I knew the answer.

When she was done we all applauded and she smiled, giving a little bow of her head. I was straining to see over the people sitting in front of me. She began to make her way over to the steps then the next thing I knew there was a "thud!" and several ministers ran over and surrounded her. It happened so fast I couldn't see her and had no idea what was happening. I wanted to run forward but my aunt held onto me and let Dad go see what had taken place.

The heel of her shoe had caught on the edge of a step and she had tumbled down, hard. She broke her leg in three places. I felt so ashamed I had not been more supportive of her singing. If only I had gone up there with her, maybe this wouldn't have happened. I watched with tears running down my face as the ambulance drivers came and took her away on a gurney. We left church and followed them to the hospital.

My father was really shaken up again. I had not seen him this vulnerable since Johnny's birth. Dolores was his rock of Gibraltar. How could God have allowed this to happen? He decided to put on a brave face for me and kept reminding me what a blessing it was my aunt and uncle were in town and able to stay with Johnny and me during Mom's first few days in the hospital. I nodded, sullenly sitting there in the waiting room area. Something felt very heavy and foreboding.

I still didn't like hospitals at all. Every time I visited one, the heavy feeling in the air was oppressive. Without knowing it then, I was not only empathic with my Dad, but also very sensitive to *many* people's feelings. Many children are, and need to learn how to do some psychic protection of the solar plexus chakra. Like imagining a white light shield there that deflects any feelings they aren't generating on their own. That's one thing I always teach in my *Mom, I Had This Dream* class, designed to help kids embrace their psychic side.

I soaked strangers' feelings up like a sponge and often had stomachaches for no physical reason. Many people, especially children, are intensely affected by the feelings of others. Today there is strong evidence showing that agoraphobics are typically very empathic. So no wonder they want to stay in the house, away from the energy flowing off of everyone in the crowd.

"How long will she be in here, Dad?"

"About a week, they say."

"Oh! I thought it would be a lot longer."

He stared at me. "Why in the world would you think that? She'll get her leg set, they'll put on a cast, get her up and around with crutches and that will be that. It's no big deal, really. She'll heal fast, honey. Your mother's a strong woman."

"I know." Suddenly I felt like my stomach was on fire. Every time *that* happened, something big was usually about to take place. It's the feeling I experienced when my precognitive dreams would wake me up. Now, I closed my eyes and took a deep breath, trying to make the feeling disappear. Instead, I had a flashback to Mom coming out of the bedroom with her sisters. In my mental "movie" this time, they were all crying. That wasn't how it had really happened. What was going on here? Not wanting to worry my father, I simply smiled at him and headed for the drinking fountain.

Sometimes I didn't like the pictures I saw in my head. Not having anyone to talk to about them didn't make it any easier. Once Mom was home, everything seemed like it would get back to normal pretty soon. Still I waited for that other shoe to drop. My "movies" usually meant something. She didn't like using the crutches, but refused a wheelchair.

"Johnny's the only one in this family who really needs one of those things," she maintained. "I'll be fine."

One day when Vesta and the boys came over to visit, the two moms disappeared into the back bedroom. This was just like what she had done with her sisters. My curiosity was driving me crazy. I told the guys to go outside and I'd meet them there in a minute.

Slowly I crept down the hall. The bedroom door was cracked and I couldn't help peeping inside. I heard Mom's voice in hushed tones and saw her lifting up her arm, then her blouse to show her friend something that apparently scared her very much.

"Look, Vesta, on the side of my breast here, under my arm. It's a lump. I found it a few weeks ago. My sisters say I should talk to the doctor about it, and I guess they're right. I was afraid they'd find it when I broke my fool leg. I tried to hide it. Isn't that silly?"

Vesta's eyes were really big. "Oh, Dee. You really need to have that looked at. I...I'm sorry." She seemed at a loss for words.

There was a sob in my mother's voice. "Oh, God, I just know it's a tumor, isn't it? Please pray for me, Vesta!"

I didn't know what all this meant, but I couldn't stand to just spy anymore. I knocked, then ran in the room.

"Hi! Um....Mom, I heard some of what you said. I couldn't help it, I'm sorry." I looked up at her as she quickly wiped her eyes on her sleeve. "Wh-what's a tumor?"

"Oh, my God!" She pulled me to her in a bear hug and Vesta stood by, still looking shocked. "I have to tell the doctor. And I have to tell your Daddy. Cheryl, would you go get him for me, please?" She did her best to smile through her tears.

"Sure. Just a minute." I ran out of the room, tears stinging my eyes. I was beginning to understand my vision, and to realize that her solo singing had been like a "peace offering" to God, hoping He would make that tumor thing disappear. Instead, she had broken her leg and the lump was still there. I felt sick to my stomach.

After the biopsy proved it was cancer, a radical mastectomy was scheduled. In those days there was precious little awareness of breast cancer; it certainly was not talked about publicly. The disease had not reached the proportions nor received the media attention it has today. Mom explained to me they were going to remove her breast so the cancer wouldn't spread to the rest of her body. She was so brave. Dad and I felt unbelievably helpless.

"God will make it all right. Don't worry, family!"

I was amazed by her resilience. I knew she must be scared, but she hid it so well. Family and church friends came to stay with us during her hospital time, cooking and cleaning in her absence. I began to take a more active role in feeding Johnny, bathing and dressing him. I told him over and over our Mom would be all right, that God wouldn't let us down.

We missed her tremendously and went to visit as often as we could. Dad was at the hospital every day for at least an hour, whenever he could get a neighbor, relative or friend to stay with Johnny and me. He took us to visit her, too, but visiting hours for kids were restricted. I could tell Johnny missed her a lot. Every time the front door would open, he'd turn his head or strain to turn in that direction. It was as if he expected her to walk through the door any minute. He was good, as always, just a bit more fussy and I certainly understood this. She was his most constant companion and had been for all his life. His crib was in her bedroom, so in her absence I moved in there to keep him company and take care of him if he needed anything. Sometimes he'd softly say, "Mama?" and when there was no reply, he'd fall silent.

The day she came home from the hospital, I made a big "Welcome Home" banner and hung it over the front doorway. Johnny was so happy to see her, he laughed, saying, "Mama, Mama," several times. She hugged us over and over, as if to make sure she was really home.

This was long before the term "chemotherapy" came along. She went through cobalt radiation treatments, which left an ugly dark blue square mark on her chest. It looked like a blue burn scar. She showed it to me because she didn't want me to stay so afraid. Mom lost quite a bit of weight while she was sick, but she was actually cheerful about that. "Guess if all the diets didn't work, this did the trick!" she joked.

In time, she went to a prosthetics store and purchased what she came to refer to as "my fake boob." She showed that to me, too. Mom was tired of being in denial about her health and didn't want me to grow up that way, either. She told me the strangest thing was the "phantom itch" phenomenon. Her missing breast would sometimes itch and she'd start to scratch it, then realize it wasn't even there! The doctors told her that was common. She tried to make everything as light as possible. Meanwhile, she subtly began teaching me how to cook, clean and increase my skills in caring for Johnny and my Dad. I didn't mind. The bond between me and the two main guys in my family was so strong, it was a pleasure to be helpful to them. I began to see my mother in a whole new light and with a new respect.

Mom, I Had This Dream...

It was May, 1967 and my fifth grade year was winding down. President Johnson was on television nearly every night, usually about "the conflict in Vietnam." As much as he wanted to protect me from the cruel reality of the world at large, my father had this "wonderful" habit of having the family view the evening news during our dinner hour. He even mounted a second television in the dining room on a platform he built over the stairway railing which led to the basement, so as you ate, you had a bird's eye-view of the tube, and the news was always the "dinner show." We didn't realize it then, but it was not exactly a great set-up to pave the way for healthy digestion!

Mom was back to her usual level of cooking and cleaning much sooner than the doctor had advised. She was not one to stay still for very long. Her first duty was to her family and she felt beyond a shadow of a doubt we needed her. We did, of course, but still Dad and I tried to get her to rest more. She refused, smiling and saying she was feeling stronger every day.

We made an appointment to have Johnny measured for a bigger "real" wheelchair shortly after she returned from the hospital. This one folded up and was more transportation friendly than the little "hoe" chair. I discovered it could do really nice "wheelies" of sorts, too. (I was still into bringing Johnny secret thrills whenever I could!)

People were still drawn to John's energy in parking lots and other venues. However, I began to notice another response that upset me quite a bit. When we'd take him inside department stores with us, people tended to have one of two reactions. Most often I would push him along, talking with him about various displays of things which I felt he'd enjoy. This freed up Mom and Dad to go shop for whatever they were seeking. The most common reactions from strangers was to either avert their eyes from him entirely, hurrying on their way, or to stare coldly right through us as though neither he nor I existed. This made me fume. He was a person, he was my brother! He had rights. Why were they so mean? The people at Evangelistic Center accepted him. Why couldn't these jerks? I complained about this to Mom. She was a much better judge of human nature than I.

"Honey, calm down. I expect most of them are more afraid than anything else."

This puzzled me. "Afraid of Johnny? Why? He's got such a sweet face. He's not some kind of monster, Mom! I don't get it!"

She smoothed my hair as she tried to soothe my feelings. "Well, maybe they're afraid they might end up in a wheelchair someday, honey. Or maybe they lost somebody who lived in one. We can't judge people so much. Maybe they just don't understand. Please try to let it go, Cheryl. Johnny has us and God to love and accept him, and he's happy with that. Why can't you be?"

"I guess so," I agreed. "But I still think a lot of 'em are just plain mean!'

She chuckled. "Well, maybe some are. But then they need our love and acceptance even more, don't they? Do unto others, Cheryl. You know that rule."

"Yes, ma'am." I still felt somewhat angry inside, but resolved to give people the benefit of the doubt more often.

Just about every day, I sang to him, and *Johnny Angel* became our special song. I truly believed then, as I do now, that in his way, he was an angel on Earth.

My precognitive dreams and the astral traveling had really never ceased, but I didn't tell Mom about them too much because she always seemed to become agitated for some reason. I was especially concerned about this after her surgery. One night I had a very real, frightening dream in which I saw newspaper and television coverage concerning a "6 Day War." The news flashes I saw in the dream were full of bombings and gunfire sounds. I had never heard of such a thing as a war that lasted less than a week, so this all seemed strange, yet incredibly vivid. I strained to see the headlines of the paper and clearly read "Israel defeats Egypt in 6 Day War."

This was the first time I had a dream with global implications. Prior to that, they had been pretty confined to my little world. This was troubling. As I made my way to the breakfast table, I decided to go ahead and share it with my mother.

She had just finished feeding Johnny and was sitting beside him, looking out the window at the birds. Johnny always loved hearing the birds sing. I cleared my throat, unable to keep my news to myself. She didn't hear me. I poured my cereal into my bowl, drenched it with milk and cleared my throat once more.

"Um, Mom?" She turned to look at me and smiled gently. I could tell from her eyes she was still tired. The surgery and the cobalt treatments took a lot out of her. I almost changed my mind, but she was waiting for me to go on.

"Yes, honey. What is it?"

"Well, Mom....I...." I took a deep breath and said words I hadn't uttered in a couple of years. "Mom, I had this dream last night...."

I waited for her to roll her eyes as she used to do, but she looked genuinely interested.

"What did you dream about, Cheryl?" she asked kindly.

This was new! I launched into my description of this crazy dream with as much detail as I could remember. She listened closely, then just shook her head a tiny bit.

"You know what? You worry too much, honey. We shouldn't let you watch the news so much. First of all, there's no such thing as a war that only lasts six days."

"I know, Mom. But it's going to be all right. Israel will win, you'll see."

"Cheryl, put it out of your head. Little girls shouldn't be so concerned over things like war to the point they're dreaming about one that isn't going to happen. Please just finish up your breakfast and get on your way to school. You don't want to be late your last week of fifth grade. Go on, now." She got up and kissed the top of my head. She hadn't done this for a long time. "Go have a great day at school and just forget all about that dream, okay?" She patted me on the back.

"Yes, ma'am," I answered. The gnawing feeling in my gut wasn't going away, however. Because Israel was an ally of the U.S., I felt their winning had to be good, even if the war in general was not a positive thing.

On June 5th, 1967 Israel attacked Egypt, Syria and Jordan. Great victories for Israel were achieved immediately. By June 10th Syria surrendered, after seeing Golan Heights come under Israeli control. That night as we watched Walter Cronkite describing the "unprecedented 6 Day War" I felt my mother's eyes turn toward me and stay there. When I dared to look up to meet them, she did not look at all pleased. This was long before remote controls were a standard feature, so she startled my father and me by getting up deliberately, then slowly walking over to snap off the television power knob.

The knot in my stomach foretold a lecture was coming, and my gut instinct was seldom wrong. She launched into a brief, "no nonsense/no discussion allowed" tirade.

"Young lady, I don't know where these dreams of yours come from. They used to be kinda cute when you'd see things that might happen to the family, or were about innocent little goings-on. But how in the name of Heaven you knew about *this,* " she gestured toward the TV, "is a mystery to me."

"What are you talking about, Dee?" my confused father asked. She shot him a look that meant, "I'll tell you later" and he quieted down.

"Cheryl Ellen, I want you to promise me something right now."

I gulped, not sure what was coming, but could feel it was important that I follow orders. "Yes, Mom?"

"You make these dreams *stop*! I don't know where they're coming from. But I think it may be the devil."

My eyes widened. I may not always have paid attention in church the way she wanted me to, but I knew I wasn't in league with any devil. She was obviously frightened by my dreams. Still, very eager to help her get well as quickly as possible, I decided not to protest my innocence.

"I don't know where they come from either, Mom. I used to think everybody had those kinds of dreams. I'm sorry. I'll find a way to make them stop." A tear ran down my cheek. "I promise."

"Well, see that you do." She stared at me long and hard before turning her attention to clearing the table. I jumped up to help her and heard her muttering to herself, "Not right that a child sees things like this. Just not right."

Basically, from that point forward I made a conscientious effort to put away or hide all things which might be considered "psychic," including my dreams, until my mother was no longer with us. I didn't dare upset her after all she had been through.

My father may not have been as upset by the things I did and saw as my mother was, but he certainly knew when I was interested in something. That summer before I started sixth grade, he noticed I was always paying attention to the way he drove, asking questions about the functions and operation of the pedals, gears and signals. I believe he sensed the tension brought about by Mom's misunderstanding of some of my "talents" and tried to find ways to make it up to me.

One afternoon I went to the carwash with him. I loved hanging out with my father, he was so easy to be around. He enjoyed my company, too. I had taken my new tennis racket (well, new to me. It was another thrift store purchase!) and was hitting balls against the back wall near the vacuum area. Dad was tinkering around on one of the machines that was on the fritz. We talked as I played and he worked.

"So, Cheryl. When are you going to start spending more time with your Mom? She really would like you to learn more about cooking and sewing, you know, girl things."

I wrinkled up my nose. "Jeez! I hate that stuff! Baking's okay, but I can't sew to save my life. I don't like it, Dad!"

He was trying not to crack a smile. Obviously my mother had urged him to talk with me. "Well, we all have to do things we don't like once in awhile. Your Mom just worries that you won't be able to ah.... well, you know. Make a good home for a nice man some day when you get married."

I snorted. "Married? I'm not even twelve years old! I don't want to get married, anyway. Yuck!" I smacked a tennis ball a bit too hard and it got away from me. After I retrieved it, my father motioned me toward our Rambler station wagon.

"Get in," he instructed.

I started to climb into the passenger seat, like always. I thought we were going home.

"No, I mean over here." He was pointing to the driver's seat. Was this some trick? "Go ahead. Might as well teach you something you *do* like, I suppose."

I climbed behind the wheel, still not sure what he had in mind.

He crossed over and took the passenger seat. Then he reached in his pocket and calmly handed me the keys.

"Seems pretty quiet right now. We've got a big ol' empty parking lot back here. Let's take her for a spin, what do you say, kiddo?" His gray-blue eyes were dancing.

"Wow!" I held the keys for a moment, then put them in the ignition, just sitting there in disbelief.

"What are you waiting for, girl? Start 'er up. You've seen me do this millions of times. I've seen the way you pay attention when I drive. Just take it nice and slow." He paused. "And Cheryl, this is our secret, yours and mine, understand?"

"Yes, sir!" I was thrilled.

He muttered under his breath, "Your mother would kill me if she found out." He cleared his throat, then pointed to the right. "Start out nice and slow, make big circles and don't hit anything. That's about all there is to it. Nice and slow, now."

We drove round and around that parking lot for about a half hour. This was the biggest surprise I could have imagined! My Dad praised me for watching so well and steering carefully.

Over the next months of summer, I went with him to the carwash at least once a week and we had our "secret driving practice." All this was well and good until Johnny and I accompanied Mom to the grocery store one afternoon.

As she got out of the car, she smiled and said, "I'll be right back. You kids be good."

Johnny immediately piped up, "I good!"

She laughed and disappeared inside. I began to talk to John when the keys dangling in the ignition caught my eye. It looked like a slow day at the store. The parking lot was pretty vacant. I made a quick decision, bolted out of the back and hopped into the driver's seat. Johnny looked appropriately surprised.

"Hey, John," I confided to my little brother. "Sissy can drive. Dad's been teaching me. Let's go around the parking lot, what do you say? Wanna go, Johnny?"

Of course he did! He threw up his hands and hooted, ready for anything that involved making the car g-o! So we went around the back of the store two whole times. What *I* wasn't ready for was rounding the corner that last time, seeing that someone had taken our original parking space! My heart sank to the pit of my stomach.

"She's gonna kill me, Johnny. Oh, God. What should I do?" He looked up happily at me, oblivious to my anxiety.

I began praying really hard that the owner of the car who had usurped our space would hurry up and return. I parked in the aisle right behind it and hopped back into the back seat. My back-up prayer was that our mother wouldn't notice we were one row back from where she had left the car. God had better things to do than help me out that day, it seemed.

As she exited the store, I saw the smile on my mother's face first turn to confusion, then as she looked up to see me peeking over her headrest, to sudden understanding. She marched up to the car, opened my door and I prepared to be pulled out and spanked right there in public. Even though I was as tall as she was now and really too old for a whipping, I figured I deserved it. Surprisingly, all that happened was the grocery bag bumped me a bit as she tossed it onto the seat beside me. She climbed in and looked at me in the rear view mirror.

"I should have known your Dad was teaching you to do something like this while you were spending so much time at that carwash. Do you know you could get us all arrested, or worse? You might have been hit by someone, or worse, hit them. What would I do if something happened to you or Johnny?" She looked like she would cry. This was a different reaction than I had expected. I felt horrible.

"I'm so sorry, Mom. I'll never do it again. I'm so sorry."

"All right." She took a deep breath. "Cheryl, I don't really blame *you*." She sniffed, then started the engine. "Not another word, now. When we get home, you go straight to your room. I have to have a serious talk with your father."

Relieved for my own sake, but feeling sorry for Dad about what was to come, I kept my mouth shut. As I carried the groceries in while he helped get Johnny out of the car, I shot him a helpless glance. Even behind the closed door of my room, I could hear her yelling at him. My parents seldom argued, but this was apparently a *really* big deal. All I could hear from Dad was a mumbled, "Yes, honey," or "Okay, Dolores," here and there.

About six months went by before my father offered to let me drive at the carwash again. I was afraid it was a trap at first, to see if I'd keep my word to my mother. I should have known better.

"It's okay. You didn't promise not to drive here when I'm with you. No need to take away all your fun. Just no more joy riding without me, okay? Not 'til you get your license in a few years."

"Yes, sir."

So our driving lessons continued less frequently, but because of this, the bond of trust between my father and me deepened even more. He began to show me basic mechanical maintenance, like "the old oil change and lube job" when he'd routinely service the car on the driveway. Mom didn't really approve of this, but she must have tolerated it because at least I wasn't driving anymore. (As far as she knew!)

I really enjoyed the sixth grade. My teacher, Miss Brockway, was a tall woman who encouraged me to "stand up straight, be proud of your height, Cheryl!" I liked her very much as she was always friendly to me, and shared a love of literature akin to my own. She recommended many wonderful books to me.

There were a number of "snow days" almost every winter. This meant school was closed because the roads were too bad to travel. Many times the snow piled up in three to five foot drifts. The ice on the roads was what made it most treacherous.

I became interested in skiing that winter. I watched movies which included that sport and thought the winter Olympics were very neat. By this time in my life I had become quite creative in finding ways to do "forbidden" things. Now, by "forbidden" I don't mean breaking any laws. I mean...well, remember the John Henry story? What I'm talking about here is similar to that.

On a Wednesday "snow day" that winter, the roads were cleared by about 9 a.m. School had already been cancelled, but my parents decided we should all go to church since it looked like it wouldn't snow anymore. Dad was a safe driver and always put studded snow tires on in the wintertime. I immediately feigned a stomachache.

"Oh, gosh. My stomach really hurts. I think I better go back to bed. I don't want to throw up in the car or anything. Would you guys please pray for me, though?" I was a sneaky little critter!

Mom felt my forehead. "Hmm, you do feel a bit warm. All right, then. Get yourself in bed and no TV, you hear? You sleep and feel better. We'll bring something good home for lunch." She turned to my father who was smiling slightly. He could usually tell when I was fibbing, but obviously didn't blame me for wanting to pass on church. After all, school had been called off. What fun could church be?

Johnny's school was closed, too, so they packed him into the car and away they went. I drank a cup of hot tea, just to give them time to really be on their way. Then I put my plan in action.

I went out to the garage and began looking around for something long, wooden and thin. I had decided to make my own skis! Nothing seemed workable until I spotted two strips of paneling leaning against the wall in the corner along with some other scrap wood. Perfect!

I "borrowed" my father's electric drill (this was as forbidden as it got!) and made two holes in each piece of panel board. Then I took some cord, ran it through the holes, and figured out how to interweave it with my shoelaces. I felt like Leonardo da Vinci!

Foolhardy girl that I was, I bundled up with a scarf, hat, and gloves, and made my way to the back yard, new skis tucked under one arm, and two brooms for poles under the other. Trudging through the deep, crisp snow, I imagined how this could launch my Olympic skiing career. Why I thought they wouldn't see my tracks, I can't explain. Kids think they have all the bases covered in these instances, though!

All I could think about was how inspiring it would be to be interviewed as a young adult athlete, regaling the crowd with the tale of inventing my first pair of skis! In those days, I changed my mind about what I wanted to be nearly as frequently as I changed television stations. Nothing seemed beyond the realm of possibility. Ah, the enthusiasm of youth!

After slipping a few times, my heart was racing. I got to the top of the biggest hill and tied on my invention. I could see my breath in the air as it flowed through the mesh scarf wrapped around my neck and mouth.

In my best Olympic sports announcer voice, quiet yet filled with energy, I pronounced, "Well, this is it. The first ski run of Cheryl Booth. And, we're off!" I pushed off with the brooms and promptly fell flat on my face!

This process was repeated at least five times. Then I got the bright idea to lean forward as I pushed and I actually traveled a few feet before falling. Never a quitter when I was proving a point to myself, I stuck with it. Eventually I got as far as the top of the second smaller hill in the yard. Exhausted, and not even realizing how fortunate I was not to have broken my neck, I finally gave up and went inside. I carefully propped the panels back where they had been, hoping they would dry off and my Dad wouldn't notice the holes, at least not right away.

The plus side was, to corroborate bailing on church I really *did* get sick from falling down in the snow so much. And the snow melted enough that they telltale tracks in the backyard disappeared. When the crew got home, I had the shivers and was headed toward a bona fide fever. So I got lots of sympathy. Dad later asked me privately about the holes in the paneling. I confessed the whole story, and he laughed until I thought he'd choke. He never punished me, but told me to think harder about potential consequences when I got inspired like that. He never told my mother. No wonder he was still one of my very favorite people!

The other thing that stands out in my memory about my twelfth year on the planet was the addition of my dog, Sam, to our family. My aunt Mary Catherine had a great cocker spaniel named Sugar. Sugar had a romantic interlude with a poodle down the street which produced a litter of cockapoos. Since I was no longer allergic, she lobbied for me to get a puppy for my birthday. Surprisingly, Mom gave in, with the rule being as soon as he was big enough, the puppy would become an outside dog, period. I didn't care. I finally had a dog of my own! I named him Samson, Sam for short.

"Such a little dog needs a big, strong name," was my reasoning.

Just like Callie before him, Sam instinctively knew Johnny was special. Once he lived outside, he would excitedly jump all over anyone who ventured into the back yard. Anyone except Johnny, that is. He would walk slowly at the side of the wheelchair, licking his young master's hand once in awhile. This sent my brother into gleeful giggling at times. He loved animals and they certainly loved him.

In other realms of entertainment, television still was a primary focus for me. In the fall of 1967, *The Carol Burnett Show* made its first appearance and I immediately decided when I grew up I'd have a variety show just like hers. Our initials were even the same! I was a big fan already, as my parents and I had enjoyed her appearances on *The Gary Moore Show* throughout the early 1960s. Carol was so funny and the cast always had such a great time. I especially loved watching Harvey Korman crack up, or getting other cast members to do so.

The Ed Sullivan Show had become a Sunday night tradition at our home years before. Of course, by 1967 we were going to church on Sunday nights quite often. At this point, we were going as often as possible to give thanks for Mom's continuing recovery from cancer, and so she could continue having hands laid on John for his healing. I missed this show, often hearing about some of the latest rock stars' television debuts from the kids at school. My father didn't like rock and roll music, no way, no how.

"Bunch of Commie pinko fags," he'd mutter disgustedly whenever The Beatles, The Rolling Stones or any other "despicable rock group" would come up in the news. Of course, I had none of their music in the house. Elvis was considered tolerable in small doses. I suppose this was because he was a nice Southern boy, a war hero and sang Gospel, in addition to rock. The criteria for acceptance in our household was always interesting!

My father was a big John Wayne fan and caught most of his movies, western and war. Dad still watched *Gunsmoke,* and *Bonanza* was also a favorite of his. I enjoyed it quite a bit because it usually had more of the family slant than a focus on gunfights. The only time I hadn't been fond of *Bonanza* was during 1963 and '64, when *The Judy Garland Show* had been on opposite the Cartwright boys. Ever *The Wizard of Oz* fan, and by then a great admirer of Judy herself, I had seen most of the *Andy Hardy* movies and several of her other films. Apparently Mom related with Judy in her own way, because she surprised me by chiming in about watching "little Dorothy's show." Dad seldom had the two women in the household gang up on him, so thanks to Judy, he went and bought Mom and me a tiny black and white set to keep peace in the family.

Television was most definitely a welcome escape throughout the troubled late '60s. The entire country was confused and appalled by the Vietnam "conflict." For a long time, they couldn't even put the label "war" on it. But that's what it was, and such an awful one, at that. Our troops were treated so horribly, both there and when they came back home.

My family's personal challenges with Mom's illness and Johnny's condition gave us additional reasons to seek out fantasy and laughter in sitcoms and variety shows. Johnny loved certain television shows. He tended to listen to them, more than watch. Focusing his eyes on the small set was quite a challenge. We could always tell when someone's music had moved him, though. He was quite vocal when he wanted to be. One of Mom's favorites was Dean Martin and Johnny always loved to hear him sing, too.

Mom discovered that Dean Martin was born on June 17, 1917, just four days after her birth date. I knew how strongly she connected with JFK, whose birthday was less than a month before hers. So I guess she found the birth year a common bond between herself and "Dino," too. Plus, she really admired his talent. *The Dean Martin Show* was pretty risqué for its day. I began to see how grown-up standards shifted at times. Things that I would have been smacked for saying or doing seemed okay when coming from certain performers.

That double standard helped me when *Rowan and Martin's Laugh-In* came along in 1968. All the kids were watching it and talking about it in school. I began to lobby to be allowed to watch it. Dad absolutely *hated* it. Mom was going to give it a blanket "thumbs-down" until I got a brilliant idea.

"Well, they sure don't say anything any worse than they do on ol' Dean Martin's show," I protested. "He acts drunk all the time and you laugh all the time. He's okay, but I think these guys are lots funnier. Why can't I watch 'em?"

My mother could be amazingly reasonable at times. This was one of those times. She watched the show clear through with me once, said, "I have no clue what you see in it, it's just plain silly. But, as long as you watch it quietly, I guess that's fine."

So I would watch on the second little set which now lived in my room. I loved mimicking Ruth Buzzy and Lily Tomlin. By the time I headed into junior high, I had worked up a number of impressions. I was not quite as shy anymore, but still pretty geeky. Making kids laugh was a way of being accepted.

Johnny was discovering new peers himself. We heard about a church school for handicapped kids and went to check it out. It was about four miles from the house. The people who ran it were nice and they had about six other kids who attended from 9 a.m. until 2 p.m. Monday through Friday. It seemed like a great idea for Johnny to be around other kids like himself. They had a physical therapist come work with the students once a week. They listened to music and did other fun things. Our parents decided to sign him up.

That school was a big blessing for all of us. It got Johnny out of the house and helped him in more ways than I'll ever know. Just the socialization must have been wonderful. He always got so excited whenever we'd get him dressed for school. There was even a little van that came and picked him up. We'd roll him to the edge of the driveway and after locking the wheels of his chair securely in, the driver would take off. Mom and Dad had more time to themselves then, which I know was very healthy for them, especially after her battle with cancer had begun.

Chapter Six

Rites of Passage

Junior high is such an awkward time for kids. I already felt clumsy, self-conscious and different. Antioch Junior High was several miles from the house, so after years of walking to the nearby elementary school, I suddenly became a "bus student." This was just one new label that was hung on me. I didn't know any other kids my age with a handicapped brother or sister, so there was really no one I could relate to about that issue. Lots of kids teased each other and freely used the slur of "retard" to slam others. I did my best not to become infuriated by this. To top it all off, nobody in my small circle of friends had ever dealt with cancer in their immediate family, so I had no peers who could relate to what I was going through about that, either.

Once again in 1968, that disease loomed large in our lives. Mom wasn't feeling well much of the time. She finally went to the gynecologist for a routine exam. He discovered a mass in her uterus. Another biopsy was scheduled, which meant an overnight stay in the hospital.

I heard my parents discussing this one night after they assumed I was asleep. I sat in the hallway by my bedroom door, hidden from their view in the living room. I was hugging my knees to my chest to keep from shivering. It wasn't cold that night, but I felt chilled to the bone.

"What if it's cancer again, Walt? How will we pay the hospital bills?" My mother's voice was shaking. I couldn't stand for her to cry. She was always so strong. I had to take a big silent gulp of air to keep from sobbing and giving away my eavesdropping.

"Aw, damn the bills, Dee! What's important is we get you well and keep you that way. I'll think of something if it comes to that. We can always get a second mortgage."

There was a pause.

"No, Walter. We almost have this home paid for, just a couple more years and it will be ours. This doesn't feel like a good idea," she protested.

My Dad was being the practical one now, however. "Well, if that's what happens, then so what? Won't be the first time, nor the last someone's had to do it. My Social Security and the carwash just barely cover our expenses now. The insurance only pays for so much. So if that's what we have to do, that's fine."

I heard him kiss her cheek. "You better get to bed, soon. Stop worrying so much." He headed for the kitchen and I heard her start to rock back and forth in her favorite rocker. I often sat in that chair while holding a pillow on my lap years after that, rocking back and forth, just to tune into her presence.

That was my cue to silently scoot back to my bedroom. Johnny had been asleep for a couple of hours. Something had made me get up. I felt a little sick, but comforted that my father had a game plan of some sort, at least. My parents had maintained separate bedrooms for as long as I could remember. They were best friends, not just lovers. Their companionship was beautiful to observe. In many ways, their relationship seemed more like a loving sibling connection, which never struck me as strange at all. If Johnny and I were soulmates, our parents certainly were, too.

I understood a lot about tightening the belt financially at that age. My clothes usually came from what we nicknamed "Monkey Ward's" bargain basement, the now defunct *Montgomery Ward* department store. For the most part, those clothes were butt ugly, out-of-date and cheap. The price was what determined what was purchased for me, so that meant the very ugliest things on sale came home with us. In addition to every other reason I felt like an outcast, my wardrobe was a major thorn in my side.

The morning after I heard my parents' discussion, I awoke to a downpour. Mom had her ever trusty cup of coffee in hand as she was scurrying to fix breakfast for me and Johnny. I had on some god-awful jumper we had bought in the bargain basement a few days before, and was feeling especially self-conscious.

"Go get your raincoat and umbrella, Cheryl. Take 'em out to the garage and put 'em in the car. I'll drive you and Johnny both to school today. No need for you to catch your death of cold waiting for that bus." She seemed like her old self. Maybe I had imagined the heaviness of the conversation the night before.

I obediently did as I was told. When she pulled into the circular drive at my school, I was mortified when she drove up onto the sidewalk.

"Mom! What are you doing?" I squawked, ducking down so no one would see me.

She laughed. "I guess my mind's just on other things. I'm sorry to embarrass you, Miss Priss." She looked at me wistfully. "You're getting so big! What happened to my baby girl?"

"Oh, Mom! I'm still your weirdo bratty daughter!" I grinned. "Thanks for the ride." Suddenly I felt guilty for being ashamed of her driving. I knew what was on her mind, but I couldn't let on. So I gave her and Johnny both a kiss on the cheek and marched into school, no longer caring who thought what about me. These were definitely not halcyon days for me. Junior high seemed like pure torture most of the time!

The results of this biopsy determined Mom had cancer of the uterus. Again, she put on a brave front, telling me they were going to do a complete hysterectomy. She explained what that meant to the best of her ability. I know now she needed another female to confide in, plus, she didn't want me to be kept in the dark and make up something that might be even worse than what was really going on.

"Heck, I've always hated my period anyway. It'll be a pleasure not to deal with that or this old menopause anymore!" She laughed.

I was a bit embarrassed, being a modest, shy kid. I knew she had suffered with migraines during her "time of the month" in recent years. During these times, she had often begged me to run get a cold cloth to place on her forehead, when she'd feel one of those awful headaches coming on. And lately with menopause, I had found her sticking her head in the freezer for several minutes at a stretch, or actually fanning herself with the screen door on our front porch! I didn't understand what she was going through at all. We simply didn't have talks about "the facts of life" in our family, or different times of life in a woman's life. Mom was extremely grateful they were showing movies to the girls at school about periods and such by the time I got to grade school.

But they didn't show movies about cancer. I began to ardently hate "the Big C." It was ruining my mother's life, all of our lives. Our house always seemed unsettled these days. Soon it was back to the dreaded hospital visits. This time, I noticed the color in Mom's face was ashen, just about every time we were there. I began praying harder, since that was the only thing I knew to do. I held Johnny and rocked him a lot during her stay in the hospital. The physical closeness seemed to ground us both. Dad wandered around the house and yard like a lost man while she was gone. I could rarely get him to eat anything.

Mom was in the hospital even longer this time. They said her surgery went as well as could be expected. One day on the way to a visit, Dad pulled into his bank. I had a feeling he was going to do that thing with the mortgage he had mentioned. He told me he'd be back in a little bit, to stay in the car and sing for Johnny.

"Cheer him and you up, Squirt. Your singing always does that. Make it some of those upbeat tunes you like so much. I'll be back in a few minutes." He was full of bravado, but I saw the worry in his eyes.

He came back out with a stack of papers, which he placed in the glove box. We went to the hospital and he never brought it up to her. We all wanted her recovery to go as smoothly as possible.

She came home just before Thanksgiving. She'd been in the hospital for my thirteenth birthday, so we had held a little party there. But none of our hearts were in it. I would have traded all my birthday parties for my mother's health.

Thanksgiving always fell within a week of my birthday. I was not skilled enough in the kitchen to make a turkey with all the trimmings, so some nice people from the church came over and did the cooking for us.

Mom took lots of naps and kept Johnny home from school quite often. She took great comfort in having him by her side. As we headed toward the Christmas holidays none of us felt exactly cheerful nor hopeful. The driving force of our home was definitely not herself, and there seemed to be nothing we could do about it. What a helpless, frustrating feeling!

Dad had purchased a silver artificial Christmas tree many years ago. I thought it was tacky and begged for a real tree, but was always voted down. That seemed a big extravagance, especially now. So this year I dutifully assembled the aluminum limbs, whose tinsel was rather bare in some places. We had one of those colored light wheels that you turned toward the tree and as it rotated, it made the tree turn different colors. Johnny always got a kick out of watching this, so I turned it on for him as soon as I finished putting the tree up, even though it was still daytime. I wasn't familiar with the musical *Mame* at that point in my life, but I knew we sure did "need a little Christmas" spirit now, more than ever.

The church folks brought a large box of food and other goodies, including stockings stuffed with goodies for Johnny and me. I felt somewhat embarrassed, but realized we didn't have much money to make a feast like my mother usually managed to put together for this special time of year.

The only present I received that year which stands out in my mind was a board game called *Kreskin's ESP*. "The Amazing Kreskin" was a hypnotist and "occult" performer who often appeared on variety shows. When I found out they had a game he endorsed, I begged for it. I didn't ask for anything else. In a moment of weakness, my mother must have given in and purchased it. It was my first experience using a pendulum. You held it over the board and asked a variety of questions. I'd seen Ouija boards at friends' homes before and didn't like the way they felt. This was different and seemed fun, interesting. It helped you trust your intuition. I played with it a lot, much more so than Mom liked.

My brother Don had moved out for awhile, but when Mom came back from the hospital he moved back into the basement apartment to be close in case there was anything he could do to help. He played Barbra Streisand records a lot and I used to plug my ears and tease him.

One day he'd had enough. I had just run down the stairs and yelled, "She sings through her nose! What makes her so great, anyway? Jeez!"

He looked up from what he was doing and simply said, "Go put on a nice dress."

"Why?"

"I'm taking you to the movies, that's why. And you know Mom won't let you out of the house in jeans. So put on a dress, okay?" he smiled.

I went upstairs and made sure this was okay. Mom seemed happy two of her kids were going to do something fun.

"Go on, enjoy yourselves. Then you can tell me all about the picture when you get back. You're so good at that, Cheryl, I always feel like I saw it myself."

I blushed. Praise from her was so rare.

"I don't even know what we're gonna see, Mom. But it will be fun, I always have a good time with Don. Thanks! See ya later."

When we joined the line at the downtown theatre, I looked up. *Funny Girl* loomed huge in the marquee.

"Aw, gosh! You're taking me to see *her*?"

I had seen Barbra on my beloved Judy Garland's show years before. She had lung power, that's for sure. But nobody could replace Judy in my book.

"You just wait. Give her a chance," he grinned. "She just might win you over."

Besides *The Sound of Music* I hadn't seen many "spectacular" level musicals. Once we settled into the cushy seats and the lights went up on the screen, I was immediately enamored of the sets, the story and especially of Barbra's talent. It was instant adoration from that moment on. In fact, to this day I am still a much bigger fan than my brother ever was. I have every album and CD she's recorded. What can I say? I was (and am) hooked!

Mom loved my version of *Funny Girl*, in particular when I regaled her with the *Swan Lake* scene. I had Barbra's Yiddish accent down.

"Vat are ya gonna do, shoot da schvans? Deese lovelies?"

However, she didn't think it was so great when I would stay downstairs when Don was out and about, playing her records over and over. She didn't protest too much, though. I imagine she was grateful I was a good kid and wasn't showing any signs of being "boy-crazy" like some of my cousins who were around the same age.

About the only "boy" I was crazy about was Bobby Sherman. Oh, those blue eyes of his! I watched his TV show *Here Come The Brides* religiously. David Soul (later on *Starsky and Hutch*) was pretty cute, too. But Bobby sang and cut records! I swooned. Some of my first 45s were Bobby Sherman records. A fellow "geek-ette" at junior high and my cousin Barbara were also Bobby fans. Somehow or other we persuaded my dear brother Don to take us to a concert where hundreds of teenage girls were carrying on shamelessly. God bless you for that, Don! Maybe you were grateful I wasn't into any hard-core rock groups. Whatever the case, you made three young girls' night by chaperoning us to that concert!

I was still taking piano lessons and singing every chance I got. Mom was never impressed unless I chose religious music. She still encouraged me to "keep the volume down." Other than that, she seldom made a comment about my singing at all.

There were some little review-type shows being put on at the junior high. I thought about auditioning for the first time in my life. I went and listened to the other kids. I knew I was as good, if not a lot better, than many of them. My shyness, however, kept me glued to my seat and when they called my name I shook my head and said, "Never mind, thanks, I've changed my mind." I figured if I did get a solo, Mom and Dad most likely wouldn't approve because it wouldn't be church music.

I was in the chorus every year of junior high. I loved it. I had not yet discovered drama class; that would kick into full swing in high school.

We were doing several numbers from *The Sound of Music* during the spring of my seventh grade year. I bought a book of simplified sheet music from the musical and applied myself to learning to play piano and sing at the same time. One day after school I was working away at perfecting this.

Mom was feeling much better by now, and was in the kitchen cooking dinner. John was in his standard place on the couch, cheering me on in his own fashion. I began to sing *Climb Every Mountain*.

About midway into the piece, I heard a loud "CRASH!" from the kitchen. Always worried about my mother's health, I hurriedly ran in to find her staring at me. She seemed fine. The only damage was a broken bowl and a lot of gravy splashed all over the floor.

"Mom? Did you burn yourself?" I asked as I crossed to her and took her arm to steady her. She seemed rooted to the floor. I was apprehensive she may have had some kind of small heart attack or something. Her voice wavered when she finally spoke.

"Your voice. It's your voice."

I felt like she was going to cry. Had I displeased her by being too loud again? We walked over to the table and I helped her into a chair. She never took her eyes from my face.

"Was I too loud, Mom? I'm sorry."

She grabbed my face in her hands and patted my cheek.

"Oh, no, honey. Goodness no! Your voice is just so beautiful. I don't think I ever really noticed before. It's like I really heard you for the first time, just now. It's just beautiful. God has truly blessed you with talent."

My eyes filled with tears as we hugged. After all my years of singing, the person I wanted as a fan the most had just become one. I silently sent up a prayer of thanks. Pleasing my mother, especially now, meant more to me than anything else in the world.

The rest of that seventh grade and most of my eighth grade year is a blur. I simply looked forward to high school more each day.

The summer of 1969, one of my favorite people passed away. Judy Garland died on June 22nd, barely two weeks after her forty-seventh birthday. I was devastated. I didn't know much about this icon's life at that point in time, but she had always represented hope and pure talent to me. I went to bed and cried off and on for two days. Mom didn't understand the depth of my attachment, but respected my feelings.

Other than my cousin Gary, who died in a car wreck a few years before, I hadn't lost anyone on a personal level. What Mom may have realized was that Judy's death brought a strange foreboding to me. She was a Gemini, born the same month as my mother. She was *younger* than my mother and she had just died. I began to think about death frequently. My own mortality became a real concept. I realized I would be forty-five in the year 2000, if that ever came along. It seemed like science fiction to talk about anything other than the 1900s back then. Death frightened me and I began to have dreams about an ambulance coming and taking Mom away from us.

I Believe in Miracles!

I sure wanted to believe in them, anyway. God must know we needed at least one really BIG miracle right now. Because of Mom's illness, we couldn't go to church quite so often. So my parents turned to a number of television evangelists to get their "fix" of religion.

Kathryn Kuhlman was one of my favorites. First of all, she was the only woman doing anything like this at the time. Her speech seemed so dramatic to me. She took long pauses and pronounced things in her own way. "God" almost always came out sounding more like "Gaahwd..." Very drawn out and majestic. She did hands on healing services, talking about miracles and "the supernatural" a lot. She was the first person I remember saying "the only limit to God's power lies within *you*!" She made me believe God could truly work miracles. Maybe I just had to believe harder and Mom would be healed. Perhaps Johnny would be, too.

We also watched Oral Roberts and Jimmy Swaggert from time to time. My father especially loved Billy Graham. We went to some of his appearances in Kansas City, always held at a large stadium. The fervor and the large crowds seemed like the rock concert version of Christianity.

Whenever there was a missionary or speaker in town who specialized in healing, we made every effort to go. In my own mind, I believed Johnny was completely happy exactly the way he was. I focused on praying for miracles for Mom, because I believed she really was the one in need.

One of her friends at church, a sweet lady named Iris, had a truly unique gift. At times, small puddles of oil would appear in her hands and she would then anoint people and pray for their healing. I had touched the oil once myself. Iris showed it to me just before she laid hands on Johnny's head and told me, "go ahead, touch it, Cheryl." It was definitely oil of some sort. I had read about all of Jesus' miracles and many others from the Old Testament for years. So this didn't seem all that strange to me. More wonderful, than anything.

Mom had her own touch when it came to miracle-working. When

our next door neighbor, Mr. Spencer, came down with devastating headaches, that family turned to us because my mother was always witnessing about God and Jesus to anyone who would listen. They realized her faith was tremendous. So they asked her to lay hands on him and pray that his headaches be taken away. She hesitated at first. I encouraged her, knowing how much she loved helping people.

"Go on, Mom. Kathryn Kuhlman lays hands on folks and they get well. Go ahead and try, it will help Mr. Spencer just to know you're praying."

So she did. He was amazed at the heat he felt coming out of her hands and jumped up after her prayer, declaring he felt much better! Mom smiled and looked toward Heaven, saying "God is truly wonderful." I was grateful for this chance for her to see how God worked through her, even if He didn't answer her prayers about Johnny exactly the way she hoped.

She still insisted on wheeling Johnny down to have hands laid on him at every opportunity. She let them lay hands on her, too, but she was still putting her son first. Johnny endured this cheerfully, bless his heart. One day I felt like he simply must get tired of this routine, same thing, several times a week. I made the mistake of voicing my opinion as we made our way to the car after church.

"Mom, I really think John's happy the way he is. What if he's already perfect the way he is? He seems so happy, I mean...."

She stared at me and said, "Stop pushing the wheelchair right now."

Dad wasn't with us on this particular day. I stopped and put the brake on John's chair because I knew that tone meant business. I was expecting a lecture.

Instead, I got the first slap across the face I had experienced in years. I was shocked and embarrassed. To be struck right in the middle of the sidewalk with all kinds of people walking and driving by! I had no clue what I had said that could have set her off. I was about to hear *her* version.

"Who do you think you are to know so much, young lady? To tell God that your poor little crippled brother doesn't need His mercy and healing? I'm amazed you could ever think that, let alone say it!" She grabbed the handles of the wheelchair, took off the brake and began pushing it quickly. I had to jog a bit to keep up.

"But Mom, I wasn't doing that. I mean, I just figure if God doesn't make mistakes, then Johnny must be...." my voice trailed off in confusion. I could tell there was no contesting this.

We drove home with only the radio for company. Even John was silent the entire ride. He obviously could feel the tension. That was the first day I truly began to understand the depth of my mother's guilt over his condition, and her burning desire to be absolved by God. If He bestowed a miracle on her son, then maybe she was a good person, after all. I remembered something from a conversation she'd had years ago with a friend, shortly after John's birth. She had said something about "the sins of the parents visited upon the child."

Sounded pretty weird to me. My parents were good, honest people who loved God. They had both been divorced before marrying each other, but lots of people did that. I couldn't think of one bad thing either one of them had ever done. So this philosophy simply didn't make sense.

When we got home, I decided to seek comfort in my ESP game. Maybe it would give me some answers, or help me to trust my own intuition. Mom walked by and saw me playing with it. She said, "hmmph!" and went on her way. An hour later she came back to find me still working with the pendulum. Something came over her and like a woman possessed, she grabbed the board, folded it up and shoved it in the box. She thrust the pendulum into her apron pocket.

"Come with me!"

You didn't cross a command like that. She was on the warpath and I was totally bewildered. I had been very quiet, minding my own business. How could that make her so mad?

She marched me out to the brick barbecue pit my father had built years before. She reached in her apron pocket and flung the pendulum into the top of the pit.

"What are you doing?" I yelled in protest. Had she gone crazy?

"I'm saving you from the devil, that's what." She tossed the whole game box in after the pendulum. Then she reached in her pocket and as I watched in horror, she poured lighter fluid in on top.

"Stand back!" she ordered.

Lighting a match, she threw it in and grabbed my shoulders, forcing me to stand there, watching as my favorite game turned to ashes.

"Why? What do you mean, 'saving me from the devil?' Do you think Kreskin is the devil, Mom?" I sobbed in confusion.

"He may be a tool of Satan. I don't know. I do know you're obsessed with this damn thing and that's not healthy. No more. No more of this sort of nonsense. We run a Christian house and you will abide by that."

She began muttering to herself. "Thinks she knows better than God what's right. Teach her to give herself airs. Praise the Lord! Burn it up, Lord! Goodbye, Satan!" She spat in the fire and looked at me. The glint in her eye was different than I had ever seen. I was so scared I thought if I moved I'd wet my pants, big as I was.

"You'll stand there until it's turned to ash. You'll never forget how powerful God is. He wins every time, yes, He does. Hallelujah!" She raised her hands as if in the praise service at church.

I wondered if some of the medicine she was on these days had driven her mad. But I didn't dare say anything else. No telling what else she might decide to burn, in the state she was in!

She marched me back in the house and I went to my room, numb to the bone. Seemed like nothing I said or did these days was right. I thought about singing to turn her mood, but didn't risk it.

The remaining spring days of 1970 drifted into summer. I focused on being docile, living in fear of what few precious possessions I had being "sacrificed" to the fire. Mom declared she was sending me to the church summer Bible camp and signed me up. I decided to look at it as an opportunity to be away from her wrath for a week, so it didn't seem so bad.

She helped me pack a bag, including a couple of postcards. "You write us every other day, y'hear?"

"Aw, Mom, it's only a week. The second postcard won't be here 'til after I'm already home!"

She snapped the lid of my suitcase closed. "Just write, and mind the ministers and church staff. Don't be sassy and embarrass us. We're counting on you to be on your best behavior."

I hadn't been anywhere away from home for this long, with the exception of periodically staying with family members during the summer. I always missed Johnny the most. I gave him a big hug before I got in the car. Dad had been delegated to drive me to church where a bus would take all of us "happy campers" to our summer Teen Revival. I was less than enthusiastic, but kept remembering how nice a break from Mom's unpredictable behavior would be.

Dad and I talked about lots of light-hearted things. He was obviously tired of discussing the mounting doctor bills and the other concerns that occupied him on a daily basis. So I enjoyed letting him tease me about catching a big fish in the lake and bringing it home so we could all "feast on it for days."

"Yeah, right. You take care of yourself, Dad. Are *you* doing all right?"

I wasn't really concerned for his health. He looked and acted fine, just pretty tired all the time. He had taken a second part-time job waxing floors at some business a few nights a week. I was more worried that my mother's erratic behavior might be taking its toll on him, too.

He patted my knee. "I'm fine, Sugar. Your old Dad is a tough ol' bird, don't you forget it. Well, we're here." He pulled up in front of the church. The drive had flown by. I didn't get to spend much time alone with my Dad these days and realized how much I enjoyed his company. He was truly a good man.

"I'll miss you, Daddy. She's made me promise to write every other day, so look for me in the mail!" I kissed his cheek, and he hugged me.

"Take care, hon. Catch that big fish, all right?"

"I'll do my best, Dad." I waved and chirped, "See ya in a week!"

"I'll be right here to pick you up," he promised. I watched him drive off as I handed my bag to the assistant minister who was loading up the bus. It almost felt like my parents couldn't think of anything else to do with me. Don was on vacation out of town somewhere, so that meant I wasn't missing out on any good movie opportunities. Might as well go to church camp.

I looked around at the other kids on the bus, wondering if most of them really wanted to be here. Some were giggling, others were stony-faced. A boy who was a year or so older than me was seated about three seats back. "Pepper" was his nickname. He was a "preacher's kid" or "P.K." for short, and he did all the typical things "PKs" had a reputation for. He cussed, he smoked, and he flirted outrageously with girls, mostly girls older than himself. He was pretty cute and he knew it. Pepper's bane in life was that one of his legs was a good four inches shorter than the other. So he usually walked with crutches, or sometimes with a cane. It didn't stop him from being rowdy, though. Popular, too. The girls liked him because he was so cute and the boys liked him because he was tough. He didn't let his handicap slow him down. They all admired that.

The bus bumped and rocked along some gravel roads as we approached the camp. It was about forty miles from home and featured a big lake. I had no real plans to go fishing even though Dad had insisted on packing a pole and small tackle box for me.

Once we got checked in, I found the cabins to be less than inviting. There was an outhouse and a community shower, one for the girls, one for the boys. Charming. I had to bunk in with three girls I didn't even know. I was glad I had brought some comic books and a couple of paperbacks along. I had hidden them under some clothes. The only reading material Mom knew I had brought along was the ever trusty Bible.

The first three days flew by. We had some arts and crafts time which I really enjoyed. I stitched a little leather coin purse, then got to use a wood burner to put my initials on it. At the last minute, I decided to put Mom's initials on it instead. Maybe she would accept this small peace offering. I had sent a somewhat chatty postcard off the day before, making it sound like I was having a great time. Inside I longed for home and my stretch of woods. I didn't go there too often anymore. When had I forgotten how special that was? I vowed to make a trek there as soon as I got home.

In the evenings after supper, we'd all head toward the lake. There were rows of folding chairs set up, with an aisle down the middle. Every night, one of the young ministers would give the altar call. I was amazed how many kids got emotional and went forward to be "saved." I had done this years ago. Some of the kids I saw going down now had answered the altar call a number of times previously at church. I'd seen them with my own eyes. I was confounded. Could it be Jesus needed to save you more than once? Maybe they just felt like they had been extra special bad lately.

On Friday night, the last night of camp, when it came time for the altar call, there really weren't too many left who hadn't already been "saved." I thought they might just cut the service short, when suddenly a commotion from the back caught my attention. I heard someone sobbing softly, and a "ker-thunk, ker-thunk" noise on the gravel path. I turned to see Pepper making his way down the aisle, real tears streaming down his face.

This really surprised me. He was the son of a preacher, and he hadn't been saved before? Still, I tried not to judge. I didn't know his story. I heard murmurs of "Praise the Lord," and "Thank You, Jesus!" coming from the ministerial staff as two of them moved down toward the boy. They each took an arm and helped him on his way.

Since he was now surrounded by about six preachers laying hands upon him, I lost sight of Pepper's head. Suddenly I heard a loud "thud" and realized he must have fallen. It was not uncommon for someone in our congregation to be "slain in the spirit" during a healing or prayer service. This meant they passed out because the power of God was overwhelming. I wondered if this was what had happened when I saw the ministers drop to their knees, praying the whole time.

Along with several other kids, curiosity got the better of us and we all edged forward. I heard a popping and sort of grinding noise I didn't recognize. All at once, there were sounds of great rejoicing and all the preachers were crying and smiling at the same time. Pepper stood up, by himself! He stood there, steady as a rock on his own two feet, sans crutches. I could see that his legs were perfectly even. If I hadn't heard that noise then seen him with my own two eyes that night, I would have missed out on witnessing my first "real" miracle. His leg bone had actually grown right then and there!

He whooped and hollered, jumping up and down. Next, he ran clear around the circumference of the audience area, shaking hands and embracing all of us as we cheered him on, shouting, "Hallelujah! Yes, Pepper! God bless you!"

Then he picked up his crutches and threw them into the lake. "I'm healed!" he hollered. "Praise the Lord, I'm healed!" He was laughing hysterically and running for the first time in his life. We all laughed with him. This was amazing. I remembered what Mom had said about not telling God what to do. Maybe Johnny could and would be totally healed someday. I knew she would take this as a sign of that when she heard the news. I was awestruck at the power of the Almighty. My faith received a tremendous jump-start that night. I was filled with happiness for Pepper and his family and promised God I would be a better person and pray more often because He had allowed me to witness this miracle.

Will The Circle Be Unbroken?

Mom and Dad were duly impressed with Pepper's story. Nothing could have topped that summer miracle for me. Nothing short of our Johnny himself being healed, or our mother's cancer being completely removed. For awhile, she enjoyed what the doctors referred to as "being in remission." This meant the cancer was dormant. I wanted to believe it would stay that way, but I kept having those dreams of the ambulance taking her away.

The fall of 1970 arrived and I headed into my final year of junior high. The most memorable TV event of that season was the premiere of *The Mary Tyler Moore Show*. I had always gotten a kick out of her as Laura Petrie and her "Oh, Rob!" tag line on *The Dick Van Dyke Show*. I immediately identified with Rhoda, the sometimes slobby sidekick. In my mind, I put other girls in the category of a "Mary;" the ones who wore the cute clothes, said the right things and had the cute boyfriends. I was still very introverted and had not even thought about a date, let alone been on one. I was and still am grateful to the MTM Show for providing many happy times in my family and for the country. The writers tended to avoid heavy topics. We had enough of that with the Vietnam War dragging on and on. My heart went out to the families of the POWs and MIAs. I wore a copper bracelet with a POWs name on it, as did many of my friends. You were supposed to keep it on until it was determined whether the soldier was alive. Mine eventually broke, and I kept it on top of my dresser, continuing to pray for my solider and all the others who were missing and serving our country.

Otherwise, that fall started out uneventfully. Johnny was growing, but was still small for his age. The doctors told us his muscles and bones were not growing or stretching much, from lack of use. "Atrophied" was a word I had never heard before that. Johnny remained as cheerful and sweet as ever. He really seemed to look forward to going to his school. Dad finally started to look his age a bit more. Lots of my friends assumed he was my grandfather when they first met him.

Mom looked haggard most of the time. Constant trips to the doctor and more cobalt treatments took their toll. She was always so sick and weak after a treatment. She began to lose a lot of weight and her hair became quite thin. I began to hate the thought of her being exposed to such severe radiation. Somehow it seemed worse than the cancer itself.

My constant solace was music. By now I was listening to records on a regular basis. My taste had expanded to pop music. I fell in love with the music of a brother/sister act who were taking the country by storm. Karen and Richard Carpenter were my main muses in those days.

So much so that I began saving money to buy a drum set in order to emulate my heroine. Most of my friends were into hard rock music by groups like *The Grateful Dead*, *Iron Butterfly* and *The Rolling Stones*. *The Carpenters* captivated me the first time I saw them on TV. Karen played the drums! I had *always* begged for a drum set, but the piano and guitar seemed to be much more acceptable instruments for a girl, in my parents' opinion. Yet here was this charming, feminine girl, usually wearing a long dress, playing the drums and singing her heart out.

My parents couldn't deny that they liked this music as well. *The Carpenters* were good wholesome looking kids who sang lyrical music, not loud rowdy rock and roll. So finally, at age thirteen, after begging for drums for years, I was given permission to buy some percussion instruments with my own money. I immediately began saving my allowance along with money from odd jobs, just like I had when I was determined to buy that first guitar. In addition to mowing lawns, raking leaves, and running a small paper route, I was now teaching piano lessons to younger kids for a few extra dollars. I envisioned drums in the basement. I was motivated, and for the first time without even knowing it, was really putting the power of creative visualization to use.

Within about four months, I had accumulated $100 hard-earned cash. After a couple of trips to music stores, I realized a new drum set cost about five times what I had saved. Upon seeing my disappointment, one nice salesclerk recommended I look in the local paper for a used set, or maybe just a snare drum and high-hat cymbal to start with.

I thanked him, ran and got the paper, and opened it up to the classified section. My finger traced down the categories until I found "Musical Instruments for Sale." WOW! I had hit the mother lode! Full drum sets were advertised for about $250.00. But I wanted something *now*! I kept looking.... "a snare drum and high-hat were a good beginning...." Aha! An ad read "Ludwig snare drum with case and practice pad. High-hat cymbal included, $100." This really caught my eye. Karen played Ludwig drums, as did many other professionals of that time. I began petitioning my parents to let me call about this bargain.

My mother was just settling into being back at home with a regular routine, of sorts. Her tolerance for noise was understandably even less than before. It became clear to me that they had never really believed I could save enough money for drums, let alone find anything for the amount I had already managed to save. Even though she and Dad were such big fans of yard sales and garage sales, it apparently had not occurred to them that their daughter might go the "used" route in order to fulfill her dream.

"Oh, Cheryl, that drum is probably not in good condition. And your Dad would have to drive you over to their house. He doesn't know anything about drums, and neither do you, really...."

My face fell. "But you said I could get drums. I worked so hard and saved my money....can't I at least call, and go see this one? I've talked to the guy at the music store about drums a lot, Mom..."

As usual, my father rushed to my defense. What a hero he was to me, time and again! "Now, Dee...we did promise the girl she could have a drum if she could save the money. And she has. All she's ever really saved anything toward is music, remember how she paid for her first guitar a few years ago? And she always buys her own piano sheet music, outside of her lesson books. She loves music, honey. We really shouldn't go back on a promise."

He smiled at her, knowing those baby blues of his could melt her pretty easily.

"Well, what if the drums upset Johnny? What if they're too noisy?" she rejoined, looking out the window. She was all too used to the two of us joining forces in persuading her to see things our way.

I jumped back into the conversation, "Oh! That's the great thing, Mom. The ad says there's a practice pad! That means a big piece of rubber that fits over the drum head so that I can practice real quietly. And I'll hit the cymbal real gently, I promise. You know, how Karen Carpenter does, just for accents. And I can set up it all up downstairs and play along with their records....I'll close the door that leads upstairs. I already have it all figured out. I won't bother you and Johnny loves their music, too. Puh-lease?"

Dad was standing with his arm around my shoulder in support. "See how much this means to her, Dee? What harm can it do to at least go take a look at these things? Maybe she won't even like them, who knows?" He winked at me, then turned a serious face back to Mom as she gazed back at us.

She sighed. "Oh, well, go ahead and call. I can't fight the two of you when you gang up on me this way. And Mr. Booth, you two be sure to stop at the store and get the things on this list for me." She shoved a piece of paper at him and walked out of the room, shaking her head. Dad grinned as I rushed to the phone.

The man who answered got a big kick out of the fact such a young girl was calling about his drum. He said to come right over, he'd be glad to demonstrate it for my Dad and me. I jotted down the address, and off we went.

A couple of hours later we came home, groceries, drum and high-hat in tow. I thought I had died and gone to music Heaven! None of my friends, certainly none of my female friends, played the drums. This felt like a real coup!

I proceeded to set everything up, then studied the music book the man had kindly thrown in with the deal. I learned about the different grips you could use to hold the drumsticks, and began to practice basic rolls, learning some of the rudiments of snare drum percussion. This was fun, although I'm sure Mom didn't think so. As I learned the various rhythms, I also worked on the subtleties of the high-hat cymbal, being careful to use the brushes rather than the sticks most of the time so as to keep the volume down.

Once I had the basics down, I played along with Karen and Richard for hours on end. My vocal range was similar to hers, so singing along made it that much more fun. When Mom and Dad would go out to run various errands, I carried my "mini-set" upstairs and gave Johnny a concert. He smiled and sang along in his own way, my biggest fan and supporter, as always!

This went on for the next few years, as the Carpenters released album after album, had their own TV summer replacement show, and their songs took over the airwaves. Many of my friends labeled me a "square" for loving their music so much, but I really didn't mind a bit. My absolute love of and devotion to their music during this time is what drew Karen to communicate with me many years later. (Check out the chapter later on in this book on celebrity communication!).

As a kind of graduation for the ninth graders, we made a class trip to *Six Flags Over Texas*. This should have been all about fun, but it involved a touch of tragedy. There were three buses, which carted us all down there. The one traveling behind mine had a major accident one night. The rest of us didn't know anything about this until we pulled into the motel and realized they were not bringing up the rear as usual.

Later that night we learned the driver had apparently fallen asleep and driven over an embankment. Nobody was killed, thank God, but one student had a broken back and several were hurt pretty badly. The rest of us were in shock. How were we supposed to have fun while many of our cohorts were stuck in hospital beds? I went to bed wondering what kind of plan God had in mind with this turn of events. I was so conditioned to believe God caused everything back in those days. The concept of "soul lessons" from life experiences would have been like trying to communicate with an alien from another planet at that time!

The next morning I called home right after breakfast, before we headed off on the last leg of the trip to the amusement park. I should have realized something of this magnitude would be on the news in Kansas City by that time. Mom was hysterical. She was relieved I was fine, then sad for the kids who weren't. I apologized for not calling sooner.

"That's okay, honey. You try to have a good time and you come home to us safe and sound. Promise me!"

I didn't know how I could promise such a thing. What had my classmates done to deserve such a fate? I was still into believing in the "blame game" on some bizarre, unexplainable cosmic level. If an accident that bad had happened to my classmates, how did I know it wouldn't befall me, too? Still, when your mother is deeply worried you promise anything.

"Yes, Mom. I promise. You just get some rest and take care of yourself. I'll see you in three days," I assured her. She seemed calmer as we hung up.

The park was fun, but a damper had certainly been thrown upon our enjoyment of it. Most of us only rode a few things and spent the rest of the time discussing what had happened. Mainly I kept questioning

God's wisdom or involvement in all of this. The church always said God had His Hand on everything. Did He cause this for some reason? Why hadn't He awakened the driver and avoided the whole incident? I was confused and mad. God didn't seem to be on the job a whole lot lately. My mother's health was steadily going downhill. My knees felt raw at times from praying so much. Still there seemed to be no response in sight.

Despite having witnessed Pepper's healing, I began to be suspicious and more confused about God than ever before. Things like this bus accident, my mother's illness and Johnny's condition seemed to cancel the good things out. Nobody had any satisfying answers for me, so I stewed about all this privately.

Within two weeks of my return from this trip, my parents informed me that Mom had to go to a "cancer research hospital" in Columbia, Missouri. My worst fears were realized; the cancer had grown stronger while she grew weaker. She was a shadow of her former self, visibly wasting away

After they talked to me, Mom excused herself to bed. Johnny and Dad and I sat in the kitchen, unsure what to do next.

Half afraid to ask, I whispered, "Where's it gone, now?"

Dad put his head in his hands. "They're afraid it's in her brain, Cheryl. We don't have any choice. There's no money left for the bills. There's a third mortgage on the house." He began to cry. "I don't know what else to do. God, please help me. I can't take anymore!" I felt selfish for not having realized how hard this was hitting him. I went up and hugged him, rocking him back and forth as if he were *my* child, as he sat there.

Over the next couple of days, my father and I had some serious discussions. He explained how he had to go to court and make Mom a ward of the state. This cancer hospital would only be able to take her if the state had control of her welfare. Otherwise she would have to stay home and get worse until she died. The only thing that seemed to bring him any hope was the chance that some of the experimental drugs they would try on her might work. I did my best to let him know I supported his decisions.

Columbia was a good ninety miles from the house. They scheduled a time for the ambulance to come and get her. My awful precognitive dream was finally coming true and I felt incredibly sick. A day or so before she was to leave, my grandmother Bertha came to see her sick daughter. My aunts and sister-in-law had been there a lot, but Grandma was getting up in years and couldn't get out too often. At least that's the story I got every time I asked where she was.

Homer, her fourth husband had passed away by now, and it was rumored among the family that she was pretty well-fixed financially. Each one of her successive husbands had apparently left her with some money. Homer had owned that farm and been very frugal, so the scuttlebutt was she was sitting pretty now. I wondered why she had never come forward to help with the doctor bills. Maybe if she had, Mom wouldn't have to go to this research hospital. I didn't understand how someone could not do everything in their power to help their own child.

Bertha visited with her eldest daughter for awhile. Then as she was leaving, she asked my father to go out onto the driveway to see her to her car. They stood there talking for a few minutes. I watched through the picture window.

Dad looked agitated and he actually slammed the door shut once she had climbed behind the steering wheel. Grandma was so short she basically looked *under* the top of the wheel when she drove. The look on her face told me she knew how mad she had made my father. I had no clue what she possibly could have said. Dad had always been very civil to his second mother-in-law. He was her junior by just about six years.

When he walked back into the house, I immediately asked him what had happened. He raised a finger to silence me, then peeked back into Mom's room. Once he was sure she was asleep, he invited me to walk into the back yard so we could talk.

"Oh, my God, Cheryl. I don't think I've ever been so mad in my life. Of all the nerve! That old biddy!" He was shaking.

"Jeez, Dad, what did she say?"

He took a deep breath as if to steady himself. He couldn't look at me, so he looked up at the sky. "She said...." he cleared his throat, "she said, 'If you pay for everything else at the funeral, Walt, I'll buy the casket. Pick out any one you want, and I'll pay for it.' *That's* what your mother's 'loving mama' had to say. With absolutely no emotion in her voice. Can you believe it?"

I was shocked. How could someone be so cold about their own child's life? Not even to hold out any hope that she might recover, or to offer any loving words to the family? Simply to offer to pay for the coffin...I couldn't come up with any words to express how that made me feel. I hugged my Dad and patted him on the back.

"Then I'm glad if you told her off," I finally said.

"Damn straight I did!" he snorted. "Told her 'Get the hell off my property, you old bitch!'" He laughed, but there were tears in his eyes. "Was that too mean? I couldn't help myself...."

"God, no, Dad! That was awful, what she said. You're under so much stress and she comes here and that's the best she can offer. Jesus!" I didn't usually take the Lord's name in vain, but this was the heaviest thing we had ever shared. Dad and I had this way of letting black humor rescue us at times. Something in me made me want to help him through this so much, I searched around in my confused brain to see what remark might bring a new light to this. I hesitated, then went through with saying what came to me. "You know, Dad, if Mom does die..."

He shot an icy blue stare at me.

"Wait now, wait. *If* she does die, let's take Grandma up on it, and pick out the most damned expensive coffin we can find!"

I tended to have a macabre sense of humor at times. I paused, wondering how he would react. He burst into nervous laughter then squeezed my shoulder.

"You got that straight, honey. You sure got that straight!" We promised not to burden Mom with any of this about her mother, then wiped our eyes and headed back into the house.

The morning of her move to the hospital, Mom called me to her bedside. "Honey, I'm going to ask you a big favor. This is something a girl your age should never have to do, but you've always been so strong and mature."

"What is it, Mom?" I took a deep breath, and tried to smile bravely.

"Well, I want to go to this damned hospital as clean as possible. I'm just too weak to do this myself." Her emerald eyes, still beautifully clear, filled with tears. "Could you give your old Mom a sponge bath, do you think?"

"Oh, of course! Don't worry, Mom, that's nothing! I'm glad to do it for you." I ran to the bathroom, gulping lots of air and wiping my sleeve to hide my tears from her. When a child has to do the things for a parent that the parent did for you as a baby, it brings up all kinds of emotions. Right then, I was scared and sad, but determined not to let her know. I prayed to Jesus to give me strength as I gathered the soap, washcloth, towels and basin. When I felt pretty composed, I returned to the bedroom, smiling and chatty about school as I respectfully cleaned her up, doing my best to get her to laugh and take her mind off a situation neither of us wanted to talk about.

When the ambulance came to get her, I stood with Dad on the driveway. She had asked that we leave John inside with my sister-in-law after she kissed him goodbye. I bit my lip to keep from crying as they loaded her in. She smiled and weakly waved.

"I love you. Take care of each other and Johnny, now. You know how, Cheryl. You're a good girl. Thank you for being such a good girl."

I nodded, unable to speak for fear of crying. As soon as they took off I broke down and melted into my father's arms.

Over the remaining months of the summer, Dad would drive us to Columbia a lot. When September rolled around and my sophomore year began, he drove down alone several times a week, or sometimes one of my brothers or my sister-in-law would ride with him. Johnny and I went along on the weekends. Mom looked less and less like herself.

On one visit she was wild-eyed and delusional. I wondered exactly what kind of experimental drugs they were giving her. She grabbed my arm and pulled me close, as if to share a deep secret.

"See that wall over there? I kicked a nurse clean through it! Told her I'd had enough damn drugs, to keep those needles away from me."

I looked at the wall, realizing there was no way this had happened. But she seemed to believe it so strongly, I decided to play along. "Well, I don't blame you, Mom. Don't blame you a bit. They sure got that wall fixed up good, though, didn't they? I hope you didn't hurt the nurse too much." I patted her arm. She still had a strong grip on my wrist.

"I hope I *did* hurt her. Damn witch. Keep that shit away from me!"

Now I knew she was high, because Mom never swore like that, at least never around me. It was funny and sad at the same time. I pulled out a recent snapshot of the housc. We had just completed painting it a really pretty forest green.

"Look, Mom. What do you think of the house? We just painted it so you can really enjoy it when you come home soon. Green's your favorite color these days, right? Isn't it pretty?"

She just looked at me and shook her head side to side. "It's pretty, honey. Not for me, though. Not for me. You enjoy it. Give Mama a kiss. You better go now. I'm real tired all of a sudden." She tried to reach up to me. I cradled her neck as I kissed her forehead, like she had done so many times to me when I was small. I was fighting the tears so hard, determined not to let her see me cry.

Dad, John and I rode home listening to country music on the radio. There was nothing to say. My mother had obviously finally given up on a miracle. And if *her* faith couldn't allow for one, how could we fool ourselves any more? It was obviously just a matter of time.

Dad was in a state of shock for real, now. He was basically on autopilot, going down to Columbia every chance he got. It became his job. I took over most of John's care, but was thankful for the help of my older brothers, my sister-in-law and some great friends from church who still came around to help any way they could. They brought us food and helped clean the house.

Aunt Kathy had come to stay with us for quite awhile, but once her sister had gone to the research hospital, she had to go home and attend to matters there.

All of the adults around me encouraged me to become involved in extra-curricular activities. I had lost some weight due to worry. I signed up for Pep Club even though I wasn't a big sports fan. Oak Park's football team was rated very high among the district high school rankings. September 17th, 1971, I came home after a game. Dad had been there when I left home, hours before, but now I found my sister-in-law and my grandmother in his place. Johnny was asleep on the couch and the two women had apparently been sitting there in silence for some time. They looked startled when I walked into the room.

I knew by the look on their faces and my own gut reaction what had happened. I looked at my sister-in-law, whom I could always count on for the Gospel truth.

"Mom died, didn't she? She's gone, I just know it." I sat down at her feet, and Doris gave me a little hug.

"No, honey, she...she just took a turn. Your Dad had to hurry down there to be with her, that's all. Why don't you go on to bed and get some rest? It's been a long day for all of us."

Grandma chimed in, "Yes, I know I'm tired. We'll put Johnny to bed, you just take care of yourself now, child."

I looked at each of them in turn. Something didn't feel right, but I knew Doris would never lie. She was one of the kindest, most loving people I had ever known. I wanted to believe her, so I did.

"Okay. I guess he'll call tomorrow and let me know how she's doing, if he has to stay overnight or something. See you in the morning."

I kissed them both on the cheek, bent over my sleeping brother and kissed his forehead as I wiped his growing hair to one side. He hadn't received a haircut in several months. I always thought he looked cute with it longer, anyway. He looked like a little angel personified, sleeping away peacefully. Perhaps he was the most blessed of all of us right now. He obviously knew Mom wasn't around, but he seemed more himself than any of the rest of us.

I put on my PJs and dropped off into a restless sleep. The next thing I remember, I heard my father's voice, as if through a tunnel. "Cheryl, wake up. Honey, wake up. I have something to tell you." He was sitting on the edge of my bed, something he hadn't done since I was a little girl. I rubbed the sleep out of my eyes. How was he here and in Columbia at the same time? I looked at my alarm clock. 2 a.m.?

"What is it, Dad?" I mumbled, trying to sit up. He gave me a hand and pulled me close to him.

"Your Mama's gone to Heaven, Honey. God took her home tonight."

All of my breath was instantly gone. I felt like I was having a heart attack. This wasn't happening, it *couldn't* be!

"What? WHAT?" I began shaking and couldn't stop. "When did she die?" I looked at him incredulously.

"About 6 o'clock last night, honey. They called and told me to get right down there. I had to sign some papers so they could release the body to bring her home for the funeral." His voice sounded so hollow.

"Then they lied to me when I came home! I knew she was gone, I *knew* it! But Doris and Grandma told me she was still here. So I went to bed thinking maybe some miracle could still happen. Why did they lie to me?" My whole world was coming apart as I ached for my mother's touch just one more time, even for one of her reproving glances.

"Don't blame them, Cheryl," he rocked me back and forth like a baby. I was still shaking uncontrollably. "I told them I wanted to be the one to tell you, that's all. I made them promise that no matter what, you'd hear this from me. I felt like I owed you that much. It's not their fault, it's mine."

"Oh, great! Why the hell couldn't you come to the stupid football game and get me, take me down there with you? God! I think I'm going to be sick!"

I ran to the bathroom and had the dry heaves for several minutes. When I came out, he handed me a glass of water and we joined the two women in the living room.

They apologized for the deception, but I no longer blamed them. My father had become a bit of a villain in my eyes, just for a split second. I continued to tremble for another two hours, no matter how many blankets they draped over me. This was a chill that had no equal.

The funeral came and went. We made sure one of Mom's favorite hymns, *In The Garden* was one of the songs. I stood there in a stupor, watching them lower the coffin into the ground, then they covered it with dirt. I just stood there like some statue, my father's arm around my shoulder. Frozen in time, feeling like the epitome of grief carved in cold, hard stone. My father was nearly seventy years old, my brother was severely handicapped. I was not quite sixteen years old, and had just lost my mother. I felt abandoned, not just by her, but by God. Would we *really* ever see her, would we all ever be together again, in Heaven or anywhere else? Would "the circle be unbroken, by and by, Lord" as the song promised? Amidst all this anger, grief and confusion, my most recurring thought was, "Where is God in all this?"

Booth family circa 1967

Dolores Booth, around age thirty

Walter during World War II

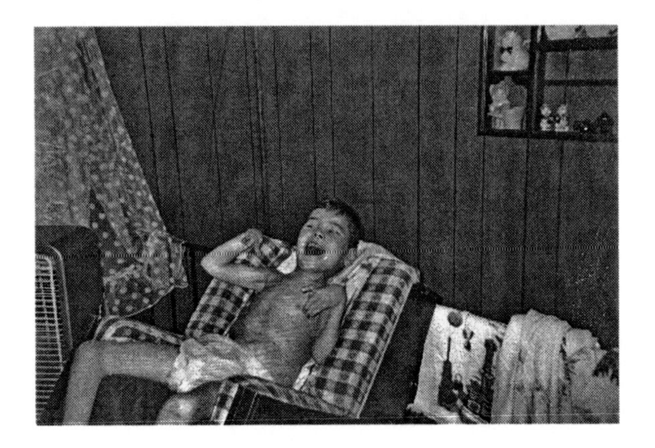

Johnny in his feeding chair; laughing
& happy, as I remember him best

Johnny with a friend's dog. Animals
always loved & felt protective toward him,
and he loved them right back!

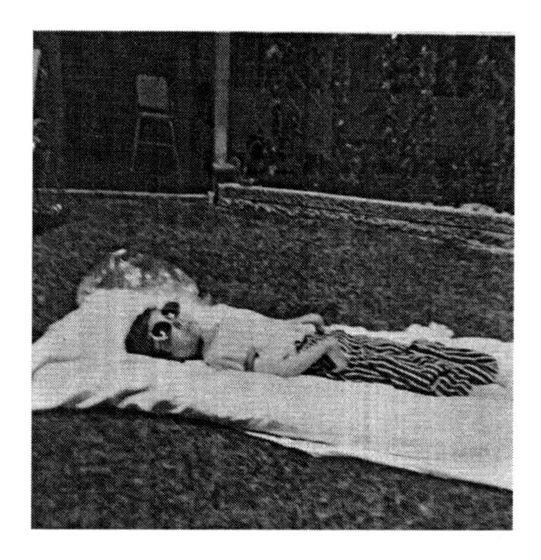

Johnny oozing "California Cool,"
wearing my sunglasses in our
sister Jeannine's back yard.
Summer of 1972, San Diego

Chapter Seven

Life goes On

Somehow, life did, indeed, go on. My sophomore year in high school was pretty much an automatic series of "going through the motions." For several months, Dad was in such severe shock he seldom had energy nor the necessary attention to think about everyday things like getting Johnny bathed, fed and ready for school. So I got up earlier to handle that, then when I came home, cooked supper for all of us, fed John and got him ready for bed. I didn't mind. My little brother was one constant factor in my life, never once stopping his outpouring of sweet, unconditional love.

For a few weeks, John would look around and say, "Mama?" I usually cried, picked him up and rocked him, saying, "She's in Heaven with Jesus, now, Johnny. Mama's not here. It's okay. She doesn't hurt anymore." But I know now she *was* there with us, giving us her strength and love from the other side. I don't believe she ever left us, not for very long periods of time, anyway. She was undoubtedly helping me not to resent giving up opportunities for extracurricular events because I had a brother and Dad who needed me. I didn't recognize this father, this man who seemed so hopeless and empty. But I understood why he had become that way. Being fifteen years Mom's senior, he never expected to outlive her or be faced with our current situation. I didn't blame him, I just prayed for him a lot.

The first clear signal that Dad was really making an effort to "get back in the game of life" came just after my sixteenth birthday. To honor that milestone, I had proudly come home from the DMV with my driver's license the afternoon of that auspicious date. I had passed driver's education easily, so as to help lower insurance rates. Now I could help out a lot more, not just drive around in circular parking lots! The Saturday morning after my birthday, Dad got up, said he had some errands to run and would see us soon. A couple of hours went by during which I fed and dressed John. We were watching TV when the phone rang.

"Hi, Honey! What color do you like better, red or green?" His voice was chipper, so I was doubly confused.

"Well, gosh, Dad, it's a little early to be worrying about Christmas decor, isn't it?" I laughed, more than a bit bewildered.

"No, I mean in a car. I'm at the *AMC* dealer and the least I can do for you after all you've sacrificed for me and John is get you a car for your birthday. What do you think?"

I was stunned. This, I hadn't seen coming at all. A new *car*? Wow! But wait, he said, "*AMC*." Dad was a big fan of *American Motors*, thus the old faithful Rambler station wagon, which had been our main form of travel for so many years. But *AMC* also sold those really cool Jeeps! Dare I dream he might pick out one of those for me?

"What *kind* of car are we talking about here, Dad? What model?"

"A Gremlin! They're real sporty, don'tcha think?"

His enthusiasm couldn't stop the flood of thoughts pouring through my brain. Gremlins were weird, downright ugly. But, they had a back seat, so I could haul around my friends. I'd be one of the only kids in my circle to have a brand new car, ugly or not. The Gremlin was probably all Dad could afford, and I wasn't sure how he planned to afford even it. But he obviously wanted to give me *something*, make my sixteenth birthday a big deal and try in some way to help me think about something other than the pain of losing Mom. The pros outweighed the cons, so I decided to get with the program.

"Sure, they're great, Dad, those Gremlins. Kinda, um, sporty, like you say! They only have red or green, though? Blue's always been my favorite color." In my teenage selfishness, I had hopes that if it had to be an ugly Gremlin, at least it would be in a palatable color.

"Sorry, hon. Only two on the lot here right now are red or green, and I can get a really good price if I take one of these off their hands. They're test drive demos, pretty low mileage, and they want to make room for some new ones. So which will it be?" He sounded so happy, I made a quick decision.

A red Gremlin would be more noticeable, possibly more likely to draw comments like, "Whoo! Look at Booth's flashy Gremlin!" Followed by hysterical laughter. That made my mind up.

"Well, green, then. Thanks so much, Dad. What a shock!" At least that last comment was honest.

"Great! I'll drive home in the Rambler, we'll pack Johnny boy into his seat, then come back down to the dealership to get your new car! You'll drive the Rambler back home, I'll take the Gremlin, because it's a stick shift. Then we'll teach you how to drive it after that." He was commandeering this like a general. It was good to hear him sounding so self-assured, so alive. "How's all that sound?"

"Terrific, Dad. I really don't know what to say, except, 'thanks!'"

After we hung up, I had a conversation with John about how neat it would be to have my own new car, ugly or not. I was actually convincing *myself* loving this thing would be easy, once I got used to its strange shape. John listened to every word, as he always did, even throwing up his arms and shouting, "I go!" occasionally, which I knew meant he understood we were "discussing" cars.

Once we caravanned back home, Dad excitedly called a few people until he found a babysitter for John. He was anxious to get me out on the road in my new wheels. All that was required was my learning to negotiate a clutch and floor stick. He was convinced he could teach me in no time.

"You can come over for an hour or so, then? Thanks, Alberta!" He hung up, happy that our next door neighbor was available to watch Johnny. "You'll see, Cheryl," he beamed, "you'll take to a manual transmission like a duck to water. After all, you've known how to drive an automatic for over four years now. Piece of cake, don't worry."

"Okay, Dad. Let's go for it!" I was actually getting excited now. Maybe I could even drive this green Gremlin over to my friend Karen's house and show it off tonight! That was the ideal script my mind worked out. What *really* happened was very different.

Dad started out driving, and I watched his every move, just as I had as a little kid when he was driving the Rambler. This clutch thing didn't look so hard. Just adding a little left foot action to the mix. No problem!

He pulled over after a few blocks and turned off the motor. "Okay, take the wheel, kiddo! Think you've got it?" He smiled, confident his tomboy daughter, seasoned veteran of driving in big parking lots for over four years, would be a natural.

"You bet, Dad!" We switched places, I turned the key, put it in gear and promptly killed it. "Oops!" I felt the blood rise in my cheeks. "Let's try that again."

He chuckled. "Don't worry, honey. You'll get the hang of it. It's just a little different than the automatic, that's all. Take your time."

Gosh, he sure was being patient. Okay, it must be a timing thing.

Turn key, slowly let out clutch after engaging first gear, press gas pedal... we jerked down the street about six feet and I killed it again.

I sat there, getting angrier with myself each passing minute. I have Virgo rising in my chart, which leaves little margin for self-created error, even when attempting a brand new skill. It tends to bring out extreme perfectionism, making one critical not just of others at times, but even harder on self. I remembered how much I hated sewing in home economics class because I simply was a no-talent seamstress. How many garments I had eventually ripped to shreds out of frustration that I couldn't sew a straight seam. I didn't want to be great at this, like Mom. I couldn't envision myself creating beautiful, hip clothes. Much easier to buy cool things when I could afford them. I simply wanted to get one of my typical "As" out of the class. That never happened. The "C" I got in home ec might as well have been an "F" by my standards. Now it felt like I was failing again. My inability to drive this green Gremlin, first time out of the chute, was causing similar frustration to well up within me. I clutched the wheel and took a deep breath.

This time, Dad's eyes rolled a little bit and he let out a sigh. It must have been a mystery to him why it had been so easy for me to learn on the Rambler and this brand, new, shiny, sporty (yeah, right!) gift car was throwing me for a loop.

"Just try it again. You'll get it."

"Oh, yeah? Don't hold your breath, Dad." I exhaled, determined to do better. "Here goes nothing." And lo and behold, this time, we got all the way down the block, with the sudden jerks and little swerves eventually smoothing out. This wasn't so bad! I drove up the hill to the stop sign, applied the brake, proud that I remembered to hold in the clutch.

"Okay, now on hills, I should've told you..." he hadn't finished before I looked in the rear view mirror. There was somebody right on our tail.

"It's okay, Dad, just let me get outta this guy's way..." I tried perfecting a "clutch and go" moment, but to my dismay, I not only killed it, but rolled back, missing the person behind me by sheer inches. He blew his horn, shook his head in utter disgust and revved around me. I was mortified.

"Give it a go again," Dad encouraged. "Just be careful..."

"All *right!* I'm doing the best I can here!" An angry tear trickled down my cheek and I brushed it away, even madder that I was acting like a weak girl. He'd stayed pretty calm, considering I'd almost creamed another car, but I couldn't say the same for myself. I was mad. I gunned it and we slowly jerked through the intersection, after about three more death sentences to the ignition.

"Pull over." Dad's voice had taken on a calm, steely edge I'd never heard from him.

"But, this isn't brain surgery, Dad. I'll get it, I know." I couldn't bear to disappoint my father. So I decided to suck it up and give it my best shot. "Just give me another chance..."

"Cheryl! Pull over *now*." He was looking straight ahead. I couldn't tell whether he was more upset with me or with his own lack of patience with teaching. I did as he said, turned off the motor and we both sat there, mad at our selves and each other for a full minute before he said, "Switch places. I can't believe this."

I got out, heartsick that I had ruined his birthday surprise to me. The only bright side was, he might take the Gremlin back and get something, *anything*, that was an automatic. But this was not to be the case. My Dad never raised me to be a quitter.

After I walked around and got into the passenger seat, he stood outside for awhile, looking at the sky, muttering under his breath. He kicked the tires a couple of times. I couldn't hear if he was asking God for help, berating all women drivers, cussing, or a combination of all three. I felt about two feet tall and very angry with myself.

As my father drove us back home in silence, I turned on the radio to check out the speakers, but an icy blue glance made me flip it back off and just sit perfectly quiet for the rest of the short trip. When we pulled up the hilly driveway, (he didn't kill it once, by the way), he parked it and without a word, set the emergency brake, slammed the car door and went inside. I sat out there, a prisoner in this homely casing of green steel, complete with white stripes and a hatchback. Hell, I couldn't even pull it into the garage to hide its ugliness or my shame. Maybe I *should* have been born in medieval England and stuck to horses. Years later, through past life regression and readings, I learned I indeed had several incarnations where horses were my main mode of transportation. But the four cylinders of horsepower under this Gremlin's hood were not about to be tamed by me. Not today. Maybe never.

I wanted to cry, but stubbornly held back the tears and went inside, slamming the door behind me. Dad and I were so much alike when it came to our tempers. We repressed and effectively "ate" almost every negative emotion until they all festered and began eating at us. (No wonder I had an ulcer by the time I went to college!)

I nodded thanks to Alberta as she headed home, no doubt wondering why Dad and I looked like we'd been through trial by fire.

He was pacing around in the dining room and I had enough sense to leave him alone. I sat down on the couch and begin massaging Johnny's feet. He always loved that, and it had a way of calming me down, too. In a few minutes, I heard Dad pick up the kitchen phone and begin dialing.

"Hi, Kelly! How you doing? It's Walt Booth."

Why was he calling the Kellys? They were a nice young couple we'd known for a few years. Dora went to our church sometimes, but her husband Kelly, refused to go (I never did know his first name. Everybody, even his wife, simply called him "Kelly"). He was a very nice person and more than a few times, I secretly envied him that he didn't feel compelled to attend church. Privately, I had begun to believe God lives in your heart, as well as out in the heart of nature, not in some sanctuary. But I knew this would not be a popular opinion at home, so I was still dutifully going with Dad and John, usually at least twice a week. I tuned back into the conversation, still curious why my father had chosen to call these particular people.

"Yeah, I think I just don't have what it takes to be a good teacher. Poor kid. We almost had a knock down, drag-out!" He laughed, but I didn't think it was that far from the truth, nor did I find it funny. "Anyway, do you think Dora would mind coming over and driving around with my kid for awhile? She *does* drive a stick shift, doesn't she?" He was obviously doubting every female's driving ability at the moment. Apparently the answer was affirmative.

"Great! When she gets home from shopping, would you have her call us, please, so these two gals can figure out when they could get together? We'd sure appreciate it. Thanks, Kelly." He hung up the phone and I heard his footsteps heading toward the living room. I feigned disinterest, examined John's toenails, then got up to fetch the cuticle scissors in order to give him a pedicure.

Dad sat down in his favorite old recliner. Not only did his prejudice remind me at times of Archie Bunker, he even had a chair that was pretty much taboo for anyone else to occupy when he was in the room! I avoided looking at him, intent on my manicurist duties, although I could feel him watching me.

"Well, guess you heard. Little Dora Kelly will be calling you soon. She's young and she also thinks more like you, well, like a woman. You're both girls. Ah, hell! You know what I mean. Maybe you can figure out this driving thing easier with her." He waited for a response, but I still avoided looking up.

He sighed. When we had disagreements, it could get *awfully* quiet.

We both hated confrontation and hadn't learned that it was okay, even healthy, to disagree at times, or ask for an explanation when feelings got hurt. I was the secretive, brooding Scorpio and he the stubborn, down-to-earth Taurus. We were almost exactly six months apart in our birthdays, just shy of it by one day. So we had lots of opposite, yet similar energy. He knew how much his daughter was like him in so many ways. So he took the plunge and broke the silence once more.

"Cheryl Ellen."

Oh, God! He was using Mom's old trick of getting my attention when I'd really been bad. But he sounded calm, not angry at all any more. I glanced up to find him smiling gently.

"You like Dora, right? She's been so nice to take you shopping a few times since your Mom passed. She's young, she's...what do you say these days? She's 'hip'? She'll be able to help you, I think."

I nodded slightly and focused on John's pinky toenail. "Okay, it may be worth a try. Dora's cool."

"Oh, 'cool', is she? Well, good." He paused as we locked eyes again. "You know, I'm sorry I lost my temper with you. I prayed, and even asked your Mom what was the best thing to do. Suddenly, I felt like I heard her say, 'call Dora Kelly.' Isn't that strange?"

He was seriously asking me a question that carried a lot of weight. If we weren't careful, we just might have a good philosophical discussion bordering on the occult. We hadn't enjoyed many heart to hearts since I was a little kid and used to follow him around, asking him questions while he built something or worked on the car. I was encouraged and began feeling better about myself and about life, in general.

"No, Dad, I don't think it's strange at all!" I smiled at him and saw his face relax a bit. "Actually, I talk to Mom a lot. I think she hears us." I paused. "I've had a couple of dreams about her, too. She's okay now, Dad. She hasn't been in pain since she left this old world behind. She looks in on us when she can, I think. So she probably did suggest calling Dora. Sounds like a good idea. That is, unless I want to turn the Gremlin into a lawn decoration or big ol' planter and never learn to drive it!"

He snorted and we shared a good laugh. I really believe what started out as a great day for us, then turned sour and was now reversing again, was the beginning of my father's decision to participate in life again. Strange how sometimes, certain events have a lot more importance than they seem to in the moment.

Long story short, Dora came over, we went out. She was sweet, patient and pretty funny. Within an hour I was driving that Gremlin like an old pro. We pulled up the driveway to find Dad standing there, looking proud, indeed, that I scaled our uphill drive with nary a jerk, and turned off the ignition smoothly.

"That's my girl!" He squeezed my shoulder. "Thanks, Dora. Turned our whole day around to have your help. Really appreciate it." He shook her hand. She was very gracious.

"Think nothing of it, Walter. Cheryl's a bright young lady. She just needed to know that practice makes perfect and to relax a bit, that's all." She smiled. "Call me in the next couple of weeks, Cheryl, and you can pick me up and we'll go to the mall again. You could probably use a new pair of jeans, couldn't you? I know I could!" she grinned.

She was a clothes horse, whom I had never seen wear a pair of jeans, but it sounded like a good excuse to hang out. Dora was sophisticated, witty and refined. She reminded me of a sweet, southern belle who had attended debutante balls and was now married to a man she loved very much. But I think being a housewife bored her, so she enjoyed being on her own once in awhile, too. We had some good discussions about music and she genuinely seemed interested in my teenage opinion on a number of things. She wasn't a mother figure, because she was only about ten years my senior. She had shared with me that she couldn't have children. So it was a nice change of pace for both of us to spend time together once in awhile.

That night when I said my prayers, I added a special note after the "Amen."

"And Mom, if you can hear me, thanks a lot for putting the idea in Dad's head to call Dora. That was so perfect! I'm so happy I have my own car. Of course, I'd rather have *you* here." A lump grew in my throat. "But not in the pain you were going through. I know you're in a much better place. Take care of yourself, Mom. We love you."

One way I was convinced she did hear us and look after us in whatever way she could, had to do with Johnny's physical appearance. His eyes had always been blue, like mine and Dad's, just a little darker shade of blue. Less than three months after Mom's death, I was talking to John when I suddenly stopped mid-sentence. I moved closer to him and stared at his eyes. He grinned, always happy to be the center of attention. His eyes were green. GREEN! Not just green, but *exactly* the shade of green that Mom's had been. I must be imagining this!

"Dad! *Dad!* Come quick!" I hollered, unable to utter more.

Dad came running out of the bathroom, shaving lather still on his face. "What is it? Are you okay? Is something wrong with Johnny?" His eyes darted from one of us to the other, in deep concern.

I just pointed. "Look at his eyes, Dad. What color are they?"

He looked at me as though I'd lost my mind. "What's wrong with you, girl? Your little brother's eyes?!? They're blue...like yours..."

"No, they're not. Not anymore, Dad. Look!" I pointed again, feeling dumb, but determined to get confirmation that I was not crazy.

He laughed. "Okay, I'll play. Let's have a look at your peepers, Johnny boy." He gently sat down at his son's side and turned John's face to gaze into his eyes. "His eyes are..." he gasped slightly, "...oh, God!" He stopped short, just as I had done. He seemed to be trembling, ever so slightly as he looked back at me. "They've turned green. Just like your mother's. That's it, isn't it?"

"Yes! It's a sign, Dad. She's still with us. You know how Mom always looked for signs about Johnny being healed? Well, she sent us one by changing his eye color. Eleven year old kids' eyes don't change color overnight, do they? Well, do they?" I was babbling in my excitement now.

"No, I don't think that's typical at all, honey. You're probably right." He looked up at the ceiling, as though smiling at her for a moment. "That's pretty cool, as you say." He patted Johnny's hand and walked back to finish shaving, almost like he was walking on air. We were all slowly making peace with her absence and finding comfort where we could.

Not long after that, I came home from school to find him with his elbows on the kitchen table, head resting in his hands. He didn't even look up when I entered the room. I crossed to his side, startled to see tears running down his cheeks.

"What is it, Dad? What's wrong?"

He just shook his head.

"Tell me, Dad. What's the matter?"

He pulled out his handkerchief and blew his nose. "Nah, you'll think I'm crazy."

"I could never think that, Dad. Please, tell me what's going on?" I pulled up a chair and sat close to him.

"Well, okay. But you asked for it, remember?"

I nodded, half-afraid he might be about to tell me he now had some terminal illness.

"I saw your mother. Just before you got home. She was standing over there at the top of the stairs. She looked so beautiful, so young. She was wearing a long, flowing red dress. I walked toward her and she smiled, then disappeared." He paused. "Am I losing my mind?"

I immediately hugged him. "No, no! I think that's wonderful, Dad. She's just looking in on you, like we talked about before. And the fact she looked so healthy and happy, that means she's doing great in Heaven. You're not crazy at all. I believe in these kinds of signs, Dad. Don't you?"

"Well, yes. Actually, I have for a long time. I just never talked much about them when your Mom was around, because she always thought such stuff was "spooky" or weird."

"Yeah, or from the devil." I knew all too well what he was talking about. I remembered my promise to her to "turn off my dreams" after the 6 Day War experience. Anything paranormal in nature had scared my mother no end. It simply wasn't something she'd been brought up to give credence to, nor ever developed enough interest in to motivate her to read about such things. I had recently begun reading *There Is a River*, about psychic Edgar Cayce. It was the dawning of my realization I was not some freak as a child, after all. That perhaps some of the ideas I was turning to lately were not wrong, nor wicked. Just different than what the preachers wanted us to think.

"Would you like to hear about some things I never told her about?" he asked.

I was thrilled. My Dad was going to open up to me about something very special, I could tell. "Yes, that would be great!"

"Well, get yourself a soda and pour me one, too. This could take a little while."

We moved into the living room to the more comfortable chairs. Dad closed his eyes for a moment as though deep in thought, then gazing at the ceiling began relating a detailed story about his mother I had never heard before. I felt like I was being allowed to peak at a never-before seen movie of my ancestry.

"Your grandfather Charlie was an interesting man. I loved my father, but sometimes I hated him. He had a still, and made his own whiskey and other moonshine. The thing is, well, y'see, he would get drunk and then beat my mother." He sighed and I tried not to look too shocked at the revelation, afraid I might interrupt his train of thought. "Being the youngest kid, I never felt I could stand up to him too much without being whipped to a pulp myself, although I did try a few times. When I was a teenager, the beatings had pretty much stopped, or at least ones I knew about."

"Did he beat you guys much?"

"Not as much as Mama. He seemed to save the worst of his anger for her, God rest her soul. You remind me a lot of her, Cheryl. She was tall and strong, never complained much. I believe in spite of everything, she found *something* lovable in my Dad. But mainly, she stayed with him to protect us from him for as long as she could. The farm needed a lot of work, and she would put on men's work boots and get in there, working as hard as any man. I always admired her determination to get things done."

"Grandma Mary sounds like a pretty tough cookie, huh?"

He chuckled. "When she needed to be, yes. But she was a sweet, soft-spoken woman who loved the Lord more than anything. And she always trusted God that everything would be all right. When I was sixteen World War I was still going on. My brothers were working at our little general store and I was bored with life on the farm. I begged my mother to help me enlist so I could see some action. They wouldn't take you unless you were eighteen. I wanted to join the Navy, see the world. Pretty funny, since I never was much of a swimmer!" He smiled at the memory.

"So, she fibbed for you?" I knew he had been in the Navy as a young man, because we had a large portrait of him in his old-fashioned uniform. In that picture, his hair looked full and straight, and when I was still a little girl, I had asked him why his hair wasn't curly in the picture. Both my parents had naturally curly hair, which I inherited, much to my dismay during my teens, since straight hair was the "in" style during much of the 1960s and '70s. Dad had laughed and told me they gave him a regulation "butch" haircut, really short. When Grandma Mary saw her baby's curls gone, she cried. After he sat for the picture, she begged the photographer to touch up the portrait and give him a full head of hair. So he did, just sans curls. That story always tickled me.

"Well, yes, she finally did. Not just yet, though. The war had already ended in 1919 when she finally gave in to my begging. I was barely seventeen, but she signed a paper saying I was really eighteen. Guess she figured I'd find a way to get in anyway, if she didn't help me. And the odds of me seeing any real action were pretty slim by that time. Back then, birth certificates weren't that easy to come by, so they would accept a signed statement from the parents. So off to sea I went, full of piss and vinegar, secretly hoping some skirmish would break out somewhere and I'd see some real battle action. But thank God, it didn't. I got to sail down to South America and lots of other places I wouldn't have seen otherwise. I felt like a man, not just a kid anymore. I was gone several months before I got leave to go home for a few days." He pulled out his handkerchief to blow his nose and quickly wiped away a tear.

"When I got home," he continued, "Mama was so sick. They told me she had been in bed for two weeks, in and out of consciousness. It was 1920. I knew she was dying." He paused. I waited patiently, knowing this was difficult. Dad and his mother had obviously been very close.

"I sat by her side for two days, wiping off her forehead with a cool cloth, and talking to her about my adventures, hoping that somehow she could hear me, know I was home with her. Your uncles Pete and Claude went for the doctor, because she seemed to be taking a turn for the worse."

"Where was Grandpa?" I was almost afraid to ask, but curiosity got the better of me.

Dad snorted in derision. "Off on a drunk. He really loved her, as best he could, despite how he treated her. He was too weak, too big of a coward to do anything in this crisis, though, so he crawled into a bottle, somewhere up in the hills. I hated him for that." He took a deep breath. "Anyway, while my brothers were off trying to get the doctor to come back with them from Roanoke, I was drifting off to sleep in the chair by her bed. Suddenly, I jerked awake to find her sitting straight up, looking out the window. I was almost afraid to say anything, because we had begun to think she was never going to come out of the coma."

His eyes got misty at the memory. "She said, 'Look out there, Walter, in the cornfield. It's so beautiful, son. Jesus is walking through the cornfield, coming to get me and take me home.' She gave me a bright-eyed happy look, then sunk back on her pillow, a peaceful smile on her face. And she was gone." He stopped and gazed outside for a long moment.

Finally I broke the silence. "Well, I know she was glad you were there with her to see how happy she was. Um, what happened with the doctor? Did he show up with your brothers later?"

"No, that's another interesting thing. I know you've been reading about Edgar Cayce. I know who he was. He lived in Virginia Beach."

I was taken aback that my father had even noticed a book I was reading. I'd been a voracious reader all my life, but he seldom seemed aware of what book my nose was stuck behind.

"Well, someone had told me Mr. Cayce talked about the kind of thing that happened next, I mean that day with my brothers. They got to the bridge to go into town, but there had been a bad thunderstorm the night before and the bridge was washed out. They started arguing about how they could get into town, and Pete looked at his watch, knowing time was running short. Just then, they both saw a red light of some sort shoot straight up out of the river, right up into the early evening sky."

I took in a deep breath, because Edgar Cayce had indeed referred to such lights rising out of the water, indicating a soul's departure from the Earth plane. I had no idea my father knew about or believed in such signs.

"Right at the time Pete looked at his watch, I had just written down the time she passed, so the doctor could put it on the death certificate. Cheryl, it was the exact same time. Isn't that something?"

"Yes, it sure is, Dad. Do you believe about signs like that, then? You must." I looked at him in a new light, realizing some of my gifts had undoubtedly come from the Booth side of the family. Grandma Mary obviously had a vision at the time of her death, and Dad knew more about this subject than he had ever shared before. In retrospect, I believe he kept such things to himself out of respect for my mother's fear of the paranormal.

"I used to, Cheryl. I know Edgar Cayce helped a lot of people get well from really bad illnesses. He had a gift from God. I do believe that. And as far as signs, after seeing your mother today, I know I still believe in those, too, when they're that strong. Thanks for listening to me, honey." He patted my arm as he crossed to the door. Think I'll go outside and do some yard work. You have any homework?"

"No, not tonight. Gosh, thanks for sharing that with me, Dad. I would really love to hear anything else like that, any time you feel like talking about it." I felt closer to him, since he had taken me into his confidence and shared a rare story about his family. I knew now why he never talked much about his Dad. Throughout my childhood, I had picked up occasional snippets of conversation about Grandpa Charlie making "white lightning", but I'd never known he was an alcoholic, nor an abusive husband. Nothing to be too proud about there, so Dad usually kept quiet about such things. But Grandma having a touch of "second sight"? And Dad actually giving credence to a psychic I truly admired? *That* was truly exciting!

"Hooray for Hollywood..."

The rest of my sophomore year was fairly uneventful. I was enjoying high school a lot more than junior high, though. I had much more freedom and the ability to take more electives. I dived into both the music and theatre departments, singing in several ensembles, acting in a number of one-act plays, learning stagecraft and lighting and lots of things I'd always been drawn to, but hadn't been able to pursue before. The performance "bug" had bitten me really hard, and I tried out for everything that came along. I didn't appreciate nor understand the fact that seniors tended to get the best roles, whether they were the most talented or not. I knew I was better than many students who wound up getting cast, or receiving the best solos in chorus. But even though I thought it was unfair, I kept auditioning. Surely someone at Oak Park High School would give me a decent part someday! My determination caused my self-confidence to reach a whole new level. Even though I didn't know it then, the teachers were taking notice that "the Booth girl" wasn't going to just fade into the woodwork.

Dad was becoming more himself, day by day. In the spring of 1972, he and my brother Don began talking about doing a cross-country trip to California, so Dad could see his daughters on the coast and Johnny and I could travel further than we ever had before. We had all gone to Virginia when I was about ten. I'd met Dad's stepmother, also named Mary (apparently Charlie Booth had some karma with that name!). Grandpa had been gone for a long while, but she was still going strong. She was very kind and loving to us, especially to Johnny, so she had won a place in my heart. Her children, my Dad's step-brother and step-sisters, were also good people. I enjoyed meeting my cousins, but we never stayed in touch much after that visit. I have often regretted that.

Dad's girls in California were a bit more involved in our family life while I was growing up. They stayed with us once in awhile when they were on vacation; my sister Jeannine and her kids visited most often. Even when they moved to Hawaii when her husband was stationed there, she had been faithful about sending us Christmas presents, which I found very exotic. Moo-moos for Mom and I, macadamia nuts and candy from Oahu. Then they had lived in Japan for a few years. Her youngest son, Walter (named after Dad) was born in Sasebo. We used to jokingly wonder if he had a "Made in Japan" label on his little bottom! Since that time, she had divorced her husband, moved back to San Diego and was raising her three sons pretty much on her own. I was anxious to see the two older boys again, and to meet young Walter in person for the first time. My sister Millie was always funny and upbeat, and her two kids were fun to be around, although they were quite a bit older than I. In fact, they were both out of the house at the time we planned this trip. Millie lived in San Diego, too. The youngest of the three girls, Norma, lived in Northern California. She was pretty and soft-spoken. I looked forward to seeing all of them and especially was excited about visiting Disneyland and Hollywood, given my recent love affair with the theatre and my longtime love of movies.

Don laughingly agreed to my pleas to "let me drive at least *part* of the way. That's thousands of miles, you know. You guys are bound to get tired!"

"We'll let you drive once in awhile, but you have to let us decide when and where that will be, okay?"

"Aw, geez. All right, better than riding the whole time," I pouted.

Having this trip in sight made that spring seem endless, but summer finally arrived and we got all the details worked out. One bright morning, we packed Don's Maverick full as can be, and I climbed into the back seat with John's head on a pillow in my lap, his thin torso laying across most of the seat. Don started out driving, Dad in the middle, and my brother's friend Jerry on the outside. Jerry had relatives along the way, too. In fact, I'm still not sure how the Booths got invited along on this trip. I think Don and Dad got to talking and decided it might be a good way for all of us to move on and have a little fun, after all the stress of Mom's illness the year before.

In some ways, that all felt like it had happened years ago. I began to realize what a funny thing time is. When you're a little kid and swinging and playing in the back yard, the days seemed endless. Sometimes, even boring. Now that I was a teenager, it was surprising to discover that usually, there didn't seem to be enough hours in the day. I wasn't yet familiar with the concept that time is an illusion. But one thing I knew for certain, I was looking forward to the time we'd spend on this trip. What a great chance to get out of Missouri and see more of these United States! I was jazzed!

At least, for the first few hundred miles, I was jazzed. There were sure some long stretches of open land. We all tried not to laugh at Dad's observation of the desert as we went through New Mexico and Arizona. He'd shake his head as he gazed out the window. "What a waste!" was his oft-repeated comment. To a Virginia boy used to green, rolling hills, that desert with its cactus, sand and amazing heat seemed like an oversight on the Creator's part.

Don was good as his word. I did get to drive on a limited basis. Much of it on those straight, flat stretches of desert and four lane highways. But it helped pass the time.

We went to San Diego first. The plan was to spend some time with the girls there, then head up to Palo Alto, see Norma, then over through Salt Lake City on the way home. For some reason, Dad was determined to see the Mormon Tabernacle there. I think it was because he loved listening to their choir on the radio. Anyhow, by the time we arrived at Jeannine's, we were all very road-weary. After feeding him, I carried Johnny into the guest bedroom, laid him down on the middle of the bed and rejoined the adults in the living room. Alan, my oldest nephew, was in college. He offered to teach me to surf, which sounded exciting. Danny, the middle son, was a quiet boy, three years younger than I, and little five year old Walter was as cute as could be, but obviously spoiled. I could tell he didn't like competing with these "strangers" for his Mom's attention.

After a few minutes of conversation, I realized it was quieter than before. Always watchful of Johnny's well-being, I glanced back through the open door to his room. I was amazed to see his little body bouncing up and down on the bed! Like a shot, I flew into the room, got down on my hands and knees and pulled little Walter, screaming and kicking, from under the bed. Now I knew why the living room had gotten quiet! This child had decided to get attention by tormenting a defenseless crippled child. I was angrier than I ever remembered being as I automatically turned him over my knee and spanked him, hard.

""Don't you *ever* lay a finger on Johnny again, do you hear me?" Swat, Swat! SWAT!!! accentuated my furious words. I had never spanked a child in my life, but every maternal instinct I had was in full swing, along with my right arm. "What an awful bully you are, Walter!"

Jeannine stood in the doorway, horrified for a moment before rescuing her baby from her sister's rage. "Cheryl! I don't believe in spanking. I'm sure he didn't mean to hurt John."

"Oh, sure! And maybe if you *did* spank him, he'd know better than to do something stupid like that. He could have bounced Johnny off the bed and broken his neck, maybe even killed him!" I was a bit over-dramatic, perhaps, but still full of disbelief at what had just happened. I didn't care that I had just met this little kid. For my money, he was a brat and one I would not trust for a moment for the rest of our time there.

We all calmed down after that. But Dad chortled a bit when we rehashed it while getting ready for bed. "Your Mom would be proud of how you defended Johnny," was all he said. I knew he was actually pretty proud, himself.

My nephew Alan took me to La Jolla and taught me to body surf. I wasn't much good on the surfboard, but this bodysurfing stuff was fun, once I got the hang of it! We had several great days in San Diego. Johnny and I especially loved the great zoo there, and when we took him to the beach, he craned his neck and laid his head over to the side of his wheelchair so that he could see as well as hear the ocean. He had always loved the water. He laughed when I put him on a beach towel, then gently buried his little feet and legs in the sand.

Walter was actually trying to be sweet toward John now, so I let him help, but never took my eyes off him. He had developed a healthy respect, or possibly just downright fear, toward me. In one way, I felt badly we had gotten off to such a rough start, but on the other hand, I believe I may have helped opened his young eyes to the world of handicapped people. He asked me some questions about John, like what he liked to do, eat, and so on, and as I patiently answered his queries, I did my best to remember he was just a little kid. Maybe a sort of rotten, spoiled little kid, but that wasn't his fault. We parted on fairly friendly terms, but I know he must have talked about "crazy Aunt Cheryl" for many years!

We left Jeannine's, then spent some time at Millie's home. I played the piano and sang for her. The rock group *Chicago* was very popular then, so *Saturday in the Park* was one of the numbers I played, along with several selections from my beloved Carpenters. She was really impressed.

"Gosh, kiddo, you're *good*! Dad, why didn't you tell me Baby Sister could sing this well?" He didn't have time to answer before she went on. Millie loved to talk and she talked *fast*. "I'm telling you, Cheryl, you've got a shot at making it as a singer. If you ever want to move out here, you can live with me."

My eyes opened wide. "Really? Wow, thanks. I just might take you up on that someday!" We laughed, but I had a gut feeling that something had been set in motion. Now I had at least three family members who believed in my talent...Don, Johnny and Millie. Dad knew I could sing, but was still most supportive when I sang hymns or country western songs. We took our leave of my oldest sister, and I thanked her again for her support and hospitality.

As we drove up Interstate 5 through Orange County, much to my dismay, I was informed we hadn't the time nor the money to stop at Disneyland. Besides, I was the only one who really cared anything about the rides. Johnny couldn't have gone on any, and none of the adult guys wanted to. I felt gypped.

"Come on now, Cheryl. You're too big for something silly like Disneyland now. Besides, you've watched "The Wonderful World of Disney" for so many years, you must feel like you've been there already!" Dad's reasoning escaped me, so I sulked in the back seat, ticked off that I was caught at that awkward stage between being a kid and a mature adult. "Sometimes, being a teenager really sucks," I thought, as I glimpsed the tip of the Matterhorn ride from the highway.

I stayed in such a sour mood that when we got to Hollywood and stopped at the Griffith Park Observatory, I wouldn't even get out of the car. Heck, it was broad daylight. Why had we even bothered to stop here? No constellations to observe. Because it was free, no doubt. Don tried to cajole me out of the car.

"Come on, this is where they shot part of *Rebel Without a Cause.* You should at least get out and check it out because of that, Sis."

Although his intentions were good, I was mad. "I've never been a big James Dean fan, he was *your* hero. Give me Judy and Mickey, Kate Hepburn, John Wayne, anybody worthwhile! Who cares about this stupid observatory and some dumb '50s movie?" I turned my head away. Dad was rolling John around outside, so I had the car to myself A perfect place to pout. Even though I had to go to the bathroom, I refused to get out. Give me Disneyland, or give me nothing, I must have been thinking.

Don was at the end of his patience now. "Fine! Suit yourself, you big baby!" He hardly ever said a harsh word to me, so I was aware I was being a jerk. When they got back in the car, I apologized. They all pretended not to hear me, and I didn't blame them.

Next, we drove through downtown Hollywood, and I was amazed how gritty it looked, compared to all the old movie scenes I'd seen. We parked and strolled along the "Walk of Fame." This was more like it. I had a bit of a sense of deja vu, but chalked it up to being such a '30s and '40s movie buff. Throughout the rest of the trip, however, I felt an underlying excitement that didn't diminish. Slowly, I grew to believe I was going to live in Hollywood someday.

We stayed in Burbank that night, then began the long drive up the coast the next morning. Northern California was so beautiful, it took my breath away. I was falling more and more in love with the west coast, and with the ocean's strength and energy. Missouri seemed pretty dull in comparison. When we got to Palo Alto, my sweet sister Norma served us vanilla ice cream with fresh blueberries. She spoke in hushed tones always, almost in a little girl voice, although she was close to forty years of age at the time. Of all Dad's girls from his first marriage, I had spent the least amount of time with Norma. She was single, had never been married, but had an engagement years ago which Dad said ended badly. He felt she had never gotten over the pain from that.

She struck me as one of the gentlest people I had ever met. She had a beautiful countenance, and constantly massaged Johnny's hands and arms while talking to him, and his eyes and smiles showed how much he loved her energy. She had worked for *IBM* for many years, and I knew from what Dad said, she made good money. Therefore, I was surprised that her home was furnished sparsely. In fact, when we left, we all talked about how she seemed to enjoy living like a Spartan. That was okay, of course, it just seemed weird in comparison to the nice things Millie had in her home or to the comforts and personal touches Jeannine had added to hers.

We made our way across more desert land to Utah, which of course prompted Dad's now familiar muttering under his breath about the vast wasteland. Don and I locked eyes as he glanced in the rear view mirror and we smiled at each other. This trip was actually turning out to be pretty good. "Who knows? I can always go back to Disneyland when I'm on my own, someday," I comforted my disappointed little inner kid.

The Mormon temple in Salt Lake City was beautiful. I really enjoyed the tour we took, learning about Joseph Smith and his vision. I even bought a copy of *The Book of Mormon* because I realized this man was also psychic, in another way. And many of his beliefs about Jesus possibly visiting the Native Americans and other cultures intrigued me.

Once we made it back to good ol' K.C., MO, we were all pretty much ready to be home and get on with "life as usual." With one exception, for me, however. Almost every night that summer, I stood out on our porch and faced the west at sundown.

"I'll be back someday, California. I promise," was my mantra.

"Hear Me...Feel Me..."

October of that same year, 1972 was the first time "IT" happened. "IT" is the way I referred to a very clear Voice, which talks inside my head so clearly and precisely, that I am absolutely certain it is not my imagination. This first instance of clairaudience, in my junior year of high school, was quite a surprise to me. Since Mom died, besides taking care of Johnny on a more regular basis, I helped Dad out with a lot of domestic things which were never before part of my household duties.

Late one afternoon, I was headed upstairs from doing the wash. Dad was working at the car wash, and Johnny was asleep. I no sooner put one foot on the bottom stair when clear as a bell, I heard a Voice say, "Go look in the suitcase under the bed." I was startled so much I looked around, even though I knew no one was there. Next, I wondered if the TV or an upstairs radio were responsible. I stopped for a second, decided it must be my imagination, shrugged it off and took a couple more steps."Look in the suitcase under the bed downstairs. There's something you need to see!" the Voice persisted.

I froze on the stairway. Needless to say, my heart was pounding pretty hard. The "bed downstairs" referred to the finished room in the basement which my brother Don had previously occupied. He now had his own apartment downtown, so when we returned from our California adventure, Dad rented this space out to help pay off some of Mom's remaining medical bills.

I liked our young renter, Alex. He was in his early thirties; quiet and soft spoken, and he always paid Dad his rent on time. Seemed like he was out of town a lot, as on this particular occasion. I was certainly not a "snoop," but this Voice's specificity stirred my curiosity. I wasn't even sure there was a suitcase under his bed. But I found myself slowly, almost uncontrollably drawn into his room, hesitating at the foot of his bed before bending down to check out the disembodied voice's instructions.

"Go on, you must see this!" the Voice goaded.

"All right!" I yelled. Feeling foolish for shouting at the air, I knelt down to peer under the bed. Sure enough, there was a suitcase! I waited a few seconds, then not wanting the voice to push me again, I gingerly reached for the handle and pulled it toward me. After taking a few deep breaths, I decided to flip the latches. What if there was something illegal inside? I closed my eyes, and pushed on the locks. Nothing happened.

"Aha!" I gloated. "Locked!" I quickly returned the suitcase to its rightful spot and stood up. "Okay, Whoever or Whatever you are, end of story. I'm no lock-picker. I've never been a snoop and I'm not about to start." I headed out of the room and jogged up the stairs.

"Wait!" the voice entreated. "The key is in the pocket of the bathrobe, hanging on the hook just inside his closet."

"Oh, man!" I was dismayed. This was getting too strange; I hated violating Alex's privacy this way. But this all-knowing, pushy voice was not going to let me rest, that was clear. "Okay, okay! I'll check out your key theory, but it better be there, or we're done. You understand, 'Voice'?"

There was no answer as I went back into the room, walked over to the closet, took another deep breath and quickly opened the door. Hanging right in front of me was a bathrobe with one pocket. Anxious to get this over with, I plunged my hand inside and felt my fingers close around a small key. I felt slightly sick, yet somewhat exhilarated. At least this Voice gave accurate information! What aroused my curiosity most at the moment was what exactly might be in the suitcase.

"Okay, Cheryl," I muttered, "Let's get this over with, and shut up this crazy Voice once and for all."

I got on my knees, pulled the bag toward me and tried the key. Of course, it fit. I wasn't shocked, given what had gone on up to this point. Praying there wasn't a bomb or anything like that, I threw back the lid of the suitcase to reveal...magazines. *Magazines?* What the...

These were unlike any publications I'd seen before. I quickly picked one up and opened it, to find myself staring at a beautiful male body builder, wearing nothing but a smile. I slammed the magazine closed in order to clear my head. I waited a moment before picking up another one and flipping through the pages...then another, and another. These were obviously magazines for men who were sexually interested in men. Homosexual magazines! I was not especially upset to put two and two together, and figure out Alex was gay. Frankly, I really didn't care. He was a nice man with impeccable manners who could be quite funny. I liked him very much. What shocked me was discovering there *was* such a thing as specialty magazines designed for this particular readership. I was an extremely naive teenager. I'd simply never considered anything like this before.

I carefully put the periodicals back in the same order I found them, and relocked the suitcase. I hurriedly slipped it under the bed to its assigned space, returned the key to the robe pocket and closed the closet door. I resolved never to go through Alex's things again. Before climbing the stairs, I decided to confront my invisible "spy." Not knowing where else to focus my attention, I looked upward.

"Okay, what was that all about, huh? C'mon, I wanna know why it was so important for me to see that, to find out about Alex's lifestyle that way. I still think he's a fine person. Whatever he chooses to do in his private personal life doesn't change that one bit as far as I'm concerned. So what was the point? Answer me!"

The Voice quietly replied, "You have discovered the point, exactly. In the future, if others berate this man or others like him, because of what you just learned, you'll know to look past that and value the person. *That's* the point."

I digested this. It made sense, but talking with this unseen Voice was creeping me out. "Okay, great. Thanks for the civics lesson, I guess. Now let me tell you something, you, you....you, 'Voice,' you! Go away! Leave me alone! I'm not sure who or what you are. You could be the devil, for all I know. Heck, I can't even tell anyone about this because they'll never believe me! If I start telling people a voice in my head told me to trespass through someone's private property, they'll lock me up for sure, for more than one reason! So just go away, you understand? I'm not ready for this, and I don't like it. *Go away!!*"

There was no reply. I waited for my pulse to return to normal before finally going upstairs. Part of me wanted to sort out what just happened, but another part wanted to ignore it, just forget it. That part won, except for the forgetting part. I never forgot this first incident of clairaudience. I didn't understand it, so simply didn't talk about it. Especially not to my Dad.

As for Alex, he was gone for nearly another week. His mother called our house a few times and we didn't really know what to say; so we told her we'd have him call her as soon as we saw him, and we prayed for his safe return. In fact, at one point Dad decided he was going to call Alex's mother back and suggest she file a missing person's report. Just minutes after he told me his intention, Alex walked in the front door. He smiled at us weakly.

"Hello there, Cheryl...Mr. Booth. Good to see you."

"Oh, good to see *you*, Alex! Are you okay? We've been wondering about you..." I went up and gently squeezed his shoulder.

He really looked like he could use a hug; he seemed pretty shaken up. I thought Dad would think that was weird, though. Hugging relatives, close friends and people at church was okay in my Dad's book, but this young man fit none of those categories. My Dad was overly protective of his teenage daughter, and I didn't want to cause Alex any more problems.

"I'm fine, really. I...I just need to talk to your father in private, if you don't mind."

He looked anxiously at my Dad, then at me, his eyes seeming to plead for just a shred of understanding. Dad nodded, and motioned with a tilt of his head for me to go down the hall to my room.

"Sure, no problem. See you later."

"Right, later." Alex seemed relieved. He looked very disheveled. Unshaven, rumpled. Pretty much the antithesis of his typical immaculate grooming.

I went toward my room and ducked around the corner until they adjourned to the kitchen table. I waited just a few seconds, then stealthily eased back down the hall, just within earshot. I hated to eavesdrop, but given my recent experience with the "Voice" I was exceptionally interested.

I discovered by carefully standing at a certain angle just inside the hall bathroom, I could see the reflection of the back of Alex's head in the mirror, and my father sitting across from him. I strained to hear as they talked in low tones.

"So...that's what happened. I'm ashamed, but I feel I owe you the truth. I'm sorry to have worried you, Mr. Booth. It was Mardi Gras, and my friends and I, well, we were drunk, and impaired judgment landed us in jail. It was awful." He held his head in his hands, and rocked himself like a small child.

My father looked at him with a strange mixture of pity and contempt. He covered his mouth, turned his head and coughed. Then he steadily fixed his eyes upon Alex, and just waited. The power of his gaze compelled Alex to finally look up and make eye contact. Years of experience had taught me this body language signaled something pretty serious was about to be said.

"Well, Alex...what bothers me the most is your poor mother didn't have a clue as to where you were. Be sure you call her right away, son. You worried her sick, you know? Whatever you do with your life is your business, but I can't have this kind of example in my house, where I'm bringing up a young teenage girl and her crippled little brother. It's just not right. You can certainly stay through the end of this month, but then I have to ask you to find another place to live. Nothing personal. I just have a family to protect from any, well, from any potential scandal. You understand, don't you?"

Alex wiped his eyes. "Oh, sure. No problem. I brought this on myself. I just wanted to be honest with you. You've been great, sir. More than fair. I've made my own bed, and...well..." He stood up and extended his hand to my father, who hesitated a moment before shaking it.

"I'll call my mother right away, then I'll start working on a new place to live. Thank you, sir."

"That's all right. Good luck." Dad awkwardly patted him on the shoulder. I scooted around the corner into my room and sat down at my desk, acting as though I knew nothing of this conversation. A few moments later, Dad tapped on my door.

"Honey, Alex just told me where he's been all this time...he's, ah... well, he's been in jail, Cheryl. He's going to be moving out soon." He stared at the floor.

"Oh, gosh. Alex in jail? That's pretty weird. He's such a nice guy." I decided not to push it by asking why he'd been incarcerated. I was pretty sure that would force my father into telling me a fib, and he looked pretty miserable already. He didn't need more pressure. I was sure it had something to do with Alex's lifestyle, though. "Well, okay, Dad. Is he all right? He doesn't have to go back to jail, does he?"

"No, no, nothing like that. I don't even think this will be on his permanent record or anything. We just talked it over, and decided it would be better for him to find another place to live. So..." he frowned for a minute then suddenly, his face brightened. "Well, hey! Y'know how you've talked about wanting more privacy, and a bigger room? Once he moves out, why don't we fix up that room for you downstairs? Would you like that?"

Poor Dad! Trying his best to find the silver lining in all this. He hated to turn out anyone in need, but his obligation to protect his family always came first. He needed to get his mind off what had just taken place.

"Oh, yeah, that'll be great! But...won't we need to take in another boarder, Dad? To help with the bills and all?"

"No, no...I don't want another boarder. Too hard to figure out what people have going on in their lives these days. We'll be just fine. I'll get another part-time job if I have to."

At this point in our relationship, I often kidded my father, calling him a "tough old bird." He loved it, he actually thrived on teasing. After Mom died, I thought Dad could be rather gruff at times. But he was still a big teddy bear underneath it all and once I figured that out, we started growing closer. He was seventy years old at the time of this incident, and as determined as ever to provide the best home he could for his children.

"Okay, or I can get a part-time job myself after school and on weekends..."

He interrupted, "Now, hold on, honey. You gave up most of your social life last year when your Mom died to help out with Johnny. Did you think I didn't notice, or that I don't appreciate that?" My father's clear, blue-gray eyes shone with wisdom and kindness.

Up to that point, I had felt on many occasions as though he took for granted my teenage wants to go to parties and belong to extracurricular activities at school. During my sophomore year, I gave up opportunities to be involved in a number of singing groups and plays, and turned down a few parties here and there, but did so willingly, for the most part. I was mature enough to realize that Dad never expected to outlive Mom, being her senior by fifteen years. He'd gone into shock for several months; family obligations outweighed my selfish wants, so I gladly took on the lion's share of Johnny's care. This was my Dad's way of letting me know he was "snapping out of it," willing to take on more care-giving duties for his son. He wanted me to enjoy the rest of high school as much as possible.

He was remarkable. Most of my friends' parents were a good thirty years younger than my father, but I didn't care. I was intensely proud of him. He was strong, self-educated and levelheaded. A very 'cool dude' in my eyes. The bottom line was, Walter Booth was a survivor, a great teacher and in many ways, he proved he was truly my best friend.

I felt sorry for Alex. He must have briefly shared some intimate details about his lifestyle with my father, moments before I overheard the rest of their conversation. Remember how I mentioned dubbing my father "Archie Bunker?" Well, I don't know whether having a "jailbird" as a boarder bothered him more than the fact the boarder was homosexual, or whether the combination was just too overwhelming. I do know he acted in what he felt was his family's best interest, and saw past "labels" at least enough to allow Alex to live in peace under our roof for the rest of that month.

Today, I consider myself to be liberal. I actually have my father to thank for that. Sometimes we learn by example from parents and elders how *not* to overreact to certain situations. Behavior patterns and prejudice are certainly not inherited. We have free will there, as in every other area of our lives. Often we receive definition of what we *do* want in our lives, by being exposed to or creating situations we do *not* want to recreate.

So, to wind up this first encounter with a Voice from another dimension, I moved downstairs once Alex left, and enjoyed more space and alone time. I nearly wore out my Billy Joel and Jim Croce records, and secretly had some "forbidden" Beatles tapes some friends had made for me, which I only played when Dad was out of the house. The basement became my sanctuary and I pretended it was my first apartment. I remember looking around there those first few weeks, repeating my admonition that I would not listen to any voices inside my head, told "them" they "just better keep their mouths shut." And amazingly, "they" did. I didn't think much more about this experience until I met Brian Hurst, then began sitting in a psychic development circle myself, fourteen years later.

Chapter Eight

Higher Learning?

I had a lot more fun in my junior year, since I had now been given permission for my schedule to include more extracurricular activities. I was in the "pop chorus", the *Oak Street Singers*. This select group performed fun, current pop tunes for many venues. I also began setting my sites on gaining entry to another exclusive group, the Thespian Society. I worked on as many crews for plays and productions as I could, in addition to taking small roles here and there, including being in the chorus for that year's musical, *Flower Drum Song*. The fact that a white bread, suburban school would even take on such a task is quite amusing, in retrospect. Dad thought I had surely gone mad. Let me explain.

We had no students of color in my class, not even in the whole school, to my knowledge. Yet here we were, doing this musical about San Francisco's Chinatown and its inhabitants. So how were all these Anglophiles going to pull this off? By dying our hair black (temporary *Clairol* products) and using surgical eye tape, cut to fit our eyelids so as to pull them back in an assimilation of Asian-shaped eyes, which was then covered with greasepaint. It was quite awhile before we could all walk around without tilting our heads backward in order to see where we were going. By today's standards, this would certainly be considered politically incorrect. But this was 1973, royalties for that particular musical were less than for others we could have done, and for whatever other reasons, the drama and music departments agreed to produce it. I was simply happy to be in the chorus and one of the featured "Hot Box Girls" quartet in a night club scene. I was paying my dues, feeling more and more confident that in my senior year, I would be rewarded with a substantial role in the musical, which would be announced at the beginning of the 1973-'74 school year.

I was still taking piano and voice lessons and performing in recitals. I had also been picking up extra money here and there teaching younger kids piano lessons, since I was fifteen. Now that I had a car, I could drive to their homes, which went over very favorably with their parents.

Johnny and Dad were doing much better all the time. In general, life was pretty good. We all still missed Mom, of course. But we kept talking with her in our own ways. I had a few dreams about her, one that had disturbed me at first. I woke up to find her sitting on the edge of my bed, crying.

"Mom, what's wrong?" I asked, reaching out to touch her shoulder. She motioned that I shouldn't do that, and somehow I knew that would make her have to leave. So I asked the question again. She didn't respond verbally, but telepathically I heard, "It's your Grandma, Cheryl. She's getting ready to come over here pretty soon and I'm worried about her."

"Why, Mom? You don't think she's made her peace with God?"

She nodded, a tear trickling down her face. "I'm not sure she's open to that. I may not get to see her too much and don't know if I can help her before she gets here. I've tried, but she's not open to letting me into her dreams."

This was interesting. Grandma Bertha always had a bit of a mean streak, to be sure, so that didn't surprise me. Mom's attempts to help her own mother were not surprising, either, but I didn't get why they might not see one another that much on the other side. Mom's image was fading, so I quickly focused on talking again.

"Well, I'll pray for her, too, Mom. Will that help?"

She nodded and smiled.

"We miss you, Mom. You look beautiful." I paused. She was thinner than I had ever seen her, like I'd seen in pictures when she was in her thirties, pretty and slender. "I wish you could talk with me more." Now it was my turn to release a few tears.

"I'll try, honey. It should get easier as time goes on. I'm proud of you, Cheryl Ellen. I love you," came the final message as she held her arms out and then disappeared.

I sat up straight in bed, unsure whether I had dreamed this encounter or had a vision. Not sure what the difference was, anyway, I was grateful to have made what felt like real, loving contact with my mother. She was proud of me! That meant so much. I told Dad about it at breakfast. He was very interested and supportive.

"Gosh, that's great she looked so young and healthy. Must mean her spirit is doing really well, huh?"

"Yes, I believe so, Dad. Don't know what to do about Grandma, though. Just add her to my prayers, since I promised, I guess."

"That's all your mother expects you to do, honey," he replied. "Everybody's relationship with God is up to them to develop, or not."

The school year ended happily. I had some new friends because of the musical. All the hours we spent in rehearsal and performance were my first taste of having an "extended theatre family." A girl who was a year younger named Donna became a close friend. Her own mother had died of the same type of cancer as mine, just that year. I was glad I could be there and help in any way I could. The similarity of our losses created a strong bond. Another girl in my own class, Martha, became another good friend. She was very popular in the music and theatre groups, a pretty girl, with a great sense of humor, and what's more, she was truly a rebel, something I admired deeply. She wore funky clothes that she got at high-end thrift shops, then gave them her own brand of class.

Several of my friends and I decided to go to summer music camp at Central Missouri State University in Warrensburg. Our music teacher, Mr. Grace, was an alumnus and always spoke fondly of CMSU. "Papa G," as we nicknamed him, was a strong, positive influence on my life and I wanted to emulate him, maybe even become a music teacher while pursuing my performance dreams.

Dad agreed I could go to the camp and wrote out a check for the expenses. He was still working at the carwash and taking on a few odd jobs here and there, along with collecting his social security check. Johnny and I had begun getting Social Security support, too, after Mom passed. So there was a bit more money coming in now to help pay down the still lingering medical bills. Dad was a bit concerned about having total care of Johnny for the whole week I would be away. We talked it over and he decided to do some research. We had no clue the results would very negatively impact our dear John.

Dad made some calls and got some brochures on a few local foster homes, which offered temporary stays to handicapped kids, who had family that needed a vacation they couldn't go along on and similar situations. The cost seemed pretty reasonable to him, and I certainly didn't blame him for wanting a week to himself. After all, I was really lucky to be able to go to music camp, learn a lot, but also would have a lot of fun with friends, while checking out what might become my future college home. Dad had been so wonderful with us since he had "come alive" again. I agreed that this might be a wonderful solution.

He decided to go with a family I will call "the Phillips." They had two full-time foster kids who were physically and/or mentally challenged, and a couple of guest beds that were open periodically for short-term visitors. We went to see their home. The middle-aged couple seemed nice enough, their home was clean and there was a nice back yard where I envisioned Johnny sitting in his wheelchair, listening to the birds and enjoying a summer afternoon. It seemed okay, so Dad gave them a deposit and we agreed to drop Johnny off the evening before I was to leave for music camp.

It was hard to leave Johnny there, in a way, because he had never been away from the family. My eyes filled with tears, but I didn't want Dad or Johnny to see me sad, so I hid it pretty well. I prayed that Johnny would be all right and we drove back home so I could finish packing for my "big week on campus."

I had a great time that week, singing in several ensembles, improving my sight-singing skills, playing in a piano recital, even working with a female barbershop quartet! Three of my friends and I shared a dorm room and stayed up late giggling, wondering what our senior year would be like. I actually had enough credits under my belt, I could have graduated a year early. But that goal to be a "star" in the musical was seductive. Besides, I wasn't ready to head off to college just yet. Dad and John needed me at home for another year, at least. The week flew by, full of fun, some hard work and a very satisfied feeling of performances well-done under time-condensed conditions. Our groups all performed well and I made some new friends from other area high schools.

Exhausted, but happy, I returned home that Sunday. The Rambler was sitting in the high school parking lot. I ran to the car, still on a natural high from the week's excitement. I started to get in the back, but Dad motioned for me to get in the front passenger seat.

"Where's Johnny?" I asked with surprise. "I want to see the little guy, hear about his big week, too." There was silence as Dad stared straight out the windshield before setting the car in motion.

"He's home, honey. Mary Beth is watching him. Something bad happened, Cheryl. Real bad." He sucked in a breath as though his heart and lungs weren't working correctly.

"Oh, my God, Dad! What's wrong? What happened to Johnny?"

He took another deep breath and in a wooden voice, said, "They hurt him at that foster home. Those goddamned idiots hurt our baby."

"What? I'll *kill* them!" I screamed, wild tears flying out of my eyes. "What did they do to him, Dad? Tell me!"

His voice remained very even. I'm sure he was suppressing his own rage. Dad didn't like getting mad, but our Irish tempers could certainly flare up, when push came to shove. I felt his fury rise as I saw his knuckles grow whiter as he clutched the steering wheel.

"I want you to prepare yourself. It isn't pretty. They, um..." his voice finally cracked with emotion, "they hit him with a hammer, or put his head in some kind of vice. I'm not sure exactly how or what, but there are two holes on the sides of his head..."

"*God*! I can't believe this! Take me over there right now, Dad. I'll kill those bastards!"

"You think I didn't want to do that? I'm going to sue them, that's the most I can do and not go to jail. I wanted to blow them away, just like you want to hurt them. But God wouldn't want us to do that. They never even told me it had happened, just gave him back to me that way. I feel sick we ever took him there. It's all my fault." He was crying in earnest now and had to pull the car over into the McDonald's parking lot down the street from the house.

"Oh, Dad, I'm so sorry. I shouldn't have gone to camp. It's not your fault. If I hadn't been selfish..."

He wiped his eyes on his sleeve. "Cheryl, stop right there. You are entitled to have a life, young lady. You didn't make these people into monsters. They did it themselves. Don't blame yourself, you hear?"

"Okay, but don't put yourself through this torture, either, Dad. Are you okay?" I put my hand over his, which was still clutching the steering wheel. His knuckles were white, he was squeezing it so tight. He was every bit as angry as I, just holding it in.

"Me? I'm fine. Don't worry about me, honey." He started the car again and we headed home. "But prepare yourself to be shocked at little Johnny's injuries. It's sick, that's what it is."

"I want to see him. How's he acted since he's been home?"

"Well, a little dazed, understandably. But he's still his sweet self. He probably even loved those sons-of-bitches while they were hurting him. He's such a little angel, y'know?"

"He sure is, Dad. Poor little guy!" At the moment, I couldn't think of taking a Christian attitude. This was unforgivably heinous, to inflict violence on a defenseless, crippled child. I bolted out of the car before it had come to a complete stop and ran inside the house. Johnny was on the couch. Mary Beth, the babysitter, saw the wild look in my eyes.

"Cheryl, it's..."

I saw the blank look in John's eyes as he moved his head slightly in my direction. Then horror overcame me and an unintelligible scream flew out of my mouth. I could see his skull moving under the silver dollar-sized hole above and slightly behind his ear. He jumped and looked the other way. There was a matching hole on the other side of his head. I now understood why Dad thought they had put him in some kind of vice grip.

I scooped John up gently in my arms, rocking him as I said in a sing-song voice, "It's okay, honey. It's gonna be all right. Sissy's home, God will heal your head." I kissed him above his wounds, which were showing signs of infection around the edges. "What have you put on these things, Dad? Any Neosporin or anything?"

"I didn't know what to do...I daubed 'em with some peroxide, just real easy..." His voice trailed off, sounding helpless and confused.

"Don't worry. I'll go get the ointment. It'll help fight the infection." I glanced at the clock. "Could we call Dr. McKendrick and get John to his office before it closes? Maybe he'll help us pin these bastards to the wall. Let's see if we can get him to examine John and make a statement that it's obvious he was injured." I was furious, blind with rage. "The hell with turning the other cheek. I want to crucify these animals! They deserve to die! How many other helpless kids have they maimed, or maybe even killed. Oh, Johnny, we're so sorry, so sorry!" I rocked him back and forth, hoping to ease both his pain and mine.

"Good idea. I'll call right now." Dad all but ran to the phone. Poor fellow. He had just picked John up earlier this same day and was obviously in shock himself. I heard him telling our family doctor a nutshell version of what happened, including giving him the name and phone number of the Phillips. He hung up, then rushed back into the room, grabbing pillows and blankets to prop around John in the car.

"That's okay, Dad. I'm going to hold him. I'll fasten the seat belt around us both. Let's just go. Dr. McKendrick said he'll testify?"

"Sure did. He's as appalled as we are. We have to hurry, though, to get in before closing. Thanks, Mary Beth." He handed her a five dollar bill. "Appreciate you helping out."

There were tears in her eyes, too. "I'm just so sorry this happened, Mr. Booth, Cheryl...I don't know what to say. Johnny is such a sweetheart. How could anyone do this?"

"I don't know," I muttered between clenched teeth, "but I plan to do everything in my power to stop them from hurting anyone else!"

We drove in silence to the doctor's office, I still rocked back and forth ever so slightly, little John's body limply pressed against mine. His breathing and heart rate seemed normal, as far as I could tell. But his eyes still had that glazed, faraway look. I began to wonder if he was preparing to die.

We rushed into the doctor's office. Dad marched up to the reception desk and I sat down with John. "I called Jim, er, Dr. McKendrick just a few minutes ago. This is an emergency. He said he'd squeeze us in."

She looked up, somewhat flustered. "It'll be just a few minutes, Mr. Booth. The doctor is finishing up with someone else."

Dad sat down beside us in the waiting room. In about ten minutes, the receptionist opened the door. I thought it was curious no one had left. There wasn't another exit...where was the person the doctor had been busy with? In fact, there hadn't been another car in the parking lot. All these thoughts rushed through my mind then disappeared as we stepped into his office. We usually saw him in an examination room, but she led us to his office door. I looked at the skeleton standing in the corner, all his medical books behind him on the massive bookshelves. He remained seated behind his big mahogany desk.

"Hello, Jim. Thanks for seeing us on such short notice." Dad reached across the desk and shook his hand. The doctor wasn't getting up to look at John. What was wrong with him? Something didn't feel right.

"Well, Walter, I'm happy to take a look." Slowly he moved around the desk to stand by my side. "Hello, young lady," he smiled at me.

I didn't return the smile. I felt sick to my stomach. "Here he is, Doc. Isn't it awful? Can you imagine anyone hurting an innocent child this way?"

He looked at the wounds, made some clucking noises with his tongue, and then returned to his desk.

"I'll write you a 'script for some antibiotics, which should get rid of that infection right away." He began doing that, his manner matter-of-fact and calm. I was outraged.

"That's not all you're going to write, is it? What about a statement as to how obvious it is they hurt him, nearly killed the poor kid?" My heart felt as though it would burst out of my chest. The doctor remained so calm, so aloof. This infuriated me even more.

"Well, I called the Phillips family to get their side of the story. They claim this happened at the dentist's office. That they took John in for a checkup and the dentist put some clamps on his head, way too tight."

I was flabbergasted. "A *dentist*? Are they insane, thinking we'd believe that? What's this dentist's name? Where's his office?" I demanded.

"Well, I don't know. There were no witnesses to this, so unfortunately, there's no real case to be made here." His voice was flat and had a note of finality, dismissal. A strong gut instinct revealed a probable scenario in my mind's eye.

Dad was speechless during what unfolded next. I carried John over, holding him against me and standing directly where the "good doctor" would have to look at us.

"Dr. McKendrick, you've been our family doctor for many years. My mother trusted you, even when you said she had to go to the cancer research hospital, where they killed her with those damned experimental drugs. I still wanted to trust you after that. But *this*? This is unconscionable. How much money did the Phillips offer you to keep your mouth shut? They bought you off so you wouldn't testify, didn't they?"

It reminded me of a scene out of *Columbo* or *Perry Mason*. I could tell by the guilty look on his face I had nailed him, or at the very least come close to describing what had happened.

"Now see here, Cheryl, I've never had a teenager address me in this way. How dare you accuse me..."

"How dare I accuse *you*? How dare you refuse to defend Johnny, to dishonor our mother's trust of you. If I believed she was really in that grave, I know she'd be rolling in it right now. You stink, Dr. McKendrick. You and every doctor who's ever given in to a bribe. You make me sick. You're not our doctor anymore. God's gonna get you for this. As far as I'm concerned, you can just go to hell!" I swung on my heel and carried John out of there, once and for all.

Dad followed, his mouth hanging open slightly.

The receptionist gave me a confused look, so I flipped her off with my free hand. The whole kit 'n caboodle of them could fry as far as I was concerned.

Dad got in the car, still staring at me in amazement. He cleared his throat. "I guess you told him off, honey. I wanted to, I really feel what you believe happened is the truth. Makes me sick I didn't have the guts to stand up to him. Thank God you did." He started the motor and began backing out of the lot. "I thought Jim was our friend. I'm really disappointed."

I snorted in derision. "His only friend is the almighty dollar, Daddy. He'll pay for this, someday. Let's get John home and ready for bed. Now, now, Johnny," I soothed as I began rocking a bit again. "It's time to go home, have a bath and go to bed. Now, now, it's all gonna be all right."

He looked up and we made real eye contact for the first time that afternoon. His eyes looked a bit clearer, and a slight smile came across his sweet face.

"I good!" he intoned softly.

"You sure got that straight, honey. You're the goodest!" We rode home in silence. I was immersed in plotting how to blow up the Phillips' house or release poisonous snakes through their vents. I don't know what occupied Dad's thoughts. My childish plans of revenge would never take form, but they made me feel a little better for awhile.

As for John, he gradually got back to being his sweet, happy self. It took months for the holes to grow new skin and heal over completely. His hair never grew in enough to fully cover the scars. It was an expensive lesson for all of us with regard to trusting others too much with such a precious responsibility. Several of our friends who saw the wounds thought we should still prosecute, but the doctor's betrayal had taken the wind out of Dad's sails. He just decided to pray about it, to try to forgive. I knew we would never forget, though.

I don't doubt Dad asked God to judge the Phillips very strictly. In my vengeful mood, I prayed someone might hit *them* on the head with a ball pin hammer, which is what we finally decided must have happened to John, according to the size and depth of the holes. I vowed to John that some day, I would find some way to tell his story and hopefully encourage other families to be cautious as to whom they turn over the care of their loved ones. After a couple of months, Dad and I silently agreed to simply never talk about it again. Dr. McKendrick died not too long after that. I wondered if he'd be held accountable in the afterlife with regard to that choice, or Heaven help him if my mother got ahold of him!

How Sweet It is

That fall, I threw myself into my senior year full blast. Because I had racked up all my necessary graduation credits, I opted for all electives, all music, theatre and creative writing. To top it off, I was doing some cadet teaching at an elementary school just a mile from Oak Park. I had a parking lot pass with handwritten permission to go teach two days a week. There were two blank spots left open, so it didn't take much for me to convince myself to forge in two more days. Hey! I was seventeen, I had all my necessary credits, I didn't technically even have to be there, right? That was my cockeyed reasoning. We were on what they referred to as "modular scheduling" at Oak Park. They divided the day up into eighteen "mods" of time, approximately twelve minutes each, I think. Most classes lasted either two or three mods. I had a lot of "free mods" for study hall or whatever else I chose to do.

My rebellious friend Martha had a lot of free mods as well, and what we chose to do when I freed the Gremlin from the student parking lot with my phony pass days was go to the movies, go to Dunking

Donuts, drive around and goof on people, whatever. We used to drive out to K.C. International airport and just watch people, observe their weird behaviors, make up stories to fit the partings and greetings we witnessed. We jokingly called it "method acting study", so figured we could try and get credit for it in drama class if we ever got caught. We flew under the radar and never did.

The musical was announced the first three weeks into the new school year. We would be doing *Brigadoon.* I had never seen this particular movie, but anything Celtic which involved that type of accent intrigued me, big fan of dialects that I'd always been. I quickly learned there was a great part for an alto, the comedy lead of Meg Brockie, and I set my cap, er um, tam, for that plum role. At the first go-round of auditions, I knew I impressed the audition panel of teachers, because Mrs. Hudson (the P.E. coach who doubled as choreographer) and Mr. Coakley (the drama teacher who had become a good friend and mentor to me) stood up and gave me a standing ovation. My idol from the music division, Papa G, however, sat there smiling and just clapped a couple of times. I was surprised and somewhat hurt. The one whose approval I most wanted wasn't giving it. What had I done wrong? Later, I overheard heard some of the kids talking backstage. I was hidden by the cloak of darkness the wing curtains provided and eavesdropped, once I heard my name mentioned.

"Hey, Booth sure can belt, can't she?"

"Yeah, but I know something you don't know!" A female classmate, but not a close friend of mine, taunted.

"Oh, yeah? There's no other senior alto that stands a chance, as far as I can tell."

"Well, Nicki sure does." The smug young lady sure gave up her secret easily.

"Nicki! The one who accompanies everything, almost every choral group we've got? You're kidding! She's a great pianist, but as for singing, I dunno..."

"Well, I do! She told me Mr. Grace promised her Meg, because of all the years she's had to sit behind the ivories, not getting enough attention."

I almost gasped out loud, but didn't want to betray my presence. I felt my face go flush, due more to what felt like a backstabbing of me rather than giving away my illicit snooping. How *could* he promise her that, after all the hard work I'd put in the past two years? I liked Nicki a lot, she was a sweet kid and very funny; but this guy was right, she was a pianist, definitely *not* a singer. And she'd never taken any drama classes. My mind began racing, trying to concoct a clever plan so that justice (i.e., my ego, would be served). Hell, I could play the piano, but you didn't see me trying to steal *her* thunder, did you? I knew I was most naturally gifted as a singer, singing always had been the part of music that came most naturally to me. And acting through singing, well, that was second nature to me. The musical theatre was my destiny. This was so unfair!

Callback auditions were posted the next day. They would be held the day after tomorrow. They had us all slated at particular time slots. I was supposed to go several people after Nicki. My conniving mind pulled up every scene from every Judy & Mickey movie about "let's put on a show" I could conjure up. What was the best way to grandstand someone? Aha! I had it! This ploy would involve a bit of acting in and of itself, but I had such a reputation as an honest "goody two-shoes" among the teachers, getting them to swallow this little white lie would be a cinch.

The day of callbacks, I waited until the person before Nicki was about done with her song. I walked up behind the panel of teachers and crouched behind their theatre seats.

"Hi! Sorry to bother you all, but I just got a call from my Dad. I have to hurry home to take my little brother to the dentist, Dad has a flat tire and there's no way he can change it on time. Is there any way I can go, well, maybe after Nicki? Would that be okay?"

Mr. Coakley smiled and squeezed my hand. "You're so devoted to your Dad and brother, Cheryl. Ain't she a good kid, Nancy?" He asked Mrs. H. "Bill, what a devoted lass this Cheryl of ours be, don't you agree?" They both smiled at his largesse. There was a reason he was the drama teacher! Mr. C had studied for the priesthood at one time in his life, then escaped that destiny and traded it to become a great drama teacher. It had taken me longer to develop a good rapport with him than with some of the other teachers, but we were friends now, and it was obvious he could see me as Meg. "It's fine with me if she follows Nicki. What do you say, Bill, Nancy? Any objections?"

"No, no, that's fine," they both nodded, falling right into my cleverly laid plot. Ah, what fools these mortals be at times, indeed!

I tried not to gloat as I made my way backstage and prepared to knock their socks off. Nicki read from the script in a rather stilted, wooden voice. Poor kid, wasn't her fault she had no acting ability. (Boy, I was conceited, but that's part of an actor's best ammunition at times! I prefer to remember it as self-confidence.) Then she went on to flub some of the difficult litany of Scottish names in Meg's showstopper song, *Me Mother's Weddin' Day*. I knew I had it in the bag for sure. As she left the stage, smiling confidently in Mr. Grace's direction, I took the stage as if I'd owned it all my life.

"I'd like to do the song first, then read afterward, if that's okay?" I gave no time for them to comment. "Maestro, if you please!" I smiled at the audition pianist. He launched into the same song Nicki had just stumbled through and I nailed it, brogue-perfect on every single stinkin' name, smiling and moving around in my best animated style. I heard them laughing at all the right cue spots and knew I had them in the palm of my hand. Then I read copy with Shawn Maples, the boy who would undoubtedly be cast as Jeff the American, flung back in time to this strange little Scottish town that appeared just once every hundred years. Meg set her cap for him and flirted her buns off, to no avail. I threw myself into it heart and soul. Again, laughter in all the right places. Another standing ovation, this time from all three judges, as well as several of my friends in the audience.

"Good show, Meg old girl! Bravo!" Mr. C huzzahed. He had called me "Meg." They *had* to give it to me. They just had to.

I bowed a couple of times, grinned like the Cheshire cat, curtseyed and hollered, "Thanks for letting me reschedule. Gotta run! See you tomorrow, lasses and laddies!"

I went home, exhilarated and not feeling one bit guilty for my one-upsmanship on poor, unsuspecting Nicki. After all, it was now or never, as far as my high school acting went. The phone rang later that evening. It was Papa G.

"Hello, may I speak to Meg, please?"

I squealed and launched into a full tilt brogue, throwing caution to the wind. "She's right here, young man! 'Tis a fine thing you're doing, William Grace. God bless ye!" I was beside myself with glee.

"Yeah, you pulled out all the stops, Cheryl. We know you'll do a wonderful job. We'll have the rehearsal schedule posted tomorrow. Oh, your buddy Martha? She'll be playing Fiona, the romantic lead. Thought you'd like to know that." I could hear the grin in his voice. Apparently he'd been outvoted regarding Nicki, but had decided to live with it.

"I won't let ye down, William, you'll see! Have a wonderful evenin', laddie!" I hung up the phone and did a bit of a jig. Dad looked at me as though I had a screw loose.

"Who in tarnation was that? Some guy asking you out or something?"

I didn't really date, and that was fine by Dad. He hadn't encouraged me to ever wear makeup or anything approaching flashy or suggestive clothes, especially since Mom had been gone. He was happy keeping his tomboy daughter safe at home.

"No, no, not some silly boy, me dear ol' Dad! T'was me music teacher, Mr. Grace. I have the comedy lead in *Brigadoon*, Daddy! You're gonna see your daughter's name up in lights some day, just like Judy in *A Star Is Born*." Judy Garland was still my ultimate musical heroine, although Barbra Streisand was right up there, too. This was 1973, remember, pre-VCRs and DVDs by many moons. I would set my alarm and get up at two a.m. so as to see rarely televised Garland films like *The Pirate* and *In The Good Old Summertime*. And I still faithfully watched *The Wizard of Oz* every single year. That story still has spiritual overtones for me. Dad thought I was slightly insane, but put up with my early morning madness as long as I didn't play the volume too loud. Sometimes when he had a touch of insomnia, or maybe was a little lonely, he'd even get up and watch the movies with me. Then I'd go back to bed, snap a few winks before it was time to get up and head toward school. It was always worth it to me, though. I still felt a strong bond with Judy Garland; Frances Ethel Gumm, the little gal with the great big voice. She was one of a kind, and certainly was a star that fought the school of hard knocks all her life. She died long before her time. I hoped from her vantage point in Heaven, maybe she'd be a kind of Glinda the Good for me; maybe Judy would look out over me and bless me with magical fairy dust as I launched my musical career!

Nothing could dull my happiness that night as I called my closest friends, especially Martha. We talked for hours about how great it would be to rehearse together a lot, as we were both in several key scenes. We probably also talked about what movie we were going to sneak out and see next! That year, we went to see *The Sting* and it was great; but the one that really impacted me was *Jesus Christ, Superstar*. Andrew Lloyd Weber was incredibly talented, that was a given, but oh, my! The script brought out so many things that my church-going years had failed to present, such as the very likely fact that Judas really did love Jesus, and felt he was helping to fulfill a prophecy through his actions. It opened my heart and eyes to that, and I no longer looked upon him as a pariah. The main reason that movie was so special to me at that time was because Dad had forbidden me to see it. "Sacrilegious!" was our church's battle cry. Some of the church members even picketed the theatres where it was shown. I never did tell Dad I'd gone to see it, although I played the soundtrack many, many times through that year and all through college. I don't think he ever realized what it was from; he never really listened to the words of my music, as long as it didn't sound like the Beatles! I still love the score to *J.C.* It's some of the best rock opera music ever written, as far as I'm concerned.

Johnny loved it that I was happy almost all the time during the next few months. He was always in tune with my moods. Thankfully, he had totally come back to being himself, and seemed to love his own school more and more. Periodically, when I skipped out on my fake pass, I'd go over to his school and volunteer. Dad thought I got credit for doing that and I let him assume that. I just went to spend some extra time with John and all the other little angels there. My rebellious side was starting to brew, under the surface, and all the other changes I was going through with my struggles about religion and philosophy could get very confusing. But being around these pure, sweet souls helped me feel grounded. We did basic exercises with the kids, most of whom were severely handicapped like John. We tried to get them to raise their heads, use their neck muscles, while holding a mirror under their faces as they leaned over their little crooked bodies.

"Bring your head up, John. Come on, Roxie! You can do it, head up! Up!" we'd encourage, clapping and hollering when they did. It took tremendous concentration for them to do even simple tasks like that with their limited range of motion. They played music for those kids and read to them. It was a wonderful form of camaraderie for them, and I was so happy John had that in his life.

Even though I was gone a lot, what with rehearsals, partying more and more with the drama freaks, costume fittings, and so on, John enjoyed hearing me sing and rehearse lines. I tape recorded all my cue lines in order to memorize my lines faster. While I *was* home, I sang almost nonstop, memorizing the entire score to *Brigadoon*, watching the film version with Gene Kelly several times, but not really liking it much. Why would I? They cut out Meg's big numbers in the edited, televised edition! Fools!

The musical would be produced in the spring. I lived, breathed and slept *Brigadoon* that winter, and also was nominated for a college scholarship during that timeframe. Resulting events proved to be a turning point in my belief system.

Edith, the Non-*Dingbat & Visualization*

Edith Lay, our wonderful neighbor across the street was such an invaluable adult for me to know. She helped me in so many ways, often took time to give me really good advice, and caused me to ponder many things my church upbringing had failed to introduce.

The year after my mother died, I complained to Edith about the general unfairness of life and God at large. She attended the Unity Church. I didn't know much about that faith, except that I'd driven past Unity Village in Lee's Summit occasionally, and read some articles and prayers in their magazine, *Daily Word*. The more I railed on to Edith, the madder I became, firing rhetorical questions at her out of my anger and confusion.

"How could a loving God allow people to die by the thousands every day from starvation and disease? And why would a benevolent, kind God strike an innocent like John with such a tremendous affliction at birth, or for that matter, what about all the other handicapped people in the world? What could they possibly have done to deserve such a fate? How could He in His 'infinite wisdom' have taken our mother away at the age of fifty-four? We need her more than He possibly can. *Why*?"

When I had finally exhausted that barrage, and sat there angrily wiping away tears, Edith smiled gently at me. "Well, those are questions that have plagued many people for many centuries, Cheryl. I don't have magical answers to any of them. All I can offer you is a consideration, all right?"

I nodded sullenly.

"Okay," she continued, "Let me ask you something. Did you ever give weight to the possibility that perhaps John *chose* the type of existence he's living in order to learn certain skills, to develop certain personality traits, and maybe to help you and your family learn from his condition as well?"

I stared at her in shock. My church certainly never offered such an explanation. I frowned, unwilling to let in this new concept simply because it *was* new. "Well, no....that's just...what do you mean, he *chose* it? Why would anyone choose to live life as a cripple? Or choose to starve to death?"

She continued, "We may never know why souls follow the paths or learn the lessons they draw to themselves. It's not our place to understand everything. That's a tremendous responsibility, wouldn't you say? But in Johnny's case, I know your mother learned infinite patience, and connected with God in ways she never had before he was born into your family. Her desire for him to be healed really brought about another type of healing for her, a spiritual and emotional healing. A feeling of being closer to God. Does that make sense, Cheryl?"

I nodded as another tear raced down my cheek. This was right at the time I had begun reading *There is a River*, Thomas Sugrue's biography of Edgar Cayce. I felt motivated to go home and read some more. Edith offered me a glimmer of hope, a new way of looking at life on Earth. That book had the same effect, conjuring up the same feelings I experienced in my neighbor's living room. I remember going home and consuming it that afternoon.

Another thought-provoking incident, indeed one that changed the whole course of my life came about courtesy of Edith's different take on life and spirituality. This occurred when a college scholarship was offered to me then quickly retracted, nearly two years later.

The mother of a good friend of mine was a member of *The American Business Women's Association*. I had known the Carvers since I was in grade school. Mrs. Carver was aware of our financial situation, my scholastic abilities, and unbeknownst to me, was planning to do everything within her power to help me realize my dream of going to college.

She called me at home early one evening. I wasn't used to receiving calls from my friend's mothers, so I was naturally curious.

"Well, hi, Mrs. Carver! What could I do for you?" A quick thought ran through my mind. Maybe she knew someone with a little kid who wanted to take piano lessons.

"Hello, Cheryl. I wonder if you might be free Thursday night to have dinner with some of my friends and me. We belong to the *ABWA*, *The American Business Women's Association*. We'd love to meet you and talk with you about some of our programs for young women."

I wasn't the least bit interested in business. I was a performer, an "artiste!" But I had known Mrs. Carver for many years, admired her and knew she was setting something in motion with the thought of helping me somehow.

"Sure, I can make it. I'll be home from musical rehearsal by 5, so any time after that is good for me. Is that too late?"

"Oh, no, no. This is pretty informal, so feel free to wear some nice slacks, just no jeans, okay? Be here at my house by 6:15, how's that?"

"Great! I appreciate the invitation. Do I need to bring anything?"

"Well, actually, yes. But I need to talk to your father about that. Is he available?" I replied affirmatively, then put Dad on the phone, totally baffled as to what he might provide for this dinner meeting. When he hung up, he turned to me, smiling.

"Honey, Mrs. Carver and those ladies are going to try and get you a college scholarship, isn't that wonderful? I have to find my latest income tax returns to make a copy for you to take, and the stub of my last social security check." He hurried back to the filing cabinet in his room.

A scholarship? I was stunned. We had discussed how much I wanted to go to CMSU, how impressed I'd been by the music department from the summer camp experience. But we had tentatively decided I should go to junior college for a couple of years, work part-time to make tuition money for Warrensburg, then transfer to finish up my bachelor's degree. I wasn't thrilled with this plan, but at least it would get me where I wanted to be, eventually. This sounded much better! I felt like I was living a bit of a charmed life that senior year...a star in the musical, more popular with the cool kids than I'd ever been, and now this!

"Thank You, God!" I blurted out.

Johnny laughed, threw up his hands and hollered, "Hallelujah!"

I joined in the laughter. "That's right, little brother. Hallelujah for sure!"

Dad came back with the necessary paperwork. "I'll make copies of this for you tomorrow," he said. "Of course, this is a preliminary meeting. There are a couple of other candidates, but Mrs. Carver sounds pretty confident they'll offer it to you. It might mean a three year sponsorship, and we can come up with the money for your last year, easy. Oh, she said you need to ask for your grade transcripts and make a copy of that, too." He was so animated, so happy for me.

"This is wonderful, Dad. I'm very lucky." I hugged him, then hugged John, who was still smiling ear to ear. I believe he knew exactly what was going on, too.

That Thursday night, I met the *ABWA* Scholarship Committee. I politely answered their questions, then briefly regaled them with some of the musical escapades. My friend, Pam, Mrs. Carver's daughter, snagged my arm as I headed out the door.

"Hey, Cheryl, I think you made a great impression. They were laughing at your jokes, and you were so polite!"

"Well, heck, my Mama didn't raise no fool!" I grinned. "This would be so cool, Pam. Thanks for putting your Mom up to this."

She smiled back. "Wish I could take credit for it, pal, but it was all Mom's idea. She's always admired you, Cheryl. The way your family kept on after your Mom passed away, how you've kept your grades up. Totally her inspiration. But I'm really happy for you, I feel like it's in the bag!" She gave me a quick hug. Pam was a wonderful seamstress, and was the costume mistress for *Brigadoon*. Her whole family was so nice, so supportive of others. I knew I was fortunate to have them in my life.

Two weeks flew by. Mrs. Carver had told me I'd hear from the committee in approximately that period of time. Sure enough, she called again, two weeks to the day. But this time her voice wasn't ringing with so much enthusiasm.

"Cheryl, I have some news for you. We want to offer you the scholarship, but..."

But? "Buts" seldom preceded good news. I bit my lip, waiting for the other half of the sentence.

"But, the national bylaws state that you have to study business. That's one of the stipulations we weren't aware of when you were telling us how much being a music major would mean to you." She paused. "They're firmer on this than I thought they'd be. I tried getting them to change their mind, just for your case. But no luck. Could you see yourself getting a business degree, and maybe studying music part-time, or minoring in it?"

My heart hurt. I knew she had tried her best for me, but I couldn't be untrue to who I knew I was. Math had always been my weak suit. I was a musician and an actor, a good writer, but not good business material. It was hard, but I decided to tell her the truth.

"Well, I want to thank you so much for going to bat for me like that, Mrs. Carver. I really, truly appreciate it so much. But I can't be a business major. I wouldn't make it. I'm just not cut out for it. I'm really sorry...I hope you understand."

She sighed, but wasn't surprised. "I thought that's what you'd say. I admire your integrity, Cheryl. Not too many young people your age are so clear on what they want from life. You'll make it, I know you will. Take care of yourself. We'll see you soon."

"Yes, ma'am. Thanks again. I'm sorry..."

"Dear, there's nothing to be sorry about. It's a ridiculous rule, if you ask me. Have a good night." She hung up.

Now I had to tell Dad what I had done, what I had said without so much as consulting him. It hadn't entered my mind to talk this over with him. I was so certain of what I wanted to become, I hadn't hesitated. By doing so, I'd opened an ugly can of worms, or so I thought.

He listened to the whole recounting of what happened without saying a word. Then he got up and stood directly across from me so we were eye to eye.

"Once again, you've made me very proud of you, honey. You didn't compromise and settle for less than your dream. You didn't try to be something you're not. Your Mom would be proud, too." He patted me on the back. "Don't worry, we'll figure out something. We always do, right?"

"Right! Thanks, Dad. It means a lot, you backing me up." I was touched by his support.

"What else can I do? You're a headstrong young woman, and most of the time, you know what's best for you. I'm glad you stood up for what you believe in. How could I not be proud of that?" He winked and went out to the garage to tinker with the car. That had always been a form of meditation for him, in a sense. A way of thinking through things while keeping busy.

Sure, I was disappointed about not becoming a music major right away. I couldn't tell him that. So the next afternoon after school, I went over to unload on poor Edith. Just as she had patiently listened to me rant and rail about God depriving our family of Mom several months ago, she allowed me to spew off about how unfair this scholarship situation was.

"Business! Could you see me getting a business degree, Mrs. Lay?"

"Well, no. Not unless it was something you were as passionate about as you are about music, dear." She poured me another glass of iced tea. "I'm going to give you some homework, of sorts. Are you willing to take it on? It's...well, maybe you should think of it as a game, instead of work."

I had no idea what she was talking about. But Edith was incredibly smart, in my book, and I'd already learned many things from her. I had been able to open my mind in new directions thanks to her kind guidance. So I didn't even question what she was about to suggest.

"Sure! I like learning new things. You're full of good ideas, Mrs. Lay."

She smiled and pulled a round magnet from the refrigerator. "Never procrastinate what you can do today. You know how people say, 'I'll do that when I get around to it'?"

I nodded.

She handed me the button. "Well, this is about as close as most people get."

I looked at the magnet and laughed. On it was written "Round Tuit"!

"Don't you put off what I'm going to suggest, either. Because even though it may seem silly to you, it's important. Can you go to the drugstore for a quick errand tonight?"

"Well, sure. Do you need me to pick up something for you?"

"No, Cheryl. I need you to pick up something for *you*! Get a piece of poster board in your favorite color. Should cost you about a quarter. Bring it home, get a stack of magazines...here, I've got lots of old ones. You can take these." She handed me a stack as I stood there, still unsure of my mission.

"Get some scissors, a magic marker and some glue. You're going to make a collage," she continued. "Cut out pictures of people singing, playing music, college kids on campuses...mostly music oriented activities, though. Paste them on the poster board, and then write along the top, 'MY MUSIC COLLEGE SCHOLARSHIP.' Put some dollar signs there, pictures of money, if you can find some, like it's raining down on top of the music students. Oh! Do you have a snapshot of yourself that you like?"

I was still confused, but this sounded like fun. "Well, yeah. What should I do with that?"

"Put it smack dab in the middle of the poster. Picture of you smiling like the world is your oyster. Do you have one like that?"

"Yes, I think so, one where I look really happy." I paused. "Then what do I do with this thing, after it's all done?"

"Put it up in your room, somewhere you'll see it every day. Don't stare at it, just somewhere you'll notice it each time you're in the room. It's a bit of a miracle-worker. You'll see." She smiled confidently.

"Okay. But how is that going to help me get a scholarship? I don't get it."

"Oh, Cheryl, that's the beauty. You don't have to 'get it'. Just play along and I believe you'll be pleasantly surprised at what might happen. You'll be opening up your belief system to allow a miracle into your life. Try it! It's only going to cost you a few cents and about an hour, right? What do you have to lose?" She held open the door, motioning me to get on with it, not when I might "get around to it."

So I told Dad I'd be right back, drove to the store and grabbed a piece of blue poster board. I came home and did exactly as she had told me. It was fun, a personal statement of my desires in picture form. Dad asked what I was doing, and I simply said, "It's an assignment Mrs. Lay gave me. Just for fun."

"Okay," was all he said, even though this probably looked like a first grade art project to him. Edith was aces in his book, too, so he didn't question me any further.

I hung up the poster board, which Edith told me I could call a "treasure map" or "prayer map." She explained this was something she had learned in a Master Mind class at Unity. I was intrigued. A church where you did artwork to make your dreams come true? Sure was more fun than standing up for hours at a time, holding your hands up and praising the Lord!

Less than a week after putting up my treasure map, Mrs. Carver called me again. I had no clue why she was ringing the house this time.

"Oh, hello, Mrs. Carver. Do you need to talk to my Dad about something?" She was always coordinating after school activities, so that was my first thought.

"No, no, Cheryl. I need to talk to *you*!" She was bubbling over. "You'll never believe this. We just got the news today...*ABWA* changed the national bylaws, with only a week to spare before we have to award the scholarship. Cheryl, we can now offer you that three year ride to school, tuition and dormitory expenses covered, based solely on your financial need and scholastic ability."

I felt dumbstruck. She went on.

"That means you can study music, whatever you want! We just want you to have it. So you better get the registration papers from CMSU right away. You're going to college, my young friend!"

"Oh, my God. This is amazing!" My voice box had begun working again. "Thank you, Mrs. Carver, and please thank all the women in the *ABWA*. Thank the national bylaw committee for me. Wow!" We chatted happily for a few more minutes, then I told Dad and Johnny the great news. They were ecstatic for me. I was on Cloud 9 the rest of the night. Just before I closed my eyes to go to sleep, I glanced over at the treasure map on the wall. I sat bolt upright and stared at it. Somehow, I knew it had something to do with the chain of events that had just shifted dramatically in my life. It was too late to call Edith, but I resolved to go see her tomorrow right after school.

I shared my great news with my closest friends at school the next day. They were all happy for me and three or four of them said they may go to CMSU, too. Sitting at Edith's dining room table that afternoon, I'd had a chance to mull over the chain of events and had a few questions.

"I'm so pleased for you, Cheryl! It was an easy technique to use, don't you think?" she smiled.

"Absolutely! So, could you tell me why you believe these prayer maps work so well? I didn't really give a lot of thought to it, once I had made the thing. I just glanced at it once in awhile, as you suggested." I grinned. "But obviously, that did the trick!"

"It surely did." She looked up at the ceiling for a moment, as though accessing a memory. "I believe the prayer map technique works because it simply helps you open your subconscious mind a bit more in a positive direction. You might think of it as giving yourself permission to allow the things you desire, or wish to manifest, to flow to you easily. That's why I said not to focus on it *too* much. Because what I've learned about the human mind is, we often get so fixated about something, we can only envision it happening a certain way. So if it does try to connect with us through another avenue, we might actually ignore it or block it, by stubbornly holding onto our own, narrow-minded vision of *how* it needs to happen. Does that make sense?"

I nodded. It felt like a light bulb was being turned on inside me somewhere. I am so grateful to Edith Lay for helping me in so many ways. She was there at times when I most needed a maternal shoulder to cry on, after Mom died. She was largely responsible for my learning to allow miracles to come into my life, as with this scholarship. She passed on in recent years, and I like to imagine her sitting at a table with Mom, drinking coffee somewhere in Heaven and having great discussions, just like they did here. I'd just like to say, "God bless you for being such a wonderful caring soul, Edith! I'm grateful you were (and are) our friend!"

So that first prayer map was really my very first lesson about the power of positive thinking, the universal Law of Attraction, how we go about manifesting things and situations. It was the first introduction I'd had about this basic fact: thoughts are things. What you spend the most time and energy thinking about is what you attract into your experience. So had I stayed focused on being mad or disappointed about those bylaws, I have sincere doubts as to whether they would have changed so quickly. By making a somewhat generic collage of my desired outcome, I had not "drawn the Universe" a single-minded map as to how to bring the scholarship to me. Rather, I had made a pictorial declaration of the result I wanted. What a simple, yet incredibly powerful tool! If kids were taught this kind of manifesting technique from the time they're four or five years old, imagine what powerful movers and shakers they'd be by the time they're adults! And the younger they learn, the less resistance or skepticism they have. That's one reason why today, I love teaching my young person's intuitive & manifesting workshop, *Mom, I Had This Dream*. We always have so much fun playing the intuitive games, and usually wind up the class by making some awesome treasure/prayer maps!

Throughout the next few years I continued to experiment with this technique. I still do! These manifesting maps are amazing! The main thing I've learned and that I share with my clients who are drawn to this technique is this: you can use one for any category you choose, any targeted, specific goal. Best not to make the mistake I did once, however, and put *everything* in the same collage. I had career, relationship, a new car...you name it, pretty much everything but the kitchen sink on there. And not a blasted thing manifested to any noticeable degree, even after a month. So I meditated and asked my guides why. The answer was simple. I had "overwhelmed" my subconscious mind. It simply didn't know where to start. In other words, if you have several goals and want to use treasure maps (I prefer to call them this, today, as you don't actually "pray" to the map!), create separate ones and hang them in individual spaces in your home. That way, even when you just notice them peripherally, your subconscious basically takes a snapshot of that one focused, specific goal. It's easier to grasp/embrace one belief at a time.

I learned a lot about visualization and the laws of attraction from many wonderful teachers, writers and psychics, including Shakti Gawain (*Creative Visualization)*, Wayne Dyer (*You'll See It When You Believe It)*, Barbara Sher (*Wishcraft)*, Terry Cole Whitaker (*Money Is God In Action* & many other books), Esther Hicks and the channeled teachings of Abraham in their 2004 book *Ask and it Is* Given and many more (visit www.abraham-hicks.com for more information).

Henriette Klauser's great book *Write It Down, Make It Happen* will help you do just that! Florence Scovill Shinn's *The Game of Life and How To Play It* is a classic study in learning to manifest powerfully. She wrote others focusing on prosperity and manifestation. There are so many books, it's impossible to list them all here, but the ones I have mentioned have all been extremely helpful to me in my personal growth.

Louise Hay, that marvelous writer, publisher and all around great human being, has taught me a lot about the power of the mind. Her library of writings is tremendous, beginning with her first big success, *You Can Heal Your Life.* When I was privileged to meet Louise Hay at a party in her home in Pacific Palisades in the 1980s, I would see how powerful this treasure map technique was in her life. You'll read more about that in the upcoming Celebrity chapter.

Or Would You Rather Be a Mule?

My senior year ended in an upbeat whirlwind of activity. I had been hanging out with a much more "in" crowd the last few months, partying at Martha's house and going to some of the "drama freaks" parties, too. I realized that, as Billy Joel wrote in *Only The Good Die Young*, that it *was* much more fun to "laugh with the sinners than cry with the saints." Oh, I was still a very good kid. I never drank or tried smoking dope in high school. But I learned to make a mean daiquiri and wasn't above passing a doobie to those who *were* imbibing. They crowned me "the coolest Jesus freak" they'd ever met! By this time, though, I had pretty much stopped going to church because many of the minister's messages smacked of hypocrisy to me. I could no longer buy into a "vengeful God" concept.

Either God is Love, as Jesus taught, or He's not. And I chose to believe He is. So although Dad was not happy with my choice, he didn't try to sway me; well, at least not most of the time! He encouraged me to watch Oral Roberts or Jimmy Swaggert on TV on the Sundays I'd stay home. Yeah, right! Look where those two wound up! Well, hindsight is 20/20. I always did enjoy Billy Graham, though, and still admire him today.

Anyway, back to good ol' Oak Park and my final days there. The musical went exceptionally well. At the annual drama awards at school, I even won a mini-statuette for Best Supporting Actress as Meg Brockie! (I still have it! I call it my "teeny tiny fake Oscar") I also was admitted into another somewhat elite group, the "Honor Thespians" for all the performance and crew hours I had put into productions at OPHS. Working on *Brigadoon* was undoubtedly the best time I ever had in high school, one that I remember fondly to this day. I'm truly thankful for that experience. In fact, the summer following graduation, my self-confidence was in such a good space, I went to the auditions for *Oliver!* put on by a large community theatre organization in Kansas City. I was cast in the female lead of Nancy, and we enjoyed a sold-out run in the open-air forum of Loose Park in downtown K.C. Sometimes there were over a thousand people spread out on the hill in back of the audience in the actual seats! It was thrilling for me, and we received wonderful reviews.

I went to the *ABWA* dinner and accepted my scholarship award. I had been accepted at CMSU months before, but had to hold off turning in the paperwork until we had the financial ability to make it happen. Now, thanks to this wonderful organization, my college dreams were to be realized.

Graduation was pretty typical. I had always been a good student, but didn't care about being valedictorian or anything. Ranking 32nd out of a graduating class of over 500 was good enough for me, and Dad was proud of me. As I accepted my diploma, I felt as though Mom was smiling down on me, too.

Johnny was doing great, back to his school routine, even part-time throughout the summer. I told him many times how much I would miss him and Dad, but that I'd be back every weekend I could to spend time with them. My two fellas had grown very close and their relationship was mutually uplifting. Dad provided all Johnny's basic human needs, and John's dauntless spirit inspired our father to keep going, no matter what. It kept them both quite healthy on every level, for a long time.

Summer flew by and before I knew it, the Gremlin was packed to the brim, and I was headed for dorm life in Warrensburg. College was a great experience in so many ways. CMSU's sports teams were the "Fighting Mules", so here I was, *officially* as stubborn as a Missouri mule and proud to be one! I did well in most of my course work. I particularly found Music History fascinating, as I had always loved reading the biographies of composers. This was the mid-1970s, so CDs were not out for several years. During exams in the class we fondly dubbed "Music Mystery", through hours of listening and study, I got to know marvelous music from many eras on such an intimate level that during exams, when the professor "dropped the needle" on a certain passage of the LP, I could immediately write down the composer's dates, what movement of which symphony we were listening to, and several other identifying facts.

I sang in many ensembles, A Cappella Choir and Madrigal Choir, most memorably. At the end of my junior year, the A Cappella group went to Costa Rica and Nicaragua (which you'll read a bit more about in the chapter *Hello Again*, dealing with deja vu and reincarnation). I worked during the summers at a variety of jobs, including waiting tables, doing some backstage work at Kansas City's *Worlds Of Fun* amusement park, and singing in a band. Dad never approved of me singing in any clubs or at parties where there might be drinking or other such activities. I didn't know exactly how strongly this disapproval went until my sophomore year of college.

I met a boy two years younger than myself shortly after *Brigadoon* finished its run. Rob had seen me in the musical and kept calling, asking me if I wanted to be in his band. I didn't think he was serious until I finally agreed to go over to his house and saw the extensive amount of equipment his parents had purchased for him, including a good sound system. He really loved the power of my voice, and wanted me to be the lead singer. The only catch was, we were just a quartet. He played lead guitar, there was a bass player and a drummer. When he found out I played piano, he was ecstatic.

"Cool! You can play rhythm then, too, y'know, fill in with chords and stuff!" he enthused.

"Well, yeah, of course I can. I just don't have an electric piano," I explained. I was getting more excited about this, now that I saw it wasn't some kid's pipe dream. He obviously had parents who backed up his performing aspirations; something I had always longed for.

"Oh, don't sweat not having a keyboard. My Dad will buy you something and you can pay us back out of the gig money we'll get from weddings and country clubs."

This kid was a man with a plan! So I went with him and his father to a music store and picked out a used Wurlitzer electric piano. They were all the rage in the '70s. This was before keyboards were commonly referred to as "synthesizers" or had a lot of different voice options. Richard Carpenter played a Wurlitzer electric, so I felt like I was truly moving into the "professional musician" category. I signed a written agreement with them, promising to pay back the $500 out of band money. Dad was never a fan of borrowing money and was already upset I had agreed to practice and actually perform "rock" music, so I didn't bother to tell him about this little contract.

We played at a number of events on the weekends throughout my first two years of college. Then one weekend when I came home, Rob called me with some disturbing news.

"Tomorrow night's the last night you'll be working with us. It's just that, um, my girlfriend's gonna be the new lead singer."

I was shocked. We didn't make a ton of money, but I enjoyed working with these young musicians. Not to be given more notice than that was a hard blow.

I tried to play it cool. "Oh, really? All right. I was getting pretty busy at college, anyway. I'll just bring my piano home with me after the gig, and I can finish paying you off in a couple of months. See ya tomorrow, Rob."

"No, wait!" he practically yelled. "You can't do that. Sheila plays keyboard and we need that piano."

There were a few moments of dead air as I let this sink in.

"You mean you're trying to tell me, that the $350 I have paid back means nothing and you're going to just keep *my* piano? I don't think so!" Now *I* was yelling. Dad poked his head into the dining room to see what all the commotion was about. "I'll find a way to bring the rest of the money to you tomorrow, Rob. That piano is *mine*! Have a nice night!" I blurted sarcastically and slammed down the phone. I was furious that he thought dumping me from the band and stealing my keyboard, to boot, would have been so easy.

I tearfully explained to Dad about the loan agreement for the keyboard. He listened, shaking his head negatively a couple of times, amazed his daughter had gotten herself into such a pickle. Then he looked up and I could see he had a plan of his own.

"I'll give you the other $150, hon. You bring that little piano home tomorrow after you work with these numnutz kids one last time. I'll go get the money out of the bank in the morning, okay?" He patted my hand. I was astonished by this show of support.

"Gee, Dad, really? That's great! Thank you so much!" I jumped up and gave him a big hug. Dad and I would show that Rob whippersnapper a thing or two about taking advantage of people, I thought.

The gig was strained because of all the personal tension. Sheila came along and played on a couple of the songs, so they asked me to sit out. She had a mousy little voice, so I knew it wasn't her talent Rob was into. I kept my cool the rest of the night, but was relieved when it was all over.

I marched up to Rob's Dad at the end of the evening and said,

"Here's the balance for the Wurlitzer," handing him the $150 cash. "Please sign this piece of paper which states I've repaid you in full." I stood there, extending pen and paper to him. He reluctantly did as I asked. "Thanks. Good luck to all of you." I didn't mean it, but didn't have the energy to get into a free-for-all. I was taking the piano with me, that was the main thing. Rob and his father looked very surprised, but simply shrugged their shoulders and walked off. What else could they do? This tall, strong-lunged singer might choose to make a scene in their ritzy private country club and God forbid *that* would happen and embarrass them! I smirked to myself, feeling that if I had lost the war and been tossed out of the band, I had at least won the battle of the keyboard.

I took the keyboard home and set it up in the corner of the living room. I played a few songs on it so Dad and Johnny could hear the different electronic piano sounds. They both seemed to like it. Imagine my surprise when I came home the following weekend to discover it wasn't there!

I stopped in my tracks, dropping my suitcase by the front door. "Dad! Where's my electric piano? I was going to take it back to college... there's this band I might be working with..."

"Well, I don't think so," he said in a measured tone. "You need to focus on your studies and not get into these borrowing money situations and wasting your time at worldly band practices."

I felt sick to my stomach. "Dad, please. What did you do with my piano?" I tried to keep my voice calm.

"I donated it to the youth group at church. They're thrilled with it," he replied.

"What?!? You can't do that! It's mine! I had a $350 investment in that thing. I would have paid you back the $150 really soon, Dad. Oh, my God! I can't believe this!" I sank down in the nearest chair. I felt betrayed and very angry. As the weekend progressed, I begged him to talk to the church and tell them he had donated it without my knowledge or permission. I pleaded my case eloquently, feeling like Perry Mason doing his best defense work. But Dad was unmovable. He staunchly refused to give in. I went back to CMSU a day early, feeling hurt and vowing to work in bands again, no matter what. He couldn't stop my dream like this!

That was perhaps the worst argument Dad and I ever had. I didn't go back home for a month after that. I would talk to him in a very flat, bored voice when he called me at the dorm. He finally got the message, and we simply didn't talk for a couple of weeks. When I did get back into the "home for the weekend" routine, we did our usual "Booth denial" routine and simply never talked about it again. I now saw how much he hoped I would never make it in music or acting. For quite awhile the hurt cut like a like a knife, every time I'd wistfully look at the corner where the little piano had briefly lived.

Yet, life continued without the Wurlitzer and so did my studies. I found a couple of garage bands to jam with around campus, but they never got their act together nor had the connections for venues to play, as Rob's family had. I played my guitar and sang in some local coffee houses here and there, just to keep my performing "chops" up. I must admit, I took great delight in telling Dad I was still doing this. This was one area of my life about which neither of us was about to give an inch.

What Kind of Fool Am I?

A big one, apparently. Fool, that is. For all the high school years I had resisted temptation and remained Ms. Goody Two-Shoes, I was more than making up for it during college. Once Dad and I had that falling out about my performing career, I gave myself permission to be pretty wild. If I wasn't high on something for at least a part of the week, life seemed pretty boring. I developed a real taste for alcohol, marijuana and around finals time, certain types of speed that kept you up all night cramming for the exam.

I had lost connection with "the Voice," didn't talk to Mom much anymore and only went home about one weekend a month. I immersed myself in what seemed to be the predominant college cultural pastime in a sleepy little town...partying every chance you got! I went to several mindless keggers, which also bored me. I had more fun with a small group of friends who would get together and drink and/or smoke ourselves silly, then fancy that we were infinitely witty and creative, although we could barely walk. On my twenty-first birthday, my present to myself was a blender so I could make all manner of frozen drinks. I even had the audacity to drive around the cobblestone streets of CMSU while blatantly drinking right out of the blender! It's a mercy I was never caught, nor ever hurt anyone. If I had been caught, my scholarship would undoubtedly have been revoked. But I wasn't into looking at the consequences, it was all about enjoying rash choices which loudly stated, "I'm young and invincible! Whatcha gonna do about it?"

All this came crashing down one night, shortly after the choir's return from Central America. I was anxious to get back into the party life after ten days of extreme good behavior under the watchful eye of our chaperone professors. We sang in a lot of churches in Costa Rica and Nicaragua. Now that I was back on American soil, I was ready to blow off some steam!

A night or two after we were back home, I called my best friend, Cindy and we agreed to get together later. I pulled on a new white top from Costa Rica which had beautiful embroidery work at the neckline. We met at one of our favorite haunts and slammed down about three Black Russians apiece, in less than an hour's time. There wasn't much else to do there, it was a pretty quiet night in downtown "Boringsburg." That's when she came up with a "brilliant" suggestion.

"Hey, I know what!" She leaned toward me, like a conspirator. I leaned toward her, too, knowing something was up. Only thing was, we were so hammered, everybody else must have heard our plan, too. We probably thought we were whispering, but that must have been an illusion.

"Let's go for a drive to sober up, 'kay?" She started rummaging around in her purse for her car keys. She drove a vintage Spitfire convertible which was very cute, but had a habit of breaking down frequently. This night, though, it was in fine form. So going for a breezy drive at 1 a.m. and letting the night air whip through our hair somehow seemed like an adventurous, fun thing to do.

"After you, dear lady," I held the door open and we stumbled to our small chariot. We stopped to put a couple of dollars worth of gas in, which went a long way in those days, and hit the open road. Somehow this flagrant illegal, stupid behavior seemed logical to us. We didn't care. Cindy and I always had a great time laughing together. As we went flying down the highway, we were laughing hysterically about something that was probably not even funny. I realize now that my rebellion was obviously due to years of repressed anger about all the overly responsible years of being quiet and behaving myself. But that night, all that mattered was living life to the hilt, damn it! Or was it?

Suddenly, she veered off the highway, onto a rural road I had never driven on before. She was still going at a good clip and this had a pretty quick sobering effect on me.

"Gee, Cin, ya might wanna slow down a little. This is a pretty bumpy gravel road," I tried to caution.

"Aw, ya big baby. Lighten up!" She gave me a wicked grin and gunned the motor. I felt nauseated as I looked ahead and saw a sharp hairpin turn, with a huge oak tree right at the center.

"Here I come, Jesus!" ran through my mind, along with several other regretful thoughts. So, this was how it was going to end, huh? How would Johnny and Dad get along without me? What an inglorious finale to a promising musical actress's career. Oh, well, too late now...

I hadn't read much about Near Death Experiences or Elizabeth Kubler Ross at that time of my life. But what happened to me next was definitely an NDE. I remember feeling like I was floating up, moving toward some misty, beautiful white light. I felt like I was zooming out of my body, amazingly free and happy. All at once, I heard Mom's voice in my head. "It's not time for you to come here yet, Cheryl. You have a lot more work to do on the Earth plane, honey. Go on back now. Go back. Learn from this. Learn..."

Next thing I knew, I sat bolt upright to find the Spitfire smack in the middle of a cow pasture. My face felt very sticky, like someone had smeared finger paint or jelly all over it. I slowly tried to sit up straight, feeling pretty woozy. When I focused on Cindy, behind the wheel, I realized she was out cold. I briefly wondered how long we had been sitting there, and remember being grateful we had at least not hit any cattle, as I took in our strange surroundings. I glanced down and saw that my previously white new shirt was now mostly red. Blood red. I touched the sticky stuff of my face and realized my head had bled profusely. Still finding it hard to believe I was even still alive, I looked back at the barbed wire fence, backlit by the street lamp from the farmhouse across the street. I saw a large chunk of my hair blowing freely in the breeze, hanging from the top wire!

Since I was apparently still among the living, I figured I'd better check on my friend. I touched her shoulder, gently at first, then shaking her harder when she didn't answer me.

"Cindy, wake up. Cindy! Damn it, Cindy, wake up! Don't you leave me here!" I felt like crying. She didn't have any blood showing on her, but I wasn't sure she was "in there." Finally, she moaned and pulled her head back. Her glasses had flown off. She peered at me, then started shrieking.

"Oh, God, you're covered with blood! I've killed you! I've killed us! Oh, my God!"

I slapped her, not knowing how else to stop the hysteria. "Cut it out! We're not dead. It's just a good thing you're short and I was slumped down in the seat. Otherwise, I'd have been decapitated. Look at all the hair back there in the fence!" I pointed.

She blanched, opened the car door and threw up. "Oh, my God, Cher, I'm so sorry. What a stupid, dumbass thing. Oh, God..."

I felt sorry for her, even though I was the one most injured. "It's okay, come on, snap out of it. Quit apologizing. You didn't hold a gun to my head or anything. I was drunk and agreed to go along for the ride. Thank God we're okay." She nodded numbly. "Look, the farmhouse has a light on. Let's go use their phone."

"No!" she screamed. "They'll call the police and I'll lose my license."

I stared at her. Perspective and priorities get really messed up when you mix chemicals and driving. We had narrowly cheated Dr. Death and now she was suddenly worried about losing her license? I was pretty sober by this time and worried about what injuries I wasn't able to look at or feel with any accuracy. Whether she wanted to or not, I was going to use these folks' phone and get myself to an emergency room, somehow.

So, looking like one of Jason's victims from a *Friday the 13th* movie, I headed toward the farmhouse door, not really caring whether my friend came with me or not. I was grateful to be alive and figured I'd better start acting like it.

The woman who answered the doorbell at about 2:30 that morning had kind eyes. She had on a housecoat and had apparently been watching a late night movie. She looked me up and down, and didn't even flinch as she held the door open and said, "Come on in. I'm a nurse. Let's get you cleaned up." Her lack of surprise made me wonder if this was a scene she had played out with other drunken college students before. The miracle that she was a nurse was not lost on me, either.

It turned out, as I told her my story and she cleansed my wounds, I had only suffered surface scratches to the scalp, but deep enough to cause a considerable loss of blood. She brought me a cup of coffee and invited me to sit down until I felt well enough for her husband to drive us home. Cindy was sitting stonily in the corner. She had apparently decided to come in while I was being attended.

"Do you think I'll get tetanus, or anything? What do you think I should do about these scratches?" I asked, more and more grateful that she was a nurse and not an easily shaken one, at that.

"No, you told me you just a tetanus shot before your trip, right?" We had shared a bit of recent history while I sat on the edge of her bathtub as she cleaned me up. "You should be just fine. Boy, you're lucky you have such a full head of curly hair. I don't think anyone else will really notice." She lit a cigarette, looking me up and down. "Let me get you a clean tee shirt to wear home. You're going to have to throw away that pretty Costa Rican shirt. What a shame!"

She went into her bedroom, and I called out after her, "Well, better the shirt than me, right?" I smiled, trying to draw Cindy into the conversation, but she was lost in her own thoughts. "Hey, Cin, they're going to give us a ride home. She knows somebody with a tow truck, we can get the car out after daylight, okay?" She nodded, so I knew she could hear me. "Come on, they're cool. They're not going to call the police, so just chill out, okay? Hello? Anybody home?" I used my best teasing voice, trying to snap my buddy out of her gloomy reverie.

She finally made brief eye contact. "Yeah, that's great. Um, I just can't believe I..."

"Shh, just let it go. We're okay, that's all that matters, right? And I gotta tell ya, I believe I have *such* a great guardian angel right now. Man!" I meant it. This was too synchronistic, to have crashed through a barbed wire fence, into a *nurse's* pasture. Silently, I was thanking God over and over, and my Mom, too, for guiding me back to pick up the pieces and move forward.

We went back the next day to watch them pull her car out of the pasture. It turned out there was amazingly little body damage, and none to the engine, whatsoever. In fact, the biggest cosmetic thing that was wrong was one of her windshield wiper blades had flown off. Truly miraculous, by every standard. I cut my hair out of the fence with a pair of scissors I'd brought along. I placed it in a baggie. I was going to keep this bloody reminder of what could have been so much worse, just for a little while. Just enough to make me think twice about doing anything that ignorant again.

For the first time, it began to dawn on me how very fragile life can be. And I knew beyond the shadow of a doubt that I had been "sent back" to do much more with my life than spend my time getting wasted, doing stupid stunts like driving drunk. It was a major revelation to recognize for the first time in my life that I was here for a *reason*. Turns out that discovering that purpose would take me a few years, and begin quite a different journey than being a big musical star as I had envisioned.

Chapter Nine

"There's No Place Like Home..." (but where IS that, exactly?)

I summoned up my courage, and on my next trip home, shared the barbed wire fence episode with Dad. That was my first "coming clean" with him about my bad habits since going to college, and it was a whopper! Surprisingly, he was pretty aware that I had been involved in such things. He was not critical, just concerned and relieved that I had survived. He told me how much he and Johnny needed and loved me and asked me to please use better judgment in the future. After talking with him I felt much better and even more aware that I had some purpose on this planet, far greater than I had tapped into so far. I could just as easily have stayed in the Light from that morning on and never written this book, for example. Then I would not have fulfilled my obligation, my promise to John to share his story to the best of my ability. And that would make me very sad, indeed. So I'm still grateful to my Guardian Angel, guides and loved ones in Spirit that I am here, able to share this story with you now.

Chronologically, Johnny was moving into puberty. When I was twenty-one, he was seventeen. Yet he was still the size of a normal ten or eleven year old child, and quite thin. His muscles never developed much at all due to lack of use. But his face was always so sweet, so open. Those beautiful green eyes shone out such love on everyone upon whom he looked. I began to spend more time with my little brother when I came home on the weekends, because I had somehow lost touch, forgotten what a blessing his very presence was in my life. How calm I always felt around him. One Saturday afternoon I was reading, holding him in the armchair, his neck cradled in the crook of my right arm, braced against the chair's arm; his lanky little body stretched out across my lap, feet dangling off the other side of the chair. I had done this many times when we were younger. I regretted having allowed my wild college ways to have ever allowed our connection to falter, and I told him so. Always my best example of unconditional love, John simply smiled up at me as if to say, "What's to forgive? I'm just happy you're here with me right now, Sis." Our telepathic rapport was still strong, and I treasured it.

As I continued reading, something made me glance down at John. He had been so still for several minutes, I wondered if he might be asleep. Much to my surprise, I saw his eyes moving across the page of my book, left to right, left to right. I held my breath, afraid to interrupt him. He finished with the page on the left, and sure enough, his eyes moved to the top of the right hand page and continued scanning, *reading* my book. I knew I wasn't imagining this, yet it felt quite surreal. I waited until he finished that page, then just sat there. He finally glanced up at me, more than likely wondering why I hadn't turned the page. As we made eye contact, I actually saw him blush, just a little bit!

"I caught you!" I blurted out. "I always felt you could say more and knew so much more than any of those old doctors could ever figure out! You can read, John, you can *read*!" I knew this was something he would most likely never repeat, something no one else would ever witness, much like the way he had finally said, "Dog!" for me and only me, many years ago. He just grinned, as if to say, "It's our secret," then closed his eyes and went to sleep in my arms. I closed the book and relaxed, content to be so near this amazing little being. I began to believe more and more, Johnny was an extremely evolved soul. All the pain and suffering he had endured in his life, the seizures, surrendering to being completely reliant on the love of our family to care for him, the loss of Mom, the horrific injuries inflicted on him by that foster family, all these he endured and survived. Always peaceful, always sweet-natured, no matter what befell him. I felt he was very in tune with the Christ consciousness. Johnny always loved it whenever I read to him, but he especially responded to anything which dealt with the life of Jesus or His teachings.

I had recently begun reading about reincarnation, and now I wondered if perhaps Johnny had been alive in Christ's time. Immediately, I got prickly goose bumps up and down my arms and felt as though I was freezing. I didn't know what this meant at that time, but those would revisit me many times, years later, when I was doing readings for others, or when my guides and angels wanted to let me know for a certainty that something was so. I have come to call them "confirmation chills." Many people experience these; others feel Spirit contact as heat. That day with John's reading revelation was the first time I recall feeling them so strongly.

I thought about telling Dad about the reading incident, but my gut instinct told me not to. Dad may have listened, but I didn't think he'd believe me. So I just enjoyed the rest of my time with "my guys" that weekend, helped with the housecleaning as much as possible and had new things to muse over when I returned to campus.

Now, I was far from being all sweetness and light from that point forward. The car wreck had been a wakeup call, for sure, yet I continued to party a bit during the rest of my college days. I just partied a little less hard and stayed clear-headed enough to use better judgment. My grades reflected my rebellion. Instead of earning mostly As, as I had in high school, I tended to be happy with more Bs, even a few Cs here and there. I still was a good student, I just didn't try as hard and didn't really care about grades anymore. Smoking dope and drinking will make you lose sight of what's important, that's no lie.

Starting my senior year, I only had a few required courses left the first semester, then the second I would fulfill my degree by doing my student teaching. I was placed at a rural school where I worked with every age, K through 12. I truly enjoyed the elementary kids' enthusiasm and attitude about music and life in general. The high schoolers were great, because they were in choir by choice, through audition. But the junior high kids, oh, my! We had a tough time reaching any sort of mutual respect. They were a bunch of smart-mouths and rowdy beyond my worst nightmares. I took this quite personally, forgetting my own fairly recent history as a kid their age. Later, I realized this is a challenging age for most teachers to handle, especially novice ones. It felt so impossible to establish any sense of control over the classes full of what I now lovingly refer to as "hormones with arms and legs." It's just part of adolescents' physiological makeup, which creates a lot of energy and confusion. But as "Miss Booth, Student Teacher" I got very upset and found it hard to take it when they were rude and unruly. I often cried myself to sleep the night before I would have to face their class.

Needless to say, I did survive this phase of my college career and went on to graduate with a Bachelor of Music Education, Vocal. I was happy to finally have the degree, but after my recent student teaching was having doubts as to whether I would ever use it!

I moved back home to live with Dad and John for awhile, unsure as to my direction in life. I took a job selling pianos and organs at a store in a nearby mall. Well, it was music-related, at least! But I soon found I didn't have the "shark-like instincts" necessary to talk folks into buying the most expensive instruments, no matter what. I tended to help them go with something more affordable, which didn't spell high commission for me and didn't win brownie points from my boss.

None of my friends from high school were around anymore. Many had gotten married, others had continued with grad school or simply moved out of the area. My pal Cindy, from college, had moved back to live with her folks in Iowa. We talked quite often, but I really missed her company. We had a lot of fun together, not counting the cow pasture episode. But even *that* we had overcome and continued to be great friends. One night when I was telling her how boring my life was now, she had an interesting idea.

"Well, Iowa's not exactly thrilling, but why don't you think about moving up here? We could get an apartment together in Des Moines. There are lots of jobs around, and you won't feel like you're living right under your Dad's nose, always walking on eggshells. Think it over, Cheryl. I'm planning on getting a place of my own in a few weeks. I'll need a roommate to afford that. This living with the parents again is for the birds, isn't it?"

I had to admit it was cramping my style, after having been unsupervised for the better part of four years. I loved my Dad and John so much, but I was feeling pretty empty inside. They had gotten along so well without me around full-time, I knew they could again. They didn't need me like they had when I was in high school

I began to save up money from my paychecks to fund a move, and in a month's time, sprung the news on Dad that I would be moving. He was a bit sad, but totally understood. Cindy was glad I'd be coming up. She told me she was sure I could find a band to work with, that there were several clubs in the Des Moines area.

I made my goodbyes to Dad and Johnny, once again. After all, Des Moines was less than 200 miles away. Further than Warrensburg, but not a bad drive. I assured them (and myself) that I would be coming home quite a bit. And if it didn't work out in Des Moines, I'd move back in and really make a go of living at home. Even apply for some teaching jobs, which was sounding less and less appealing. I'd half-heartedly applied around home right after graduation, but nothing had panned out. The emotional wounds from my junior high teaching fiasco had prevented me from even looking at that age group as a viable option.

So I headed north with what few personal possessions I had. I cried a few tears on the way out of town, worrying about what might happen to "my guys." Dad was still getting along really well, but he was seventy-six years old now. He insisted they would be all right and not to worry, but I knew things wouldn't stay the same a lot longer. Still, I felt driven to make a major change in my life. So ready or not, Iowa, I was on my way!

The four years I spent in Des Moines seem a bit blurry when I think back on them now. I taught music lessons, was in several bands, and did a number of odd jobs, including waiting tables, in order to make ends meet. The first really good band I worked with were all musicians in my age range, some a few years older. We called ourselves *Midnight Blue*. (I have always been a big Melissa Manchester fan).

I had the best time singing some of the greatest pop music ever written (who knew, at the time?) I just knew then what I liked, songs that spoke to my heart. Now, in the 21st century, when rap and hip-hop are much of the rage, I still take great comfort in these older, melodic songs with stories to tell. Songs by artists like Melissa Manchester, Jim Croce, Billy Joel, The Eagles, Paul Simon, The Carpenters, Harry Chapin, Linda Ronstadt, Barbra Streisand...I still had a great admiration for La Streisand, and was now lead singer in a band who learned many of the songs from her version of *A Star Is Born*, because I told them I loved the soundtrack. In many ways, I was in musical Heaven. I was actually getting paid to play music I loved. We had a lot of fun at rehearsals, we all became good friends. We played at some kind of rough C & W bars, where we mostly stuck to Patsy Cline, Hank Williams and Grand Ol' Opry standards. Bob, the guitarist, was an amazing self-taught musician who didn't read a note. Yet I have never met a more naturally gifted player. He went out and rented a violin, and a week later, came to a gig and whaled on *Orange Blossom Special* like he'd been playing it all his life! I was having a lot of fun again with performing, and felt like I was at least more on track than I was right after college.

We made some rough-cut recordings from some of our live performances. I proudly sent a tape off to Millie in California, and to Dad, too. Figured he'd at least approve of the traditional country stuff. He did, he was just fairly non-committal. I'm sure the thought of his daughter playing in bars to a lot of drunks was not exactly appealing. And many times, that's exactly what was going on. I can't tell you how many times I was hit upon by unsavory characters who thought all singers were sluts. Or of the countless times when there was no stage and we literally had to play right on the dance floor level. You could almost count on someone stumbling into my mic stand, nearly knocking out my teeth. That part was *not* fun. But I endured it, because it was at least a fringe aspect of show biz, and it was rebuilding my confidence that my future lay in that direction.

After we'd been playing about two years, more and more folks would come up and say things like, "What are you doing still wasting your time playing here in The Holiday Inn in Podunk, USA, Cheryl? You've got a great voice, so much power. You need to go to California or New York!" I began to seriously consider this, remembering my teenage vow to live in L.A. one day.

I went down to K.C. every few months and spent a few nights with John and Dad, usually during the week, since the band played mostly on the weekends. By this time, the band was making enough money I let my other part-time jobs go. John and Dad were getting along pretty well, but I noticed Dad didn't have that old spring in his step anymore. It worried me that he moved a lot slower now, and talked more about his arthritis pain. Johnny was growing a little bit, and that meant he was heavier to move and carry. So it came as no great surprise to me when in late 1980, Dad called to tell me he felt it best if we placed Johnny in a nursing home.

"I don't know what else to do with him, Cheryl. I just don't think we can go on like this. I'm afraid I'll drop him when I'm giving him a bath or moving him from his chair to his bed."

There was a pregnant pause. I had felt this coming, but had pretended it wasn't real. Now that the actual words had been spoken, I knew differently. I cleared my throat.

"Do you want me to move back home, Dad? I will, you know." I meant it. I would have done anything to help them. Dad could tell I was sincere.

"No, no, honey. We'd just be postponing the inevitable. And you have a life of your own, remember? We've had this discussion before, just not with these exact circumstances. I still want you to get on with your life, that's important. You have a lot of talent." That last comment was very low volume. I almost shook the phone to make sure I had heard him right.

"Well, thanks, Dad. That means a lot. But how will we get him admitted some place on your retirement income? Nursing homes are so expensive, aren't they?"

It turned out my father had done his homework. He had already applied to make Johnny a ward of the state of Missouri, just as we had to do with Mom and the cancer research hospital. That was the only way he could find of getting Johnny around the clock care in a nursing facility. Tears rolled down my cheeks at the thought of little John living full-time amongst total strangers for the first time in his life. The horror of the foster home situation flashed through my mind, along with the fact that we would lose total control and say-so in his care, once the state ward status was granted. Just like we had with Mom, which had enabled them to perform as many experimental tests with drugs on her as they had seen fit. I shuddered, knowing none of those exact scenarios would play out again, but still feeling really helpless. I decided to put on a strong front for Dad. Being a crybaby now wouldn't help him feel any better about his decision.

"Okay, sounds like you've got a plan. Where will he be living? Close by, I hope?"

"Well, no. The only place that has room for him is down in Warrensburg, where you went to college. Isn't that funny?"

Funny, not so much. Ironic? Absolutely. I had fled "Boringsburg" just two years before; now Johnny was going there to endure God knew what at the hands of strangers. Ostensibly, to spend the rest of his life there. Too far away for Dad to visit often, to know exactly what was going on there. I remembered what Edith taught me about life choices. On some level, maybe John had agreed to go through this phase of his life when the time came. And the time was now.

They would have a bed available for him in a month. I made plans to come home and ride down in the state van to move John into his new home. I knew the trip would wear Dad out physically and emotionally. There was no way I was letting Johnny go through this move all alone. The least I could do was go along and talk to him about what was happening. I held him all the way, talking in low tones to him almost continuously. I didn't give a damn what the van driver heard or thought. This was my baby brother and all that mattered was that *he* understood me. And I knew he did. He always had.

"Daddy and I are so sorry about this, John. It breaks my heart to do this to you." My eyes filled with tears over and over. I wiped them on my sleeve as he looked up at me with those trusting eyes. "We love you so much, but Daddy just can't lift you any more, you're such a big guy now."

John listened closely. I felt like he already knew what I was telling him, probably already knew where he was going. He showed no fear of his new circumstances. He just smiled sweetly and made some comforting sounds, trying to help *me* in my grief. I felt as though he was sending me the message, "It's going to be all right, Cheryl. Don't cry. God will take care of me."

The van driver hadn't been happy about it, but Dad and I insisted on moving John's big "eating chair" down with him. This was the chair Dad had made so many years ago out of an old TV cabinet. I was determined to convince the workers in this nursing home to give my brother the closest possible approximation of attention and care he had received all his life.

When we arrived, they escorted us up to John's private room. The place looked clean enough, which was a mercy. I gently laid him on his new bed and brought up the rest of his things. The driver said he would give me a few minutes to say goodbye, then we needed to head back to Kansas City.

I hooked up John's portable radio and turned it on. "He really loves music," I explained to the director, who was standing nearby. "Could you make sure this is on for him, as often as possible?"

She looked hardened and somewhat callous. No doubt she had seen her share of tearful goodbyes over the years and just removed herself from any emotion. "Well, we can't allow anything to disturb the other patients," she flatly replied.

"Oh, no, I understand. You can keep it low volume, like this," I adjusted the dial. "There's nothing wrong with John's hearing, in fact, it's always been very sharp. He's quite sensitive to loud noise, himself." Johnny was looking up at me as if to say, "Just let it go, Sis. It really doesn't matter."

"Your brother will be fine, Miss Booth. You and your father can come visit him any time." Her toneless voice failed to assure me. I knew visits would be few and far between because of Dad's failing health and my distant living situation. I demonstrated how the feeding chair worked and explained how much easier it was to get John to eat good meals by using it.

"It takes about an hour to feed him. Takes a lot of patience, but he really loves to eat good food. He's such a beautiful soul." I had to step out in the hall to avoid breaking down in front of this tough customer. I ran to the hall restroom, because I didn't want John to hear the heaving sobs I could no longer control.

I took a few moments to compose myself, splashed cold water on my face, then put on some semblance of a smile before I reentered his room. The sterile, institutional atmosphere really depressed me. I looked down at my little brother, alone in his new surroundings, trustingly looking around the room; he seemed to know on some level he would be fine here. I held his small hand and knelt down beside the bed.

"I love you more than anything, Johnny. I wish things were different. Mom will watch over you, and Dad and I will visit whenever we can. Please forgive me for leaving you here." I hugged him really tight, then kissed his forehead. He smiled up at me one last time before I hurried down the hall to the elevator. I thought to myself, "He truly is totally in God's hands now."

"He always has been, honey," I swore I heard my mother's voice. "John is God's child. He'll be fine."

I blew my nose, composed myself, and then quickly made my way to the van. The driver opened the door for me. I thanked him, then sat looking out window all the way home, in a helpless daze. I couldn't believe what had just happened. John had already outlived the doctor's predictions. Most of them thought he would only survive to age fifteen or so, due to the severe curvature of his spine. They said it would likely cause a lung puncture or collapse. But here he was, approaching his twenty-first birthday, no bigger than a small twelve year old, still very much alive. I wished for the thousandth time that I had the money to provide around the clock care for him and keep him with me. This was not God's plan for John, though. That day was one of the hardest lessons I ever had about surrender.

I put on my best cheerful face to describe the place to Dad. He listened, but seemed far away somewhere. Finally, I put my hand on top of his to make sure he had heard me. "Dad? Y'know, God will watch over him. You didn't have another choice. I know that. I'm sorry I couldn't help more. I know what a tough decision this was..."

He looked out the window, then turned his gaze back to me. "Yes, it was a rough one, for sure. But it was the best I could come up with." He got up to get a glass of water and cleared his throat before turning back to face me. "I want to talk with you about something else, now."

I sat back and waited. Obviously, this wasn't the end of Dad's plan. What would come next, I wondered.

"Honey, I'm nearly eighty years old. I can't take care of this place anymore, not just John. It's too much of a burden." His voice sounded wooden, rehearsed in a way, as though he had gone over this speech for the entire five hours I'd been gone, moving John to his new home.

"Then what are you going to do?" I was almost afraid to ask.

"Well, I'm going to sell the house, and move into a retirement home."

I caught my breath. I hadn't seen this coming so close on the heels of Johnny's relocation. But I knew how logical my father was, once he set his mind to something, so I did my best to be supportive.

"Well, if that's what you feel is best, I know it will be fine." In a sense, I was relieved. I had never wanted to deal with placing my father in a nursing home, myself. Now, he had prevented me from facing that dilemma. It was obviously something to which he had given a lot of thought.

"I'll be going into a nice place called Kendallwood. They call it a retirement home, but it's really an upscale nursing home. Clyde took me to look it over last week. They have good facilities and a nice staff." He produced a brochure and pushed it toward me. "They can take me in a couple of months, and hopefully the house will sell by then. If there's anything you want to take from the house, you might want to pack it up before you head back to Des Moines. Unless you can come back again, before that." He gave me a half-hearted smile.

"My God, Dad, there's nothing here that I really want. Maybe just some pictures, a few things like that. Will you be able to take anything with you, or is the place completely furnished?" This all felt so weird. I was glad this was most likely the last surprise I'd face at home. I didn't think I could take anything else.

"Well, I can take my chair," he finally gave a real grin. "And clothes, of course. You'll come see me there, won't you?" He squeezed my shoulder.

"What? Are you kidding? I'll be down to see you so often they'll think I'm moving in. Maybe I'll buy a blue wig so they think I'm a resident, too! And thank goodness you can take your precious chair! I'd hate to think of you without that treasure by your side!" We both chuckled now, trying to take our minds off the reality that was sinking in for both of us.

"Well, can I see this place while I'm here? I'd like to look it over, check it out, if that's okay."

"Sure, sure. Let's go tomorrow. You've been through enough, today." He looked me up and down. "You must be exhausted. I know that was really hard for you, Cheryl. Why don't you go take a nap, then we'll go grab a bite of dinner later, okay?"

"Yeah, that sounds fine, Dad. I could use a couple of hours' sleep." We hugged, a bit tighter and just a few seconds longer than usual. We both knew we had come to the end of a major part of our lives as a family. Everyone would be settled into separate, private living situations. No more playing the piano for my guys. No more laughing at some silly TV show together. I glanced out the window to the back yard on my way to lie down. No more playing for hours on end in the safety of that huge yard, or climbing the trees, reading for hours on end as I had done so many times. I wasn't a kid anymore, which was clearer than ever before. The times they were a-changing.

Chapter Ten

Time Passages

The years after college certainly brought major upheavals to the whole Booth clan. What had been a predictable, loving home environment was turned topsy-turvy. There was Dad, coping to the best of his ability with the aging process. Sweet little Johnny, outliving the doctor's grim predictions, seeming perfectly happy, wherever he went. Content to be a little minister of love in whatever surroundings he found himself. And me, sort of living my dream by singing professionally, yet knowing Iowa was definitely not my final destination.

I'd like to share one of my favorite Albert Einstein quotes with you. It goes like this: "When you sit with a nice girl for two hours, it seems like two minutes. When you sit on a hot stove for two minutes, it seems like two hours. *That's* relativity."

As this amazing genius knew well, time truly is an illusion in many ways. Sometimes it feels it goes on forever and ever, other days there simply is not enough time to get everything done. Looking back now on all that happened in my life, especially the personal loss of family members, I've wondered if I did have it to do over again, would I have spent more time with some, less with others. Pondering those kinds of things doesn't serve a lot of purpose, until I always come back to this conclusion: everything happens in Divine Right timing and all I can do is commit to being here and fully present and aware *right now*, living each day of my life in the best way I know how. I share this with you because so many of us tend to get hung up in the past, feeling guilt for things we weren't even responsible for, really.

I believe life is all about choice; that's the very definition of free will. All you can do with your choices is make the best ones you see fit, without malicious intention. How others react is *their* choice. Many clients who come to see me for hypnotherapy are so stuck on the way their parents treated them, or something that happened many years ago. I do my best to help them see that dragging around a lot of emotional baggage from the past is preventing them from being fully energized and focused in the present. No wonder we have so many dis-eases like Chronic Fatigue Syndrome, anxiety and panic attacks, and a boatload of antidepressants pushed at us about four times during any given hour of prime time TV.

Where the mind goes (what it dwells upon most), the body will eventually follow. It's exhausting to continually dredge up negative memories and experiences from the past. I encourage you to take the positive learnings from your past experiences and apply them to your present life. Let the rest go! Try it for a week and see if you don't feel better. Start out by trying it for a day. And if you feel inundated by "all the negative energy out there in the world", take a media fast for at least a week. Detoxify yourself from the news, including newspapers, TV, radio and online reports. Just live your life and be focused on being the best, most productive, peaceful and happy human being that you can. I believe you'll find the results are truly amazing. Mass consciousness is so powerful, that I like to imagine what might occur if every last one of us on the planet participated in such an experiment for 24 hours? And we can call upon the Higher Consciousness of all our loved ones in Spirit to join with us. I know the results would be amazing. Every time we have World Peace Day or a similar conjoining of group consciousness wonderful things happen. Or not so wonderful things *don't* happen. For example, I believe positive mass thinking and many prayers have helped prevent "the big one" in California. All the predictions by Edgar Cayce, Nostradamus and many other modern "seers" are all subject to change, if enough of us believe the change can occur. In a great movie that combines quantum physics with metaphysics titled *What The Bleep Do We Know?* (visit www.whatthebleep.com for more information), a documented experiment on the positive effect of mass consciousness through conjoined meditation actually lowered the crime rate in Washington, D.C.

Peace must begin within each our individual hearts before it will ever spread worldwide. Wonderful recent leaders, teachers and authors like Gandhi, the Dali Lama, Shirley MacLaine, Wayne Dyer and James Twymann, just to name a few, exemplify similar prescriptions for everyday living

In my work as a medium, I have learned that in the Spirit World, there is no sense of linear time as we know it here. They are not ordered about by Day Timers or Palm Pilots. Many times, predictions that have come through in readings I've given (and received) have happened quite some time after the session occurred. Clients have verified this for me, sounding so surprised when they replayed their audio tape from months, or even years ago, many of the names and situations Spirit had described through me had finally manifested. Because in Spirit's "mind," things already *are*, if they're strongly meant to be part of our soul growth lessons here at Earth School. Situations arise which serve a purpose, cause us to enact a choice, a reaction. The timing happens if and when it's in Divine Right Order, then it's up to us what we make of it.

That being said, I'll move on to what was one of the most difficult portions of this book for me to write. It doesn't matter if you're a medium, or personally in close touch with your loved ones on the other side. As long as *you're* still grounded here, you go through times when you miss them like crazy. You're happy they're in a wonderful place and out of pain, but sometimes, it would sure be nice to be able to hug them, look them in the eye again, wouldn't it? I know all about this. The loss of my wonderful family members prepared me very well for the work I do today. I know they help me, all the time. I am so grateful for that, for the compassion and understanding that coping with their loss has opened up in me. But I still miss them, just like you miss your folks. I'd be a liar if I said anything different.

Once I returned to Des Moines after my guys made those major moves in their lives, I often wondered what motivated Johnny to hang around here. What quality of life could he possibly be enjoying, especially now in that nursing home? How long could he survive there? I didn't like to think about it too much. My own guilt still nagged at me sometimes. I'd be singing a ballad and tears would well up in my eyes and voice. People would tell me how moving the song was for them, and I'd smile and thank them, knowing I had just found a small bit of catharsis for myself, yet they had believed it was about something else, something mysterious and sad. Songs are a great way to act, to release emotions. I've always found that to be true, but perhaps at that time of my life, more so than ever before.

Times were changing in that part of my life, too. My band somehow or other fell apart, as bands are wont to do. I went on to be the lead singer for another band with good musicians, but didn't have the same energy or kinship I'd felt with Bob and the guys. My heart wasn't really in the performance anymore. Those comments of, "You should move to California or New York" kept ringing through my mind.

It was 1982. Johnny had been in his nursing home for nearly a year and a half. Dad sold the house and moved into his facility as planned. He'd been there for a little over a year. I remembered the last time I visited Dad at the house, just before escrow closed. It was good confirmation he had made a wise choice to move. I walked from the garage into the kitchen and was engulfed by smoke pouring out of the oven! I quickly grabbed the fire extinguisher, yelled for Dad to run outside and save himself, then gallantly opened the oven door. When the smoke cleared, I burst into laughter.

Dad had tried to bake one of those frozen coconut creme pies, which you are supposed to eat cold, after they've thawed to room temperature! I kidded, "Hey, what in tarnation you trying to do, ya old coot? Burn down the house before you sell it? I'm gonna tell them not to let you near the kitchen in Kendallwood!" We both had a good laugh over what might have turned into a bad situation.

You may think it's awful I talked to him that way, but for as long as I could remember, my father had called himself an old coot, an old fart, and many other less than loving nicknames. And it actually tickled him when I joined in the teasing! He got me back later though, from the Spirit side of things. I also used to tease him sometimes about being "gimpy" when his arthritis was flaring up. A few years ago when I had some challenges with a knee and was walking rather stiffly, I heard him singing the theme song from the TV comedy *The Real McCoys* in my head, "Grandpappy Amos and the girls and the boys, and the family known as the real McCoys!" Then I heard him chuckling like crazy. Now, for those of you too young to remember this show, the importance of the phrase about Grandpappy Amos was, that was Walter Brennan's character's name, and he walked with a strong "hitch-along in his giddy-up." So what goes around, comes around! And never let it be said those in Spirit lose their sense of irony or humor...far from it!

I went back to Missouri to see my two favorite fellas as often as I could, which was never enough. The very first time I returned to visit Johnny, about a month after his admittance, I was shocked to find how radically things had already changed for him.

First of all, his feeding chair was in the corner, piled full of things like bedpans and other equipment. They had inserted a feeding tube almost immediately after he had checked in, removing his only real physical pleasure, the taste of good food. When I questioned the people in charge, they simply said, "We can't waste an hour for every meal on one patient. We'd never get anything done. He's getting the nutrition he needs through the feeding tube." And they moved on to the next patient's room, undoubtedly to give their family members some similar story.

The radio I left in his room was missing. Stolen. I hotly asked two or three attendants if they had seen it, or observed anyone taking it out of the room, but they just shrugged. I was appalled at the lack of concern or regard for my brother's rights as a human being.

Johnny looked paler than the last time I'd seen him, but was still cheerful. As time went on, subsequent visits showed they were not taking care of his teeth. We had always brushed them every day and taken him to the dentist for regular visits. Now his breath stank and his teeth were turning yellow from lack of cleaning. His beautiful little face, always his best feature, had begun breaking out in pimples and the hint of a wispy mustache showed. In his twenties, he was finally going through puberty. It was harder to see him each time, harder to realize he took longer to recognize my voice. We had always been so in sync, it hurt so much to see how their impersonal treatment of him had effectively squelched his personality.

My sister-in-law went with me one of the last times I visited him. She led me out of the room, her arm around my shoulder. I was devastated and felt like such a creep for letting this happen to John.

"Now, Cheryl, you know God is everywhere. He's certainly there with John when none of us can be. My brother Kevin lives here in Warrensburg. He's offered to come and talk to John once a week or so. In fact, he's brought his daughters here to visit him a few times already."

I sniffed and wiped my eyes. "He has? Oh, that's wonderful! Anyone who can come and sit with him, someone to become a familiar voice and just spend some time and attention on him, that's such a blessing! Please thank him for me!"

"I sure will. He's happy to do it. Kevin likes sports, so he talks to John about that."

"Oh, it doesn't matter what he talks to him about. That makes me feel so much better. I'll have to send Kevin a thank you note."

From that point forward, Kevin was faithful in his visits to John for the years he lived in that home. I shall always be grateful for his kindness and understanding; for providing a friendly voice and face for my brother to look forward to in what must have been an incredibly lonely situation for him.

For his part, Dad had made himself one of the staff's favorites at Kendallwood. He harmlessly flirted with the nurses, teased them about different things, listened to their stories about their families and basically endeared himself to them. He was one of the more "with it" residents, and they lavished as much attention on him as they could without making the others jealous. Many residents lived in a silent stupor, day in, day out. Others periodically repeated whatever was stuck in their mind, like the poor old fellow who sat in the corner, singing over and over to the tune of *The Old Rugged Cross*, "On a hill far away, stood an old Chevrolet..." then he'd cackle at his own pun, and sing it again and again, just that one line.

Dad shook his head and made me promise not to ever let him get "that far gone." On one of my trips down, I brought up something which had been pressing on my mind. "Well, you seem to be thriving here pretty well, Dad. You've got the nurses wrapped around your little finger, huh?"

His eyes twinkled. "It's fun to flirt and know I'm too old to have to do anything about it! They're really sweet girls. They tell me about their families, show me pictures of their kids. And they listen to me tell them about you and John, too. This place isn't all that bad, honey." He adjusted the electric bed so that he was lying back a bit more. I was seated in his armchair, beside the bed. I paused, not sure how he'd feel about what I was about to say.

"Well, I'm glad they're good to you, Dad. I wish Johnny had more people like that taking care of him." He nodded, sensing I had more on my mind.

"Um, Millie and I have been talking. I've sent her several tapes of my band, and she's always told me she felt like I could make it, singing professionally."

He was watching me closely, but still smiling a little. Encouraged, I continued. "She thinks I should move to California, Dad. And I really want to. I'm sick of Iowa. Nothing's ever going to change for me there. I feel like I need to give this my best shot before I'm too old. What do you think?" I was almost afraid to ask.

"Hmm...I think she's right. You are a great singer. I've played some of your tapes for a few of the people here and they all think so, too."

I was astonished that he had been proud enough of my pop music to let anyone else hear it. "Really? Wow, that's great, Dad. You mean it? You think this is a good idea?"

He nodded his head. "Yup, I do. If you're bored and unhappy in Des Moines, get out of there while the gettin's good. I'm not going anywhere for awhile," he smiled. "John's as set as he's going to be. You may as well move forward in your life as best you can. Now, let's get a plan put together to get you out there." I could scarcely believe my ears. This was going over so much better than I had dared to dream. We talked for a couple of hours, even calling Millie and Jeannine in California to work out the details. Millie and her husband Jack had said I could stay with them, but they simply didn't have the space. She suggested I start out living in San Diego, since Jeannine had more room. Then once I had made enough money, I could move up to the L.A. area where the opportunities to perform would be more plentiful. I was very excited. This was more like it!

We worked out the details, which included, at Dad's insistence, flying my brother Don back to Missouri to drive out to California with me. Don now lived in Oregon.

"But Dad, I'm twenty-six years old," I protested. "I can drive cross county by myself. I'll be just fine."

"The point is, you don't have to do that," he replied. "Don said he'll be happy to do this, and you two have always been such good friends. Come on, humor your dear old Dad. You know you'll have a good time. And I won't worry nearly as much if Don is with you."

I agreed this was probably a really good thing, not just for the safety factor Dad was worried about, but because I loved my big brother so much and knew we would, indeed, have fun on the long trip.

My sister-in-law suggested I could move down to Missouri for a few weeks and stay with them. She'd get me a temporary job on swing shift at the plastics factory where she was the HR director. That way I could earn money for the trip and spend time during the day with Dad. This all felt good, like the inertia I'd been stuck in was about to explode!

So that's what happened, basically. I told my current band members I was "outta there," had a yard sale to lighten my load, gave away a few other things, and pulled the rest back down to Missouri in a little rental trailer. I moved into Jesse and Doris' house and went to work inspecting plastic pieces as they came off the assembly line from 3 to 11pm. Boring work, but a mission in and of itself...raise that moving money! It wasn't stressful, and working that shift allowed me to spend some quality time with Dad.

I'd arrive at his room every morning to hang out with him for a few hours. We talked about all kinds of things; sometimes I'd sing and play the piano the dining area. We calculated I could put enough money together in six weeks to make this work, so that's how most of my summer was spent in 1982. Don was scheduled to fly back so we could "hit the road" in September.

I went to visit Johnny one last time before taking off for the coast. His eyes seemed to be focused on some point even further in the distance than the last time I'd seen him. He showed some signs of recognition toward me, but not much. I realized that he intuitively might be trying to help me detach a little more before making my big move. I picked him up and rocked him, like in the old days. Then I gently put him back in his bed, washed his face, and did my best to clean his teeth. I teased him a bit about his mustache growing in more, and wondered if anyone would bother to try and shave him.

"I'm going to California, John. I have to give this a try, y'know? It's kinda now or never. The music business is all about who you know and how young you are, it seems."

He didn't react, but I felt he was listening on some level.

"You always were my best audience. Really, you and Dad are my best friends. I love you. I'm going to miss you guys so much. You hang tough, little brother. Keep talking to Mom and Jesus and all the other angels who come to visit you. I know Kevin is here sometimes and that's great. But I have a funny feeling you have visitors on a regular basis that no one else can see, huh?"

He smiled, and I caught a faint glimpse of the happy, carefree Johnny who had been such a blessing in our lives and home. I knew he understood that last comment, for sure.

"Well, this is hard, but it's something I have to do. Here's a kiss from Dad and one from me." I kissed his forehead twice, then hugged his frail little body once again. "I love you. I promise you, someday I'll tell the world about your life. I'll write a book, so people will understand there's so much more to you than meets the eye. You helped me know people who come here with such severe challenges are special beyond normal understanding. You've been a great teacher." I brushed away a tear.

I tried to avoid a sad goodbye, but it was impossible. Somehow, though, I felt better about surrendering his care to God than I ever had before. "I have to go now, honey. You keep being a good boy. You're *good*, Johnny, you know that? You're so good!"

I hoped to prompt him, to hear him to speak that old familiar phrase, or to say *anything*. He remained silent, however. The peace I felt from him on that "just one more hug goodbye" helped me walk out the door, holding my head high. I knew his soul was so much more magnificent than his present surroundings and circumstances reflected. I vowed to keep my promise to write the book about him, the one you're reading right now. Sometimes, my friend, promises we make take a long time to be fulfilled, but when we are able to make good on the ones that really matter, that's truly soul growth.

The sense of comfort I receive these days, when I feel John's beautiful Higher Self along with Mom and Dad watching me from Heaven is indescribable. So I take a moment to encourage you to believe in yourself and your promises. This book was a dream that took over ten years to finally see in print. It's the fulfillment of a promise to Johnny, and one I'm euphoric about, seeing it finally achieved. The fruition of dreams often takes a lot longer than we may have anticipated, but never give up on yourself. Always allow space for miracles in your life.

I drove back to Dad's new home in silence, reflecting on the passages of time. My father looked thin these days, but he usually ate the fast food I brought him. Oh, yes, Walter had changed his tastes. He who scorned fast food for years now craved the flavor of *anything*, even a somewhat greasy hamburger! The food in the rest home was pretty bland. I couldn't blame him. His doctor was a bit concerned about the weight loss, and encouraged me to get him to drink a beer or a glass of wine once in awhile. "It can't hurt him at this point and might actually put a little weight on him," was his comment.

Dad had undergone a hip socket replacement earlier that year, but it was unsuccessful. In fact, he was in more pain afterward than he'd ever been before. But he braved it, preferring to walk with his cane instead of living in a wheelchair, whenever he could. He was on several pain killers, though, and that concerned me. He had a little chart he made himself, and he was very aware of when he was supposed to get his Demerol. It was obvious he was addicted to it, since the only time he really got irritable with the staff was when that particular med was delivered even ten minutes late.

One weekend, I took Dad over to the little town of Sugar Creek, to visit Aunt Kathy and her current husband, Don. They owned a bar there called "The Do Drop Inn." Aunt Kathy and Don obviously loved each other a lot. I hadn't seen her happier with any of the husbands I had known. But this time, neither one was too happy. She had been diagnosed with cancer, almost identical in nature to the kind that had taken Mom. Her strength was failing, and she wanted us to come over for a visit. She told me in private about the personal hell she'd been going through, and it brought back memories of Mom's battle. She wanted us to share a few laughs, though. She was always a great kidder. So after we'd had our "girl chat" she insisted we all share some wine. It went right to Dad's head, because he started reminiscing in a way I hadn't heard before. He looked at me as though he were about to disclose some big secret.

"Honey, there's something I've never told you," he began.

"Oh, God," I thought, "here comes a skeleton out of the family closet...we really *are* related to John Wilkes Booth!" Having been teased about it from such an early age brought this very real possibility to mind first.

"You know how I always told you I graduated from 8th grade?" he continued, looking quite guilty.

"Well, sure, you never made a big deal out of it. I knew you had to skip high school to help out on the farm and all." I wasn't sure where this was headed.

"Well, it's all a lie, big fat pack of lies!" He sounded disgusted with himself. "I was ashamed, ashamed to admit to my baby daughter, my favorite daughter, that I never even finished the sixth grade. What do you think of me now? Nasty old liar, huh? Dumb ol' sailor!" He grunted.

I was touched by his display of honesty; sharing something he'd secretly feared I'd be ashamed of, and kept to himself all those years. "Dad, don't you know how much I love and admire you? You're without a doubt one of the brightest people I've ever met. It doesn't matter you're mostly self-taught. So was Abraham Lincoln, remember? You're my Dad and I love you. Nothing will ever change that!" I got up to reassure him with a hug. I hadn't seen him smile that big in a long time.

As I've said many times, my Dad will always be one of my heroes. I have written poems and lyrics from the time I was very young. He wrote a few poems in his day, too. I'd like to share a short poem I wrote for him on Father's Day, 1982, shortly after he shared his "deep dark secret" about his lack of education. I still have the photo album in which he lovingly kept it.

A Letter to my Father

June 17, 1982

If I could write a special poem for you on Father's Day,
I'd take my pen and ink in hand and this is what I'd say.
I'd start, "Dear Dad," (for you are dear as no one else could be),
"I can't begin to tell you all the things you mean to me.
You're always there to understand with sympathetic ear,
And always offer me a hand whether I'm far or near.

You're stronger far than many see, and prove it every day.
The care you gave to John and me was the best in every way.
And so I guess I'll close my rhyme for mere words cannot say
How I appreciate the time and love that you convey.

You've been the very best good friend a girl has ever had.
Just want to tell you once again, your daughter loves you, Dad."

So, just in case you had any doubt about how I *really* feel about "the old coot," hopefully that clears it up! That afternoon in Kathy's living room, he regaled us with stories about how big of a moonshiner he was before, during and probably for a few years after Prohibition, helping Grandpa Charlie sell quart jars of "homemade hooch" out the back door of the kitchen. It was quite an epiphany and we all laughed a lot.

Aunt Kathy passed away not too long after that visit. It was a blessing, because she was a shell of her former self, much the same way Mom had wasted away. I was happy the sisters were reunited and out of physical pain. I knew I would miss Aunt Kathleen tremendously. She was such a cut-up and so good-hearted where our family was concerned. She loved flashy showmanship, in fact, she adored going to see Liberace in Vegas. I imagine she has taken Mom along to at least one concert of his in the Spirit World! I know she's having a great time over there, and am so grateful she chose to come through so strongly to me, that first time I went to see Brian Hurst.

The summer went on, and I socked away my moving money, right on schedule. Dad was really good about not talking about our time together growing short. He was content to converse on any number of topics, just happy with each day we shared companionship. He told me he took comfort when he'd wake up from a little nap and look over to find me zonked out in his armchair, dozing peacefully. I found a lot of peace just being in the same room with him, too. It was the only thing approaching normal family time, in a long while.

About two weeks before my scheduled departure, we got a call from Millie. She was pretty panicked. "Hi, you two. Listen, I'm gonna make this quick," she said breathlessly. Millie always talked quickly, so that part was no surprise. But there was an edge to her voice. "I'm going in to the hospital a couple of days before you head out here. They're going to do a double lumbar laminectomy. Basically, they'll be scraping my lower spinal vertebrae to remove the arthritis down there. I know I'll be fine, but I want you two to pray for Jack." Her voice had a definite catch in it, and I heard her blow her nose. "They've found some kind of cancer, some unusual, wildcat kind that just basically attacked him a few days ago. We're going to be in adjoining hospital rooms while they figure out what's next for Jack. Being so close to him will help my recovery, too. I want you and Don to drive real safely, Cheryl. We'll be here and more than likely doing great when you arrive. Just wanted to let you know what is going on and ask you and Dad to please pray for us, especially for Jack." She finally paused for a breath.

"Oh, Millie, I'm so sorry! Of course we'll pray for you. We'll say a prayer as soon as we hang up. Here, talk to Dad for a little bit." I handed him the receiver, shaking my head side to side to further emphasize it was not good news.

He calmed her down a little bit, I believe. She certainly had a full plate to deal with. We bowed our heads and Dad said a wonderful prayer for them. He always was a great believer in the power of prayer. In fact, I often thought had he received encouragement as a young person, he would have made a great minister. As I reflect on these things, I realize how often we tend to allow the disapproval or non-support of family members to define the direction we pursue. Breaking free of that definition and exceeding our parents' accomplishments is a natural chain of events, along with the evolution of time "marching on." I was certainly glad to finally have my father's support about my music pursuits. I planned to go up to L.A. and spend some time with Millie and Jack after I settled in a bit in San Diego.

Dad and I discussed some very serious things those weeks we sat there in his room. I believe Aunt Kathy's passing affected our subject matter in many ways, and the "confession" he had made at her house somehow let me know it would be all right to tell him just about anything. So I told him about my belief in reincarnation, and much to my surprise he did not refute it. He simply listened closely and said,

"Well, nothing is impossible to God. I sure don't claim to have all the answers."

Interesting! Here was a man just past his eightieth birthday, willing to be open to something he had not considered feasible all his life. We went over the burial plan he had picked out for himself as well as the one he was preparing for John. One day he asked for my input on that, which touched me deeply.

"Well, Dad, I don't know how you'll feel about this, but here goes. I look at John and see what a courageous soul has been trapped in that little twisted body, all his life. He loved California so much, especially the ocean." I took a deep breath before continuing, "What would you think about having his body cremated, then I would take the ashes to the ocean and scatter them? I believe he might like that. Seems like a symbolic freeing of that crippled body, to me. When it's my time, I want to be cremated, myself." I paused, hoping I had not gone too far.

"Hmm," he pondered. "That's really a good case you make there. After all, once we're gone, the body's pretty much done for anyway. Isn't cremation is an ancient tradition in lots of cultures?"

I nodded, surprised he knew this. But Dad had always watched lots of news programs, as well as several *National Geographic* specials. He read quite a bit in the years after Mom passed, too. I meant it when I said he was one of the brightest people I had ever known. For someone with a sixth grade education, he had certainly taken it upon himself to learn a lot!

He went on, "You are probably closer to Johnny than anyone else. You two have always had such a special bond. That meant a lot to me, watching you grow up. To see how much you accepted and loved him, how you were always willing to fight for him. Okay. It makes sense to me." He folded up the paperwork and handed it across to me. "Can you go to the funeral home in the next couple of days and tell them we want to go with cremation for him? They can call me to verify it. There's a blank check clipped to those papers; you just fill in the amount when they tally it all up. That will include a plaque for him at the cemetery that will be by your mother and me." His own plan already included an interment with her resting place. He chuckled. "Knowing you, you wouldn't go visit any of us, anyway. You always knew the soul doesn't hang around a cemetery!"

"I'm so glad that didn't tick you off!" I smiled. "It just seemed morbid to me, making all those treks there on holidays and so on. I guess it makes lots of people feel better, but not me."

"I know," he said. "Never really made much sense to me, either.

But for those who do take comfort in it, it's a nice thing. I know you'll do what's right by John and me, Cheryl. I don't know if I can hang on longer than he does. I'm amazed he's survived in that nursing home this long."

"Yeah, me, too." I hated going there, seeing John in those conditions and had no clue how he tolerated it. Lately, he had been going in and out of the hospital, due largely to complications from his feeding tube. Digestive problems, often compounded by breathing difficulties, were causing him trouble. It was painful for both of us to know he was going through that, unable to be there on any sort of regular basis. Sometimes I wondered if Johnny was "God's little secret agent" who had a mission that nobody else could understand, but which he was determined to fulfill. His tenacity and stamina were amazing.

"Now, if I do cross over first, I know you'll see to John's arrangements. I'm beginning to think he might outlast me, don't ask me why. I trust you to take care of things when that happens. You're strong and you've always been a very responsible girl."

I felt a lump in my throat and tried to lighten things a bit by changing the subject. "Yeah, until I drove through that barbed wire fence!" I laughed, but he didn't join in.

"God spared you that time, for sure. I know you'll be more careful from now on. You don't always watch out for yourself too well, honey. I mean, you've always done the right thing for others, whenever you can. That's a wonderful thing." He closed his eyes. "I'm pretty tired now. Think I'll take a little nap before supper."

I crossed to the bed and kissed his forehead, like I usually did with Johnny. Dad was pretty fragile these days, so thin and almost childlike. It's odd how we switch roles with our parents in many ways, as the aging process moves along. Talking with him about seeing to details regarding death and funeral arrangements hadn't really been scary, though. I felt like he was at peace about it all, and that put me more at ease.

"Love you, Dad. I'll see you tomorrow. I'll stop by the funeral home to take care of this before I come back, okay?" I turned and waved from the door, but he was already asleep.

Before I knew it, I was walking away from the boring job at the plastics factory, greeting Don at the airport and preparing to make my goodbyes. I did a better job of not breaking down in front of Dad than I had with John. He and I both classically rose to our best shows of bravado and kept the whole thing upbeat. My father was so remarkable. As with John, I knew he would be all right. It was obvious people at Kendallwood cared about him, and my brother and sister-in-law and the Lays came to visit him quite a bit. We promised to call each other regularly, and I assured him I'd call him from every overnight stop of the move. So there were no tears this time. Not in front of one another, anyway.

It was September 1982. The plan was, once I got established a bit, I'd come home for the holidays. Don and I planned out our route and one bright fall morning, we hit the road. The first night of our journey, when I made my call to Dad to check in, he had some sad news.

"Honey, Jack died this morning. That wildcat cancer took him, just like that. Millie is still recovering from her surgery and now she has to deal with this, too." He was concerned for his eldest daughter, and so was I.

"Oh, I'm so sorry to hear that. I don't know if we'll even get there in time for the funeral, then. We have a good three days ahead of us. The trailer really slows us down." I felt helpless.

"Yes, well, she's pretty much in shock. Norma will be there for her. After you get to Jeannine's, you can figure out the best thing to do, as far as spending some time with Millie and so on. Just wanted to let you know. Keep her in your prayers, she's in a lot of pain right now, in more ways than one."

"I will, Dad. Poor Millie. Well, you take care. We'll talk tomorrow, okay?"

The rest of the trip was fairly uneventful. Don and I shared some good conversation and some laughs. We had always had such an easy rapport. I was so glad he was able and willing to make this trip with me. It made the move easier in so many ways.

After we got to San Diego, Jeannine had already discussed a possible change in plans for me with Norma. She suggested I move up to L.A. and live with Millie, as she would need someone to help with the housecleaning, fixing her meals and so on, during her recovery. The surgeons were predicting it would be two months before she'd be able to return to work. Now with Jack gone, she'd also needs lots of emotional support. I shifted my mindset immediately. In fact, this would be best for me, too, since living in L.A. was my actual goal. Interesting how the Universe works, isn't it?

So I moved to Glendale, a nice suburb of the San Fernando Valley. Millie's little house was charming, and what had been Jack's office was quickly converted to my bedroom. Millie was uncharacteristically quiet. Life had dealt her a very hard blow. She had planned to spend the rest of her life with Jack, someone I had only met by phone, who sounded so jovial and full of life each time we talked.

That fall, I accepted a few part-time temporary jobs through an agency, and helped Millie in every way I could. We grew very close and she loved hearing me sing. In fact, she helped me rent a piano so I could write songs and "keep my chops up." I joined the Burbank Civic Light Opera, and was immediately cast as Eliza Doolittle in their production of *My Fair Lady*. I was thrilled! Back on the musical stage in the L.A. area, and in one of my favorite musicals within two months of moving... "not too shabby!" I had always loved the music of Lerner and Lowe. The role of Eliza gave me a great chance to show off my Cockney and British accents. I had a blast! Millie was able to attend one performance and was always proud of me.

Dad enjoyed hearing about my success and commented that I must have, indeed, made the right move. He was very understanding when I couldn't make it home for Christmas, because several performances were around the holidays. And Millie wasn't quite ready to be on her own yet, either.

I made several new friends from that experience in the musical, and began to feel more and more comfortable finding my way around L.A. The traffic was incredible, but I adapted pretty quickly. You had to, if you wanted to get around. Public transit was not great in L.A. in those days.

Around the first of the year, I got a temp job in the production department of *Warner Brothers Records*. At least I was involved in some aspect of the music industry in a real way. After I was there a month, they offered me full-time permanent status. Thinking this might be a really good "in" in my chosen industry, I accepted. Filing, typing and answering the phone for one of the many vice presidents there was neither as exciting nor glamorous as I may have hoped, but there I was, right in the heart of the music biz. I learned a lot and saw a few artists here and there, like the very young, diminutive Prince; Ricki Lee Jones, who was quite popular then, and a young, unpolished upstart named Madonna, who was married to Sean Penn and hadn't even thought of studying the Kabala way back then. She originally signed on the *Sire* label, one of WB's subsidiaries.

The production department was not recording production, however. We were concerned with getting all the details of the album jackets correct, the artwork proofed, the liner notes correct, and so on. We were just down the street from *Warner Brothers Studios* in Burbank, and I often walked over to the lot for lunch at the commissary, or strolled down the streets of various back lot movie sets, when permitted. It felt like I was really starting to "break in" to the biz!

On February 4th, 1983 a coworker motioned me over to her cubicle. She had come to a couple of the "open mic" nights where I'd sung, and she knew I was a huge Carpenters fan. "Sit down, Cheryl. there's something you need to hear." She turned up her portable radio. The announcer was talking about Karen Carpenter. She had died that morning, just short of her thirty-third birthday, due to complications from something that wasn't well-publicized back then, anorexia nervosa. I couldn't work the rest of the day, I was so stunned. I felt like I'd lost one of my closest friends. All those years I had sung along with her, so happy for her and Richard's success. How could this have happened? I had seen her on a recent Olivia Newton John special and she'd been so thin, I'd barely recognized her. But her voice was the same, melodious, pure, true alto it had always been. I remember being a bit worried about her, but this disease was a largely unknown enemy in those days. I figured she'd bounce back from whatever was wrong.

I called Dad that night. "Yeah, honey, it's a shame. I knew this would tear you up. She had a great talent. Seems like such an awful thing, a young woman like that being taken." He sighed. "Hard to figure things like that out sometimes, isn't it, kiddo?"

"Yes, it sure is. She must have been very unhappy for a long time. Thanks for understanding, Dad. I don't feel too well. I think I'd better hang up now, but I'll call in a few days, okay?" I had a headache from crying all the way home. This was as hard as Judy Garland's passing had been for me. Karen was so young! I just didn't get it. I wished there was something I could do for Richard and their parents. I did the only thing I could think of—prayed for them to somehow find some peace about this horrible loss.

I sang in more venues and got some good response, but L.A. was such a different animal than Des Moines or K.C. This was a tough crowd. More often than not, you had to pay to sing! This was back-asswards! But many musicians were doing just that, paying to play, willing to cough up some money to buy time on a stage where they hoped someone with clout would hear them and rescue them from obscurity. I found lots of open mic situations, won a couple of talent contests, but didn't feel like I was really making a lot of headway. The musical had been such a positive note on which to begin my L.A. life; everything after that seemed like a let-down somehow.

It began to dawn on me what a tough business this could be. You couldn't take rejection personally, nor could you stop giving 110 percent every single time you performed. Each performance was an audition on some level. Karen's passing opened my eyes even more, helping me comprehend why not just aspiring actors and musicians, but even successful ones, often fell prey to depression, chemical dependency, and self-abuse via such demons as eating disorders.

Working at *Warner Brothers* provided me a pretty decent paycheck, but that was not inspiring. I submitted a tape of one of my original songs to a producer in Nashville. He got excited about it and pitched to Anne Murray's people. But as happened more often than not with unknown writers, singers, actors...it led to zip, nada. He finally was kind enough to tell me that they had too many similar songs scheduled for Anne's upcoming album. Small comfort.

Millie called upon her resilient disposition and grew stronger and happier, little by little. By mid-summer, I moved in with one of my new friends, who just happened to live a few blocks away from my sister. I was happy about that arrangement, as it gave us both more freedom, yet we were still easily accessible to one another.

Dad and I talked on the phone at least once a week, often more than that. He always seemed to know when I was going to call. He'd pick up the phone and say, "Hi, honey!" or "How's my girl?"

"Aw, I bet you say that to all your women callers!" I'd tease.

"No, I knew it was you. I can tell it by your ring." I could hear the smile in his voice. After all the years of being so in tune with Dad, I believed he probably *did* intuitively know when it was me on the line. I made plans to come home and see him and John for Thanksgiving. He was happy about that. His voice sounded pretty tired, most days. But the thought of an in-person visit perked him up a bit. I looked forward to it, too.

As my second California November approached, I was happy to be in sunny L.A. for the winter. Not having to drive in the snow every day was a real treat to a Midwestern girl. I had my tickets to fly home, though, and was looking forward to Thanksgiving dinner with Dad and making a visit to John, too. I was going to fly out early the morning of the holiday. Late the afternoon before Thanksgiving, on November 23, 1983, I got a phone call at work. It was our friend, Clyde Lay. He often visited Dad at the nursing home. He was speaking in kind of hushed tones. I soon understood why.

"Cheryl, I'm sorry to disturb you at work. I'm here at your Dad's nursing home and he's acting kind of funny. He keeps telling me he's dying, and he insisted we call you." He paused. "I didn't know what else to do."

"Oh, that's all right, Clyde. You know, Dad has told me he's dying off and on for years! He gets in pain when he doesn't get his meds on time and..."

Our friend interrupted me. "No, this is different, somehow. I've heard him say that before, too. But he's very agitated right now. He's picking at the buttons on his pajamas....I've just never seen him act quite this way. He wants to talk to you."

I drew a sharp breath. Just a couple of days before, I had read an article about how people sometimes pick at their clothing just before they pass away. It's almost as though they're uncomfortable in their own skin anymore. I cleared my throat and tried to sound cheerful. "Sure, put him on, Clyde. And thanks so much for being there with him."

Dad took the receiver. "Hi, honey! How are you?"

"Well, I'm fine, Dad. The question is, how are *you*?" His breathing sounded labored.

"Well, not so good, but not so bad, either. I had to call and talk to you. I'm ready to go home. I've had a good, long life. I'm tired, Cheryl. I want to go home and see your mother." He sounded tired, indeed, but so matter-of-fact, I was startled.

"Well, Dad, I understand that. You know I'll be there tomorrow afternoon, right? We can talk all about this then. Maybe you need to go to the doctor and get some new medication or vitamins or..."

He chuckled. "No, that's not it. I know what's going on." I fleetingly wondered if he had a vision of Jesus coming to get him, as his mother did. "I just had to call and tell you, I have no regrets. I know you'll take care of Johnny, when his time comes. You've been a wonderful daughter to me and a great sister to him. Thank you for everything."

I was crying openly, now. Several coworkers looked my way, but I didn't care. "Dad! Wait, Dad. That's really sweet, but listen to me...I'll see you tomorrow. Maybe you should take a nap, or..."

He sighed patiently. "Maybe we'll see each other tomorrow. I just knew I had to call you tonight. I want to tell you something, and I want you to really hear it. You ready? Here it is. I love you, sweetheart."

I sniffed. "I love you, too, Daddy." What I really wanted to do was scream, "Don't do this! Don't talk this way! You're tearing me up, I have to fly thousands of miles tomorrow to see you..." But I felt deep inside that he knew what he was talking about. I could only pray he would hang on until I got home.

I heard Clyde's voice on the line again. "That was what he really wanted to say, Cheryl. Are you okay? We'll see you tomorrow," he said encouragingly.

I wiped my eyes. "Yeah, sure. I'm okay. I'm so grateful you are there with him, Clyde. You're right, this is different than any way he's been before. See you tomorrow. Thanks so much." I put down the receiver, feeling hollow inside. I realized Dad and I had not said goodbye, but our last words to one another were "I love you."

I asked my boss if it would be okay for me to leave an hour early, and he kindly gave permission. The car somehow found its own way home, because I don't remember driving there. I was packing, determined to make my father feel better once he saw me, when the phone rang.

Almost afraid to pick it up, I tentatively said, "Hello?"

I heard quiet sobbing on the other end. "Miss Booth? This is Rhonda at Kendallwood Retirement home. I'm one of your father's nurses."

"Yes, Rhonda?" I already knew what she was about to say.

"I'm so sorry to tell you this, Miss Booth, but your father passed away. He was gone so quickly." She was obviously crying, and I could hear someone else doing the same in the background. "Jenny and I were walking your Dad to the bathroom. He paged us to help him. He said he wanted two beautiful escorts to walk with him, so we each took an elbow and were heading that way, when he just kind of slipped out of his body and slid to the floor, very gently. We couldn't catch him. He was gone before we could get him back up on the bed. I'm so sorry."

"Yes, thanks. I know you are. Thanks for being so good to my Dad. Thanks for being there for him at the end." I was staggered. *I* should have been there with him. Why couldn't he have hung on just one more day?

"Oh, we should be the ones thanking him. He was so special to us. Almost always cheerful and pleasant. Certainly one of the sharper residents here. We all enjoyed talking to him so much." She paused. "He said you are coming back here tomorrow, is that right?"

"Yes, I'll be there. I'll, um, have to see to the funeral arrangements. I'll make sure and get all his personal things out. Some of his stuff can be donated to other residents, if they can use it..."

"Oh, honey, don't worry about that now. Just let us know if there's any way we can help you, once you're here. Again, we're so sorry, Cheryl." She was very sweet. I could tell Dad had indeed won over a number of the staff there. Why wouldn't he? He was such a great guy.

I woodenly went through the motions of finishing packing, after calling relatives with the news. Millie, Jeannine and Norma got busy booking flights back to Missouri. I called the funeral home and they set the date for Dad's service. He had lost so much weight; in the last pictures he sent me, he looked like a ghost of himself, but was still smiling brightly. I told the funeral director to please plan for a closed casket service. I wanted to remember my father as the robust man who had always been my biggest hero. Our age difference had never mattered to us. We truly were best friends.

Somehow, I got through all the machinations of the funeral, attending to Dad's affairs and so on. I was grateful he had sold his home; that was one less thing for me to deal with. Doris, Jesse and Don drove me down to Warrensburg so we could all see Johnny, the day after the service. I was pretty much all cried out by then, just operating on autopilot.

I looked down at my little brother, so helpless, yet perfectly at peace. I had a feeling Dad had already visited him, telling him he and Mom would be waiting, whenever John chose to come be with them in Heaven. I don't remember exactly what I said to him, something about our parents being together again, and how much we all loved him. Whatever I said, I felt as though John really got the main message. He even said, "Ohhh..." to me in a comforting tone, like "Don't cry anymore, Sis. It's all right, now." I knew if he could, he would have given me a big hug and patted me on the back. The fact that he couldn't didn't matter. He knew what pain I was in and wanted to make it better.

I sat beside him and held his small hand for a few minutes. Just sitting silently, together, helped me a lot. Our relatives left us alone and it was a very special time. I kissed his hand, then his forehead, brushing his hair off his forehead. I pulled myself together enough to wash his face and attend to him in a basic, loving way. Then I hugged him and told him I loved him. No goodbyes, just like my last conversation with Dad. I realized how important it was to me that the last words my father and I had spoken to one another were, "I love you." He had wanted company when he crossed, so he had buzzed the nurses. But he hadn't wanted me to see him actually pass away. I realized there truly are no "goodbyes" only "see you laters."

Dad's service was well-attended. I wound up any unfinished business with the retirement home and took a few of his "treasures" back home with me, like a pocket watch I had given him years before, his photo albums of his kids and grandkids. On the flight home, it occurred to me why he had found it so imperative to call and tell me he was leaving. It was his way of making it up to me about delaying the news of Mom's death, twelve years before. He knew how much it had upset me that he'd gotten Grandma and Doris to fib, to make me wait until he came home from the cancer hospital that night. He thought he was being sensitive, wanting to be the one to break the news of her death. And he was, but at age fifteen, I didn't recognize his sensitivity, only how it compounded my own pain. Now here, with his own death, he made sure

I heard it directly from him, just a couple of hours in advance. Once again, he didn't want anyone else to tell me, but this time he wanted to be sure I didn't have to wait, either. Walter Booth truly was an amazing human being.

Somehow, I went through the motions of getting back to work at *Warner Brothers*. But my heart wasn't in it anymore. I found myself dialing Dad's phone number a couple of times, out of habit. We had talked twice, sometimes three times a week since I'd moved to California. I'd drop the phone like it was a snake when I realized what I was doing, freaked out by a habit which no longer had meaning.

In the spring of 1984, I was on a trip with a friend to Seattle. Sleeping on her relative's couch, I had a curious dream. Ever since Dad died, I had a number of dreams about him, all peaceful in nature, letting me know he was okay. This one was different.

The dream started out with a phone ringing. I picked it up, and heard Dad's voice say, "Turn on your TV, honey, there's something important you need to see."

I knew in the dream that he was dead, that this was really a "long distance call," but I didn't question that. I wanted to see what message he felt was so important he had to call me from the Spirit World.

I turned on the television, and in the lower left hand corner saw the words "New York City." People on the screen were running, crying and screaming. Tall buildings in the background were swaying and there was lots of smoke. Given my recent life in L.A., I figured it was some kind of earthquake in New York, wreaking horrible havoc.

"What *is* this, Dad? It's awful!"

"Just be safe. This is going to happen. I want you to stay away from New York, okay? You're better off in L.A., or anywhere else for awhile. I love you." With that, he hung up.

I sat up on the couch with a start. Very quietly, I turned on the television to see if this had really taken place in the "real" world. There was nothing about New York. I breathed a sigh of relief. The dream was so vivid and specific, though, not just a typical dream filled with scattered images. It reminded me of my precognitive dreams from childhood. For years, I hoped I would not hear about some terrible earthquake in New York. Then on September 11, 2001 I knew what the dream had been about. It wasn't an earthquake at all, but the heinous attack on the Twin Towers. It took seventeen years for that dream to make sense. Why would Dad have warned me, but not given me a date or more specifics? I'm not sure. Maybe he wasn't allowed to. More than anything else, I believe he really just wanted to warn me off moving there, since we'd had that discussion many years before, about me trying my hand on Broadway. There was certainly nothing I could have done to prevent this awful act. I believe he simply wanted to warn me to stay away, well in advance.

I believe on a soul contract level, everyone who passed in that tragedy agreed to check out at that time. Their mass crossing raised the world's awareness of many things; especially it brought home the fact that we need to love and appreciate each other every single day, to be present in the moment. I feel the same about the tsunami in Asia just after Christmas 2004, Hurricanes Katrina and Rita...the devastating loss of life that took place in all those events, as well as in deadly earthquake in India and Pakistan in October, 2005. There are more Earth changes to come. We have not been the best of custodians for Mother Earth, and she is a living, breathing entity, after all.

I do firmly believe we can all start on an individual basis to turn things around. To do our best to be good people, to be kind to others and ourselves. Every single day! Because beyond the present, none of us truly knows what is there. Predictions of probabilities can be made, but the fact is, life is tenuous. The course of it can turn on the spin of a dime. If we aren't grateful for what we have right here and now and don't take the time to validate and appreciate our loved ones, we may never have that opportunity on the Earth plane again. That's why I'm so thankful my father's and my last words to one another on this physical level were "I love you." I usually close each conversation with a loved one in that way. No one ever hears those words too much, do they? I don't believe that's possible.

It's time to return to the chronology of my story now, and doing so requires a bit of a flashback to the mid-1980s. I left Warner Brothers before the end of 1984 and enrolled in acting school, something I had always wanted to do. Dad had left me a little bit of money, and I believed that was one of the best investments I could make, one in myself and my talent. I felt like he approved.

I continued to write songs and appear in open mic venues. I tried singing with a few bands, but didn't fit the image most of them were looking for, some kooky Cyndi Lauper look or vintage Madonna "slut" image. I focused more on acting and really enjoyed it tremendously. I took a few classes in voiceover and found a new outlet for all the impressions and accents I had done since childhood.

By this time, I was living in a countrified setting, outside of North Hollywood about ten miles. I loved it there. Many neighbors had horses, it was a great change of pace from downtown L.A. and Hollywood. The little two bedroom house I rented is where I was living when I went to see Brian Hurst that first time in 1985, when I first heard from Aunt Kathy from the Spirit World. And just a few short days after that, I was there when I got the call that Johnny had passed away. I was glad for him in many ways. He was reunited with our parents, and finally free of that twisted little body. As Aunt Kathy had said, he was now, "perfect" in his spirit body. I was happy for him, actually. Happy and relieved that he no longer was confined or restricted in any way. Having had that reading just prior to his passing helped me have that attitude. Because I knew for a fact, stronger than ever before, that this life here on Earth is far from "all there is." I knew then that there is an afterlife and that there was absolutely no reason to fear death.

I flew back to Missouri, because I wanted to be the one to give my brother's eulogy. I couldn't stand the thought of some detached preacher who hadn't known anything about John's life standing there pontificating on this "poor little soul's life that had drug on and on" or anything along those lines. I also made arrangements to bring his ashes home with me, then Millie and I would have a memorial aboard a boat called *The Tribute* which provided a legal venue for scattering ashes offshore.

On the flight back to Kansas City, I looked out the window and realized Missouri no longer felt like home. The plane made its final approach, and I reviewed my notes for John's eulogy one more time. When I called to make plans for this trip and the arrangements for the funeral, Jesse and Doris suggested the minister from their church perform the service. I politely thanked them, but told them I'd handle it, adding that if one of my nephews wanted to sing and play his guitar, that would be great. I knew I could speak John's tribute, but singing as well would have been too much. He used to love it so much when I'd sing for him, but I wanted to stay strong for him. I knew speaking most likely wouldn't tear me up as much as singing. I wanted everyone in attendance to remember the positive impact John's life made upon the lives of so many others, how my little brother was the happiest, most peaceful soul I ever met.

Stepping into the terminal of Kansas City International, I saw my sister-in-law over in the corner, waving to me. We hugged, and walked to the baggage claim area. She talked about the weather, her sons, her work, and of course, how Johnny was no longer suffering.

"He's with the Lord, now, Cheryl, so we know he's all right." That statement triggered something in me. Most likely, it was because I was still so jubilant over the information Brian had so recently shared with me. At any rate, I began babbling excitedly to my dyed-in-the-wool, "born again Christian" sister-in law about the fact I'd gone to a medium. Her eyes widened as I rambled on about this wonderful fellow who was able to get in touch with Aunt Kathy, who in turn gave all this incredible evidence and comforting messages about John. I told her how all this had given me such peace of mind because I knew John was now absolutely perfect, safe, whole and happy.

She listened politely, and when I'd run the gamut on this track, she took a deep breath and looked at me squarely. I literally felt a dark, invisible curtain drop between us as she said, "Well, Cheryl, the devil can talk through a lot of people, too. You can't allow yourself to be deceived."

Her slow, sweet Midwestern drawl contained an edge I'd never detected before. This was one of the most accepting, sweet, nonjudgmental people I knew, but I had just crossed a boundary that was taboo. Brian had talked about God's love over and over, so I knew there was nothing evil about the work he did, nor in the fact I'd gone to see him. This was my first personal encounter with the fact certain folks didn't even want to talk about mediumship. Just because I found truth in it, didn't mean everyone would. Sort of like discussing religion or politics. Some things you just don't bring up in certain circles.

I determined not to broach this topic with her again, nor with any family members during this trip. Our encounter didn't shake my conviction nor reduce the comfort the reading had delivered to me; it just brought home very clearly what a valuable gift is discretion.

John's service was sweet and simple. My nephew Jeff played and sang a lovely song. Here's the eulogy I gave.

TRIBUTE TO AN ANGEL

"John Howard Booth was the most uniquely talented person I have ever had the privilege of knowing. Some people would not understand that, because so many people cannot look past a misshapen body...they cannot fathom why a benevolent God would permit such a small, helpless individual with a twisted, non-walking body to enter into this world. How could a soul trapped in that type of deformed structure possibly be of any use? This is where their special gift enters the picture...the gift of LOVE, pure and simple. John was LOVE personified. From the moment he was born he became an unselfish human dispenser of it in quantities that had no bounds. Special Earth-bound angels such as he are, in fact, far more powerful than any "Superman" ever imagined.

And the only thing these small angels ask in return is to bask in the reflection from that LOVE they so willingly give. Anyone who spent any length of time with John marveled at his glowing countenance and ethereal sweetness. He taught a countless number of people, including me, patience and compassion. Surely this is the highest form of existence we should all aspire to, rather than getting so wrapped up in ourselves. Whenever I get bogged down by life's little pitfalls, all I need do to regain perspective is remember John in his contented silence. No problems weighed him down, although many would say his life was full of heartache. He took delight in the simple offerings of nature—a bird singing, the bright sunshine, a rippling brook. He loved music and laughter, and all the best things in people, and had malice for no one or no thing. Although he never spoke more than a few words, his smile and laughter were infectious, and far more eloquent than any words which language has to offer. All too often we so-called "normal folks" take for granted such priceless possessions as good health, loving family and friends, and our most generous and boundless Creator. Each terrible "trial and tribulation" we so begrudgingly endure is, in fact, just another opportunity to grow in faith and love.

Johnny was more than a perennial baby brother to me. He was often my most attentive listener, my favorite playmate, and my most valued instructor. He only offered love and support in place of criticism and anger, which the rest of us fall back on too easily. I wished many times that I had been able to keep him with me somehow, because his last few years at the nursing home seemed so dreary. Yet I realize now he was able to touch that many more lives, and so continued his life's work, even as we all must. I shall keep the good memories of times at home, and be joyful that he is free at last from the physical shell which was his own private prison. The LOVE and LIGHT he spread will continue for a long while, and knowing that, I'm sure John is smiling somewhere.

My brother and the many others like him are Bearers of Light in a world that is progressively growing darker due to fear and ignorance. The Light they put forth is an unconditional LOVE for all mankind. If we can channel and spread it, how much better everything would be. These must indeed be very evolved souls to have chosen such a non-self-serving existence. Many might say, "What a waste. How futile an existence." In truth, they have the greatest gift of all; being special missionaries of LOVE and living testimonies of FAITH and TRUST in a GREATER POWER. This surpasses "normal understanding" until your life is personally touched by one of these beautiful souls. So, rather than pity these whom we consider so unfortunate, the energy would be better spent in striving to follow their precious example, and just LOVE them in return the best we can."

While waiting to get on the plane back to L.A., I felt nervous about carrying the small box which held my brother's ashes. I'd never done anything quite like this. When they scanned it at the security checkpoint, the woman asked me what the "powdery substance" was. She must have thought it was drugs.

"Cremains," I quietly replied.

"What? Please speak up!" she demanded.

I steadied myself and repeated, louder, "Cremains." Still no registration of understanding. I raised my voice even more. "Human, crematory remains. Those are my brother's ashes, okay? I'm taking them to California to scatter them."

She looked down and mumbled, "I'm sorry ma'am. Please continue to the gate." I guess this particular item didn't get carried on that often! On the plane, that experience struck me as funny. Ironic. I knew John would think so, too. I was still nervous, so I ordered a gin and tonic as soon as I could, to help me relax. These were unusual circumstances, to say the least. John's remains were neatly tucked under the seat of the unsuspecting passenger in front of me.

The day Millie and I went to Marina Del Rey to scatter the ashes, the weather was gorgeous and strikingly clear. Unusually so, even our boat's captain commented on it. In my mind, I could hear Streisand singing "On a clear day you can see forever, and ever...." We took a dozen roses to scatter after the ashes. When we got to the proper mile where this activity was deemed legal, the captain opened the container while Millie and I looked out over then ocean. Then he gently asked me if I would like to spread the remains.

I didn't know what to say. I hadn't thought about who would do that part of the ceremony. I nodded, and he handed me a little light blue bundle that looked somewhat like a disposable diaper. He told me it was a biodegradable material which was legal for such use. I could feel little pieces of something inside. I realized with a shudder it must be tiny bone fragments. I leaned over the railing and gently dropped the tiny package, then looked up at the sky as Millie and I scattered our roses.

"I hope you like this, Johnny. You loved the ocean. It was the best thing I could think of to do. I love you," I added in a whisper. "Be happy, honey."

Millie and I had a nice dinner, then went home. I was glad she had accompanied me. It felt good to have her support. She was doing really great by this time, fully back in the swing of things at work and even dating once in awhile. Millie was another inspiration to me, and she was one of my biggest fans. It meant so much that she always made time to see me perform, whenever I invited her.

In a subsequent reading with Brian, he told me he saw my face on the cover of a book I had written, as well as on a CD cover. I still had dreams of making it in entertainment, but began making notes for the book I had promised Johnny I would write one day. The one you're reading right now. I began to realize my spiritual life was more important to me than anything, and even though I continued working on my career in the entertainment field, I now began studying and reading about metaphysics more than ever before. I became a big Shirley MacLaine fan, greedily reading each book she cranked out. I absolutely loved the television movie of her book *Out On A Limb*. It gave me major chills! Life was taking some interesting turns. I knew my family in Spirit was around me much of the time. I could feel their love and energy. I loved going to Brian to talk with them, attending his group meetings and watching him share his gift. What I didn't know at the time was that I would soon be studying to become a medium, myself.

Part II

The Medium Awakens

Chapter Eleven

Tuning In

After my first meeting with Brian described in Chapter One, I got into the habit of having a reading with him once or twice a year. He refused to book appointments with people more often than that, because he believed the client would not receive new or different information. I also believe it was his way of encouraging individuals to learn to trust their own discernment. I strive to help my clients do the same.

Two years into our friendship, the readings with Brian almost always included one common theme: I was very psychic and should probably find a way to start doing readings on my own, that I could help people in this way. It reminded me of the dreams and visions my mother had forbidden me to share, out of her fear. And of course, it reminded me of my teenage experience with "the Voice."

I wasn't sure I was ready for this, even now. I was beginning to work with a lot of creative visualization techniques at this point in time, and decided to "invite" this opportunity to develop, if it were truly so important. To release any blockages I might have. And wouldn't you know it, within days of that invitation to the Universe, Brian gave me a call.

"Cheryl, how would you like to sit in a psychic development circle?"

"What's that?" I was puzzled.

"Well, it's an opportunity for a few like-minded people to sit together once a week in the hopes of developing whatever spiritual, psychic gifts they have. This is a common way to increase your abilities in England. You must be willing to commit to a long-term situation, however. At least six months, maybe more, one night a week, at the same regular time. That allows the helps the energy of the group build, and the talents develop strongly as a rule. My friend Sara has offered to start such a group and asked me if I knew anyone who might be interested. You were one of those who came to mind."

"Sounds good so far. How much does it cost?"

He laughed. "Nothing. It's a commitment to help others by helping yourself. Shall I have Sara call you?"

I paused. I had blown this stuff off for quite awhile. Seeing Brian work inspired me very much. Once a month he held group sessions at his home which thirty people or more would attend. I went as often as possible, because I knew he was genuine, and was fascinated by the work.

"Okay, sure. Please ask her give me a call. I'm in."

"Oh, great! I know you'll get a lot out of it. She'll ring you straightaway, I'm sure. Take care, Cheryl."

"Yes, thanks. Talk to you soon, Brian." We hung up, and I wondered what I had just gotten myself into.

Sara was a British healer who had been confined to a wheelchair for a number of years before learning to harness the power of her mind, and actually heal herself. After that, she began performing healing energy treatments on others. She lived in a mobile home park in Pacific Palisades, high atop a mountain. Her deck had a breathtaking view of the ocean. She confirmed the negative ion theory about psychic vibration, and told me she chose to live there because of the ocean's healing, soothing power.

The first night we got together, six of us were present. Sara wanted to keep the number at eight or less, so she was very pleased by the turnout. Besides myself, a young man was in attendance who would become quite well-known in a few years, writing several books, even having his own TV shows about mediumship, *Beyond* and *Ghost Whisperer*. Chances are since you're reading *this* book, you are already familiar with James Van Praagh. James was ready to do readings at the time we met. I was just opening up and not ready to read for anyone else, nor to trust my own messages all that much, yet. So I went to him a few times, and he was always helpful. Because Brian was limiting his readings to just one ninety minute session per day, he often referred people to James.

Sara began each sitting by lighting some incense, then placing a bowl of water in the center of the circle to draw the spirit energy. We had a long paper device which looked like a tall, thin dunce's cap. This was a "conical trumpet." It was placed on a paper plate, then one of us would trace a circle around its base. The trumpet was there to determine if anyone in the group was what was known as a "physical medium." After the session, we always checked to see if the trumpet had moved at all. It never did during the entire course of time the group sat together, which was nearly two years, for many of us.

Physical mediumship involves a number of phenomena. As far as the trumpets went, they were said to be capable of flying about the room, and often a spirit voice would speak through the trumpet. Because mass consciousness was opening up more and more and people were accepted mediumship more readily in the 1980s than 100 years previous, this type of physical demonstration was becoming pretty rare. Clairaudient/clairvoyant mediums such as Brian, James, John Edward, myself and many others are usually referred to as mental mediums, because the information we work with is telepathic. Through Brian, I met a well-known British voice medium (one category of physical medium) named Leslie Flint. (I'll share more about Leslie in another book. His life and work were fascinating!)

After we were all seated in our circle, Sara would light a candle, and douse the electrical lights. She then played a recording of *The Lord's Prayer*, either a spoken version, or a musical one. This was for protection, and to get us all in alignment with our intention for the evening. We joined hands as she led us in a brief, affirmative prayer. This basically stated that we were only sitting for the good of all present, and for the good of all creatures upon the Earth; that the only type of information or activity we invited was to be of the Light, and positive in nature. Then we dropped hands, and sat in the still darkness until someone felt moved to speak, or a significant shift in the energy was noticeable, and we'd begin to stir. These sessions might last an hour, or even two. Once the silence was broken, we'd turn the lights back up and share what, if anything, had been seen or heard by each member of the circle.

On the evening of our first meeting, James described seeing a woman standing behind me, first tapping me on the shoulder, then almost knocking on top of my head, trying to get my attention. We all laughed, and he said he believed this was my mother, striving to get me to open up and hear her. He said she was around me more often than I thought, often with messages to share, but I had not yet learned to open the channel enough to hear her. This made sense to me, and I resolved to spend more time in meditation, clearing my mind as much as possible in order to hear better.

One night in our group, I got a vision which I shared with a young man I'll call Jerry. Someone in Spirit showed me a talisman that belonged to him. He told me this necklace had been given to Jerry several years ago, and he hadn't worn it for some time.

"This is unusual for me," I told him, "because I'm just starting to get more clarity through pictures during our meditation. He shows me a quarter moon with a star attached to one point, and it's made of silver. Does that make sense to you?"

He stared at me and gulped. "Y-yes. A teacher, a mentor of mine gave me that necklace several years ago. It was for protection and to open psychic awareness. It's in my jewelry box."

"Yes," I went on, still in a slight daze, "he says his name is Miguel, and he is in spirit now. He would like you to wear the talisman. He calls it a talisman, not a necklace. Anyway, he'd like you to wear it again for awhile. Perhaps while sitting with our group here. He feels it will open you up a little faster." I opened my eyes and looked directly at Jerry.

"Yes! Miguel, that's him! He died three years, no, four years ago. Wow, this is amazing!" He grinned at me. "I'll wear it next week and show you!"

Huge goosebumps ran up and down my arms the entire time Miguel had been speaking with me and showing me images. Jerry's confirmation encouraged me and made me believe more strongly that I was on track by being willing to develop this ability. I was beginning to feel like a "psychic telephone" between Heaven and Earth!

This sort of activity grew stronger each week, with everyone becoming more confident and open in sharing their visions and what they heard during our evenings together. James broke off from the group after awhile, and started one of his own in his home. I stayed with our core group. It was one of the most enlightening experiences in which I have participated, and it certainly stimulated my desire to become more attuned. (I will include detailed information on how to start your own psychic development circle in my upcoming book devoted to that topic).

James was beginning to do quite a lot of private readings at that point. I went to see him two or three times. His information was accurate, and I felt comfortable going to "check in" via his abilities between readings with Brian. I'll briefly share some of the highlights of one reading James did for me. Of course, this was years before he began making television appearances. In addition to being a medium whose gifts have helped many, James is a best-selling writer. Perhaps you've read his books, *Talking to Heaven*, *Reaching to Heaven, Healing Grief* and others.

In 1987 and '88, I was beginning to receive more and more "direct contact" from spirits, which was very exciting to me. One of the first people outside of my own family to speak with me was a well-known celebrity. I shared some of her communication to me with Brian, because at first I thought I was imagining it. There's more about her in Chapter Sixteen, but I mention her here because she significantly figures into the reading I'm about to describe.

During one particular reading with James, he asked if I knew someone named Norma. I smiled.

"Well, yes. I have a sister named Norma, but she's still on the Earth. We don't really talk much, she's more than twenty years older. I also have contact with a certain Norma in the Spirit World. Which one does this seem to be, James?"

He rocked to and fro just slightly, concentrating on what was being transmitted. Then he opened his eyes wide and said, "My God, she says it's Norma Jean. Norma Jean Baker! Has Marilyn Monroe talked with you before?"

I laughed. "Yes, yes! That's the Norma I felt it was. This is great! It's the first time she's come to me through someone else. Now I really know what happened before is real! What does she want to say?"

He still looked at me with some surprise, then conveyed Norma Jean's message of love and support for me. Whenever I have heard from her, either directly or through anyone else, she has always referred to herself as Norma Jean, never Marilyn. Her basic message delivered through James that day was to encourage me to pursue my psychic work, and she offered to help in any way she might be able.

I thanked her, and that was about all there was to that portion of this particular transmission. [As I mentioned, there's more detail about our connection in Chapter Sixteen, which is about contact I've had with a number of celebrities now in Spirit].

After a few moments of silence, James visibly shivered. "Oh, God, Cheryl...there's a John here. He's very evolved...incredibly spiritual. Who *is* this? Maybe John the Baptist, or St. John? God! The chills are so strong!"

"No, this time it's nobody famous, James. That's my brother, John. Doesn't he have amazing energy?"

James nodded. "He sure does, incredibly strong. Your Mom is with him, she says she's so proud of him. That she and your dad are actually in awe of him. She says John doesn't dwell in the same area of the Spirit World where they are, but he comes to visit them. He is off with Master Teachers, studying and learning, even doing some teaching himself. She is impressed by his spiritual level, and loves him very much."

I felt the same way. "Yes, that makes a lot of sense. I'm glad he spends time with them. What sorts of things do they do when they get together?"

James went on to describe how my mother and John had recently gone for a trip in a boat on a lake in the Spirit World. Knowing how much John always loved the water, this didn't seem strange to me in the least. And she said he sometimes took her to musical concerts, which they both enjoyed a lot.. The more I learned about the Spirit World, the more interesting it became! I was so relieved it wasn't boring in the afterlife, because our church led people to believe that basically, as soon as you arrived in Heaven you were issued a cloud, a harp and told to "Have a nice Eternity!" That always struck me as incredibly boring and non-growthful. [There's a lot more about what I've learned about Spirit World activities from the readings I've done, a bit later on]

John himself talked a bit through James, too. He was an eloquent communicator by this time. Much evidence was given, and some mention made of potential future events. My mother chimed in here and there, but for the most part, John did the talking that day.

"Cheryl, your brother loves you very much, the power of his love is almost overwhelming. Again, I must tell you, he is incredibly evolved."

James wiped away a tear, and I did the same. Sometimes the emotion a person in the Spirit World conveys touches the medium strongly, too. "Oh, this is so sweet. He says, 'Sis, you took such good care of me when Mom died, that I promise you this, I will always be there to take care of you. Believe it.'" James shook his head. "Wow, that's powerful."

"Yes, it is." I had so many questions for John, but primarily was interested in some of our past lives together. Especially one where we were an Irish husband and wife song & dance team had come through in my first past-life regression (Check out the chapter called "Hello, Again). I had a strong feeling that was not our only previous incarnation.

"John...can you tell me about any other lives we shared, other than the Irish one, and this one?"

James responded, "Yes, he says to tell you that he doesn't want you to worry so much about money. Says you were a brother and sister in France during the French Revolution; very well-to-do...he says, 'Tell my sister I was not a nice fellow in that lifetime...I was actually a bit of a cad, where the ladies were concerned. But *she* was kind to everyone, and always held a special place in my heart. She was good to our servants, to everyone, really. She did not misuse or abuse our inheritance. Partly because of my cold-heartedness in that lifetime, I chose to manifest in the person known as her brother John most recently. There are other reasons my soul chose that form, but...'"

John seemed to pause, or else the "link" was fading, I couldn't tell which. After a deep breath, James continued, "John says, 'Tell her she will have money again, and be able to manage it wisely. I'll always help her any way I can.'

"Wow...thank you, John. And thank you, James. I know your energy is getting drained a bit...could I ask him just one more question?"

"Oh, of course, Cheryl," James smiled. "He's one of the clearest communicators I've talked with in a long while. It's a pleasure."

"Thank you so much. I wonder, I know John has had many incarnations, and I'm sure I have, too. How does he look at the various lives he's led, and what seems to be the most important thing he's learned, if he could share that, please?"

James waited a moment to allow John's response to come through. Then he repeated my brother's words. "I have learned to look at my lives much as you might see the bows on the tail of a kite...each life represented by a different color, each one rising higher and higher, the learning and understanding more and more clear, closer to the sky... more and more light and love in each life..."

There was a pause as James sighed, then said, "What a lovely image."

I sensed the transmission was complete, and that was fine. That session brought me a lot of comfort and insight.

"Yes, my brother's very articulate for someone who only chose to say a handful of words in his last physical appearance, isn't he? I love him so much. It's really helpful that you tuned into him so well, James. He must feel comfortable with you."

"Oh, he's very strong and clear in his transmission! You're blessed to have someone so evolved around you, protecting and guiding you. And his love for you, well, again, it's just amazing."

We parted company, and I felt John around me off and on the rest of that evening, just basically sending me little electrical impulses of "warm fuzzies." Meeting Brian, Sara and the others in our group had changed my life in such a positive way. I no longer had any fear of death whatsoever and wanted to do everything possible to help others find the comfort I had found. That, coupled with the strong desire to finally have complete two-way communication with my beloved Johnny, inspired me to become the best medium I possibly could be.

Chapter Twelve

Bless The Children

In my work as well as from my personal experience with death and dying, I've discovered loss is never easy. As I mentioned in one of the Case Studies at the beginning of this book, the type of loss which strikes me as perhaps the most difficult is the death of a child, because parents simply never expect to outlive their children. It seems unnatural.

A common theme regarding babies that has occurred many, many times in readings I've done may bring some comfort to you or someone you know. I've had several mothers who've come to receive a reading about other issues, only to have the fact that they lost a baby to a miscarriage, one that was stillborn, died very young or even one that may have been aborted come through with a message they weren't expecting to receive. These wee messengers invariably want to emphasize that they don't wish their parents, especially their mothers, to carry around any more guilt, and to do their best to release any more pain about their passing. They often tell them they knew, on a soul level, they were not going to live to maturity on the Earth plane and that they still derived great benefit by being with the mother, even for such a short while. Because many of them are old souls, who may have had a number of lifetimes where they were rescuers, leaders, extremely responsible caregivers in one way or another. And this pattern of repeated giving, over and over, tends to make one forget what it's like to receive. To remember that is a very important thing to do, too, in order to create balance. So being in the womb is one way, on the physical plane, to recapture the feeling of just receiving. Being unable to do anything else, in fact. Many have said it has helped them tremendously in their soul growth. Others have promised to try and come be with the family as another child, at another time. Many women have received great comfort from this, and been able to shift their own perspective on that shared experience into a new light.

Despite the loss of my mother, father and my beloved John, I have never been a mother in this lifetime and therefore can only empathize with the depth of sorrow and grief the loss of a child brings. The bond between parents and children is usually loving and exceeds that of any other type of relationship. However, there are exceptions to every rule, and some parents are unfit to be the custodians of trusting little souls. This chapter deals first with one of my personal experiences in detail, about a wonderful mother and her daughters. Following that is a journal entry describing psychic messages I received about a well-known murder case involving a mother and her sons, along with its karmic implications.

Jan is one of the best friends I made while living in L.A. She had two beautiful teenage daughters, Becky and Stephanie. Becky was a dancer, an extremely attractive girl. She was stunning in appearance and graceful in her demeanor, so much so that she struck me as quite ethereal. It almost seemed to me her feet didn't touch the ground. Stephanie, the younger girl, is an actress, who is also very beautiful and talented.

The girls were teenagers when I met them in the late '80s. Jan and I thoroughly enjoyed discussing spiritual matters and the girls would sometimes sit in and ask questions and offer opinions, which I found refreshing and interesting. Becky was seventeen at the time I'm referencing, Stephanie not quite fifteen. I'd only known this family of women for a couple of months. Jan and I met for dinner in Toluca Lake one fall evening and in the middle of our meal, she became agitated and distracted, basically picking at her food and shifting around in her chair. I asked if everything was all right.

"Well, Cheryl, I don't really think so. I'm not sure why...I just feel uneasy, that's all. The girls both have dates tonight. I believe I need to go home right away."

"Oh! Well, you're very intuitive, Jan. I understand. You head on home and I'll talk to you tomorrow." I stood up, we hugged goodbye, and my friend hurried out the door, a strained look on her face.

I was still sitting in the psychic development circle one night a week, and studying a lot of metaphysical books. I attended Brian's monthly group sittings on a regular basis, and always learned a lot simply by observing him "in action." I wasn't quite ready to do professional readings myself, only did a few here and there for friends, just as practice. I wanted to be sure I was going to be helpful and as accurate as possible, so took my time learning and building my confidence in trusting the messages. I was doing some voiceover work, going to broadcasting school, and made much of my income from doing transcription and secretarial work. I was also learning about the movie industry from the inside out, because I was considering becoming a director one day.

For a future director, one of the best on-the-job training grounds is to become a script supervisor, the one in charge of what they refer to in films as "continuity." You work closely with the director, taking copious sets of notes which the editor will utilize when doing her/his job. This is an intense assignment. In fact, in movies where you've noticed incongruities from one scene to another, for example someone's hair suddenly changing style, or a cigarette ash changing length, etc., it's usually because the script supervisor neglected to insist upon more footage being shot so that the editor can cut things together believably. So though this job is very detail-oriented and often stressful, it's a great way of learning all about shots, camera angles and editing.

The morning after Jan and I had dinner, I was due on the set at 8 am to be the script super on a UCLA student film. Just the week before, I had moved into a spacious one bedroom apartment in a lovely house. My landlady was out of town this weekend; her home was full of many lovely antiques, had a nice big, backyard, and the energy there felt good. After Jan and I parted, I went home and read myself to sleep after setting my alarm for 6 a.m.

Instead of my alarm, the grandfather clock in the hallway awakened me and not at 6:00, but at 4:00. What startled me into waking consciousness was that it loudly struck not four, but thirteen times! It had never done this since I had been living there. I sat up, startled. Rubbing my eyes, I decided I'd get up for a glass of water, then grab a couple more hours of shut-eye. But I tossed and turned, wide awake and antsy. I felt a different energy, a presence, in the house. I wasn't afraid, but definitely aware of someone there who was not in a physical body. I wondered if it was my landlady's deceased husband. I decided to quit driving myself crazy with my musings and just get up.

Part of the arrangement in renting this room was that I had use of the kitchen and all utensils as long as I cleaned up after myself. Many of my belongings were in storage; I was sorting out bits of past relationships, career path changes and so on. I had rented this room as a temporary refuge to clear the clutter and better help me further my metaphysical studies. I started a pot of coffee, then sleepily reached up and grabbed the first mug my fingers closed around. Pulling the cup down, I was surprised to see it had writing on it, unusual writing at that.

There was a cute picture of a leprechaun on the outside. Being Irish myself, I smiled back at him as I read the writing around the rim. "May the Good Lord take a liking to ye...." Then my eyes focused on writing *inside* the cup which continued, "...but not too soon!"

"Huh!" I sputtered. "That's kinda weird!" I went about my business, reading the paper, took my time showering and dressing, deciding to make the most of my extra time to prepare for what promised to be a long day. I still felt an energy around the house, but it seemed calm and peaceful. I looked over my shoulder a few times, and even asked, "Does someone have a message for me, please?"

The only response was a sweet voice which said, "Just know everything is all right."

Bemused but not upset, I continued with my preparation for work. At 7:30, I was out the door on the way to my car, when I heard my phone ring. "The answering machine will get it," was my first thought, then another voice said, "No, this is important. Go back in!"

I hurried back in and grabbed it just before the answer machine started. "Hello?"

There was labored breathing on the other end and tears in Jan's voice. "Cheryl? Oh, my God....Cheryl....something awful has happened!"

I sat down and took a deep breath. "Jan....breathe nice and slow... I'm here for you. What happened?"

"Oh, God....I can't believe this....Becky died in a motorcycle accident early this morning. The police came to the house to tell me what had happened."

The goosebumps were back, stronger than ever. "Jan, was that around 4 a.m.?"

"Yeah, how did you know that?" she asked. I told her about the grandfather clock incident and the strange little message on my coffee cup. I realized it must have been Becky, trying to let me know that "everything is all right," knowing I would share this visitation with her Mom.

"Listen, Jan...I'm going to call the director and tell him I'm bailing today. I'm supposed to spend the day with you, I know that."

She objected, but weakly. I could tell she needed a friend more than she ever had in her life. This took precedence over anything else. I called the student director who was certainly miffed, but I really didn't care. My friend was in worse agony than I could begin to imagine and I knew I had to do whatever I could to help her.

Becky had been riding with her boyfriend and another young couple was following them on another bike. They were taking a big curve on Sepulveda Boulevard, one of the preferred thoroughfares from the Valley into L.A. It was a way to avoid the 405 Freeway, but obviously a potentially dangerous one. The kids on the cycle in back saw Becky's date lose control of his bike, then skid into a large tree at the peak of the curve. The impact threw Becky off the back and she landed on the street, right on her head. Her friends watched, helpless and horrified as her body shuddered once, then went limp on the pavement.

Jan heard Becky's friends' account of the accident, then went with the police to identify her daughter's body early that morning. Everything seemed so surreal, so slow motion and sickeningly nightmarish. She was in advanced shock when I arrived at her apartment. I put blankets around her and made hot tea for her and Stephanie, and just sat there between them, one arm around each or them. We sat there for hours, discussing the un-realness of it all. Becky had been so vital, so alive and happy just the night before.

"She didn't ever wear a helmet when she rode on one of those damn motorcycles...she was afraid she'd mess up her hair! God, I can't believe this is happening!" Jan sobbed.

I did my best to console her, and Stephanie numbly agreed with me that at least her sister had gone quickly and not suffered. Jan went completely silent for several minutes then suddenly stood up.

"I've got to go there!"

I was confused, knowing she'd already been to the morgue. "Honey, the funeral home will call you when they're ready...we can't really go there yet...."

"No, no! We've got to drive over to Sepulveda, where it happened. I won't believe she's really dead until we go there!" Her body seemed calm and controlled, but her voice was shaking. I realized she was in shock, and probably would be for some time. Not knowing what else to do in this circumstance, I agreed to drive over to the accident site.

About a year before this happened, when Brian was doing a reading for me he had gotten the message that one day I would help locate missing people, using maps, working with the police and so on. At first I had objected, thinking that kind of work would be morbid and too emotionally taxing for me.

My mentor gently reminded me, "It won't be anywhere as tough on you as the uncertainty has been on the families. Your guides and angels will hold you up. You have a gift, Cheryl. Even if the people you help locate are dead, at least their families won't expect them to walk in through the door any day. You can help them get closure, then perhaps help get messages between the two worlds for them later on..." His words echoed in my head as we got into my car. This might be tough, but it felt like the right thing to do at the time.

We took our time driving over the hill. Stephanie was not prepared to go with us, and had climbed back in bed. Some of her friends and Jan's sister stayed at their apartment to make sure she would be okay. Becky's friends had given a detailed description of exactly which curve, and which big single tree had been the point of impact. I slowly pulled off the side of the road, parked, and watched Jan get out of the car, moving as if in a dream.

I stayed close by her side, not sure what her emotions would lead her to or through. She deliberately made her way to the tree. I could see it was the tree in question because there were skid marks on the pavement, indicating the path the motorcycle took to its head-on impact. Jan stopped about five feet from the tree, and I heard a sharp intake of breath.

"Oh, look...." she pointed at the trunk. There, to the right was a mirror that had broken off the handlebar, along with some other pieces of plastic and glass. What she did next surprised me. She walked up to those twisted broken pieces and picked them up, cradling them against her heart. Silently, the flood of tears began once again, and all I could do was hold her. She shivered for awhile, then turned back to the car.

"Oh, Jan...are you sure you want those things? We can throw them away..."

"No! You don't get it, you just don't get it!" Her eyes flashed with hurt and confusion. "This is my proof. This makes it real to me. I need to keep these with me, they're mine now!"

I helplessly nodded, completely unsure as to how I might have reacted in her place. She rocked back and forth, holding those inanimate objects as though they were her child. Obviously the last physical imprint of Becky's energy on them was somehow comforting and at the same time convincing proof of the tragedy that had taken place. We rode home quietly. Still carrying those broken bits like a cherished treasure, Jan climbed the stairs to her front door.

Because Becky was a very popular girl, on the day of the service the funeral home was crammed full of young people from school, from her dance class, and other friends. I had never seen so many teenagers in tears. Jan's sister had agreed to do the eulogy. The chapel area was so crowded, I stood out in the small foyer, planning to listen, and then follow the funeral procession to the cemetery. Looking out the door at the clear California sky, I smiled. I felt Becky's spirit acknowledging my delivery of her message, then heard her young voice whisper, "Thanks for helping my Mom and Steph. I'm all right, keep reminding them, Cheryl. I'm in the Light." I jumped as a hand touched my elbow.

"Sorry to startle you, hon," Jan whispered.

I turned and hugged her. "No problem. Can I do anything for you?"

"Well, actually...yes, you can. My sister is way too choked up to give the eulogy. These kids need something to connect with...something to help them go on. You're the only one I can ask to do this, Cheryl...would you mind saying a few words?"

The only other eulogy I had done up to that point in time was John's. I felt his now familiar energy shoot through me, and heard him inside my head. "It's okay, Sis...you know how to do this. The angels will put the right words in your mouth, don't worry. Just go." I smiled at Jan. "Of course, Jan. I'd be honored."

Her squeeze of my arm and the gratitude in her eyes spoke volumes. The angels must have indeed done the talking for me, because I don't recall what I said. I just know several of the young people hugged me tightly as they made their way out the door and thanked me for paying such a nice tribute to their friend.

As the weeks went by, Jan gradually began to talk more about Becky; there were many more tears, but there was also laughter about the good times they'd shared. Becky was quiet psychic herself, so much so that she had told her mother just a week or so before the accident that if she were to die, at least she'd have nothing to regret. At the tender age of seventeen, she felt that she had lived a good life, had good friends who reflected back to her the strength of her character, and was content. She'd even had a precognitive dream where she and Jan were wearing white clothes and many of their relatives were in the background as the two of them walked away, calling after them, "Come back, we're sorry...it's not time to say goodbye yet...please come back!" Eerie? Not really. Many people have premonitions of their deaths; few are fearless enough to share them with others, perhaps believing that if they don't talk about it, it won't happen. Many times dreams about death and dying are symbolic of some situation or project coming to an end. In Becky's case, it was obviously literal in the prophetic sense, but her sharing of it actually brought her mother some solace.

"She wasn't afraid to die, so I'm glad she told me those things," Jan sighed. "And because of you, Cheryl, I believe her soul is still very much alive, and she's in a beautiful place."

I smiled. We had received a few messages from Becky in the last few days. Nothing incredibly strong, but evidentially accurate so that

Jan knew it was her who was "transmitting." Jan continually told me what a gift I had, and was really the first person to encourage me to start doing readings professionally, not just as a free service for friends.

"You're too good not to charge, Cheryl. People won't value your services if you don't set a price."

I nodded, still not certain I was ready for that part of my life to begin. Up to this point, I had "tapped in" for friends only; many of them had validated information which came through, but I wasn't completely confident as yet. A few days later, I came across a quote by Thomas Paine which brought Jan's words home.

"That which we obtain too easily, we esteem too lightly. It is dearness only which gives everything its value. Heaven knows how to put a proper price on its goods."

I meditated upon this for awhile, feeling encouraged to move to the next phase of my mediumship. Shortly thereafter, I went and ordered my first set of business cards and began to give them out to friends. I placed a few in New Age bookstores. It took awhile for the calls to come in, but come in they did. Word of mouth began to spread, and satisfied clients who had received comfort from a session with me proved to be my best advertisement. So I owe Jan, Stephanie, and especially Becky a great debt of gratitude. God bless you all, ladies! Jan and I are still in touch, and she has developed into quite an accurate channel and psychic herself, which thrills me. I love seeing people become empowered and tap into their own intuitive abilities. That's why I teach seminars on this topic. The more of us who embrace this side of self on this planet, who learn to work with forces of the Light, the more the consciousness of the Earth is raised. The higher the vibration is attuned, the more understanding can spread.

Infamy Be Thy Name

This next experience depicts how notoriety can have strong karmic repercussions. I include it here because it involves children, specifically Susan Smith's little boys, and how they reached out to connect with me from the other side. I'll use a journal entry to share this, because the detail is fresh from the date it took place.

November 3, 1994—Thursday night

"At approximately 7:40 this morning, I found myself singing *Where Is Love?* from the musical *Oliver!* I became thoroughly hysterical. I thought it was related to my own loss of my mother, but that seemed odd, because we are in rather constant psychic contact these days.

Later on, by early evening, I realized I had tapped into the fact that the two little Smith boys who were missing had been found, and they were not alive. I also was pretty convinced their mother had been involved.

Earlier this week, we saw a bit on the news, video clips of the boys and then their mother telling her cockamamie story about how the "carjacker" had "forced her out of the car," held a gun on her and took off, without even taking time to remove her babies from the back seat. It struck me as a lie from the get-go. In fact, I told my roommates I believed Susan Smith had killed her own children. They shuddered, and asked why I would think such a thing. Here's why:

They found the boys' bodies tonight, and even though I already knew in my heart that they were dead, I lapsed into being quite emotional. Then tonight in my roommate Donna's car as we were sitting in the parking lot of the grocery store, they contacted me, the little Smith boys. They told me some fascinating details, including the fact their mother had planned their murders, and that she had also murdered them in various other incarnations. She had always gotten away with it until now. They kept repeating, "We got her! we got her!"

Later on during our communication, they told me that some of their dirty diapers would be found in the trunk of the car in a diaper bag, that she had been driven almost to the brink of insanity and was blaming all her problems on the boys, right down to not being able to stand changing their diapers. They also said she has been diagnosed as clinically manic depressive.

The little guys told me they had "been granted a dispensation to have access to her brain track," so they planted an improbable story, which she shared with the media, in a tiny chip in her brain, not unlike a computer chip. The story would have obvious holes in it. They went on to say she had gotten away scot-free on many previous murders in other lifetimes, and they had made a contract with one another that they would bring her evil to light in this life, thereby putting a stop to her murderous ways.

The boys told me she had first encountered them during the Spanish Inquisition when they were man and wife. Then she was a male who ended up impaling them after a series of torture treatments. What was throwing me the most about them contacting me was how they would switch from the perspective of very old souls to being little boys. For example, when we were walking down the cereal aisle, they flitted around, saying, "Oooh! Coco Puffs! Fruity Pebbles!" Then they'd return to being the old souls! I asked them to try and ground more, because all this was making me dizzy. I had to go sit in the car to center.

They promised to try, just remarked how it was a bit harder since they had been off the Earth plane for such a short while. They were not fully back in the Light just yet. There was no malice or vengefulness in their tone whatsoever as they talked about Susan, just glee that she would be stopped from hurting others and escaping justice, along with the fact they would never have a karmic incarnation with her ever again. They said she has a diabolical soul, but this time around, it was given various maladies to deal with, such as the manic depression, so that she was unable to act as shrewdly as in the past. They mentioned an incarnation she'd had as a serial murderer in London, who was fascinated by and actually copied Jack the Ripper to a degree. With a role model like that, this is obviously a very disturbed soul.

The boys told me not to be sad or to worry about them. Also, while we were sitting in the parking lot, they moved a shopping cart which had been sitting perfectly still towards our car, but stopped it a few inches short. They also made the car sitting opposite us flash its lights and beep its alarm. Because no one was near it, the owner had been away from it for several minutes and did not reappear after this occurred.

Donna feels strongly I need to coordinate the evidential aspect of this information and send it to the police in the small town where they were from. I also got that the boys had kidney infections; she had been neglecting them a lot lately. They said she was taking them to see their paternal grandmother, whom I feel will one day come forward and say she had suspicions that she was abusing the boys. She had insurance on her sons, which she was planning to cash in and use to run away. Several of the boys' toys will be found in the trunk, including a brown and white spotted stuffed dog."

I did send the details to the local sheriff's department. I never found out if any of it was validated, because I sent it anonymously. In 1994, I was not ready to have notoriety, myself! Maybe someone who reads this will know more details of the investigation and contact me to validate a few things. Whether that happens or not, I believe it was real. When I asked the boys why they were contacting me, so many miles away from where their murders took place, they said, "Because you're nice, and you are open. We have been talking to lots of psychics, trying to get our message out."

I was doing readings on a local scale, but wasn't ready to have more exposure. Today, I am always pleased to work with the police in any way

I can, to help solve murders, find missing people, whatever I can do to be of service. The Smith boys' story is an unusual one, but it made sense to me on a karmic level. I'm so glad they finally broke free of the dark karmic cycle and have moved fully into the Light.

Chapter Thirteen

Healing

I have come to believe healing takes place by individual choice, just as John so brilliantly demonstrated by his life choice. Healing can have many forms, on many levels, including physical, emotional, mental and especially spiritual. This chapter is going to deal with various forms of healing which I have personally experienced and witnessed on all of those levels. I want to share something I recently became aware of which may help you or your loved ones. I wouldn't normally stop midstream in a book to endorse something, but this particular healing tool has made such a huge difference in my life, I feel I must share the details with as many people as possible. So here goes. In the beginning of this book, I made mention of a wonderful massage therapy bed called *Ceragem*. I wish this had been around for Johnny and our parents to use, because I truly believe it is a healing tool which already has helped many people, myself included, and it will continue to help countless others, if we continue to spread the word.

This amazing therapeutic tool "saved my bacon" while this book was in the editing process. During what should have been a relaxing, healing massage, the therapist got a little overly zealous and stretched my limbs a bit further than my body was willing to allow. I'm not sure what exactly happened on the internal level, only that I was miserable the next morning, with an aching back that made it nearly impossible to move. A friend "just happened" to call that day (you see why I believe there are no "accidents" in life, by now?) and told me how *Ceragem* had been helping her and her father feel better from a variety of things including his arthritis, her indigestion, and a number of other maladies had improved since they had been going to the *Ceragem* center. And here was the big surprise about all this—the forty minute treatments they went to receive several times a week? Absolutely free of charge!

And the center they attended happened to be just about a ten minute drive from my home. So I hobbled out to my car and immediately went to check it out.

On the window of the center located at Tatum and Thunderbird in Paradise Valley were written the words, "Love, Service, Kindness." I went in and signed a short standard release form, which is all they require you to do, just the one time. The only other requirement is that you arrive fifteen to twenty minutes early in order to insure you'll be able to receive a treatment at the session time you have chosen (they offer several times throughout the day, six days a week). This particular center currently has seventeen beds, and room for a few more when they get enough folks.

Each center operates a bit differently, but the basics are the same. They have a video they will show you about the benefits of the bed. They will also show you a bed with the jade rollers and carbon heating element exposed, and talk with you in detail about how this process generates far infrared light, which has tremendous natural healing properties the body just soaks up. The FDA has tested the product, and states that the intended use of the Ceragem-C Thermal Massager is to provide muscle relaxation therapy by delivering heat and soothing massage, and it provides radiant infrared heat for 1) Temporary relief of minor muscle and joint pain, and stiffness, 2) Temporary relief of minor joint pain associated with arthritis, 3) Temporary increase in local circulation, and 4) Relaxation of muscles.

Long story short, I felt better the very first time I visited the center, and have continued to frequent it ever since, noticing different improvements in my overall health, the more I attend. They will never hit you with a heavy duty sales pitch, in fact, they wait for customers to come to them and ask about purchase details. They won't even sell one unless someone has used it for thirty days and really *knows* the depth of the benefit they're receiving. Seriously! They know that word of mouth and actual experienced healing from users will generate enough sales to keep them going. So you can understand why I, who am walking straight again with virtually no pain after dealing with this back injury for two weeks (at the time of this writing, but by the time you read this, I will be in tip-top shape!), am anxious to spread the word about this company and their wonderful product. They make healing accessible to people of all ages and incomes, free of charge. Amazing, in this day and age! I am so impressed with this product, that it has become a dream of mine to invest in at least one center of my own, down the road, and continue to share the benefits. It has been a long-time dream to either own or be involved with a number of healing centers around the country, practicing hypnosis for healing, energy balancing techniques and more. And believe me, I will tout the benefits of this bed every chance I get, hopefully convincing many such centers to incorporate *Ceragem* as one of their offered modalities.

I experience a general overall feeling of peacefulness after each treatment, my posture is better, my digestion has improved (always a nice perk!), and my joints and muscles feel wonderful. There are many other such testimonials out there. The best thing I can urge you to do is visit their website, www.ceragem.com and find a center near you, if possible. Be sure to read up on it while you're visiting their site. They are now in over half of the United States, and parts of Canada. If there's not one near you now, make note of where they are and if you have a reason to visit a city where they can be found, be sure to make time to go try it out. I obviously feel very strongly about this, and why not? As someone who has experienced many types of healing treatments, including chiropractic, acupuncture, energy balancing, massage and more, I have found *Ceragem* to be thoroughly therapeutic on multiple levels and couldn't be happier to do whatever I can to help others experience it for themselves. My only motivation for including this in my book is my desire to share this gift. They have given me free treatments (I *will* buy a bed soon, though, trust me!) and whatever I can do to give them some free recognition, is simply from desire to create some reciprocity and hopefully inspire many others to try this out for themselves. That being said, I will now move on.

The remainder of this chapter deals with a variety of healing experiences I was connected with in some way at different times in my life. Each situation is unique, and personally inspiring.

When Johnny was born, I began to hear words like "special," and "handicapped" and in the 1960s, "retarded" was used quite freely in reference to someone with a condition such as that of my baby brother. He was termed a "birth injury." I've already shared much of our early lives together, but wish to emphasize once again my personal belief that because he manifested in this way, he is an extremely evolved soul. I prefer to refer to those others think of as "challenged" or "handicapped" as "LBOTHOs"..."Light Beings Of The Highest Order." I believe in many cases they are Master Teachers, come to Earth to enlighten us. This is my devout feeling, due to my experience with John.

Therefore, I'm so thankful for the opportunity to interact with such lovely beings, to learn from them virtues such as patience, acceptance; the ability to look beyond the physical in order to value real emotions and God-given gifts which exist in each and every one of us. For the miraculous thing is, these lessons most certainly can overlap into our dealings with *everyone*, if only we allow this to take place. I'm still very much in human form, and frankly, I love being here at this time in Earth history. After all, I chose to be here now, so why not enjoy it? The trick to self-created drama is not to buy into it and turn it into a full-blown theatrical extravaganza. Shakespeare's "all the world's a stage" is so true! It's much simpler to find humor in situations, in your own reactions if you don't expend time and energy creating drama. Realize you are the creator of your experience, and if you don't like the results, simply focus on what it is you *do* want to create. Don't dwell on negativity. Otherwise, your pain grows and increases each time you tell the story, each time you "plug into" the negative emotions, all that does is magnetically attract more of the same.

Better to step back a bit, quickly notice what's going on as objectively as possible, see if there's a significant message to retain for positive learning, then release your attachment. This process can become almost instantaneous with practice. You'll then be quite pleased to notice you have more productive, happier time to spend doing things you love.

As far as I'm concerned, Earth School is the fastest place to really get your lessons. I believe once we fully absorb the course of "soul study" we came here for, we move on. I do look forward to that time on many levels; meanwhile, it's a fun ride being an "Earthie!"

One way to accelerate self-healing is to do your best to stay focused in the now, because it's obviously when you have the most power to affect positive change. I'm always fascinated by the power of the subconscious mind to assist us in creating whatever we want to experience. One reason I became a hypnotherapist is because I love to see people actualize their own creative power. Hypnotherapy is just one wonderful, quick path to empowerment. Guided visualization is another, and certainly meditation allows the subconscious and Higher Self to communicate and interact more freely. There are many terrific techniques and tools readily available today to assist you in these areas, largely because mass consciousness is expanding so quickly at this time in our planet's history.

ANGEL DUTY

Some people definitely have a gift where healing is concerned. They are instruments, channels or conduits of this Power, and have learned to allow it to flow through them into the body of the person desirous of healing. I believe that no human being heals another. Rather, people heal themselves with their thoughts, the strength of their faith, and the wondrous unlimited power of Almighty God, Who most certainly moves in mysterious ways at times. If not, we probably wouldn't be so impressed! We're pretty spoiled in this age of special effects in the movies, television, computer technology, phones that are cameras, stereos and who knows what's next? So instead of getting all caught up in our gadgets and thinking we have it all figured out, when a good old fashioned, non-technological miracle comes along and knocks your socks off...well, I believe that's one way we're reminded of what's really important.

A conduit of miraculous intervention is one of my psychic heroes, Edgar Cayce. Long before a lot of the technological brouhaha we have at our fingertips today, the "sleeping prophet" had the ability to accurately diagnose and offer healing treatments to people while he was in a trance state, and they got well! This amazes me! My admiration of Edgar Cayce and his gifts has inspired me to develop my own skills with both hypnosis and psychic work. If you'd like to learn more on Mr. Cayce, there are many books written by and about him. Recently, a wonderful movie about his life has come out, entitled *Beautiful Dreamer*. You can learn more about this film by visiting www.caycecures.com/Holiday/catalog/beautiful.htm While you're there, peek around the rest of the site to learn more about this amazing soul whom I'm so blessed to have as one of my guides.

If you're unfamiliar with his work or that of the A.R.E., I highly recommend doing some research. (The Association for Research and Enlightenment, founded by Cayce in 1931, is a non-profit organization that makes available concepts from his vast body of work through a variety of activities, products, programs, and services) There's a wonderful A.R.E. clinic in Phoenix, complete with a store that offers many of his remedies. The main location is in Virginia Beach, Virginia and they have an online store, too.

I was fascinated by the story of this simple man with these incredible abilities. Edgar Cayce also clearly saw auras around people, and this intrigued me very much. There was no talk of auras at my childhood church, of course. One of my favorite stories about this remarkable man still gives me chills, every time I share it with people. Here it is:

He was in a skyscraper with a friend one day. After finishing their business there, they were waiting for the elevator to take them to the ground floor. When the elevator doors opened, his friend started to get on. There were several people onboard, but plenty of room for two more. He felt Edgar's hand grab his elbow and pull him back out. This gentleman knew enough of Edgar's talents not to question him when he quietly said, "We'll take the next car."

His friend nodded and the doors closed. Suddenly, there was an awful groaning sound as the cable snapped and the car whooshed to the bottom, instantly killing all those inside. His friend gulped and turned to Edgar. "Just tell me, Edgar, how did you know?"

"Well, none of them had the lights around them, no auras. Their souls had already gone on. It would have been like getting in a car with a bunch of dead people, and it was their time, but not ours."

The concept of the soul exiting the physical container in advance of a sudden death, especially one brought about by an accident, has become a familiar theme in my own work. When they've asked me to share this with their loved ones, it has brought a lot of comfort to them, knowing that their family member or friend didn't endure suffering, but went straight into the Light. I encourage you to read as many books by and about Edgar Cayce as possible, because you will undoubtedly learn much, or at least be stimulated to consider things in new ways. His assistance in my readings is so appreciated, and he's helped open my eyes to many things with no seemingly "logical" explanation.

Another friend based in the physical dimension has been a great source of encouragement and inspiration to me as well. Interestingly, he, too, clearly sees auras. By the time I moved to L. A., I was receptive to a lot of different paths of study and knew that "When the student is ready, the teacher appears." Enter Merlin.

A wonderful mentor for me in many ways, Merlin has a PhD in psychology. Merlin's Apache by birth, and the medicine man/shaman of the tribe mentored him as he was growing up. He told me many stories from his childhood which involved this. The one that impressed me most follows.

When Merlin was twelve, his mentor gave him a headband with a single stone in the center and told him to it wear every day. The stone covered the area of his "third eye" in the middle of his forehead. When it came time for Merlin to perform his "rite of passage into manhood" at the age of thirteen, he was taken to a very desolate desert area and given only a knife. This is an arduous ordeal for a young man, oftentimes lasting for two or three days. The knife comes in handy not only for killing food, but for obtaining fluid for sustenance from certain types of cactus.

Merlin was successful in his trial, and upon his return to the camp was next sent down into a kiva (a small underground cavern of sorts, in this case) and given some peyote to chew upon. The peyote was to invoke a "vision quest," a spiritual journey whereby he would receive clarity on his life purpose. The peyote button makes one violently ill in most cases, and Merlin was no exception. He had many strange visions in the kiva, and when it was time for him to emerge, his teacher was up above, reaching down to give him a hand up. It was late at night, and the stars were incredibly bright. Merlin was weak from his experience, and the medicine man had him lie down flat on the ground.

He gently removed the headband from the boy's brow, and Merlin began screaming, "Make it stop! Make it STOP!"

The medicine man shook him lightly and asked, "Make what stop? Calm down! What are you talking about?"

Merlin covered his eyes, thinking he was still having an hallucination from the peyote. "The colors! The colors all around you, all around the stars, around everything! Make it *stop*!"

His mentor emitted a loud belly laugh. "Young fool! Why do you think I made you wear this headband with this stone all this time? It prepared you for this. It was all in order for you to see the colors, not to make them stop! This is one of your gifts. Learn to use it wisely."

So Merlin began seeing auras on an almost constant basis. He learned to discern health conditions in others by the color of the aura around various regions of their bodies. He is a complex, caring human being who astral projects into the future, seeing visions, and tuning into helpful information for others. He is one of the most fascinating people I've known personally. What I'll share next are some examples of situations involving Merlin and healing, one of which directly affected me.

When I met him, Merlin was teaching classes on many topics of metaphysical studies, including astral projection, future projection, the values of meditation, accessing the Akashic Records and much more. Once he said he felt such gratitude for the abilities with which he had been blessed, he asked his spiritual guides if there was anything he could do in return. The answer surprised him.

"Yes, Merlin, there is something."

He was excited, willing to give something back to the Source, to All That Is. "What is it? Please tell me."

There was a pause. "You will begin to experience some feelings of intense drowsiness. This will take place at times when you are not at work, so it will not interfere with that schedule. But when you notice this sleepiness reaching a state where you cannot resist it, you must go lie down for awhile. There is work you will be doing in another dimension, time traveling, if you wish to call it so. You might even wish to refer to this work as 'Angel Duty.'"

Merlin was stunned. "Angel Duty? I'm no angel, I know that...I don't understand...what...?"

"Follow your body's inclination to lie down when this occurs, your understanding will soon follow. Thank you for offering your services. This will not go unnoticed."

There was silence, and he pondered whether his imagination was working overtime, or if he had really just received valid communication. His gut instinct/third chakra verified for him on a physical level that the instructions were valid. So he accepted them as such, and released worrying about where or when this might take place.

A few days later as he was driving home from work, Merlin began to feel incredibly tired. It was mid-afternoon, so he was surprised by the drowsiness until he remembered his guides' instructions. Upon arriving home, he went straight to bed, not knowing exactly what to expect. He began to dream, and realized he was bypassing the astral plane, seemingly moving through time and space very effortlessly. He emerged in the middle of a cornfield, and heard a painful moaning sound not far from where he stood. He made his way toward the sound, and saw a woman writhing on the ground in pain, blood all around her.

"Oh, my God!" he thought. He wasn't sure if the woman could see him or not, and something within him instructed him to send her his thoughts in a focused manner. He looked down at his own body, and saw that it was permeable, almost ghostlike, compared to the solid appearance of the woman and her predicament. He immediately sent her as much healing energy as he could muster, and focused upon sending her a thought. "Hello. I'm a friend from another point in time. I've come to help you, I can feel the intensity of your pain. Are you dying? I'm not sure why I'm here right now, but if I can help you make your transition to Heaven, then that's what I'll do..." He was startled by her laughter.

"Dying?!? You idiot, it's my time of the month! And granted, sometimes I wish I could die 'cause this hurts like hell, but I have a lot left to do in my life. I came out here to check on the crops, and this hit me like a ton of bricks. If you want to help me somehow, go tell my brother in the farmhouse back yonder to bring my horse out here so I don't have to crawl home." She peered at him closely. "I can see right through you. Who, or what, are you?"

He didn't quite know how to reply, and was now experiencing incredible pain in his second chakra region. His empathic ability to tune into the pain of others had carried over into this time traveling. Fascinating! He began to focus on sending her more positive healing energy, and found his own pain lessening. The woman was still staring at him.

"Oh, I...yes, yes! I'll go put the thought in your brother's head that he needs to bring your horse to you. Right away. I hope you feel better soon, ma'am."

He made a sort of polite bow to her, then projected himself back to the farmhouse, where he telepathically told the brother to take his sister's horse out to the fields. He watched as the brother's face registered consternation, then tried to "shake off" Merlin's message. Again, he sent the same message, with more intensity. After about the fourth or fifth time of planting the thought in the young man's mind, Merlin watched as he saddled his own horse, bridled his sister's, and began to make his way out into the field where the young woman was waiting. Satisfied he'd completed this mission, Merlin found himself floating back "through the ethers," then returned to his own solid, physical body and awoke.

When he told me this story, he laughed a bit, but a pained look crossed his face. "Believe me, Cheryl, after feeling her suffering, I never again doubted when a woman friend would tell me about her cramps. I became a champion of women who were on their periods. 'Oh, you poor thing! Let me get you a footstool, or a heating pad...'" He shook his head, smiling at the memory.

I was puzzled. "Well, I know you're empathic in your conscious state, but why do you think it was necessary for you to feel her pain so strongly there? Have you had more instances like this?"

"Oh, yes," he nodded. "I'll share one more with you that really brought it all home for me. Do you have time?"

"Are you kidding? Sure, this is great stuff!" I always learned so much just listening to him, and his experiences were always so intriguing. He told me about another "deep sleepiness" episode, where he laid down and immediately went into an altered state of consciousness. As he checked out his surroundings, he realized he was in the middle of pioneer days, out in the middle of the wide, open spaces. He saw an overturned wagon, and as he got closer to the scene, had to avert his eyes in horror. A young man and his wife lay dead, scalped in what he recognized as Apache style slaying. Because of his heritage, Merlin knew his ancestors' history very well.

"What can I do for them?" he wondered. "Their spirits are long gone to a better place..." he looked around at the remains of their belongings. His ears picked up what sounded like a child sobbing, and he made his way in that direction, concentrating on appearing as solid as possible. "I don't need to scare this poor child anymore," he told himself.

As he rounded the corner of the wagon, sure enough, there was a little boy crouched down behind some cooking supplies. Merlin smiled at him, but couldn't tell if the child could see him yet.

"Hello, son. What's your name?" he asked kindly.

The boy ran to his mother's body, and threw his arm about her waist. "Wake up, Mama, wake up! The Indians are gone. Oh, please, won't you or Pa wake up?" He cried as if his heart would break.

Merlin felt incredibly sad, too, then realized he couldn't help the boy if he allowed his emotions to cloud his mission. He crossed over to the child, focusing on projecting a material image. This boy was about seven years old. What a tragedy! The Apache were vicious in this day and time; Merlin knew they tended to either take children back to their camp in such a case, or left them to survive or die. They seldom killed children, however, and he now saw why he'd been sent here.

Merlin bent down beside the boy, and tentatively reached out to touch his arm. Then he thought better of it, wondering if his hand would pass right through the child and frighten him even more. He cleared his throat, and this time the boy looked up at him.

"Hello, son. I'm a friend. You need to come with me now, so we can get you to someone who can help you. There's nothing we can do for your mother and father. I'm sorry..."

"No!" The boy screamed. "I'm not leaving. They'll wake up soon, and we'll go find us some land and build a house, just like my Pa promised!"

Mustering all the power he could call forth, Merlin took a deep breath, then looked down at his hands. It worked! He looked almost as solid as his surroundings. Perhaps now the child would respond to him more positively. He'd seen a Bible in the wagon, so decided to try another approach. "I know this is hard to understand, but your Mama and Pa have gone to Heaven, son. They're not here anymore. These are just their bodies. What made them live, their spirits, have gone to Heaven. Do you know about Heaven?"

"Sure, I do. My Mama used to read to me about Jesus and Heaven a lot." He wiped his eyes on his sleeve and took his first long look at Merlin. "My Mama told me not to talk to strangers, either. So you just go away, mister. I'll be all right." His lower lip trembled, and he turned his back on Merlin.

"Well, let me see..." Merlin was buying some time, when inspiration hit. "I'm sure your mama told you about angels, didn't she?"

The boy looked up at him, his eyes shining brightly. "Oh, yes! Angels are wonderful! They work for God." He looked Merlin up and down, and solemnly asked, "Are you an angel, then?"

Seeing this would convince the boy to trust him, Merlin nodded. "Yes, that's exactly right. I'm an angel. And it's important for you to come with me so that we can get you to shelter and some people who can help you. That's what your parents would want." He watched as the boy stood up and dusted himself off. "What's your name, son?"

"Timothy. Say...you don't 'xactly look like an angel. Where's your wings?" he asked suspiciously.

"Well, Timothy, we can't just go around flapping our wings when we visit Earth. That would scare too many people, see? And besides, I'm really a very new angel, so I really don't have any wings yet. Come on now, look at me real close. Don't you notice anything different?"

Timothy looked at him, then almost giggled. "Well, you don't have any feet!" he pointed, and Merlin looked down. Sure enough, his feet were missing. He laughed, then sent an extra "zap" of concentration below his knees, and his feet gradually came into view.

"Well, you're right, Timothy. It's tricky doing 'angel duty' here on Earth. The atmosphere is different. Like I said, I'm new at this angel stuff. I've been assigned to you so I can earn my wings. So you help me out, and go right ahead and point out to me if something is invisible, okay? Then I can get practice on how things work here, and fix it. Are you willing to come along with me now?" He looked at the mountain range ahead. It was springtime, so that was in their favor. But no sign of a town for miles. Not wanting the boy to see his concern, he quickly looked back at Timothy and smiled.

"Oh, yes, I can go with you if you're an angel. That's different!"

They went back to the wagon, and Merlin instructed his young charge to pack a small bag of supplies. There wasn't much food, but Timothy found a few pieces of bread, a little jug of water and some jerky. He packed his one clean shirt, a pair of pants, and insisted on bringing his small Bible. Merlin told him how to pack it all tightly as possible. The boy didn't seem to think it was odd taking orders from this "angel."

Since he was so etheric, Merlin had to content himself with helping verbally rather than physically. His main regret was being unable to carry the boy part of the way, or to at least hold onto his small hand to comfort and steady him. Timothy, however, seemed content to walk close to his new friend, and happily pointed out to him whenever a foot or hand would momentarily disappear.

They began their long journey, and once they reached the edge of the mountain, Merlin began to tell Timothy where to grab the best handholds, and to make sure his footing was solid before moving forward. He felt pretty helpless as he "float-walked" alongside the young boy, but soon realized his positive attitude and wilderness training were great survival skills to share with Timothy. The boy complained very little, slept soundly each night, and was determined to please his "angel" and make good progress by day.

After traveling nearly three and a half days, they reached the crest of the mountain. Merlin spotted a small town in the valley below, and excitedly pointed it out to Timothy. "Look there, Timothy! You did it! There are people there who will help you, son."

The boy jumped up and down, shouting "Yay! Let's go, Merlin!"

"All right, all right. Take it easy now. We'll be there before supper time, that is if you don't fall and break your neck. Have a care, Timothy. You've learned some good skills. Let's use them as we go down the mountain." He chuckled under his breath as he gave the gentle admonition. It did his heart good to see the child so animated.

Time seemed to fly, and soon they were standing at the edge of a small farm. There was an apple tree just outside the farmhouse fence. Merlin told Timothy to rest there until someone came to fetch him.

But where are you going, Merlin? Won't you come back?" the boy pleaded.

"Well, Timothy, once I've got the message through to someone to come out here and help you, then my job with you is over. There's someone else who needs my help. But you sure helped me a lot. I know I'll get those wings now!" He leaned down, and without thinking, grabbed the child and hugged him tightly. He smiled as he realized he was momentarily solid. Contact felt so good! "You be a good boy, now, you hear? I'm not sure who's gonna come help you, but someone will. You just wait. I won't leave until I'm sure they understand that you're out here, all right?"

Timothy sniffed. "Okay. I understand if ya gotta go help somebody else. You're a good angel." He looked right into Merlin's eyes. "Thank you. You saved my life."

Merlin almost choked on a tear, but fought it. He wanted the boy to stay happy. "My pleasure, Timothy. Thank you!" He smiled and waved, then float-walked up to the farmhouse porch. He made himself fully invisible and then floated inside the kitchen, where a farmer sat next to his wife, his arm around her as he talked.

"There now, Clara. I know you want a child. But seems like we can't have one, since you lost the baby a few months ago. The good Lord moves in mysterious ways, though. Let's be thankful for what we do have." He stood up and walked right through Merlin, who was startled at first. The farmer paused at the door. "I'm going back out to rub down the horses...well, I'll be!" His mouth fell open as he looked out in front of their home.

Merlin smiled and thought to himself, "This is too easy!" He quickly looked up, "But that's okay, thank You!"

"Clara? Come look out yonder, just past our fence." His wife sighed and pushed back her chair, slowly crossing to where he stood. "Do you know that child, honey?"

She gazed in the direction her husband was pointing. The sun blocked her view at first, then her vision focused. She squinted, then shook her head. "No, Adam. I don't. He's mighty small to be alone, though, out here in the middle of nowhere, a good two miles from town...oh, look! He's got some stuff tied up in a cloth...what on earth...?" she was already making her way down the steps, fairly running to get to the child. She flung open the gate and dropped down to her knees to talk with Timothy.

Merlin smiled again. His job was truly done. Next thing he knew, he was back in his body, in his own bed. He sat up and stretched gingerly before making his way to the bathroom, and glanced at the clock. 8:30 p.m.? How long had he been asleep? How many days? What had this "angel duty" business cost him in terms of the waking world? He grabbed the phone and called his friend Paul.

"Paul? Hi, it's Merlin. Hey, this is a silly question...what day is it?"

Paul snorted. "It's Wednesday, all day. I just saw you when we knocked off at 4 today. Have you been smoking something wacky, you crazy 'Injun'?"

"Very funny, Paul. No. I just, well, my alarm clock doesn't work right, and I wasn't sure if I'd lost a day or something. Never mind. See you tomorrow." He hung up. The "dream" had taken place over what seemed like three full, real days, yet he had only been asleep for a little more than three hours. Amazing!

As he wrapped up this story, I fired another question at him. "Okay, that was really cool. But why do you think you were sent back to those particular people, to help in those ways? How could you feel their pain so strongly? What pulled you to that woman and Timothy?"

"I thought you'd never ask," he teased. "I meditated and asked my guides the very same questions. And the answer I got was really wild. The woman and Timothy were both earlier aspects of me! They were previous lifetimes, earlier incarnations that I was allowed to return to in an objective state, and do some healing. It's some of the best time traveling I've ever done. And I'm not sure, but I think both of those people might have died if I hadn't been sent to work with them. So I basically healed my own past lives by being given a second chance. And those are just two stories. I've got more...."

Merlin is the first person who was able to explain the concepts of simultaneous time and parallel lives to me in ways I could understand, ones to which I could give serious consideration. He provided me with valuable tools such as how to do astral travel. He has so many talents and abilities. I'm fortunate to call him my friend, and to have had him as a teacher. We haven't been in touch in a long while, but I know if it's in divine right alignment, he'll get a copy of this book and certainly know how much I miss him. I want to share one more story where he helped me with some of my own healing in a powerful way.

In 1989, I moved away from L.A. for awhile. The last few years, I had done some readings, but was still reluctant to trust and do it full-time. Many personal stresses were piling up and I needed a change of scenery. This helped for about six months, but because my new location was a difficult place to find a good a job, I moved back, knowing I was always able to find some type of work in L.A. I also was in the position of not having a car. Now, in L.A., this is not a good thing, at least at that time, it was not, because the bus system left much to be desired. So I began to save money, and within a few weeks, I had enough to purchase a used motorcycle. When my Dad passed away six years prior to this, I bought a brand new cycle, and drove it all over the city for a full year before deciding to sell it. I never had a bit of trouble with that bike mechanically, and certainly was never in any accidents. So I really didn't think that much about purchasing another motorcycle. It was cheap, reliable transportation, period.

Within three weeks of purchasing this used bike, I was riding home in a very upbeat mood, singing to myself, watching the road carefully. I'd just finished teaching a children's acting class, and was actually feeling pretty good about my decision to return to California. I stopped at a red light, then when the light changed, looked at each angle of the intersection and started forward. In about two seconds, courtesy of peripheral vision, I caught sight of a car to my right, approaching at breakneck speed. Caught in the middle of the intersection, I suddenly got that sick feeling in the pit of my stomach as I realized he was blasting toward his red light much too quickly to stop. I was bound to get hit whether I sped up or hit the brakes...it was my choice. My reflexes chose the brakes, and a split second later, the car slammed broadside into my bike.

I immediately began praying, and somehow knew I was not going to die, even as I was flung up into the air about ten feet. It was dreamlike, really trippy. There was a "CRASH!" and I must have gone numb from the impact of landing on the hood of the car. In slow motion, I saw an elderly lady's face inside the car, her mouth contorted in a scream as I rolled off the vehicle. There was a second jarring "THUD" as I hit the pavement in the center of the intersection, flat on my back. I lay still, continuing to pray, mostly that I wouldn't come out of this thing a cripple. I knew myself too well; I'm an excellent caretaker, but a lousy patient. Growing up with John had increased my patience and tolerance for others' conditions, but not for my own. I couldn't stand to be sick in any way. The only person available to take care of me in such a happenstance was my brother Don, in Oregon; I couldn't bear to think about putting him through that.

All these thoughts and more spun through my head as I lie there for ten minutes, probably longer. It was one of those situations where time becomes elastic. Not once did I worry about dying. I had completely lost my fear of death after seeing Brian that first time. I was more worried about living in a physical body which might not function the way I needed it to.

No one ran to my aid before I tried to move. I was shocked to realize I *could* move, and warily stood up, moving very slowly. First I wriggled my fingers and toes, then carefully stretched and moved first one arm, then the other, then each leg. Amazingly, nothing felt broken! I took off my helmet, allowing my hair to fall down around my face. Pieces of the helmet lay on the street. "Better it than my head!" I thought.

I could hear witnesses on each corner of the intersection, talking with each other, and with policemen who were taking reports. I realized then I must have been lying there for quite awhile. Why hadn't anyone come to check on me?

The voices were saying, "Oh, look! It's a woman rider! She's moving, thank God..." "Yes, officer, Totally his fault. He came right through the red light and ran right into her..." but I tuned all this out. The reason it didn't seem so important to me at the time was because I looked at the man who had struck me with his car, and saw that he was still sitting in his primer-gray, old, beat-up Pinto, just staring at me. His mother, or grandmother, I wasn't sure, was still sitting beside him, crying and wailing. Suddenly my adrenaline kicked into high gear.

I walked over to his car door, and yanked it open with righteous anger. "Hey! Who the hell do you think you are? You nearly killed me, you jerk! And you're just sitting there? You didn't even get out of the car to see if I was dead or alive. What's your problem?" I was breathing heavily, and he must have thought a she-devil had come back to life to torment him. He sat frozen behind the wheel. I was in shock; pure adrenaline replaced any traces of the milk of human kindness or forgiveness that may have been present in my veins. I was righteously enraged, and he knew it!

"Ah...look, lady. You're okay, don't cry. You're okay."

I was dumbfounded. "Okay? OKAY!?! You idiot! You freakin' maniac, I oughta..." I was about to haul off and hit him, when my elbow was grabbed by John Q. Law. I turned to glare at the policeman.

"Listen, lady, why don't you go have a seat in the squad car over there, before you get hurt..."

"*Me* get hurt? Ha! Officer, I just walked away from the jaws of death...I'm incredibly protected for one reason or another. But this imbecile here deserves to get hurt...he just said..."

"Yeah, yeah, I heard what he said. Why don't you let me handle this and just go have a seat, please?" The officer firmly guided me toward his car, and began to question the driver. I sat there, fuming. As I gradually calmed down, I gingerly tested each finger, each toe for any signs of breakage. I was sore and shaken up, but so obviously protected. This was the second time I had walked away from an accident that by all rights should have been my ticket into the Great Beyond. I began to count my blessings, and to take stock of what I was doing with my life. I realized I wasn't working on my writing, nor making significant progress toward doing spiritual readings for people as a profession, although I had received the message time and again that was part of my mission. I resolved to change those situations. Long story short, the driver was from El Salvador, had no license and no insurance. I had waived uninsured motorist's coverage from my insurance (never a good idea!), and had no health insurance. So, I had lots of time to reevaluate where I was going with my life as I healed up. I was off work for about two weeks, because even though nothing was broken, I was pretty banged up and bruised, and didn't walk too well for several days.

The main physical condition which concerned me was my right leg. By my choice to brake, the car had caught the fork of the bike's front wheel, and my right leg had been slammed into the gas tank as the motorcycle spun out from under me. Whatever or Whoever helped me choose to brake was profoundly wise, however. 20/20 hindsight made me realize if I'd tried to speed up, the gas tank may have been hit directly and I'd have either been a crispy critter, or else minus my right leg, at the very least. As things stood, I had a large black, blue, purple and yellow area on my inner thigh, accented with several purplish black blood clots that showed no signs of dissipating.

I decided to call Merlin for advice. This next part may seem bizarre to you. When he first told me about this aspect of his healing abilities, it struck me that way! Merlin had described "inner body" health readings which he had performed on a number of people. This story has a Jules Verne sci-fi *Incredible Journey* flavor to it. After obtaining permission from the person he'd be examining, he'd astral travel to his/her body at a time when he/she planned to be asleep. Then by the power of thought, Merlin would reduce himself to minuscule proportion, an infinitesimal dot of pure positive energy; then he'd enter the sleeping person's body through a tiny pore in the skin. From that point on, an interior "scan" was done on health conditions throughout the person's entire system; a check on all organs, circulatory, respiratory and pulmonary functions, a "tuning in" investigation. The following day, Merlin would call the person to report what he found. At that point, they'd discuss healing alternatives. While he remained in his tiny, lightning quick state, Merlin could send healing, mending energy wherever it might be needed, but he always made a report first, knowing he could return upon invitation. He is a firm believer in obtaining permission and cooperation before taking any action. That's a great model for any healing facilitator, no matter how conventional or unconventional the treatment.

I had never asked him to perform this service for me, but now I was in a quandary as well as a great deal of pain. I had no health insurance and limited financial resources. Those blood clots were looking pretty angry, and I'd heard how dangerous they could be. I trusted Merlin implicitly. I had experienced a number of his talents personally through readings he had given me, and by techniques I had learned from him. I knew I needed to take action quickly, so I picked up the phone.

"Hello, Merlin? It's Cheryl Booth."

"Cheryl! Haven't heard from you in a long time. You're back in town, now?"

"Yeah...ahm...Merlin...the reason I'm calling today is this: I was in a pretty bad wreck a few days ago, and there are some things going on with my body that are disturbing me. I was really lucky and I'm so thankful it's not worse. Nothing's broken, but...I really need to see somebody about this, I think...trouble is, I don't have any health insurance at the moment, so I want to make the doctor's visit as productive as possible..."

He sensitively interrupted, "Would you like me to do a scan for you? I can do that tonight, if you like. What time will you be asleep?"

"Oh, that would be great, Merlin! I'm sleeping a lot, because that's about the only time I'm not hurting some place or the other...I'll be asleep by 9:30 tonight, I'm sure."

"Okay, I'll visit you and do the scan a couple of hours after you've been asleep, then give you a call in the morning to let you know the results."

"Wonderful! Thank you, Merlin...I really appreciate it."

"Hey, no problem! I haven't done one of these for awhile, and need to keep my chops up, y'know?" He laughed. "I'll give you a call between 8 and 9 tomorrow morning. Will that work for you?"

"Perfect. Thanks again. Talk to you then."

I went to sleep that night, not knowing what to expect, but feeling very peaceful, a first since the accident. I slept through the night for the first time in days, and woke up in anticipation of what my friend had discovered. I read and meditated, and moved the phone beside me, picking it up on the first ring.

"Good morning, Cheryl. Here's the deal...I would suggest you get yourself to a good chiropractor A.S.A.P., because your tailbone and your three lower lumbar vertebrae are really out of alignment. Once you do that, the blood clots in your right leg should break up and be cleaned out of your system normally. That guy must have hit your bike really hard to shock your leg that much. Those clots can't move right now because that spinal pressure is preventing solid blood flow. But you need to take care of this right away. Restoring full circulation will help them break up and just disappear. If they stay as big as they are right now, though, one of them just might break off and go to your heart. Don't mean to scare you, but it's important you move on this right now. Does that make sense?"

This was remarkable! Not only had I not even mentioned the fact I was riding a motorcycle during the wreck, I had certainly not told Merlin about the blood clots, nor where they were located. He had apparently seen a mini-movie of his own, like I often did during readings I was giving. He had come through for me again!

"Oh, yes, Merlin. All of it makes perfect sense. You're right on target about the blood clots, and my low back is where most of the discomfort is centered. I'll call a chiropractor today. You're amazing, my friend. I can't thank you enough."

"My pleasure. Let me know how it turns out, okay?"

"You bet. Talk to you soon."

I got a referral from a friend to a good chiropractor whose office was nearby. I was not surprised in the least when he confirmed Merlin's assessment, treated me accordingly, and in a couple of days, the blood clots began to disappear!

So "Angel Duty" is something I learned about from my teacher and good friend Merlin. I'll finish up this section by telling you how John performed his own version of "Angel Duty" during that same timeframe.

About three weeks into my chiropractic treatment I was resting at home, watching a TV movie. I was feeling a lot better, but mobility was not yet completely restored. I was moving pretty slowly. I sensed John's presence, so I grabbed the remote to turn off the television. This was common practice for me now. I knew to eliminate as much electrical sound wave interference as possible in order to get the clearest communication from Spirit. I sat in anticipation.

"John? What do you want to say? I know you're there..."

"Come out, come out, wherever I am..." his voice teased me. I laughed. "You're getting good at this, Cheryl. So...*when* are you going to start doing readings for others on a full-time basis?"

"Oh, that again! I know, I know...if I can help others by doing that, I need to. Okay, already! I do free readings for people once in awhile, you know. I just get worried about whether I'll give them wrong information, or..."

"Worried about being human, just like they are? Get over it, Sis. Don't do this out of ego, do it out of the willingness to be helpful. Then it won't matter if you're wrong once in awhile...all that will be outweighed by the help you can offer, the comfort. You know how much working with Brian and others has helped you..."

"Yes, I sure do. So, Little Brother...it feels funny to call you that, knowing how evolved you are..."

"Well, that's what I was most recently to you, so I like it when you call me that," his voice had a smile in it.

"Okay, Lil Bro, did you just come here tonight to harass me into doing readings? Because I know I'm supposed to. I've been through the training classes, I've observed Brian for years now. You, Mom, Dad, and Aunt Kathy have certainly been great communicators with me directly...so if you're saying I'm ready, then so be it."

"Well, you're the one who has the say-so when you're ready, and you know that. It's your choice. I just know how much you love to help people, and this is definitely a special gift you have. I'm just encouraging you to share it, that's all. Also, I came here to ask you a favor."

"Really? Well, sure! Anything I can do for you, you know I will."

"I have been studying some healing techniques with my Teachers, and was wondering if you'd be willing to let me practice on you, since you could use a little extra help right now."

This was a new twist! "Well, yeah! Absolutely...I'm just confused. How will this work? I know you can do a lot from your current perspective, but are you gonna jump in someone's physical body and ring my doorbell, or what?"

He chortled. "Actually, that's not a bad idea! It just takes longer to find a willing person to help that way, that's all. I'm going to work on you energetically...you'll feel some tingles and hopefully some other good stuff. I just need you to lie down on the floor, face down, if you will."

I shook my head in wonder. This was a magical time in my life, escaping near death encounters, learning and experiencing all these unusual methods of healing from people I loved. A few short years ago, I would have thought I needed to be committed to an asylum! I chuckled to myself over that one as I moved to the center of the carpet, and slowly got down on all fours, then stretched out in prone position as instructed. "Now what, Dr. John?"

"Just focus on your breathing for right now, and relax as much as possible."

I closed my eyes and began slow, rhythmic breathing, just as though I were going to meditate. Different areas of my back got warm and "tingly" and a couple of vertebrae startled me by popping rather loudly. Then it felt like a cool breeze swept over me from head to toe.

"Great," John's voice said quietly. "Now, roll over, and I'll tell you how to move your arms and legs in order to finish the treatment."

I rolled onto my back, and he had me extend my arms all the way out to the side, palms up. I felt invisible hands reach under my torso, and gently pull up along my spine. Like a non-physical massage combined with healing. What a treat! Then John instructed me to cross one leg over the other, much as the chiropractor would do during certain adjustments. My back popped again, and I felt more open, as though I could take deeper breaths without as much effort.

"Okay, we're done. How're you doing?" my brother's voice reminded me he was still present.

"Great! That's so cool! Hey, John, you've got a great 'floor-side manner!' I'm just kidding. I feel lots better. Thank you, honey!"

"You're welcome. Thank *you*! I need all the practice I can get. It helps build my confidence."

I felt like he was getting ready for some "final exam" or something, but since he didn't bring it up, I decided to wait. I was certainly curious, though. "Hey, John...you mentioned 'getting into' a physical body takes more time. Have you done that? Have you materialized on the Earth plane since you've been gone?"

There was a pregnant pause. "Yes, a few times. I wasn't going to tell you, because I thought you'd wonder why I didn't come see you that way."

"Well, the thought does cross my mind, but I don't know all the rules on your side of things, so that's no big deal. My feelings aren't hurt or anything...I just find this all so amazing! When you have done that, what do you do here?"

"Pretty much what I just did with you, but I use a physical body... or what appears as a solid physical body to the people I'm around. You wouldn't even recognize me, Sis...I look so different when I show up there!" His voice became animated, and even though I knew what an old soul John is, just then he sounded for all the world like an excited young man, of the same chronological age he would be if he were still in this dimension.

He went on to tell me how he usually chose to appear unshaven, wearing dirty, baggy fatigues and a trench coat...looking like a "walking army surplus store," he laughed. He explained that he hung out with homeless people because they not only need healing on the physical level in many cases, but mental and emotional healing as well, and that gave him an opportunity to practice many techniques simultaneously.

"I usually show up with a bottle in a brown paper bag, and after talking with someone my Teacher and I have chosen for me to work with, I offer him or her a drink, just to break the ice, basically. It's just iced tea, but to them, it tastes like booze."

"Wow! What a trip! Then what?" I could see the scene unfolding in my mind as clearly as if I were watching a movie.

"Then I find an excuse to touch them in a healing way. I either put my arm around their shoulder for a little while, or I'll touch them on the back, or hold their hand a little extra while when we shake hands goodbye. I shoot the healing energy into them, concentrating on the area that needs it the most. Lots of them ask why my hand feels so hot, and I usually tell them I'm just getting over a fever, but it's not contagious!" he laughed.

It was clear he had fun doing this, but at the same time, it was a strong calling for him. I couldn't have been more proud of him if I had just watched him receive a medical degree.

"Wow, John, that's so wonderful. Hey! Your 'signal's' starting to fade a little...do you have to go?"

"You always can tell, Sis. Yes, in a minute. The really neat thing about all this is, I'm allowed to go back and visit these people a few weeks later. I usually don't appear, I just check in on them and run a health scan of sorts. The great thing is, they're getting better, Cheryl. That's what's so gratifying. It makes me so happy to help others."

"That makes perfect sense to me, John. And I'll follow your advice, I promise. I'm going to talk more with Brian about seriously starting to do readings professionally. If I can help others that way, I'd better get to it, huh?"

"That would make me happy, if it makes you happy! I gotta go, Cheryl. We'll talk soon. I love you!"

"Oh, I love you, too, Little Brother. My back feels great! Thanks so much for the treatment."

"We'll do another one soon. Take care!" and with that, our communication disconnected.

John was as good as his word. He worked with me several times during my recuperation and I know I mended more quickly because of his loving attention and special healing talents. I knew he was preparing for something, it was just not quite time for me to know exactly what at that time.

I soon got to experience a connection such as John had told me about. An up close and personal encounter with someone based in Spirit operating through a physical body, but it wasn't my brother. Shortly after I healed up from my motorcycle accident, I got a part-time job working for a friend in Burbank who did video production. This helped out a bit, but I was just barely squeaking by financially. I was doing a couple of readings a week, too, just by word of mouth spreading. I still was reluctant to charge much, though, and since a girl's gotta eat and pay rent, I decided to take on some additional part-time work. Only problem with that was, the job I landed was in Woodland Hills, which is located at the opposite end of the San Fernando Valley from Burbank. Now, for someone without a vehicle, this may seem absurd. But there was a much grander plan than just my gaining familiarity with the bus route from one end of the Valley to the other and back again. Let me explain.

Because the job in Burbank was actually overseen by the City of Burbank, I was qualified to join their credit union. So I did, and continued the back and forth long bus trip five days a week for several months. My friend Barbara at the production company encouraged me to apply for an auto loan.

"Well, Barbara, I only work part-time here. Do you really think they'll seriously consider a loan application from me?"

She smiled. "The people at this credit union are so nice. It can't hurt. And you're actually making pretty good money between the two jobs. So what do you have to lose?"

I thought it over and realized she was right. So I started the auto loan application process that week. The following Monday, I got a call from a loan officer at the credit union, asking me when I could come by and get my letter of credit to take to a car dealership of my choice. I was approved! I was ecstatic, to say the least.

Barbara told me to take a couple of hours off, go to the credit union and have some lunch to think over what kind of car I was going to get with the funds that were now available to me. I excitedly caught the bus, completed the paperwork and got my letter of credit. I happily walked back up the hill toward a favorite nearby restaurant where I was going to relax and spend a few minutes envisioning myself driving my new car. It felt like my feet weren't even touching the ground!

Suddenly, I felt a touch on my elbow. I looked beside me to see a tiny woman dressed somewhat like a Russian peasant. She wore a long dress, a sweater with moth-eaten holes here and there, and a scarf on her head. She looked to be about sixty years old. I smiled at her. I was smiling at the whole world, at the moment!

"Yes, ma'am? Can I help you with something?" I asked.

"Yes, please." She replied. "Please, you know where is bus goes to Woodland Hills?"

I laughed. "Oh, I know that bus all too well! I've been taking it every day for a long time. The bus stop is right across the street, ma'am," I pointed, "and number 132 should be along soon. One runs every twenty minutes. Have a nice day!" I patted her on the shoulder and turned to continue on my way when she tugged on my sleeve once again.

"No, please. You take me, please take me to bus." Her eyes burned bright, pleading that I just do this one little thing. It was a short walk to the bus stop, and I was in such a wonderful mood, I thought, "Heck, why not?"

"Okay, sure!" I answered. She smiled, and I saw that several of her teeth were missing. She held onto the crook of my arm as we walked, and I sent her some special healing energy, much the way I imagined John did when he was doing his work. Interestingly, I felt even more uplifted almost immediately.

My companion began talking in her broken English. "My daughter, she in bad accident recently. But, thanks God, she okay."

I smiled down at her. "Really? Wow. Same thing happened to me just a couple of weeks ago. Guess your daughter and I are really lucky, huh?"

"Yes," she nodded. "My daughter, she very, very happy right now. Because that accident left her no car, but today she find out, she able to get brand new car."

What a day of wonder, filled with synchronicity everywhere I went, it seemed! "Huh! That's exactly what I just found out. Imagine the chances of that!" I was still in my euphoric cloud, not paying close attention to what I was in the middle of (and I'm not talking about the intersection we were crossing!)

"I know," she replied. "Yes. It's good, very good." We stopped at the bus stop bench and she sat down with a peaceful smile on her face. I guessed she must be happy for her daughter and to have gotten to the right stop. I had no idea how right I was.

"Well, ma'am, the bus will be along any minute. You have yourself a great day now, okay?" I smiled and as I turned, she pulled at my sleeve one last time.

"Thank you Cher....Cherie," she reached up and patted me on the cheek in a motherly fashion. The full impact of her nearly saying my name (which I had not told her) still didn't faze my walking on air state of mind.

"You're welcome, ma'am. God bless you!" I smiled and as the light turned green, walked back toward the restaurant.

"God bless *you*!" I heard her call after me.

I threw up my hand in a wave, over my head, and kept walking. I was glad to have helped her, but wanted to get on with my lunch and my new car visualizing. About midway across the street, everything that happened in the last five minutes quickly replayed in my mind. I "woke up" to the import of what had just transpired and spun around in my tracks to look at her. She was gone!

I knew her bus hadn't come, because I was walking with the light, going straight across from her, east-west, and the 132 bus ran north-south. I blinked, and jumped as a car honked at me. My light had turned red, and I was still five feet from the sidewalk. I scurried over, moving backward to the curb, scanning up and down the opposite side of the street. Where had my little Russian lady disappeared to?

I got really strong chills as I realized what a miracle had just occurred. When I called Brian that night, he confirmed what I already knew to be true.

"Oh, Cheryl, that was definitely your mother! She took a physical form you would never associate with her, so as not to startle you. She wanted to physically connect with you, to touch you and let you know how happy she is you're getting a new car. Also that you're starting to do the readings, at long last, I'm sure. Isn't that something?" I could hear the smile in his voice. He and my mother had become old hats at communicating over the past several years.

Tears welled up in my eyes and as I wiped one away, I told my mentor, "Yes, Brian. It really is. Thanks for the validation. Have a great night." I hung up, and gazed at the ceiling. "And thank you, Mom. I don't know what else to say. I'm really blown away here. Thank you!"

I felt a loving warmth envelope me, just like her hugs made me feel when I was a little girl and I knew she was proud of me. I was sure John had helped her pull off this earthly manifestation, and felt so blessed that my family was still all around me, always letting me know how much they cared.

Chapter Fourteen

Heaven on My Mind

This segment deals with details of life "over there" in the Spirit World, Heaven, whatever you are comfortable referring to when it comes to letting go of the physical experience here on the Earth plane. These things have come through in readings I've done for others, as well as some which have been done for me. I also have included some insight about communication with that dimension which I've gained over nearly twenty years of being involved in this work. I'll be releasing a book about how to best open and develop your own intuitive/psychic abilities, including mediumship, in the very near future. This book which will be more detailed on this topic, including exercises you will find helpful, along with instructions on how to start your own psychic development circle, just like the one I was part of "way back when!" It will also address getting in touch with your Spirit guides and angels more clearly. I am so grateful to *all* of mine!

First of all, I'd like to stress what clear channels so many of our children and young people are. Especially since the Harmonic Convergence of 1990, there are many old souls coming to the Earth plane to help raise the vibration of the planet. I believe they don't really need to be here so much to learn their own lessons; rather that their desire is to bring as much Light to Mother Earth and the rest of us as possible. Read up on Indigo Children and Crystalline or Crystal Children. It's pretty fascinating stuff. Many of them are getting misdiagnosed or labeled with things such as ADHD. It is our duty to help them remember who they are and how to best stay on their path. They certainly need to be allowed and encouraged to have fun, happy childhoods; just be aware they may knock your socks off with some of their innate wisdom. And the younger they are, the more in touch with Spirit, is often the case. Just think about it for a moment...they have a much more recent memory of what it's like to dwell in the light. I'd like to illustrate this with a quick example.

I was in Chicago in July of 2005, and stayed with a lovely family in one of the 'burbs there for part of the trip. They told me about their two year old nephew who had recently demonstrated he clearly was in touch with his grandmother, who had passed away a few months before. This lovely little boy had not spoken in complete sentences prior to the incident I'm about to describe.

One day when he was playing, he started laughing and clapping. His mother looked around, but the TV wasn't on, nothing unusual was taking place. So she asked him, "Honey, what's so funny? What's going on?"

And clear as a bell, as he pointed across the room, a wide grin on his face as he answered, "I see Grandma!"

His mother was floored! This little child, far too young to make anything like this up, had uttered his first full sentence which also confirmed for her that her own mother was coming to visit them from the Spirit World!

Because I love working with kids, I offer a special workshop to help them develop their own intuitive skills and gifts called *Mom, I Had This Dream* (I know my own mother appreciates the tribute there!). I plan to expand the teaching of this class, and to create a playbook for kids, which includes the fun, interactive exercises. (Please email me if you'd like to set up a *Mom, I Had This Dream* seminar in your area, which parents are also welcome to attend.) I immediately expressed an interest in meeting this tiny Earth angel.

Soon after, Tommy's Mom brought him to her sister's home, where I was staying. He was shy toward me at first, which they told me to expect. His uncle was holding him, so we were on eye level. I kept talking to him quietly, while he hid his little face in his uncle's sleeve. When I asked him if he saw his Grandma sometimes, he peeked out at me and a huge grin started to form.

"*There* you are, Tommy! So, Grandma does come to visit you, huh? Does she have angels with her sometimes?"

He laughed and nodded. Encouraged, I went on with my "interview."

"Does she do funny stuff to make you laugh?"

He grinned and nodded once more, then stuck his thumbs in his ears and wiggled his fingers, to demonstrate what Grandma did! A few minutes later, we all sat down at the kitchen table, and he kept stealing peaks at me, so I winked at him and did the typical goofy stuff I do with little kids, like my Donald Duck impression (I have been able to do this since I was about eight years old. It has come in handy many times over the years when babysitting!) I decided to ask him one more question, very curious as to what his answer might be.

"Hey, Tommy, do you remember when you were in Heaven with the angels? In the beautiful Light?"

He nodded, solemnly this time and pointed at me as he said, "With you!"

I wasn't expecting that one. Here was this child, still less than three years of age, conversing about memories of being in the Light, hanging out with angels, as well as his present day ability to see loved ones in Spirit who were making Earth visits! Far too young to make anything like this up. Like I said, these kids coming in these days are truly amazing!

It's extremely helpful and encouraging to psychics when clients and friends for whom we've done readings are kind enough to take the time to let us know when validations pop up. Many times I have given names of relatives who have been long gone, some who were in Spirit before the client sitting across from me was even born! Although not everyone over there is interested in doing communication through a medium, many are. Some simply prefer to connect directly with their loved ones here on the Earth plane through dreams, or through signs of various types. One thing you may have experienced for yourself, without totally knowing it, or wanting to, is Spirit contact through the sense of smell. They will send an odor which you would relate to them when they were on the Earth plane, such as a particular cologne or perfume, the lovely aroma of their favorite flower, sometimes pipe or cigarette tobacco (not one of my personal favorites!), the smell of something they loved to bake or cook...and these olfactory signals occur at times when you know they could not be emanating from anywhere else, like in your car, or in an elevator, or in your home when no one else has been around or could have created that "smelly" trail! You see, those in Spirit who have had physical incarnations are well-aware that the sense of smell is a strong memory evoker. They typically will try sending their loved ones a thought form, first of all. But we may be too absorbed in our daily activities to allow it to come in, or talk ourselves out of it as being something they are sending. But when they clearly send an odor that is unmistakable, *that* gets our attention, as a rule! I guess they figure, "Well, he/she has five other senses, I'll start trying to get their attention through one of those, next!"

And of course, they are quite adroit at using electrical energy as a signal. Flickering lights, appliances that turn on or off by themselves, things associated with vehicular operation (of course, loving beings will never create anything that will harm you, but might actually alert you to something you should know)...all these are ways they may attempt to get us to focus on their presence and message. Again, it simply takes practice to improve how clearly you receive. Be willing to sit quietly and still your mind for even a few minutes whenever something like this occurs, and you'll be amazed at how quickly you start tuning in. Give it a try!

Many in that dimension have told me time and again their motivation for communicating, for lending their energy to projects, to help us heal, or just to feel better, is that doing so creates a win/win situation. Their descendant, now having the reading, may be the first relative in generations open enough to allow a message to come through, and therefore those "over there" are willing to help in any way they can. They may have been knocking on previous generations' consciousness for decades, and become very frustrated when it was written off as "nonsense" or sheer imaginative caprice. Now, they finally have a chance to be of help, and because it also helps *them* to evolve in their plane, they usually are excited and informative. So when clients who are not into genealogy can't confirm names on the spot, I always tell them to just listen to their tape later, make note of the names they don't recognize, and if and when possible, check with some older relatives to see if anyone remembers that person. Friends of the family often will come through, too, because sometimes they don't have any of their own family members currently on the Earth plane. It's been very gratifying when clients have called or emailed me to let me know someone in the family *did* know exactly who had been talking during their reading. Keeps me from thinking I'm totally crazy!

Another thing that has kept me going with this work through the years has been confirmations of things that did not make sense on the day of the reading, but that did unfold as time went on. Sometimes as much as three years after the fact, or more. I believe part of the reason these futuristic predictions of possibilities come through, is to give those of us here a bit of time to decide how we might choose to react, if and when those events cross our path. Free will on our part can certainly divert things which look like a "done deal" from the Spirit side, too. So I always encourage clients to put such things on the back burner for now, and to simply pay attention if certain people or circumstances that resonate with information from their reading start to show up. I've been blessed to have many clients share hundreds of those situations with me over the years, and I appreciate it more than I can say.

As I mentioned earlier, there is not a linear sense of time in the Spirit World as we mark it here. My mother told me there is no darkness in her corner of Heaven, and if she wants the illusion of darkness or night, she simply sends a mental request that the drapes in her house close, and they do! She also talked about how those in Heaven needn't sleep, because there's no physical body which needs to rest. Just that some souls who had a rough time on Earth such as a long illness or a lifetime which had been filled with a lot of negativity might need more time to recharge. This is similar to what Michael Newton wrote about in *Journey of Souls*, where his clients described needing a shower to "wash the negativity of Earth off their soul" when arriving back in the Light, between earthly lives.

Once my mother decided communicating with us here was "okay," she actually became an excellent guide when it came to describing her experience on that side. Brian and Leslie Flint had taught me that things in the Spirit World are made up of the substance of etherea, or thought forms. Mom brought all that home in a very real way to me with some of the descriptions she gave of what goes on there, from her perspective.

In one of the first readings with Brian where she came through in a strong way, she described her Spirit World house, "constructed" by the sheer power of her thought. As more and more clients' relatives in that dimension talked with me over the years, many of them speak of their houses there. I have come to believe this may well be what Christ was referring to when He said, "In my Father's house are many mansions." Just something to think about!

Mom told me that one day, sitting in her living room, she began to think about how much she used to love coffee. It's true, she was a dedicated coffee drinker the whole time I knew her here; seemed like there was always a pot percolating on the stove, filling the house with its aroma. Fortunately, I liked the smell! Anyway, as she sat there remembering how much she enjoyed it, the thought crossed her mind, "Gee, it sure would be nice to have a cup of coffee now." And no sooner had she thought it, than a cup of the steaming liquid appeared on the table beside her!

She was amazed. This was pretty early on in her "awakening" to being back in Heaven, and still kind of remembering what powerful creators we all are, made in the Master Creator's image. She took the cup of coffee in her hands, and enjoyed the aroma for a moment. It smelled *wonderful*! Even better than she had remembered. She took a tentative sip, not sure what to expect. It was the most delicious cup of coffee she had ever tasted! And why wouldn't it be? This was Heaven, after all. She totally enjoyed it, savoring it to the last drop. It was at that point she realized, "Hey! This was great, but I don't have any sort of buzz, like I did on Earth." She pondered this for a moment, then realized because she no longer had a physical body, and that she and the coffee now were basically made up of thought ethers, strong sensory memories of things enjoyed on Earth were simply that. Pleasurable memories. The coffee obviously had no caffeine. She had no physical body, just one made of light. Therefore, no "kick" was attached, as it had been when she was on Earth. So she decided then and there that even though it had been a good experience, she had no real reason to keep manifesting a daily cup of Joe! Made sense. I asked her about other types of favorite memories or addictions people in that dimension might choose to manifest.

"Oh, honey, it's easy now for me to spot people who are strongly attached to such things. I see them walking around smoking a pipe or cigar, or cigarette...some carry around a snifter of brandy. Doesn't bother anybody else at all. Since it's their thought form, nobody else is affected by it, so nothing like secondhand smoke exists here. And again, with no physical body to rev up or injure, well, it's more like a satisfying magic trick than anything else. A comforting memory which helps them adjust to their surroundings, I guess. Seeing that kind of thing is not uncommon here, really. That's just in my neighborhood, usually. When I have visited Johnny in his, that sort of thing doesn't go on. I just figure some of those Spirit folks are "newbies" and haven't released their earthly trappings. Nothing wrong with it. I figure if it makes 'em happy, it's all good!"

"Wow! Can you tell me more about the neighborhoods you speak of there, please?"

"Sure. Seems there are different sections of Heaven, which I look at like neighborhoods. It's basically different levels of consciousness, where like-minded folks tend to hang out most of the time. Not too different from Earth!" She chuckled. "We can grow, evolve, if we choose to, just like you can there. Some people are more willing to learn and move forward here than they might have been on the Earth plane. And there's nothing wrong with us going to visit loved ones in another neighborhood, just like I mentioned when I go see Johnny. He's in that place where he studies with some of the ascended masters, and it's so beautiful. He has taken me for boat rides on a picture perfect lake. We've gone to some musical concerts together...you'll be pleased to know I've taken a liking to classical music, as well as other kinds."

"That's so interesting, Mom! What about Dad? Does he live with you in your house there, or somewhere else?"

"I wondered when you were going to get to that. You and your Dad were always so close. He will start communicating with you more soon, I know. You remember how hesitant I was, the first time you had a reading?"

"Of course! And I'm thrilled you opened up to it. It means so much to me. Yeah, I've wondered why Daddy is so reluctant to communicate much."

"Well, sweetheart, don't take it personally. When he first got here, he laid down on a park bench not too far from my house. I'd go there quite often, talking to him, trying to get him to look at me and talk. But he'd just lie there, his hands folded across his chest, looking for all the world like he was still resting in his coffin. I didn't get it. This went on for a long while...a few years, by Earth's marking of time. Finally, I went over to him, determined to get his attention. I leaned down and shouted in his ear, '*Walter*! You sit up and talk to me right now!'"

I chuckled, envisioning the whole scene as she described it.

"He finally opened one eye and leaned on an elbow, looking at me like I was some awful person. 'What do you want, Dee?' he grumbled. 'What do I *want*? Well, honey, I want to share Heaven with you! Why are you acting like this?' And Cheryl, you know what his reply was?"

"I have no idea, Mom." I was anxious to hear it.

"He said, 'I have to wait until the last trumpet sounds before I can wake up.' Well, that took me aback, until I realized it had taken me a long time being back in the Light to remember a lot of stuff. We do bring our belief systems over here when we first cross, and he was always stubborn, y'know! With his Southern Baptist upbringing, he just couldn't imagine anything other than what he had been taught to believe about the afterlife! I laughed and pulled him up to stand beside me. Then I said, "Walt, not everything they told us down there is exactly that way. It's time for you to wake up and get with the program. This is the new reality!' And he's been fine ever since!"

She went on to share with me that once Dad got "with it," she explained to him that he could have his own house, if he so chose. He was eager to do this, so they gathered some like-minded relatives and friends together who collectively asked Dad what type of setting he would like for his house. It wasn't surprising to me that his preference was to have it situated at the bottom of a mountain. He had loved Virginia so much, this made perfect sense. They all focused on his description, and then step by step, went through a "house-raising" where no physical building was necessary at all, simply their conjoined focusing on each aspect and detail he wanted his house to have. And it appeared exactly as he wanted. Mom said that when they work as a group over there, it just helps make the manifestation take place more quickly, and that sometimes people have great ideas to make things even better. Not all that different from any type of group endeavor or mass consciousness effort here on Earth! She told me that they often visit each other in their separate homes and spend quite a bit of time together, but actually like having their own space.

"It's not uncommon for folks who were married to have a bit of distance here. We realize we are all One, yet each is a unique soul. Sometimes it's easier to learn when we have some private time to meditate, pray, or work with our teachers on our own. We can always choose to do things together, too."

Her detailed portrayal made a lot of sense to me, and when I've had vivid visitation dreams of my parents, spending time with them in this way, I understand more and more. In fact, it's such an amazing feeling to be there, even for awhile. I always know I'm dreaming and must return back to Earth because my work here is not done. But while I'm there, the beauty is breathtaking. Everything seems to breathe or vibrate subtly...even inanimate objects. I suppose this is due to the fact that everything is thought forms there. Everything appears solid, but it has this slight transparent quality to it. The colors are so brilliant, especially trees, grass, sky...it's like an utterly non-polluted, pristine version of the world. You're probably not surprised I'm always a bit bummed when I wake up here! Don't get me wrong, I love Mother Earth. It's simply that this place in Heaven is so ideal when compared to what mankind has done to the Mother's aura and body with our greed, industrialism, our raping of her resources. These dreams always make me feel like taking a more active role in environmental causes, and raise my awareness about being a good custodian while here.

One of the most recent dreams I had of visiting my parents found us in a '50s diner. Being a product of that era, I shouldn't have been surprised. Again, there are no physical bodies over there, so food is not necessary for sustenance. But the memory of favorite places and things, including tastes, is something they can conjure up and enjoy. What I found most interesting about this dream was the fact that in their present light body forms, my parents both appear younger than I am now! They both look to be around their mid-thirties, when both were healthy and basically in the prime of life. Since it's their choice as to how they appear, why not? As I looked around the diner I saw children, seniors, and souls of every age in between. Some people prefer one age over another, perhaps due to the fact that's when they had the best time during their most recent earthly incarnation. The one thing I noticed all the folks in that diner had in common was that everyone moved with great ease, obviously free from any type of restriction or infirmity. Again, it's Heaven, so why should that be surprising?

Although I have done this work for many years, I am certainly not immune to the pain associated with grief and loss. Up until ten years ago or so, on the anniversary of my mother's death, I still would find myself quite sad and often in tears. Then one such day, she sent me warm, comforting waves of love that washed over me like a powerful hug. I heard her sweet voice in my head.

"Cheryl, honey. I'm sorry this day makes you feel so sad. I wish you could learn to look at it the way I do."

I sniffed, and breathed in the consoling energy. "How is that, Mom?"

She replied, "Well, I look at it as my graduation. I finally released all the pain and suffering and moved into the Light, which is more like graduate school, or hanging your diploma on the wall and feeling proud of all you achieved. The road to get there was really worth it, and my family certainly always did and still does make me proud to have helped them any way I could. Does that make sense? Does it help?"

It certainly did, and still does. I seldom get the blues about her passing, or that of any other loved ones. I know they're in a wonderful place now and am happier thinking of them celebrating their graduation. Perhaps that can help you look at loss in a new light, too. I hope so.

Let's go back to talking about manifesting in the Light, the seeming ease of it all, compared to how much we may struggle when creating here. Remember, struggling is also a choice! Growth opportunities abound which don't necessarily require pain and suffering. Learning to allow is much better, isn't it? Anyway, after spending some time back in the Light, can you consider that perhaps all that instantaneous manifesting directly from the essence of pure, focused thought might after a fashion become too simple, in a sense? Or if there were certain things that you had a difficult time mastering while enrolled at Earth School, it seems to me that coming back to have a physical experience with improved results would be a great opportunity. Earth is a great place to remember how to manifest, to balance some karmic situations, to connect with other souls we love so much we wouldn't miss it for the world. There are many good reasons to consider coming back. We can also help others who perhaps haven't taken responsibility for their own creations and how important the power of thought is, to focus on their desired results and know right down to the core of their being that no one is a victim, rather we are all creators. If you've never visited www.abraham-hicks.com, I urge you to check it out to get really great information on all of this, via tapes, CDs, books, you name it. I've been an Abraham fan since I first became aware of them in the early 1990s. If this topic really calls to you, please read *Ask and It Is Given* by Jerry and Esther Hicks. Dr. Wayne Dyer wrote the foreward, and it's published through Hay House. It really gets to the point about manifesting your desires and contains empowering exercises to help you get there. It's all about how we're emotional creatures and at the core of things, it's our *feelings* rather than our thoughts, that really determine the level at which we manifest. Great stuff! Doing readings is a continual learning process for me, and sometimes it's quite surprising. I love the new insights and clarity I receive as I pass along the information to my clients. Here are a couple of examples.

One day I was in the midst of a session and asked a client if an "Aunt Ruth" was passed over, because this lady was being very chatty with me. My client looked quite surprised and informed me that Aunt Ruth was still alive. Puzzled, I asked my unseen friend to please straighten me out. She told me she was dealing with Alzheimer's, but that when she was asleep, her soul was on "walkabout," so to speak, and able to communicate quite lucidly. This was the first time this happened, so I was taken aback. However, when the niece confirmed her aunt was suffering from dementia and Alzheimer's, it opened a new window of understanding for me. Since then, a number of folks who deal with that particular situation, as well as people who are comatose, have come through fairly frequently. So this brought it home to me that people with those challenges are still aware on some deep inner level of what's going on. So it is, indeed, important for their loved ones to know that they can hear and understand what they tell them. Much the same as its been proven people under anesthesia often recall what was said in the operating room, so doctors and attendants in those circumstances need to be very careful of what they discuss.

One other fascinating insight that I learned, due to the frequency of its repetition in many readings over the years, is the explanation of what is often referred to as a "life review." What I've been told, many times, is that those who cross over may view their most recent life, much like a movie. Mainly, the "highlights" are accentuated, giving them the chance to understand and experience soul growth by witnessing various choices they made in that lifetime. However, the "highlights" shown are sometimes a bit difficult to watch, at first. For they might include such scenarios as a volatile argument, or their unkind treatment of another person. The difference in observing these scenes from an objective "audience" standpoint is this: once the interaction with someone is completed, instead of going on about their own business as they did in the moment, they next watch and actually experience the emotional response of the other person(s). Many in Spirit have told me that this is an incredibly growthful situation, which helps them open up to be more tolerant, considerate and empathetic to others. Just as many who arrive there become more open to counseling and expanding through that modality, the life review experience is apparently a powerful soul-altering opportunity for expansion, to release prejudices and narrow-mindedness. If we'd just do our best to tune in to what others are feeling when we are engaging in such situations here on the Earth plane, just think how much nicer we'd be to one another!

There's so much to share with you, I'm trying to cover as many bases as possible. A lot of this you may already be aware of, and if so, that's great. But if this happens to be one of the first books you've read concerning metaphysics and specifically, mediumship, I hope you find it truly helpful. I'm going to move on and talk about dreams a bit now, and how they can be a viable, uplifting way to make contact with loved ones who have passed on.

Just as I mentioned earlier in this chapter about people in the Spirit dimension choosing to manifest at younger ages, it's also not uncommon to have dreams of those who lived to a pretty ripe old age being much younger, active and vital. You may also dream about them interacting with you in your current daily life. This is one way they have to let us know they *are* here visiting, or looking in on us frequently, and reminding us they do care about what goes on with. It's much easier for many of us to allow them to appear to us in a dream than in a vision or meditation. The mind is simply more relaxed. It's perfectly fine to invite them to visit you in a dream, too. I'm going to list a few suggestions that might make enhance this.

If you have a picture of the loved one you would like to have a dream visit with, it can help convince them to do their best to appear in a dream if you will write them a brief note and then place it in plain sight, by their photograph. This also can be quite helpful in persuading those in Spirit to come through in a reading you might book with a medium. When my mentor Brian told me of this technique years ago, I was puzzled.

"Brian," I queried, "Don't they know on a telepathic level that we'd love them to communicate with us? Is this picture deal really necessary?"

He said, "Of course the ones closest to you can understand your mental and emotional requests and very often do respond without you needing to write the note. However, just because the physical body has died, it doesn't mean that the ego has! It is flattering to them to see that you keep their picture and often touches their heartstrings that you have actually taken the time to harness your thoughts and actually write out a formal invitation, of sorts. It just lets them know how important they still are to you, and some who may not be as willing as others to come through in a reading, or in a dream, just might make the extra effort. It does take a lot of energy on their part to do this, so if they see your desire to connect with them is as strong as theirs to reach you, then it's more likely to happen. Does that make sense?"

It did. And I have had many clients report successful results when they've done this, both with dreams and in readings they've had. The other technique is a simple one, indeed, and that is to send a very clear, sincere request to the loved one you would like to connect with in a dream just before you drop off to sleep.

You can say something like, "Hi, Mom! I'd really love it if you could pop into my dreams tonight, and let's both intend that it be a happy, pleasant visit for both of us. And anything you and my Higher Self can do to help me remember it when I wake up, that would be terrific. Thanks so much for whatever you can do to make this happen!"

You may have to repeat the request several nights in a row. It's not that they don't get the message or understand you, it's just that they may have other activities going on that particular night, or even more likely, *you* may not allow yourself to completely relax as much as possible in order to let them come through. Sometimes when we realize we're dreaming about a loved one who has passed on, we get so excited we immediately wake ourselves up. So send yourself a message, too, that you will stay relaxed and allow the dream experience to unfold nicely, and that you wish to remember the details when you awaken. With practice, you can become very good at this.

One other thing about dreams I'd like to mention here. Many people over the years have asked me, "Why did my Mom come through so clearly in a dream to my friend Barbara, when she really didn't know her well? Doesn't she know how important it is to me to dream about her? She is my Mom, after all!"

The odds are, your Mom or other loved one has been trying like gangbusters to get through to you in your dreams. *But*, the closer we are to someone, the more deeply we tend to grieve, and that grief can be an exceptionally tough barrier to break through. So many times, they will appear to someone else who is a little more detached and objective, knowing that person will most likely relay the dream to you. They are simply going through a "middle man" to reach you, not unlike giving you messages through a medium, really. So accept those messages from "Barbara" as validation that your loved one is, indeed, making the attempt to connect with planet Earth. I urge you to keep practicing, keep inviting them, keep believing it will happen. It will, in the perfect right timing, you'll see. You just need to relax, allow and believe.

In addition to using the photograph and written invitation technique to invite them in through readings or meditations, I'd like to give you another way to open up your frequency channel between dimensions. Try to do this at a regular time of day, on the same day of the week, if you decide to commit to doing it weekly. Establishing routine in this practice helps you develop the mindset of opening to receive messages as well as letting those you want to connect with know you are seriously interested. It's like anything else truly worthwhile, you get better with practice. That psychic "muscle" needs some stretching and working out, just like any other physical, mental or emotional muscle.

Once you've picked your scheduled time (I would highly suggest putting this in your Day Timer or Palm Pilot. Make it a priority to keep that time slot open for this communication and don't let anything else interfere, just as you would with any other type of class you are very serious about). You may wish to say a brief prayer of protection before you start, just stating that you are only interested in working with energies from the Divine Light, then call in any angels and guides you wish to surround you with a loving circle of light. Light a candle, if you like, and either focus on the flame, or close your eyes and take slow, deep breaths. Keep your hands on your lap in a palms upward, open position. This puts your physical self in a stance of receiving, allowing. I always tell folks, "Hold your hands out as if someone were going to place a gift there, because that's really what they're trying to do."

Then just send up a mental request or speak it aloud, if you prefer, that goes something like, "Hi, Dad/Mom (whomever you would like to reach). I'm going to be quiet for a few minutes and just want to invite you to do your best to send me a picture, some words, a strong feeling... whatever you are able to, just so I can get used to our communicating this way. Thanks a lot. I love you!" You can use your own words, of course. Just try to keep it short and sweet, and then take slow deep breaths to help stop your mental chatter. Try holding the tip of your tongue still against your lower teeth. It's a physical point of focus and actually is very effective at stilling the mind for many people.

Then willingly receive whatever comes, doing your best to accept the first impression that comes through. The more we allow our analytical left brain to engage and question, the more likely we are to talk ourselves out of a great message. It's true! Your loved one may choose to get your attention through imagery, words, they may even send you the scent of something you would associate as a strong memory of them, as mentioned earlier. They figure if they can't reach us on a pure mental stream, we've got five other senses, and they'll start tapping into those! So don't be surprised if you get a signal that way sometime. If so, great! They've got your attention. Now it's time to relax and follow the other steps in order to see *what* it is they'd like you to know. Practice, practice, practice. Be patient with yourself, and with them. Some of them may not have believed in this type of communication during their most recent earthly experience, so it's pretty new to them, too!

Sometimes when we ask them for a sign, it might be so literal, you'll tend to ignore it. For example, when my Dad "got with the program" over there, as Mom says, he started communicating with me directly through signage. So his "sign" to me, often is a real *sign*. Such as the time a truck pulled up beside me at a stoplight with signage declaring, "Walt's Office Supplies" or "Waltco." Yes, such companies exist, I realize, but when I get the familiar chills in conjunction with noticing these things, signaling Dad is really pulling out all the stops to get me to pay attention, I definitely know it's time to close my eyes, settle down and listen to what he might have to say! Recently when driving, I felt his energy but was caught up in frustration over the traffic due to construction activity. He didn't give up, though, bless him, and my eyes were drawn to a real estate sign on the side of the road which had a smaller sign hanging beneath it urging, "Call Walt!" So I calmed down, laughed, and we had a nice conversation. The slower traffic provided a nice venue for it.

Remember when I said they might be "busy" doing other things at the exact time you are attempting to have them enter a meditation or dream? I believe they have many wonderful things they can do over there, such as the concerts, classes and lectures in that dimension which my mother tells me about. They study with their master teachers quite often, or they may be visiting other loved ones either in that dimension or on Earth. They often have wonderful "jobs" over there that I've been very interested in learning more about. Here are a few of the really great ones they've shared with me.

In the beginning of this book I mentioned the paramedic teams who assist people who cross over quickly in acclimating to their return to the Light. I feel like this must be a very rewarding endeavor. I've also heard there are huge task forces who help usher the mass arrivals who cross together, such as from the tsunami, hurricanes, the India/Pakistan earthquake, etc. My teacher Merlin believed that people who choose to cross en masse (on a soul level, before they ever make an appearance in that particular lifetime) are more comfortable doing it that way, and often select that type of crossover because the media attention such a large disaster attracts can serve to raise the consciousness of those of us still here. This type of huge statement helps us appreciate each and every day more, reaching out to help one another more often, being reminded of the Oneness we are part of.

When we wish to connect with angels and guides to request their energetic assistance with various things going on in our earthly lives, I believe they are more than willing to help in any way they can. We don't even have a clue as to how much they work on our behalf every day, and we don't need to know exactly how they do it. Remember, I mentioned that ancestors and other loved ones often love to help us because it is one way to actually further their own evolutionary soul growth on that plane. Angels really appreciate the invitation to assist because it allows them to do so without interfering with our free will choices. Whomever you're requesting help from, I think it's always a great idea to be sure to say, "Thanks in advance for whatever you can do," release it and move forward with whatever *you* can physically put in motion with the visualization of the desired end result held clearly in your heart and mind. The *how* is what can really trip us up, if we get too involved in that aspect!

People have often questioned me as to why I sometimes only get a few words out of the messages being transmitted, other than full sentences. It's true, they are sending complete thoughts, almost always, but the incredible amount of energy it takes to do so can get dispelled between the dimensions. Brian described it to me perfectly, long ago. He said, "Have you ever seen little children playing in the swimming pool? Often they'll try to sit down on the bottom of the pool, playing tea party, or staying underwater as long as they can hold their breath. Well, imagine someone up at the surface who leans down and says something to them. The words kind of bubble, bubble down toward them and 'pop!' They might hear an inkling of a word. Frequently that's how hard it is to catch someone's exact thought from the other side. It's a true blessing when they can really let it flow!"

It is, indeed! I have had many readings where it flowed, and it's gotten easier as the years go by. But there were several times it was not unlike getting just a few key pieces to a jigsaw puzzle, then having to ask for further clarification, or to have the message transmitted in another way to fill in the gaps, like with pictures instead of words.

Just as group energy is beneficial to us here on the Earth plane, so it is in the Spirit World. Simply because someone's physical body has died, it doesn't mean their soul automatically knows how, or even wants, to communicate through a medium. However, they know how much it will mean to their loved ones if they give it their best shot, so many times they will enlist the aid of like-minded folks in that dimension to join with them in sending the messages. I explain to my clients that I imagine a big living room of sorts over there, where those interested in communicating during a particular reading gather ahead of time. I happen to believe there's some sophisticated way of getting the word out over there, beyond what we can totally comprehend from this side of things. Perhaps some sort of grand scale telepathic announcement, but because my guides like me to keep a good sense of humor and pass that along to others whenever I can, I've taken to saying to clients, "I imagine there's one of those rotating signs with the revolving red letters, a really big one, that says something like, 'If you know Bill Jones or anyone strongly connected to him, he's having a reading with Cheryl on June 23rd at 2 pm Earth time, and if you'd like to get a message through, you can gather in the Heavenly Message Lounge'!" Now that adds a whole new meaning to long distance communication and "can you hear me now?" doesn't it? Something along those lines makes sense to me, because there are often messages which come through for people not even present at a reading, but their loved ones in Spirit have someone found out that *you* are having a reading, and they know you know their relative or friend who's still on Earth. They are determined to get their messages through, and this has happened so often in my work. Many times, getting a vicarious message through a friend who's attended a reading has convinced that person their loved ones really are around them, more than anything else possibly could have. Heavenly residents are very generous about sharing message time. I sometimes have to ask them to be extremely focused and keep it short and sweet, because it is the client's time, after all! My experience with this type of thing has been that most people are very gracious and happy to pass on such messages when they come through.

Other questions I've been asked many times concern those who have been murdered or crossed over in the midst of some violent act.

Once they are in the Light, these souls usually release vengefulness toward whomever caused it; they simply don't want anyone else on the Earth plane to suffer or be hurt by the person(s) responsible. That seems to be their primary motive in helping to solve crimes from the other side, not to be a ghostly vigilante. They also know their loved ones need the closure that a balance of justice affords.

Another frequent inquiry is with regard to the act of suicide. I do not believe those who commit suicide are punished in any way, shape or form. Many have told me once they're in the Light, they have counseling made available to them and they're often more receptive to allowing that in their new dimension. The only punishment they go through is what's self-inflicted by their thoughts of guilt, much like the wife in the movie *What Dreams May Come*. They have told me they know they will most likely have to come back and "do it all again" in order to get the full value of the soul lesson which prompted them to come to Earth School in the recent incarnation, which was cut short by their choice to take their life. I will share a story with you which really explained this in a clear way to me and to the clients involved.

Two sisters came to see me a few years ago for a reading. A number of their older relatives came through, and then a friend they knew quite well identified himself by name. He started talking about their brother in very active terms. He was saying things like, "Adam's in jail now, but I hope he'll get out soon. He's really punishing himself far too much. I go to visit him every day, but he won't let me in."

From the way this guy talked, I concluded he meant he went on a Spirit visit to the prison where their brother was locked up. He went on to describe various things their brother had done and when I looked to the sisters for validation, they nodded their heads so I knew they understood. Yet there was a strange look in their eyes which puzzled me. So I paused and asked, "What's confusing to you here? You're brother's incarcerated, is that correct?"

One of them shook her head "no" then explained, "That's what we're not getting, Cheryl. So many things our friend Bill is talking about are right on target with Adam. But Adam's not in jail. He committed suicide recently."

"Oh, I'm so sorry," I said. "Bill is such a clear communicator, though. Let me just ask him to clarify this a bit more so we can put all the pieces together and hopefully make some sense of all this." I closed my eyes, took a few deep breaths and requested a more thorough explanation from Bill. Soon I understood.

"He says that out of his guilt for crossing himself over, Adam has literally built a prison around himself over there. Everything in that dimension is made of thoughts, and his are so negative toward himself, he feels he deserves some awful punishment. He's obviously sorry for what he's put the family through. And when Bill says he goes and tries to get him to come out into the Light and experience God's love and acceptance, Adam either doesn't respond or just yells that he should go away. I know this may seem confusing, but there are many levels of understanding in the Spirit plane, and your brother seems to be a bit stuck, to say the least. Would you be willing to do an exercise with me, which I believe might help him?"

"Oh, we'll do anything we can!" they replied.

I asked Bill to be our proxy there and transport himself to Adam's location, to do his best to open the lines of our communication in such a way that Adam could hear clearly what we, as a group of three, were sending to him. We closed our eyes, and I led them in a prayer on Adam's behalf, asking that his eyes, ears, heart and mind in his Spirit body be open to knowing, right down to the core of his soul, that he was not being punished by anyone or anything other than his own guilt. That his sisters and family remaining here on Earth wanted him to step out into the Light where Bill was and start to understand more about himself and God's love. His sisters sent him some personal messages, too. In a few moments, I had a vision of the prison bars melting, and Adam blinking at the brightness of the Light as his friend Bill hugged him, happy that his healing and knowledge could now move forward. Adam was able to communicate a bit after that, and I'm sure he's been able to appear to family members here in dreams since that time, and brought them comfort, knowing that he is truly all right.

Self-esteem, or the lack thereof, is such an important quality to cultivate. Adam's story illustrates that the lack of it can carry over even after death. There are those different planes of consciousness there, too, remember? We often worry so much about what others think of us, it taints our words, our behaviors and subsequently, the quality of our lives. Terry Cole Whittaker wrote a book whose title I absolutely love, *What You Think Of Me Is None of My Business*. Isn't that great? And so true. We should never let ourselves be defined by what others might think of us. One of my real-life heroines who came out of the metaphysical closet in such a big way about twenty years ago, obviously decided to let go of caring about that. I'm talking about Shirley MacLaine, whom I mentioned a bit earlier. I admire her so much, I don't mind paying her a bit of additional homage! She has been an inspiration to me and millions of others. I'm very grateful to her for not letting what others might think prevent her from speaking up and writing some great books about her spiritual beliefs. In fact, some of the best roles of her life came along after she let the cat out of the bag! If you've never visited it, check out her website www.shirleymaclaine.com

If anyone has judged you harshly, or treated you badly; if there is someone you wish you could have shared important information with, or told off, *whatever* it is you feel you lost the opportunity to tell them, it's really never too late. Here's a simple technique that is incredibly cathartic and healing. I didn't make it up, it's been around a long time. Take some time to yourself, and really pull out all the stops. Sit down and write a letter to the Higher Self of anyone like this; whether they're still living or have passed on makes no difference in the effectiveness of this. Just let your stream of consciousness flow unfettered, letting them see all your pent up emotions laid bare through your words. When you feel you've gotten it all out of your system, take the letter and walk with it and a lighter or matchbook, to the fireplace or sink. Just before you set fire to it, tell the person, along with your angels, guides, whomever you feel comfortable sharing this with, something to this effect:

"I'm so weary from carrying this around all these years. I know keeping these feelings locked up inside has been self-destructive and hurts *me* more than anyone else. So I'm willingly releasing them right now, once and for all. I wish you the best wherever you may be, too. As the smoke dispels from this, my intention is to feel lighter and freer. And so it is." And then light it and watch it burn. You should immediately feel like a boulder has been lifted off of your shoulders! This effective tool was passed along to me through one of Hanna Kroeger's students who taught a healing class I attended. Hanna was an amazing person who did amazing work with herbs, energy healing and more. If you'd like to learn more, just do a search on Hanna Kroeger—lots of wonderful stuff, including her books, will pop up. Her work is fascinating, and very healing. When this technique was shared with me, Hanna hadn't taken credit for it, either. It was something a psychologist she knew during World War II told her to try. When she did, she was amazed by how much better she felt. So she asked her friend why she didn't share it with all her patients.

The wise doctor replied, "Because if I did, I wouldn't have many patients, now would I?"

It's so true that some many powerful techniques are deceptive in their simplicity. Don't write them off, just because they're easy. Many amazing breakthroughs can occur through a strong belief in a simple action.

Readings, Nothing More Than Readings...

Many years ago, a funny friend of mine was curious as to why my work was called "doing a reading." Larry said, "Well, if you're mostly clairaudient and you get the messages by hearing all this stuff from the other side, shouldn't you call it a 'listening' instead of a reading?"

That was pretty funny. But pretty on track, with regard to clairaudience. When I first started practicing readings, I was very stuck on working with the assistance of psychometry, which involves holding an object that belonged to the person that they touched a lot, so it had their energy on it. Such as keys, jewelry, a pen, etc. This can be an effective way of tuning in, and I'm in no way negating its use. It's just that after about three years of clutching such objects tightly, all the way through a reading, my guides collectively ganged up on me to tease me a bit.

Inside my head they shouted, full-force, **"CHERYL! Can you hear us?"**

I was surprised and a bit miffed. I telepathically shot back, "Yes, of course I can hear you. Why?"

The loving response which had a smile running through it was, "Then put that thing down. You don't need it. It's become a crutch."

They were right. They usually are! Psychometry is a wonderful tool, which can help to tune in more accurately to loved ones energy. I simply had outgrown the need to use it in every single reading. But today, when dealing with missing persons or murder cases, I find that having access to that person's energy through a picture, a piece of clothing or another personal item can often amplify my tuning in ability and accuracy.

I've made reference to a future book about developing your psychic abilities, and I will release it soon. Also, I want to mention that when my schedule permits it, I do private mentoring of students, ages eight on up, to help open up your intuitive abilities, whether you want to do this for your personal use, or to do readings yourself some day. This can be done in person, if you live close by me, or also is extremely effective via telephone and email correspondence. Either way we can do many interactive games and practice techniques which can really accelerate your growth in this area. Email me at lifeofspirit@gmail.com or call my toll-free number 1-877-271-8218 for more details, if you're interested.

One of my main goals with my work is to reach as wide an audience as possible. That's why I'm focusing more on writing, traveling and seminars these days. I had an internet radio show for a short time in 2004 called *Soul Survival*. You can hear those archived shows over your computer by going to www.achieveradio.com/showpages/cherylbootharch.htm. I plan to have another show someday soon, and will keep you posted via my website. Whether it will be internet or satellite radio or the more conventional airwaves, at the moment, I'm not sure. I just know that having interesting guests who can discourse on a wide variety of metaphysical topics is something I really enjoy being part of. So I'm open to suggestions, and certainly to being a guest, myself, on such shows!

I will address a few aspects of the topic of psychic development right now, since I want to be as helpful as possible. Please remember, cultivating the psychic "muscle" takes practice, just like any other skill or talent, in order to reach its full potential. You have to be willing to work it out, baby! We live in such a technologically dependent society, we have lost patience when sometimes that's exactly what is required. I often equate it to an old Joan Rivers joke where she spoke of an overweight celebrity standing in front of a microwave oven and screaming, "HURRY!" That's really how many of us in Western culture are geared these days, and in some ways, it's a shame. Taking the time to really learn the various subtleties of certain techniques is very important. There's something to that old joke, "How do you get to Carnegie Hall?" "Practice, practice, practice." Same with sharpening your intuitive skills. You need to allow time, commit to practicing, including sitting in a Psychic Development Circle, if you're led to go that route, and above all, be patient with your own development.

Please don't misunderstand and think I'm blatantly putting down technology. So many amazing advancements and achievements have catapulted forward as a result of it. With regard to this particular field, I am anxiously awaiting the announcement of something Merlin saw years ago in a dream state, when he projected ahead in time. He said within my lifetime, scientists will find the means to visually capture the image of someone in Spirit who is talking with a medium, and even be able to hear the voices from those in the Spirit dimension. Given the electromagnetic nature of Spirit contact, and its effect on electrical devices, I believe this is true. I know it has been in R and D for some time in Europe. And because so many things Merlin shared with me have come to pass over the years, I have no doubt this will, too. To have other people be able to hear and see for themselves things I've been blessed to experience is a great concept. I would always advise doing a prayer of protection when doing this, just as I do with *any* type of spirit communication.

When opening up to Spirit communication, it's important to declare what your intentions are, and that you feel safe. There are energies in the lower astral planes which you may not wish to deal with. That's best left to my next book, or for you to research in current existing books. Do some research on psychic defense and psychic protection. See what resonates with you. I will just say here that I have been involved in doing energy clearings for a number of private homes and businesses, places where the occupants have noticed unusual paranormal activity, like objects flying through the air, doorbells ringing on homes where there are no doorbells, fun little things of that nature! The first time I went to do a clearing on such a place, I was understandably a bit nervous. Armed with sea salt (it dispels negative energy), lavender oil (it's great for blessing ceremonies and many other things), sage (bundled sage has been burned for centuries by Native Americans and other cultures to assist in cleansing/clearing), and a white candle, I drove toward my destination. I needn't have been anxious, though. Right before I pulled up to the place, Johnny sent me a very funny message in the form of a song. I told you those in Spirit have a great sense of humor, and often try to help us lighten up about things here, remember? I clearly heard the theme from *Ghostbusters*, with the words slightly altered to: "Who ya gonna call? My sister!" This cracked me up, gave me an extra dose of courage, and the clearing proceeded without any problems. People for whom I have performed clearings and cleansings have reported that the "weird activity" stopped, afterward. Anyone who has a strong faith and a commitment to create a peaceful environment can learn to do this. Read up on it! There are a number of reference tools out there. I will be including some instructions in my next book, but there are already several tools and methods available, if you only are willing to do the research.

Exploring our own "shadow self" can often lead to great enlightenment. I'm not talking about Darth Vader, witchcraft or other topics typically considered part of the "dark side." Rather, it could be rewarding to take a mind-expanding journey within the recesses of your own psyche. An excellent book that can guide you through this is *The Dark Side of The Light Chasers: Reclaiming Your Power, Creativity, Brilliance and Dreams* by Debbie Ford and Neale Donald Walsch.

I'm going to return to talking about mediumship, specifically, for a bit. I always encourage people to know that we here on Earth can all talk *to* those in Spirit without going through a medium. Your loved ones get your messages, they understand your thoughts when you direct them with earnest sincerity, with the power of your emotions behind them. They're connected to *you*, after all, not any medium. It simply takes dedicated practice to learn how to interpret what they're sending back, and that's where a medium's services can come in handy. Again, be patient as you are working toward developing the ability to hear/see/feel/understand what they are sending back. Over the years I've done this work, inevitably people say, "Please tell him/her...." And I smile and say, "You just did. They can hear you just fine!"

It's been my experience that someone's core personality will pretty much stay intact once they're in Spirit. In other words, folks who were quiet and shy here are not going to be "Chatty Cathy" once they're there. These retiring types may be more inclined to send a medium (or you!) pictures, rather than words. The more gregarious ones still tell jokes, are more pushy, outspoken. Many still cuss. I've heard it all, believe me! I do my best to use the exact verbiage (when it's offensive, I usually give a warning beforehand) that they're giving me to pass along. This is often one of the most convincing factors to their loved ones here, that it really *is* them doing the talking!

Those in Spirit often can influence those here to help us in ways we might never have imagined. They truly don't mind being asked for help as long as we thank them in advance, as I mentioned previously. I've had loved ones in Spirit influence people here on the Earth plane to say certain things to me, do favors for me, including get me gifts that I will recognize as being from *them* in Spirit, something that I know they would give me if they were physically able to. Some friends have even said, "I totally had something else in mind to give you, so I'm not sure why I got you this particular birthday present/card, etc. I just felt like I needed to." *I* know who influenced them to be the physical "courier" most of the time, and it's a delightful surprise when those types of things occur.

I believe it's impossible to disturb those in Spirit by talking to them, if your intention is based on love and a desire to achieve healing, growth, or comfort. If, for whatever reason, they don't want to communicate or are busy doing something else at the time, it seems they have something over there similar to "call screening" or "voicemail." It may sound silly, but I believe it's true! And remember, not everyone there chooses to communicate through a medium. They look at someone like myself as a total stranger whom they may not be comfortable connecting through. Because of this, they may prefer to "go direct" and come into your dreams or send you messages and signs without using a "middle man."

Some clients have said after a reading, "Gosh, I was really hoping my Dad would have come through really strongly today" and when we talk a bit more, I've learned (over time) to ask, "Do you dream about them often, or feel them around you?" "Oh, sure, we talk all the time," is often the response. So when that's already going on, those in Spirit look at coming through a medium as a waste of effort/energy. It's kind of like a rerun, isn't it? It takes a lot of energy for them to come through. So try not to be too attached to getting Grandma to give your pet name she used when you were four years old, or to tell you where her long lost brooch may be. First of all, she knows *you* know that nickname, so why should she waste her energy repeating that for you, when she might have other valuable insight to offer from her new perspective in the Light, which has more to do with your current or future experience? And she may not even know where that brooch ever got to. They do lose attachment to material objects once they're in the Light. Now, I'm not saying great validations like that aren't convincing, so that you know beyond a shadow of a doubt it's really them talking. In fact, I love it when those kinds of things do come through. It's kind of a "bonus," but I'll let you in on a secret. It happens most often when people come to a reading with an open heart and mind and are not fixated on hearing just one certain thing. You just might deny yourself a wonderfully helpful message if that's *all* you are obsessed with hearing.

Finally, I just want to mention a couple of other things about human nature and offer some suggestions of things which may inspire and enlighten you. As I've mentioned, I believe more and more movies and television shows are being channeled these days, in a manner of speaking. The retelling of inspiring real life stories is also making a comeback, thank goodness! I really got so much out of the wonderful film *My Left Foot*. If you've seen it, you'll know why. Christy Brown's true courageous story, how he was born with cerebral palsy and his only controllable limb was his left foot, is indeed remarkable. He became an artist, using that left foot. The fortitude of his family and his creativity are very stirring. Parallels exist between his story and John's, in a number of ways. Rent it, if you've got the opportunity. Daniel Day Lewis gave the performance of his life in the role of Christy. You'll understand why it touches me so deeply, once you've seen the film. In fact, this book you're reading now has actually been referred to as a mixture of that story with a bit of *The Sixth Sense* thrown in!

Chapter Fifteen

"If We Could Talk to the Animals..."

I believe Dr. Doolittle himself would be pleased with the present trend toward animal communication. *The Pet Psychic* show was pretty popular, and many books on the subject are available. There are gifted animal communicators who are able to assist in clarifying behavior problems and health situations your pet is experiencing, even after veterinarians, trainers and other professionals have tried everything else. I've done my share of animal communication, and find it very touching, enlightening and often just downright fun! I've been able to successfully find a number of folks' missing pets over the years, and that always is such a great feeling. I love working with animals; in many ways, it's easier and less stressful than dealing with people, but people are my main thrust. It's always best to contact someone who has a particular area of expertise in any field, so I'd like to recommend a friend of mine, Marla Steele, who is a wonderful animal communicator located in northern California. You can visit her website, http://marlasteele.com to learn more about her work and to sign up for her always interesting newsletter. She does a lot of work with horses, as well as other animals and pets.

Of one thing I am certain when it comes to animals...they have souls and are God's creatures, just as human beings are. Ones who have passed over often come through to me in readings I do, usually by showing me a picture of themselves, sometimes by giving great detail about something they shared with their human companion(s). I also have reassured many clients over the years that they are *not* crazy when they feel like a beloved dog or cat who has passed on has once again rubbed against their leg or jumped up on the bed as they used to. I believe they can come by and say "hello" if they want, in their own way. Earthbound pets are also good indicators of when you have human visitors from Spirit. It seems cats can actually see these spirits, and dogs often get excited and sense their presence. I also believe pets can find a way to reincarnate and come back to be with the same human(s) again, if it serves everyone's mutual good. Sometimes they may even choose to change species, as you'll read more about in this chapter. All in all, animals have so much to say, if we are only willing to tune in.

I once asked my Merlin, if pets could have a future incarnation as a human.

"Why just future?" he shot back.

"Well, come on, wouldn't it be going backward, evolution-wise, to be a human then come back as an animal? Kind of devolving?" I asked, forgetting my Apache teacher often had quite a different take on things than I.

He snorted. "You're a snob!'

I blushed. "What? Why do you say that?" I felt foolish without knowing why.

"Well, why wouldn't someone, a soul, who has had a rough lifetime or two decide to come back in a different form, in order to achieve different things? For instance, if you wanted a lifetime where you could be with others like yourself when you wanted, but also could be self-sufficient, finding food and water on your own, enjoying solitude, not having to pay any bills...why wouldn't you choose to come back as a panther? Or a wild mustang? Or any animal form where you could learn and enjoy those experiences you had not, as a human?"

I couldn't come up with any reason why that was inconceivable. Merlin always provided me good food for thought. I was reminded of another Merlin, King Arthur's magician. I was always fascinated by the stories of how he turned the young Arthur into a variety of animals in order to sharpen the future king's awareness and to open his mind to other ways of thinking. *That* Merlin is one of my guides now, in fact, he always has been, I've learned. He is the same soul who incarnated as St. Francis of Assisi, St. Germaine and Joseph, Jesus' earthly father. He's part of the Brotherhood of Light (there are more websites on them than I can begin to enumerate here. Again, do some research and find what truth resonates with you to learn more about them). I channel messages from these ascended beings which I send forth in a monthly email newsletter. If you'd like to subscribe to this free email newsletter, please send me a note at lifeofspirit@gmail.com and I'll add you to the list. I mention Merlin the magician here because I'm so grateful to have a connection with such a powerful soul. He has a great sense of humor and tremendous love and patience. I often call upon his St. Francis personality to help with healing of animals. I encourage you to do the same. He's always willing to assist!

I would like to share a couple of special stories with you about pets I have met and worked with. Remember how I talked about my childhood pets seeming to know that Johnny was a special needs child; how they were always respectful, loving and protective of him? I feel animals are incredibly intuitive to our situations, especially if we are loving and kind to them. Many of you who have animals have seen how they instinctively know when you're not feeling well or are sad. They tend to stick really close to you when you need a comforting presence; to be a clown when you most need a laugh, and always offer unconditional love and acceptance to you. We can learn a lot from animals, if we're open to it!

In my experience, most of the communication I've had from dogs has been in pictorial (clairvoyant) form, while that from cats is quite verbal in nature. Although, some dogs have sent clear thoughts along with the pictures, so it depends upon their style and your link with them, I believe.

Some animal communicators specialize in talking with horses or other creatures quite successfully, often saving the owners lots of time and money and in many cases, helping to save the animals' lives, modify behaviors and so forth. My own primary experience has been working with house pets. Next, you'll find a few examples of memorable pet readings I've done.

Several years ago in Phoenix, I was asked to participate in a Psychic Pet Fair by a promoter of that event. I had not done much of this work up to that point in time, but since I've always had such a love of animals, I felt it would work out well.

A senior couple came by my table with their three dogs. The woman asked if she could bring them over one at a time while her husband held the other two, and I agreed that was a good plan. Her husband rolled his eyes a bit, as if to say, "Oh, brother, what a crock! I can't believe I even agreed to come here with her!" Then he went and sat down several yards away with two of their dogs.

Each dog had a bit to communicate which their human "Mom" felt was helpful. But when she pulled out a picture of their cat, I began to get the "tingle chills" and felt something more explicit was going to come through.

"We didn't want to bring her here in person because she gets so nervous around strange dogs," she explained. "I wonder if you could tune into her picture and tell me anything about her, Cheryl? Her name is Maisie."

I held the picture and closed my eyes, seeking to tune into Maisie's vibration. It didn't take long before she was chatting away and showing me a little mini-movie, to boot!

"She's showing me a curious behavior she has toward your husband. He's lying down on the couch, and she's perching on his shoulder, on her haunches, then extending her front paws and head, which she gently rest upon his heart area, in the center of his chest. She tells me that she's trying to help heal his heart. Do you understand this?"

Her eyes widened. "Oh, my, yes! She does *exactly* that!" she said excitedly. "And what's really interesting is, he had bypass surgery just last year! You mean the cat knows about that and is trying to help him?"

"That's what I feel," I smiled. "And there's something more." I glanced over at her husband, who apparently hadn't heard any of this. He looked extremely bored. "Would you ask him to come over here, please? I'd like to share this next part with him."

She went over and coaxed him to join us. He reluctantly did so, looking at me like I was a nutcase. I didn't care. I felt he needed to hear this.

"Sir, your cat is talking up a storm with me here. She just showed me how she gently places her head and front paws upon your chest when you're lying down. She says she's a healer, trying to help heal your heart. Your wife confirmed you had heart surgery recently, so I find that very intriguing."

He perked up a bit and showed some interest. "Yes, that's something that cat does," he conceded.

"Well, I have something else to ask you here. That's why I called you over. Do you remember a little white dog that you adopted when you were a little boy, about eight years old? You brought this little scraggly stray home and begged your mother to keep him. Do you recall that?"

He paused before answering. "No, I...oh, wait! Yes! That's right." He looked at me with more curiosity now. "What about that dog?"

"Well, the cat is telling me you only had the dog for a couple of weeks. That you were heartbroken to come home from school one day and find that your mother had given the dog away without telling you she was going to do that. Is that correct?"

He looked wistfully sad. "Yes, she sure did. I was pretty upset, I remember. But why is our cat telling you about that? I haven't thought of that for so many years!"

"Well, as hard as this may be for you to believe, your cat now was that little dog, then. She reincarnated and came back to find you, because you showed her such love and care when she was the dog." I waited a moment, knowing this might be hard for him to swallow. "I believe animals can find ways to be with us again, if their desire is strong enough. And not always as the same species."

He nodded, mulling this over.

I continued, "Thanks for coming over here and helping me know I was getting the story straight. All you need to know is that your cat loves you a lot. You may, of course, believe any of the rest of it if you choose." I smiled at them. "Thanks a lot, folks. Have a great weekend."

They walked away, the wife beaming happily while her husband's look showed me he was at least giving all this "nonsense" some serious consideration!

Another lady brought her black Labrador over for me to read. He was very friendly. I petted him, asked his name, then closed my eyes to see what he might have to say. Now, I know for years many experts have said animals do not see color. I would tend to disagree, from my experience with this beautiful dog, and that with several other pets who have sent me pictures of things in their homes, with full color pictures their owners verify are correct.

Peabody was this fellow's name, and he showed me his spacious kennel with a purple and blue plaid pet bed. He said, "I really like this new bed. It's much more comfortable than the other one." I described all this to his "Mom," who verified she had recently purchased such a bed. He went on to tell me how happy he was to have so many other dogs around him. She confirmed she was a breeder and that there were always several dogs there. Then he said, "I miss my mother," and sent me a picture image of her. I could tell this dog had passed over. I believe animals know when a human or one of their own leaves the planet. Peabody certainly did. "She's honey," he kept saying. I thought he was describing her color, as she was a blonde Lab. I told his human Mom what he said. Her eyes filled with tears.

"Honey was her color, that's right. And she has passed away. But Cheryl, her name was Honey. That's what he's trying to tell you!"

"Oh, good boy! Good job!" I hugged Peabody and he wriggled happily. "You are a great communicator!" He grinned up at me. He gave several other details about his home life, in such accurate detail that she hired me to come to her home in a couple of weeks and do readings for several other dogs.

Another doggie story which I got a kick out of involves a sweet dog named Bear. His owner brought him to me and asked if there was anything he wanted her to know. He sent me pictures of her cooking his special dog food, complete with vegetables and high quality meat.

"I thought all dogs got to eat such good food," came his thought. "Until we went to visit a friend's dog. When I met him, the first thing we asked each other was, 'What do *you* eat?'" (I laughed because this seemed so like the way a dog's mind would run!) "He said, 'Come 'ere, I'll show ya!' so I followed him to his bowl in the kitchen. It was full of all this dry, yucky looking stuff. I looked at him and said, 'You're kidding!' I couldn't believe his humans didn't cook for him the way my Mom does for me. Please tell her thank you for being so kind to me. I didn't know I had it so good!" He licked her hand right at that moment, as if to emphasize his gratitude.

I repeated all this to her as we went along, and she just stared, first at me, and then at Bear. Finally, she spoke.

"That is so amazing! We just went to a friend's house to feed his dog while he was out of town. Bear and this dog had never met. Sure enough, the first thing they did after sniffing around each other to say hello was run off to the kitchen, and Bear did look at his food bowl, smelled it, then backed away, like it was something awful!"

We both laughed. "Well, he certainly loves the gourmet stuff you make him! You're a great Mom!"

Here's one more quick kitty story that tickles me, still. A friend of mine has several cats, and had just adopted a new little kitty. Like many kittens, he was playful, but there are several unique things about Jelico. For example, he sits with his front paws splayed wide apart, just like a dog. He also pants a lot, just as a habit. Like a dog. And he fetches like no cat I have ever met before. Most cats who learn the fetch trick will do it five, maybe ten times, if you're lucky. Then they get bored and move on to something else. Hey, they're cats! Nonchalance is part of their job description! Not Jelico, though. One night while visiting, I threw his little spongy textured ball fifty times. No joke, *fifty* times! He brought it back without fail and dropped it in my lap. Every time, just like a dog. So of course, I'm convinced he was a dog in his previous incarnation. He's a delightful cat, too. It's really neat that he is so unusual.

These are just some of the heartwarming incidents I've shared with amazing pets. We've all heard about pets who have saved their owners from a fire, or from drowning or other dangerous situations. Animals seem to have a built-in clock, and often know exactly what time their master is due home, crossing to wait at the appropriate door just a few minutes before their arrival. They appreciate a kind word and a pet so much. They really love to connect with us and ask so little in return for the countless hours of love and fun they bring us. When some owners have asked me what their pet likes to do, I have been shown a variety of things. Some put on little hats, to indicate to me what they see as their job around the house. Some have worn police hats (their job is to guard), others a nurse's cap (healers), some a clown hat (entertainers). Some have shown me their favorite place to sit and watch TV with their owner (This was always verified. Along with my belief that they can discern at least shades of color, I also believe the ones who choose to focus on the TV screen see two dimensional images).

Animals are a true blessing upon the planet. They never exhibit naughty behavior just for the sake of tormenting us. There's usually an emotional cause behind it. A good animal communicator can help you discover what is out of alignment and offer suggestions as to how to correct it. Mainly, what I've learned from animals is they are full of such unconditional love, acceptance and trust, it is amazing. I believe many of these lovely creatures are evolved life forms. We should learn as much as we can from their simple, honest example.

Chapter Sixteen

Mystery Guest, Sign in, Please

(A.K.A. Hobnobbing with Heavenly Celebrities)

A long-time fan of game shows, as a kid I loved *What's My Line*, especially when they had a "mystery celebrity guest" who tried to fool the panelists. As I got older, the shows like *Hollywood Squares*, *Password*, *The Match Game* and *The $100,000 Pyramid* were always a lot of fun to watch. I liked the witty banter people like Paul Lynde and Charles Nelson Reilly always provided at the drop of a hat. From that very young age, I always felt like I could be a successful contestant on a good game show, and after moving to L.A., I actually appeared on three of them! I won *something* all three, by the way; most noticeably $10,000 on the *The $100,000 Pyramid,* thanks to the help of David Graf, a talented actor probably best known for his role as Officer Tackleberry in the *Police Academy* movies. He's a genuinely nice guy, and not only helped me win $10,000 the day I was on the show, but when he was paired with my opponent, he helped her do the same thing! So I'm grateful to David, and hope he might someday read this and smile.

Show business has always intrigued me; that's why I took a shot at it before I realized the main reason I was in L.A. was to meet my mentor Brian and to open up my spiritual path. So this chapter has to do with some contact I have had from celebrities who have passed away.

Now, I know what you're probably thinking. "Oh, brother, here comes the *real* wacky stuff!" Well, maybe you're not, but the first time a well-known person made contact with me, those were basically *my* thoughts. In the summer of 1987, I was driving over to Brian's home for a cable TV show taping. They were going to interview him, and wanted some people present who were willing to attest to the validity of Brian's gifts. He had helped me so much, I was more than happy to accommodate.

Brian lived in Hollywood at that time, near the old Paramount Studios lot. I lived in Burbank, so if you know the Valley and L.A. at all, you'll recognize the route I took. I was driving through the Los Feliz area, past Griffith Park, then the road bends to the left after awhile and you're suddenly in Hollywood.

At this time I was doing lots of "open mic" nights, singing and doing some comedy shtick, including a number of celebrity impressions. I had "done voices" since I was a kid. I always had an ear for unusual or well-known voices. I toyed with the idea of becoming the female equivalent of Rich Little for awhile. On this day as I drove to Brian's, I was having a mini-rehearsal, preparing for an open mic night just a couple of days away. I started singing *Diamonds Are a Girl's Best Friend* and was very surprised to notice that I sounded more like Marilyn Monroe than ever before. It was as if I was standing outside myself for a few moments, listening like an audience member. I got a warm feeling on the right side of my face as the song ended. It felt almost as though someone had tenderly caressed my cheek. Then I heard, "Hello, Cheryl. This is Norma Jean." I nearly sideswiped the car next to me, I was so startled. A stoplight was just ahead, so I took a deep breath in an attempt to collect my thoughts, wondering if I had truly taken leave of my senses this time.

As I tried to formulate something to say in response, I glanced across the street into a store window. I was in the heart of Hollywood now, so normally this would not have seemed unusual, but staring down at me from that window was a large poster of Marilyn, wearing that notorious white dress blowing up, the famous still from *The Seven Year Itch*. I was a bit nonplussed, to say the least. I still felt the presence in the car with me, so I said something incredibly intelligent like, "Um.... hello. May I help you?"

She laughed sweetly. "I just want to say hello, and thank you for paying tribute to me. Imitation is the most sincere form of flattery, right?"

The light changed, and I slowly continued on my way to Brian's home. "Well, so they say. Did you just help me sound more authentic? Was I sort of, well, channeling you?"

"You could say that. Listen, I just wanted to wish you luck on the show today, and on your gig that's coming up. Have fun. We'll talk more later, okay? God bless, Cheryl."

And she was gone. "Yeah, thanks, God bless you, too." I could tell she was already gone, but her presence lingered like a delicate perfume. My left-brain logic was screaming at me, "*Hey*! Just because you have been in that psychic development circle, don't go giving yourself airs that someone as famous as Monroe would talk to you!" I drove on, musing about what had just happened until I pulled up in front of Brian's house.

After the taping, I hung around for a few minutes. I wanted my mentor's feedback on what had happened on the way over.

"Am I crazy, Brian? Why would someone like Marilyn contact me? Do most mediums go through phases where they question what information is coming through, or is it just me? Am I losing it?"

He chuckled. "Well, Cheryl, I don't find it strange at all that she would talk to you. Marilyn Monroe was interested in spiritual matters. It was another facet of her personality that helped make her so complex. The fact that you're developing your mediumship and are an entertainer as well, I think she must find that absolutely fascinating. Coupled with the tribute your impression of her pays her memory." He patted my arm in reassurance. "Imitation is the sincerest form of flattery, after all. No, my dear, I don't believe you're 'losing it' at all!"

I felt relieved. Brian always gave me his gut impression of things, and I trusted him implicitly. Unfortunately, it turned out the producer of the show we had taped had less than pure motives, and was actually on a "debunking" mission. Seems he simply couldn't find anything about Brian to "debunk!" Brian is an extremely talented medium, a gifted painter and writer. In 1999, TV's *Hard Copy* did an excellent feature on him entitled, *The Miracle Medium*, which paid a wonderful tribute to his abilities.

More recently, John Edward broke major ground for mediums with *Crossing Over*. James Van Praagh had *Beyond* for awhile; now he is co-producing the show *Ghost Whisperer. Medium*, starring Patricia Arquette, won an Emmy its very first year. Just a few short years ago, in 1990, this genre of a show would not have been given a shot. What a difference ten to fifteen years makes! I'm so thankful to James and John for pioneering the topic of mediumship via television's mass impact. Awareness has been raised so much, and many skeptics (like I started out, years ago!) have changed their thinking about mediumship. The fact that so many mediums' books have become bestsellers shows just how hungry the public is for information on this subject. A quest for confirmation that there is life after death; something beyond our earthly experience.

Shows like *Crossing Over* had the way paved for them by some earlier shows. One of the early ones to hit mainstream consciousness about such "otherworldly" topics was *Highway To Heaven,* and more recently, *Touched By An Angel*. These two shows are easier for the mass consciousness to accept because nearly everyone believes in angels, or finds them at the very least innocuous, no matter what their religion or lack thereof. (Speaking of *Highway to Heaven*, Michael Landon will be mentioned again a little further into this chapter) There are several other shows in recent years which feature(d) recurring characters who have passed on; the mother (Concetta Tomei) in *Providence,* HBO's now dearly departed smash hit *Six Feet Under* had the father and others in Spirit who periodically connect or appear with the family members, and a recent Showtime entry with a dark humor twist on the afterlife, *Dead Like Me*, unfortunately was short-lived.

Another favorite show of mine which broached the subject of time travel and using it to affect positive changes in people's lives was *Quantum Leap*. Thanks to these pioneering shows, others have followed, such as *Early Edition.* I suppose at the heart of it all, we have Rod Serling to thank. Many of the original *Twilight Zone* episodes don't seem nearly so improbable today, do they? Interesting how perspectives shift and change with time.

Of course, I have to again touch upon the blockbuster movie, *The Sixth Sense.* Basically I really liked it, but found it to be heavy-handed on the sensationalism side, in particular the scenes of people who had passed on still being shown in their death condition, or in pain. From my experience in doing this work, that simply isn't the case. After all, why would any soul want to remain in a state of torment or pain? Especially children, who were the primary focus of those who had passed over in this film? Having lived in Hollywood and been involved in aspects of show business for many years, however, I completely understand the box office appeal of straying a bit into *The Exorcist* mode. The young protagonist of *The Sixth Sense* was most assuredly a medium, although they were careful never to mention that term in the movie.

I understand full well the controversy that still clings to that label in many circles. When I first began doing readings, I had business cards printed up which basically said, *Cheryl Booth, Psychic Spiritual Readings,* and gave my phone number.

I originally was very hesitant to use the word "medium" as an identifier. About three years into doing the work, my guides were having a laugh at my expense (typical for them, really. We take ourselves far too seriously here on the Earth plane, according to them, and I must agree. Seems it has a bit to do with the density/gravity of the planet). Anyhow, one day they said, "Cheryl, what does the word 'medium' mean? Have you actually looked it up in the dictionary?" I opened up my *Webster's*, knowing they would not relent until I had done so. I read aloud, "a person thought to have the power to communicate with the spirits of the dead." I paused, a bit sheepish that I had never bothered to officially research the term prior to this.

"Uh-huh. And what is it that you do, Cheryl?"

"I hear and speak with those who have died."

"*Exactly*! Then please begin calling yourself a medium, won't you? It's one of your specialties. It will draw people to you for the right reasons. Don't be afraid of who and what you are, ever!"

"All right. Thank you, friends." And I proceeded to go to the local print shop and order some new cards, now identifying me as "Cheryl Booth, Psychic Medium." I continue to use the word psychic on my cards and literature today, because it still helps qualify what I do. After all, in addition to "talking with the dead," I also get in touch with angels and guides to help folks get clarity on relationships, career, finances, health and more. By the way, all mediums are psychic (I actually believe all *people* are psychic. That's why I love teaching psychic development workshops). Conversely, not all psychics are mediums. They may be wonderfully gifted with a variety of psychic talents, but talking to the dead might not be one of those. Some psychics are channels, which I also do. My channeling is usually in the written form, while others do wonderful work as trance channels, who actually let the spirit(s) "pop into" their body. Similar to what you saw happening to Whoopi Goldberg in *Ghost*. Speaking of that movie, I just want to stress once again that I truly believe the writing of it was strongly influenced by Spirit. Many of those in that realm have told me that *Ghost* hits pretty close to the mark in a number of ways.

Other intuitives work effectively with tools such as astrology, cards, runes, crystals and pendulums to gain access to psychic insight. These are simply that, *tools*. There's no power in these tools by themselves, just as there's no "power" in the carpenter's saw, hammer and lathe. It's what your intention is, what your end goal is, that counts. And when using *my* tools, I have always considered myself a mere conduit for a Higher Power to flow through. I deem it a privilege to be a circuit, a "telephone" between dimensions, through which messages flow, to bring those on the Earth plane comfort and support.

Now, back to Marilyn, or Norma Jean, as she's preferred to call herself when talking with me. That first communication with her took place that summer of 1987; then the reading with James Van Praagh (referred to earlier) followed that fall. For the most part, the information she shared with me was filled with loving encouragement, yet I felt quite honored she chose to talk with me at all. I had never been a huge fan of hers, yet always felt empathy toward her; saddened by where the path and seduction of fame and show business eventually led her.

In 1988, I was working for a networking organization of businesswomen. We operated out of the owner's home, located in a well-kept older neighborhood of Sherman Oaks, CA. I was out driving, running errands on my lunch hour one day, and Elton John's *Candle In The Wind* played on the radio. The song had just received a resurgence of popularity, so it wasn't unusual to hear it. What was unusual was the gentle brush of energy against my right cheek, and the awareness that *she* was there in my car with me, once again.

"Hello, Cheryl, it's Norma Jean. How are you today?"

"I'm great! Good to hear from you again! Do you enjoy this song that's playing?" (I knew that the energy of the song had probably played a part in her desire to communicate with me again.)

"It's a beautiful tribute to me, yes, I like it very much. He's a wonderful songwriter. Listen, I'd like to talk with you on a more personal level, if you're willing. Would you light a candle tonight at 8:00? I'll come back and talk with you then, when you're not driving, and able to concentrate more completely on our conversation, all right?"

I wasn't about to refuse this invitation! "Oh, sure, terrific! 8:00. I'll be sure to light a candle...." Her energy had gone just as quickly as it arrived. I pulled into my parking space and went back to work, bemused by these events, but easily pulled back into the worldly activities of business.

My boss had asked me to housesit for her that evening, as she and her daughter were going on a little overnight journey. Their two dogs did better when someone stayed in the house with them. I did quite a lot of pet-sitting and house-sitting in those days, so I was happy to comply. I didn't even think about my "date" with Marilyn again until I glanced at the clock around 7:45 that night.

My eyes widened as I remembered what I had agreed to do. "Oh, my God! I don't even know if there's a candle in this house!" I rushed around, rummaging through a couple of kitchen drawers until I found the perfect white candle and a book of matches. I set the candle on a plate, and took it to the living room. I grabbed a pad and pen in order to make notes. It was now 7:55.

At 8 p.m., I lit the candle, and Marilyn's face appeared in the flame! I was startled, and the first thing I said to her was, "Wow! You're so prompt. It's 8 on the button!"

She let out a full-throated laugh. "Yes, well, I've learned how to be on time on *this* side. Isn't that just the living end?" Living end, indeed.

The end to a physical existence which had been quite painful; so much so that she often arrived for events quite late, probably having struggled many times over whether to even show up at all. Living, in that she was here giving me proof positive once again that the soul does *not* die when the physical body does.

She proceeded to give me lots of encouragement with regard to my spiritual growth, as well as for my continued interest and involvement in the entertainment field. I took notes quite fast and furiously, much in the way that I did when practicing automatic writing, not really looking at the page. I was transfixed on watching her facial expressions in the candle flame, which was serving as my own mini-movie screen. Amazing! She told me quite a lot about her own personal drama and trauma, and warned me that show business is certainly full of pitfalls and temptations, but that we have to be aware of them and make wise choices. She clearly recognized her own free will as the vehicle which took her the direction she headed. I won't go into great detail about the mystery surrounding her death; let it suffice to say that she confirmed what many have speculated, but that she knew her own addictions and behavior allowed the cover-up which occurred to seem credible.

"There are no mistakes, Cheryl. I learned a lot of lessons. I must say I'm learning much more here, though. Bless you for the work you're doing. You have quite an interesting path ahead, you know! Keep your eyes open, and stay connected to your Source, and you'll be just fine. I have to go. It's been wonderful spending time with you. God bless you, dear Cheryl."

I thanked her, and sat watching the flame die down after her departure. I glanced at the clock. Just thirty minutes had gone by, but it had seemed more like a couple of hours. I tried to watch some TV, but couldn't focus on it after what I'd just experienced. So I meditated a bit, attended to the dogs, then prayed and went to bed.

Around noon the next day, my boss and her daughter returned. I grabbed what few things I had packed, asked them about their little trip, and told them everything had gone just fine. Then I headed out the door.

"See you Monday, Nancy!" I was pulling the door closed behind me when I heard her call after me, "Hey, Cheryl?"

I pushed the door open again, and stepped back inside for a moment. "Yes?"

"You're a big fan of old movies, right?"

I was surprised by that question, seemingly coming out of nowhere. "Well, yeah, I've always had a soft spot for certain classic films. Why do you ask?"

"Well, I don't really know why. Just occurred to me I haven't told you this before.... Did you ever like Marilyn Monroe?"

I froze. "Oh, ah, yes, sure! Who didn't like Marilyn?" The familiar goosebumps were all over my arms at this point.

"Well, I can't believe I never told you. She's actually been in this house. Isn't that funny?" I moved back toward the kitchen to look her in the face.

"When? When was she here, Nancy?"

She looked up, startled by the intensity of my question. "Oh, back in the late '50s, from what I understand. One of her boyfriends used to own this house, his name was Bob something or other, I think. Just something the realtor told us when we bought it, and I thought you'd find it interesting, that's all."

"Yeah, very interesting indeed. Thanks for sharing that. I'll see you Monday." I practically flew to my car, started the engine, and burst into laughter. "Well, no wonder you wanted to talk to me last night, Norma Jean! You knew I was going to be staying in a house where you'd actually spent time when you were alive. That must have made the contact that much easier, or at least familiar! Thanks!"

I felt her presence, just lightly laughing with me, glad that I had put two and two together. Many of those in Spirit have such a delightful sense of humor, and Norma Jean most definitely is no exception! I'm thankful to her for our connection, and have included a tribute to her in my one-woman musical show *Medium, Rare*. I get the feeling she enjoys that. Speaking of which, I plan to take this show on the road quite a bit in the next few years. If you'd like more information on it, please let me know!

Another celebrity in Spirit helped inspire the two original songs I wrote for that show. Dudley Moore, in addition to being a great comedic actor, was also an accomplished musician and composer. He approached me one day when I was in the midst of writing *Medium, Rare* and said he would like to help. I loved him in *Arthur* and many of his other film roles. I really appreciate his assistance. One of the songs we "collaborated" on took me less than ten minutes to composer, lyrics, music and accompaniment. Now *that's* efficiency, Dudley! Thanks so much!

Michael

Besides loving Laura Ingalls Wilder's books as a child, I also was a big fan of Little Joe Cartwright on *Bonanza*. Well, who wasn't? Michael

Landon was cute and funny, cocky yet vulnerable in that role. Men, women and kids found him extremely likeable and believable. When he launched *Little House on the Prairie*, I gained a whole new respect for his talents. The quality of television he brought into our homes was so pure, so inspiring. He was not only an excellent actor, he was also a wonderful director and writer. Then when *Highway to Heaven* came along years later, I realized he was a very spiritual man as well. He went way up in my estimation as I recognized what a remarkable human being he was.

I'd like to share with you an entry from my journal, dated May 11, 1999, when I lived in Phoenix.

"This is starting out as such an INCREDIBLE, BLESSED DAY! I was eating breakfast when a voice distinctly told me to turn on the TV to channel 7. It was about 7:40, so I didn't know what might be seen, nor even what the programming on that station was. It was a *Little House on the Prairie* where Charles takes his son James, who is severely ill, out into the wild. There, God tells him to build an altar of mortar and stone. So he does, placing a cross at the top. This is an altar tower. Charles is almost feverish in his labors, and an old man comes and gives his son some soup from a bowl, which is the first food the boy has eaten in several days. Prior to that, he'd only sipped liquid from a glass straw the doctor had given them. A family friend, Isaiah, came to bring them home, and Charles told him he knew the old man had been sent by God, and refused to go home with his friend. Isaiah went home to tell Charles' wife, and they decide to go back that night. However, a storm is brewing and as he sits in the wagon waiting for her, the old man appears and tells him they need to wait until morning, because that night is special.

The old man goes back to be with Charles and James. Lightening is crackling, the wind is blowing like mad. He tells Charles to go the altar. Charles asks, "Will He save my son?" The old man, who is an angel, says, "Only He knows. Will you lose your faith if he doesn't?" And Charles replies, "No." He then carries his limp-bodied son to the altar and stands at the base of it. It looks as though lightening strikes the cross and sends an aura down all over Charles and the boy. They are knocked to the ground. When Charles awakes, his son is touching his face, and asking, "Pa, are you all right?" Teary-eyed, he quietly exclaims, "James!" over and over, hugging the boy tightly.

I got chills all over during this last scene especially, and then Michael Landon came to me in Spirit and basically told me he wants to help me. That my work, especially my writing, will make people feel the same inner warmth that scene just evoked in me. He reminded me that faith without works, and works without faith are dead. It takes both. The example of how he slaved over that altar made me realize how crucial it is for me to buckle down and do my work. He then asked how he could best help me today, and I asked him to help me stay focused on the tasks at hand and not to lose sight of my dreams. He went on to say he wants to work with me writing screenplays and teleplays. He is as excited as I that we will work together. What a blessing! There are not many I can tell about this just yet, but I plan to include it in my book about Johnny someday. I felt okay about telling all this to my friend Ann, since she likened me to Michael Landon last year. I had talked about wanting to move out of the desert, but not feeling it was time yet. She said she felt like I was staying here helping her help others through our work, kind of like Michael's character did in *Highway to Heaven* and that if I left too soon, I might not discover what my true purpose for being here was. I feel so very alive and blessed to have been chosen by Michael to help continue with the type of work he loved so much!"

Since that time, I have heard from Michael a number of times. He is a dedicated worker and quite the perfectionist. He expects that same commitment from anyone with whom he chooses to work now, just as I have learned he did when he was on the physical plane.

Karen

When I was in junior high school, most of my friends were into hard rock music by groups including The Grateful Dead, Iron Butterfly and The Rolling Stones. I, on the other hand, had a very special place in my heart for a brother/sister duo whose soft, soothing tones charmed many people (most of them considerably older than me). I've written about them earlier in the book, but just want to spend a bit of time talking about The Carpenters. They took me by storm the first time I saw them on TV. Karen played the drums! I had ALWAYS begged for a drum set, but the piano and guitar seemed to be much more acceptable instruments for a girl, in my parents' opinion. Yet here was this talented, feminine girl playing the drums and singing her heart out. My parents couldn't deny that they liked this music as well.

After I purchased the snare drum and hi-hat I wrote about previously, I practiced until I had the basics down. Then I played along with Karen and Richard for hours on end. When Mom and Dad would go out to run various errands, I carried my "mini-set" upstairs and gave

Johnny a concert. He smiled and sang along in his own way. My biggest fan and supporter, as always!

This went on for the next few years, as the Carpenters released album after album, had their own TV summer replacement show, and their songs took over the airwaves. Many of my friends labeled me a "square" for loving their music so much, but I really didn't mind a bit. My absolute love of and devotion to their music during this time is what drew Karen to communicate with me many years late.

After she passed away, there were several times I would get chills when performing one of their hits at an open mic or an audition. I felt like she was thanking me for keeping their music alive. As I developed more as a medium, I have actually sat down and contacted her a number of times, just to get to know her. I had always wished we could have been friends. In a sense, I believe that we are, now. She's told me how she basically began to believe all the pensive, sad love songs about being unfulfilled. Her own love life mimicked many of the songs, especially *Goodbye To Love*. She is a kind, sweet spirit whose crystal clear voice brought pleasure to millions. I'm glad to count her among my friends/ guides in Spirit.

Other Contacts & Present Day Inspirations

I have felt connected to several celebrities as time has gone on, including Judy Garland, John Lennon, Danny Kaye and Elvis. In fact, I happen to believe we can connect with anybody's Higher Self, as long as they are willing to work in this way with someone here on the Earth plane. I have often encouraged clients to send thoughts or messages to people they have admired, asking for help (energetically or inspirationally) with projects they are working on. You might even choose to get a picture of that person and put it in a conspicuous place. For example, a musician would put a bust of Beethoven, or if your taste leans more toward classic rock, perhaps a photo of Jerry Garcia, near the place where you play or write music. If you're a writer, consider placing a picture of a "writing mentor" near your computer or writing station. I have one of Mark Twain, because I've always loved his work and besides, I feel like he tells me a great joke once in awhile!

In a recent group reading in someone's home, Emily Dickinson came through strongly. She told one of the women in attendance she wanted to act as a guide to her. The woman gasped, listened to the message, and then validated the connection by saying, "She has always been my favorite poet! In fact, I've started writing some poetry myself, and now I know why!"

Madame Curie has come through more than once to talk to various people who have had readings with me. She has a powerful, wise energy. What else would you expect?

I believe many celebrities have challenging circumstances to overcome in life because it's part of their mission. So do many non-celebrities, like my brother John. We're all One, remember? I just feel that those who are more strongly in the public eye have a tendency to call more of us to action. Christopher Reeve, for example. Look at all the changes in health legislation his pro-activism created. What an inspiration he was, and still is! He certainly can fly now, and truly was a super man.

Michael J. Fox and Montel Williams also come to mind as being in that category. There are many more. Thank goodness beautiful souls like these are here on the planet, and that they don't give up. They help those of us with lesser challenges keep going. They are wonderful examples of the resilience of humanity. Their dedication helps people understand more about various diseases/conditions and motivates the rest of us to get involved in helping. Just like Johnny. God bless all such souls, indeed!

Louise Hay

Since I've been talking about modern day, Earth-based celebrities, it seems like a good time to share this experience with you. I had a personal encounter with Louise Hay in the mid 1980s. For anyone unfamiliar with Louise, first of all, where have you been the past twenty-five years? (I'm just kidding, but she really has become an icon of healing and metaphysics!) Secondly, do yourself and favor and go pick up one of her books. *You Can Heal Your Life* is s a great one to start with. Also, her company, Hay House, publishes many other brilliant writers, many of whom cover metaphysical territory.

In the late '80s, I was fortunate enough to be invited to attend a party thrown at her lovely home in Pacific Palisades. She had recently moved in. The grounds were gorgeous, complete with terraced flower gardens. The home was large yet inviting, filled with her loving energy. I sat beside her on the couch for awhile. She acted as if she'd known me for years. She treats everyone that way and it's a marvelous feeling to be so completely accepted! At one point, she offered to give a tour of her home. She took my hand and led me along, with a few other people behind us.

The attention to detail in the home was awesome. She talked about how she had first envisioned each room, then witnessed it become reality. As we went down a long hall, I stopped and let her take the others into the room-size walk-in closet. Hanging on the wall, my attention had been riveted to a large construction paper star, hanging there by a push pin. In the center was a magazine cut-out of a Jaguar convertible, and across the body of the car she had written in bold letters, "Louise!" Shades of my experience with treasure maps! When she came back down the hall and took my hand once more, I said, "So, a Jaguar is what you're manifesting next?"

She winked at me. "You bet! It's pretty basic stuff, but I tell you what, it really works!"

I knew that it had worked for my college scholarship and a few other goals I had used it for. But here was evidence that it worked for someone who played on a larger manifestation scale than I had dared yet imagine. I'll always be grateful to Louise for her hospitality that night, and for allowing me to see that you're never too successful to use the power of a simple, genuine tool!

Chapter Seventeen

Hello, Again

Even today reincarnation remains a touchy subject for many people. In the movie *Contact,* in answer to his daughter's question about the prospect of intelligent life on other planets, the father replies, (paraphrasing) "If there's not, sure seems like a waste of space." In kind, to totally negate reincarnation seems to me to be a great waste, with regard to possible solutions and answers about soul growth, opportunities to do healing on various levels and other "mysterious" situations worthy of consideration. For example, why we feel immediately comfortable or uncomfortable around certain people as soon as we meet them; it's as though we've "recognized" them on some level. Or why we have talents, gifts or fears that do not seem to be based upon any present life experience. I plan to write a book which focuses on past life work someday. Meanwhile, this chapter shares some of my experience and thoughts relating to the subject.

Like most children, I continually questioned and sought solutions or explanations to things which puzzled me. For example, how could Mozart write symphonies when he was less that five years old? Where did that knowledge come from? Granted, his father Leopold was a musician and composer, but exhibited nothing near Wolfgang Amadeus' clear genius as a prodigy. The more I learned about reincarnation, the more I began to see certain plausible explanations.

J.S. Bach lived to be sixty-five years of age and died in 1750; he was a master musician and composer whose wives bore him twenty children, seventeen of whom lived beyond childhood. Mozart was born in 1756. I often wondered, "Is it so far-fetched to consider that Bach might have returned to experience a different life, a new form of celebrity, as the child prodigy Mozart?" In addition to their extraordinary musical prowess, they had another thing in common; both could be great jokesters who loved to make people laugh. Mozart had six children, only two of whom lived beyond infancy. An incredible genius with much sorrow in his adult life, Mozart died at the young age of thirty-five. While majoring in music in college, such biographical facts rang a poignant note within me. I became intrigued by the possibility that these two musical masters may have shared one soul. It just makes sense and feels true to me.

My friend Merlin often consulted the Akashic Records for a variety of reasons. He is a big fan of Elton John, and once asked permission to know who Elton might have been in a previous lifetime. The answer? Beethoven! Again, very possible. Why wouldn't a reclusive, tortured soul like Ludwig van Beethoven want to have a really FUN incarnation where his talent was fully recognized and appreciated, as well as to and be known for his outrageousness and differences, rather than trying to hide them? Food for thought, that's all I'm saying.

Remember the earlier story about my survival of flying through the barbed wire fence, virtually unscathed? You might recall I mentioned just prior to that, my college choir went on tour to Nicaragua and Costa Rica, because we'd been invited to sing with those countries' national symphonies. It was quite an honor, and quite intimidating in some ways. I had never flown on a plane before, not even a short hop, let alone to a foreign country. I was a bit apprehensive. I needn't have been, though, because from that first flight on I discovered that flying felt quite natural to me.

Our first layover in New Orleans occurred very late in the evening. The crisp February night inspired several of us to check out The Big Easy. So we bundled up, caught the bus downtown and were off on a stateside adventure prior to visiting foreign soil.

Strangely enough, I felt extremely comfortable roaming around the French Quarter at 1 a.m. Given my sheltered background, this surprised no one more than me! I went into a some sort of trance state as we walked here and there, telling my companions what we'd find around the next bend, and then staring in consternation at the confirmation of my "prediction" a few moments later. This happened more than once. I was never a strong history buff, yet "something" told me clearly that if we went up the next block and around the corner, there would be a statue of Andrew Jackson. I shared this with my friends who responded by teasing me.

"C'mon, Cheryl! Andrew Jackson? He wasn't from New Orleans, was he? Are you tripping out on us, or what?" They were confused yet intrigued by my strange behavior and couldn't help themselves from following me in my daze. I quickened my pace and pursued the route the voice inside my head directed, and we came face to face with a large statue of our seventh president, a commemoration of his defeat of the British in New Orleans in the War of 1812!

"Okay, enough already. You've been here before, right?" My friend Pam raised an eyebrow in suspicion.

No one was more shocked than I! "No....well, at least not in this lifetime!" I made a feeble joke, but my gut instinct told me something of consequence was going on. Just prior to that trip, I'd had my first "past life" dream and had given my roommate a start in the process.

Precognitive dreams were a regular part of my childhood, as I've already shared. But this particular dream was quite different from anything I'd experienced before. I remember a feeling of floating very high, almost like I was in a balcony, watching the action below. There was an open arena where two gladiators were battling. Suddenly I became aware that I was also seeing through the eyes of one of the combatants...a split perspective, or double vision, if you will!

I felt the soldier's heart beating fast, his breath very short. He had just been disarmed and his wounded horse lay dying, off to his side. He stood firm as his opponent charged at him, the point of his enemy's lance looming larger and sharper. I heard the horse's hooves bearing down, but knew that he/I would not move. It was a point of honor to face death courageously. This soldier was not about to become a coward and run. I was fascinated, horrified, and confused. This was more real than many aspects of my waking life! Everything was so vivid, so intense. And still that double perspective was intact. I steeled myself for the mortal blow headed straight for my chest, and as the tip of the lance pierced the breastplate I yelled loudly, waking myself and my roommate, who ran wild-eyed from her bedroom.

"What the hell was that? It sounded like someone broke in here and killed you or something!" She looked around nervously, then seeing no one else, glowered at me, struggling to catch her breath.

"Yeah, I think someone just did...." She didn't find that humorous in the least, and I couldn't begin to explain in any logical manner. "It was a really bad dream, Cindy, sorry. Try to get some sleep. I'm going to get up and read since I don't think I want to invite an instant replay. Good night."

As I learned more about dreams in years to come in my work as a hypnotherapist, I found the "double vision/split perspective" was a common modality of reliving a past life experience while simultaneously watching the overview from the Higher Self's viewpoint.

Returning to the New Orleans incident, during one of my early readings with Brian some helpful validation with regard to that lifetime came through. He was touching in on some things that were pertinent to my present day life when suddenly he asked, "Who is Felicity?"

That name had come through in a previous sitting, but we hadn't spent much time on it, because it simply didn't "link up" for me. "I don't know, Brian. Her name came through about a year ago, too." I felt puzzled; Felicity was trying her best to be heard, but I had no clue what to do with her connection.

This time, however, she was able and/or willing to give much more information. Brian continued, "Oh, this is so sad, Cheryl. She says she was your sister in a past life, and you were her older brother. You were killed quite tragically, in a war....you were only nineteen or so, and she grieved for you the rest of her life. She's available to be a guide to you now, she hasn't chosen to come back to the Earth in all this time..."

"Wow! Well, please tell her thank you...what war is she talking about, will she say?" I was glad we had more to go on; during my brief exposure to this communication at this time, I had learned to be grateful and happy to identify those in Spirit who care about us and are willing to work with us, no matter from which lifetime.

"It's the Civil War, Cheryl. She says you were non-violent, and didn't want to join the army, but you were compelled. Your family lived in the South...."

"In New Orleans," we said in unison as strong goosebumps ran down my arms. When these "confirmation chills" were this strong for me, I now knew it was Spirit's way of saying, "This is truc, this is right. Trust it."

Brian smiled at me. "Oh, you know about this lifetime, then?"

"Not much. I just had a strong deja vu experience in New Orleans a few years ago; knew where things were, what had happened in certain areas of the city, yet had never visited there before in this life."

He was back in "conversation" with my long-lost sister. "She says you vowed not to kill another human being. You couldn't stand violence, you were going to study to become a doctor when you had to join the army. It was compulsory, you see, expected of you." He paused. "Oh, this is the tragic part...she's showing me that you were frying some fish while making camp by a river's edge. A Union soldier came up behind you unexpectedly. You turned to him and said, 'Welcome, brother. I have no desire to hurt you, or anyone. Won't you join me for supper?' That apparently stopped him in his tracks for a few moments, then he screamed a battle cry and charged at you. Oh, God!" Brian gasped as he looked at me. "She says he ran you through with his bayonet. How awful!"

My heart beat faster, and the chills intensified. I knew Brian was a sensitive soul, so I tried to lighten things up. "Hmm. Well, that's not the first time I was shish-ka-bobbed!" I proceeded to share the gladiator dream with him.

"My, my," he sighed, then paused. I could tell a bit more detail was being given to him. "Ah! She says to tell you you'll not pass violently again. You've grown to a point where that is unnecessary. Nothing for your soul to learn from it. When you die this time, you'll be quite an old lady, well over ninety, is what she's saying. And you'll go quite peacefully in your sleep, yes." He smiled.

My mentor, Merlin had shared similar information with me just a few weeks before. Merlin is great at doing future projections, and when he did one to check in on what was ahead for me, he said, "You're going to live to a ripe old age. Into your nineties, anyway. All your family in Spirit will gather 'round you while you're sleeping, and simply lift up the corners of your sheets and gently carry you to Heaven, Cheryl. That's what they want me to tell you."

That had given me great comfort. Here was separate validation of the same thing. Brian and Merlin didn't know one another, so that made this all the more conceivable. Double or multiple confirmation(s) from independent sources translates to, "Best to pay attention to this!" Past lives, my potential future in this life, all were quite fascinating possibilities. If I'm likely to live that long, I realized I'd better take good care of my physical body as well as my spiritual development!

Those are simply a few of my personal experiences and exposures to the concept of reincarnation. The rest of this chapter deals more with a past life I shared with John, and a very interesting twist that I never would have expected. When I've worked as a hypnotherapist conducting past life regressions, many fascinating cases have come to light which help people understand present day relationships, fears, talents and more. I actually believe it's possible to contact the Higher Self of someone who has reincarnated on the Earth plane. It may be a bit more difficult to get a really clear connection with them, than when they were in Spirit, but from my own personal experience, I know it's possible.

Hypnosis is a remarkably valuable tool, in so many ways. I've been privileged to facilitate a number of cathartic releases of phobias, negative habits, healing karmic situations and relationships. The main thing I'd like to stress about the subconscious mind is that its basic function is that of a computer hard drive. It does not have discernment nor judgment to signal you when you are feeding it negative programs (repetitive thought patterns) Its response to whatever you send it will always be, "Yes, that's right. Yes, that's right." Again, let me emphasize that thoughts are things. Whatever you spend time and energy thinking about will most definitely show up on the physical level in some form. So do your best to resolve to become a careful "thought monitor." Focus on what you *do* want as your results/outcome, or you'll keep creating more of the same self-sabotaging, negative situations over and over again. It takes a dedicated person willing to spend a minimum of twenty-one days to retrain yourself to feed the subconscious mind only positive input. That's been scientifically proven. In order to shift a habit, an attitude, a behavior—twenty-one days, minimum. That's why so many self-help programs are geared to a thirty-day timeframe. The creators are hoping you'll stick with it at least three weeks, if not the entire four.

Past life regression and the entire field of hypnosis are so fascinating, I've decided to write a separate book focusing on the benefits I've observed people receiving from their use. There are so many success stories from clients whose hypnosis sessions I've conducted, I plan to launch a new website in the near future dedicated to this topic in its various forms. [My current website (www.cherylbooth.com) has some information about the personalized CDs I create for hypnosis clients. As far as the completion and release of any upcoming books, the launch of my hypnosis website, and so forth, the current site is the best way to stay up to date with such things, as well as to see dates of upcoming book signings, performances of *Medium, Rare*, my travel and seminar schedule, etc.]

Past life regression work has afforded me much insight and clarity about my present life. It has also helped me assist clients in their own self-discovery. I'd like to share just a brief excerpt about reincarnation from the transcript of my first session with Brian in 1985.

BRIAN:"I had a lady here awhile ago...her son came through, and she wanted to connect with her brother who was killed in the second World War, shot down over Germany, and her son said, 'Mom, he's been reincarnated. He's living in the body of a young German man, and you'll go to Germany and meet him, but he won't look anything like your brother used to.' She went to Germany, and she telephoned me a couple of months back and she said, 'I met the man and I know it's my brother. I just feel it, I know it!' she said. 'There was an immediate rapport between us.' And that was predicted before she went there. It was very interesting..."

Little did I know how strongly the theme of that story would affect me ten years after my reading. I'd wondered many times if Johnny and I had shared previous incarnations. During my first hypnotherapy session in 1987, I had strong direct validation of that.

Merlin had a very interesting way of looking at how we choose our families and what our soul contracts' terms might include for each incarnation. This also includes what I have come to look at as a loving way to deal with death and dying. Allow me to explain.

Merlin and I were discussing free will choice, soul groups and reincarnation one day. As a matter of course, the topic of death and dying worked its way in as well. I'm paraphrasing a bit, but basically, here is what my mentor had to say.

"I like to look at all this in the same way you might go about chartering a bus to go on a really fun family excursion, let's say to Disneyland. I'm going to use Disneyland as a metaphor for Earth, okay? All right, for this adventure, you would undoubtedly invite friends and relatives along you know you would have fun with, as well as some who would be the responsible ones and keep an eye out for everyone else, right? Everybody has a role to play in everybody else's experience, as well as getting their own benefit from this trip. So everybody gets on the bus and heads to the theme park. Once you arrive, everyone kind of takes off in the direction in which they're most interested. Sometimes you'll find yourself in line waiting with certain people to go on a certain ride or attraction together. Other times, you might just wave at them across the park, staying in touch but not always having to be attached at the hip. With me so far?"

"Yeah, it all makes sense," I replied.

"So at some point, some of the folks you haven't seen for awhile come and track you down, maybe holler across at you as you're waiting in a long line. They might say, 'Hey, Cheryl! I had a lot of fun. Hope you did, too. I'm pretty tired now, though, so I'm getting on the bus and going back home. See you later!' And you're okay with that. You might feel a bit sad that you won't see them for awhile, but somehow you know you will hook up again down the road. And you also know the bus will be waiting for you, to take you home when it's your turn."

"Wow, Merlin, that's really a beautiful way to look at this. Thanks for sharing it with me," I said.

Continuing to work on raising my spiritual awareness during the mid-eighties included a renewed interest in hypnosis, especially past life regression. I decided it was time to personally investigate this.

So I booked a past life regression session with a highly recommended

L.A. hypnotherapist. I was quite surprised when Terri told me I would be able to hear and remember everything that was said, as well as any images or experiences, so long as they served my Highest Good. She would simply get me into a very relaxed physical state in order to access my subconscious mind and we'd go from there. I agreed that sounded fair, and stretched out upon the couch in her office.

Once she talked me into a deep relaxation, I was surprised how easily pictures began to form, almost as though a movie were playing in my mind. And the now familiar "split perspective" was in full force. With minimal prompting from her, I began to describe what follows:

"I'm a dancer...quite a good one, too, if I do say so myself." (When I listened to the tape of this later, I noticed I lapsed into an Irish brogue easily at this point. I was also amused, because dancing in *this* lifetime was not among my natural talents. In fact, I often referred to "my two left feet.") "My husband and I are a team, we're hoofers, y'see? Molly and Charlie, that's us! We're quite a song and dance team. We're Irish, but we work the London vaudeville circuit. That's where the money is, the crowds."

Terri interjected, "What year is it, now?"

My voice took on an incredulous tone. "Ye don't know? It's 1896, dearie. We just finished a tour of a number of theatres....well, um, stages. All right, so lately we've been performing on street corners, but we're still a good team! *Sweet Rosie O'Grady, Love's Old Sweet Song,* we love doing those, especially. We played The Old Vic awhile back. We'll get back on top of things, soon." Molly/I coughed. "I've been sick quite a bit lately, so we don't make the rounds so often. Charlie's nursing me back to health, though. I'll be right as rain, never you fear."

The tape went on to tell how Charlie got sick and passed away before Molly, then a strange opportunity presented itself. I saw and described my own death in 1904, after a long, lonely battle with lung disease. "T'was the consumption that took me, dearie. All alone in my little room I was, no one brave enough to come check on me or visit the last few weeks."

"Why would they have to be brave?" Terri asked.

"Tch!" the clucking sound rang out on the tape. "Are ye daft? It's catchable....what did that doctor fella call it? The last one who came to see me—contagious, he said it was. Even *he* wore a face mask. Can't blame folks for not comin' round...When the angels and me mum and dad came to get me, t'was so peaceful, such a beautiful light filled the room as we floated up, up toward Heaven..."

Terri honored the memory of that moment, then gently asked,

"Molly, see what answer comes to you for this last question, please. Think of Charlie...does Cheryl know Charlie in this lifetime? Did he reincarnate with her this time around?"

There was just the slightest pause. "Sure she does. They're brother and sister this time together. Her brother John, he's Charlie. What a great love they've had, many times in many lives." She sighed, and was silent. Molly had said her piece. Terri brought me back to waking consciousness.

Dazed but not altogether surprised, I hugged and thanked her. I headed home, profoundly moved by the revelation. A few weeks later while listening to the tape again, the memory from when I was not quite five years old came rushing back, when I told my mother that John and I had danced together "when we were big." This really hit home in a new way now!

I later did a bit of research and discovered Molly's "consumption" was a synonym for tuberculosis. In retrospect, I found her weakened lung condition to be a parallel to my current experience, having been plagued by chronic bronchitis from the time I was a teenager until the time of that regression. Interestingly enough, I've dealt with it very little since that time. Soon after this session, I began to read up on "soul memory" of various conditions the present day body might house, carried over from a past life experience

Eight years later, I was to learn of a totally unexpected twist in my reincarnation travels with Johnny. Please "fast forward" with me to October of 1995 and the following journal entry:

OCTOBER 26, 1995

This is a most unusual night...for the past two weeks, I've experienced a different type of psychic contact...Something akin to someone gently rubbing my shoulders with a soft cloth...very warm, very comforting, perhaps an arm in a sleeve made of soft material. I felt an extremely strong vibration along with this as I was backing my car out of the parking lot at work yesterday—such deep chills, and a voice which told me to turn off the motor so I could hear the message clearly. I pulled the car back into the parking space and asked who was trying to speak; the vibration was strong, but not totally familiar. I received confirmation that is was Grandma Mary, my Dad's mother...I had little visitations from her previously, but no real discernable words. This was different. She told me I "had to get on with it..."

When I asked what she meant, she added, "Get on with your

happiness, with what makes you happy." Shortly after that, my mother's voice chimed in. "We're here together today because something special is going on, Cheryl." Their combined energies made me feel a bit dizzy. They were joining forces to tell me something important; I realized I needed to pay close attention.

"Well, you've never teamed up before, ladies. I'm listening, please go on."

What Mom said next was rather surprising. "Johnny has come back to Earth." She went on to tell me he was a little Native American boy, and he was physically perfect this time; he'd been born just a few weeks before. She said he came back to be a healer, which seemed so perfect. I began crying, because I knew this was something he had been wishing to do for some time. Selfishly, I was afraid I wouldn't be in contact with him anymore. Mom and Grandma Mary left me feeling a mixture of happiness for John, along with a bit of loss. John had been my strongest link to the other side for several years.

Now, what happened tonight has me amazed! Just a few moments ago, I tried asking John if we would ever be able to communicate again. I had no idea if he could still hear or feel my thoughts. I realized as he became more involved in his new life, he might not be able to continue with our connection. His recognizable intense vibration was immediately there...I got an image of him sending me telepathic communication from his crib! A very wee baby, doing this...once again, a small child holding this tremendous spirit inside...

Stunned, I cried, "How are you doing this? You're just a baby!"

He roared with laughter. "*How* long have you been doing this work now, Sis? I'm not a baby, not my soul, not any more than yours is. I'm simply living in a baby's body in my present earthly experience. I promised you I'd always find a way to take care of you, to stay in touch. And I meant that. As long as this child is sleeping or not in any danger, I can take time to check in with you, no matter where either of us might be."

The feeling of love was so strong. "Thank you, honey. What should I call you?" I was in a happy state of shock. I had heard of children in India remembering past lives and making a pilgrimage to find their past life family, but I never expected this particular experience to cross my path!

"Oh! You want to know my name? It's Sam," he replied. "I'm Native American on my mother's side." He went on to give me his last name, current location and more details on his new family, assuring me he'd find ways to keep me updated on his life, and that we would, indeed, meet in person one day.

That was the end of that journal entry. In subsequent connections with Sam/John, he told me we were to meet on his fifth birthday, and he'd give me more details as that time approached. Some details of my quest to find John/Sam follow. Yet another interesting turn in our lives, make that *many* lives, together!

Chapter Eighteen

On The Road Again...

As time went on, I did indeed hear from Johnny once in awhile, and of course, I have always enjoyed our connection. These days, I tend to call him "John/Sam" usually, because he will always be Johnny to me, but as I mentioned, his present life name is Samuel (after a paternal ancestor). He told me his birthday was in mid-October, and one night during a "conversation," he told me that he really wanted me to do my best to come be part of his fifth birthday party. I was elated at the possibility, but unsure as to how this all could work.

"Well, I've given you my last name, and you know the area where I live," he went on. "If it's meant to be, you'll find me."

"An exact address would help, y'know!" I didn't get a response to that, and figured it was one of those details I needed to let go, and simply plan the trip based on faith and our strong bond. "How will your mother and siblings feel about me showing up?"

To bring you up to speed, John/Sam had told me his parents had divorced about a year prior, and that he had two siblings. His father, French Canadian by birth, had returned to his homeland, but the children were still in the states with their mother, who is Native American. His plan was to study alternative medicine as he grew older, and every type of healing he could. This was no big surprise! They lived in the Southwest, not too far from me, but in a different state. It wasn't all that far away, and I could feel the excitement mounting as we were telepathically discussing this.

"She's fine with it. The Native American culture, and especially my mother, is pretty accepting of this type of thing. So, will you be there?" I felt his energy shift back and forth a bit, from the old soul I knew him to be to the anticipation a young child has at seeing a relative they really love visiting.

"You know I'll do my very best to make this happen. Let me look into renting a car, getting some maps and praying for guidance about it all. I guess you're not allowed to give me more particulars on your exact location, huh?"

Again, there was no response, so I took that for a confirmation of my feelings. It felt like the energetic connection was fading, so I sent him a quick, "Thanks for the invite!" and prepared to take one of my biggest leaps of faith ever.

I knew most people would think I had surely, *finally*, lost my mind completely. Going to find a family without a definite address, and just a strong feeling about the town they lived closest to? "Cheryl's really gone off the deep end this time," I could hear some of them sighing and clucking their tongues. "Poor thing. Bound to happen sooner or later when you spend so much time talking with those in Spirit."

I decided to avoid that inevitable raining on my parade, and just told two really close, understanding spiritual friends. One of them said, "Hey, if I thought there was any remote possibility I could see my folks again, I would do everything in my power to do it. I don't think you're crazy at all!"

That's what it boiled down to, really. I knew if I didn't make every effort to carry this out, I would regret it the rest of my life. So I rearranged my appointment schedule to give myself a full week to make the round trip. I decided to rent a car in Phoenix, since it was about a day's drive each way, and I would need a car to go exploring once I arrived in the designated area.

I made several attempts to call information, trying to get a phone number on anyone in the vicinity with the last name John/Sam had provided me, but none were listed. There was one that showed up, but it was non-published. Truly a test of faith. But I was up for it! If I could see and actually hug and talk with my dear little brother once again, see him in a healthy physical body living a "normal" life, it would all be worth it.

The morning I drove out of town, I felt something that surpassed happiness...utter jubilation fits the bill most accurately. I had my cell phone, some of my favorite CDs, plenty of snacks for the road to minimize stops, and the brand new rental car had less than twenty miles on it when I picked it up. I was ready!

About two hundred miles into the journey, I was still "up" but some little nagging doubts were trying to creep in. I told them to "get lost!" and after taking some deep breaths, focused on my driving. Just then, a big semi-truck pulled alongside me, and I had to smile as I glanced up at the logo on the side. *J.B.Hunt* is a well-known trucking company, but this was the first one of their fleet I had seen so far on this trip. To me, that was definite confirmation that the "John Booth hunt" was underway!

One last thing (for now!) I want to share. It was obviously no accident that the funding for this book's first print run was available and sent out to "seal the deal" on John/Sam's tenth birthday, 2005. I know he is thrilled that his story is finally reaching the many, rather than the few.

For the time being, I wish to say, "Namaste'" and encourage you to never doubt what you feel deep in your heart. Hold onto your dreams, for when we do, they have this miraculous way of coming true. As one of Wayne Dyer's book titles proclaims, *You'll See It When You Believe It*.

Thank you very much for joining me in this retelling of some of my more interesting and amazing personal experiences of communication with those in other dimensions. As far as that journey to my brother's fifth birthday party and what has happened since then, we'll have to cover that another time. I'm not sure if I'll be the author of it, or possibly that will be left to John/Sam. What I do know for certain is that a sequel will appear when the timing is right. Stay tuned!

Lyrics to the song Medium, Rare
from Cheryl's One Woman Show, *Medium, Rare©*
by Cheryl Booth

Life's full of twists and turns, bumps, bruises and concerns
That often just don't seem fair.
So, why do bad things happen to good people?
Don't know, but when they do I know that's when they'll seek a Medium, Medium Rare.

They call me up and say, "Oh my God, Cheryl, can you please see me today?
My life is falling apart! I think my guides are mad at me, 'cause they're not communicatin'
Like the Church Lady says, I think I'm plagued by 'Satan!'
And it's just breaking my heart.
I miss my Mom and my Uncle Joe, they were always so wise, y'know?
Can't you please establish a connection?"

"Well, I'll do my best to satisfy, I can't guarantee, but I'm gonna try,
You know, you don't become a genius when you die...
But they do want to help us if they can."

One thing I've learned for sure, if your intention's pure,
They're gonna hear you without me.
You've got to tune into your Inner Voice and listen,
We ALL have a soul contract and a mission,
It's not at all hopeless, you see.

Because you're a creator and psychic, too,
If you look inside your heart, that'll get you through,
You'll start to feel your own way.

Don't get too reliant on an outside source,
There's only One Divine Universal Force,
So start connecting today!

When folks cross over there, they still love us and care,
They're simply in a new dimension.
So remember the good times that you had together,
You'll all meet again and it'll be even better
When your soul makes its ascension!

Now, I hope that helps a bit. Never just say, "I quit!"
Keep meditating, and don't forget prayer.
One day you'll get a message and you'll see
That you, too, have the ability
To be a Medium, Medium Rare.
Medium Rare.......Medium Rare!

NOTE: There is another original song in this show. The run time is just under an hour. A DVD of it will be available in the near future, and Cheryl is open to booking live engagements around the country. For more information, get in touch with her using the Contact Information on the next page. Thank you!

Author & Contact Information

WEBSITE: www.cherylbooth.com
EMAIL ADDRESS: lifeofspirit@gmail.com
TOLLFREE PHONE: 877-271-8218
PHOENIX AREA PHONE: 602-316-8763
MAILING ADDRESS: 4730 E. Indian School Road, Suite 120—202, Phoenix, AZ 85018

For more information on Cheryl's work, to book an appointment, learn more about her private mentoring program for psychic development, or to schedule a lecture, seminar, or book signing in your area, please use the contact information above, and be sure to visit Cheryl's website: www.cherylbooth.com. A fully detailed list of workshops and seminars is available upon request. Readings and hypnosis sessions are available either in person or by telephone. For long distance clients, a recording of the session will be mailed to you. The only type of hypnosis she will not do by phone is past life regression. In order to insure her client's Highest Good in those sessions, she needs to be able to calibrate their facial/body postures to help them stay objective and just report on what they are experiencing. Therefore, regression work must be done in person.

Cheryl also does healing energy sessions, including the use of Reiki, chakra and aura balancing, somato-emotional release techniques and more. Energy work may be incorporated into hypnosis sessions.

Please use the same contacts to book engagements of her one-woman show, *Medium, Rare*, to schedule radio or television appearances, or other events.

To hear archived internet radio shows from her show "Soul Survival," please visit www.achieveradio.com/showpages/cherylbootharch.

htm. She intends to have another radio show soon, and is open to brainstorming about this with producers and others working in the fields of conventional, internet and satellite radio.

Email is the preferred and most expedient way to check appointment availability, subscribe to her monthly newsletter, and learn about her upcoming travel schedule including book signings, seminars, and performances of *Medium, Rare*. Please understand that she cannot personally answer each and every inquiry and does not do free readings. She donated the first three years of her practice without charging, and her guides have made it clear that was plenty!

Cheryl plans to move from Phoenix in 2006; however, her website, email and toll-free number will remain the same. For updates to her contact information, please check www.cherylbooth.com

Made in the USA